SCHAUM'S OUTLINE OF

GERMAN GRAMMAR

Third Edition

•

ELKE GSCHOSSMANN-HENDERSHOT

Former Instructor, Rutgers University

LOIS M. FEUERLE

Adjunct Assistant Professor, New York University/SCE

•

SCHAUM'S OUTLINE SERIES

McGRAW-HILL

*New York   St. Louis   San Francisco   Auckland   Bogotá   Caracas   Lisbon
London   Madrid   Mexico City   Milan   Montreal   New Delhi
San Juan   Singapore   Sydney   Tokyo   Toronto*

ELKE GSCHOSSMANN-HENDERSHOT, a native of Germany, received her formal schooling in Regensburg, Germany, and completed her post-graduate work at Rutgers University, New Jersey. She has teaching experience at various levels, from elementary school through college. She designed programs for the Army Language School and served as supervisor for Deutsche Sprachschule. Her most recent teaching assignment was at Rutgers University, New Jersey.

LOIS M. FEUERLE received her B.A. in German and English from the University of Vermont, her J.D. from the New York University School of Law, and her doctorate in Germanic Languages and Literatures from the University of Kansas. Dr. Feuerle also spent two years at Christian-Albrechts-Universität in Kiel, Germany, in addition to her studies in Vienna and Salzburg, Austria. She has taught German to students of all ages in a variety of contexts including the University of Kansas Intensive Language Institute in Holzkirchen, Germany, Marshall University, the German Language School of Morris Plains and Montclair State University. She is currently Adjunct Assistant Professor of German and Translation in the Department of Foreign Languages at the New York University School of Continuing Education, where she headed the Translation Studies Program from 1991 to 1995. She has translated numerous books, law review articles, and a wide variety of other legal materials from German into English. She is the coauthor of the three book series *Communicating in German: Novice, Intermediate and Advanced* in Schaum's Foreign Language Program.

Schaum's Outline of
GERMAN GRAMMAR

2 3 4 5 6 7 8 9 10 11 12 14 15 16 17 18 19 20 PRS PRS 9 0 1 0 9 8 7

ISBN 0-07-025134-7

Sponsoring Editor: Arthur Biderman
Production Supervisor: Pamela Pelton
Editing Supervisor: Maureen Walker

Library of Congress Cataloging-in-Publication Data

Gschossmann-Hendershot, Elke.
    Schaum's outline of German grammar / Elke Gschossmann-Hendershot,
Lois M. Feuerle. — 3rd ed.
        p. cm. — (Schaum's outline series)
    Includes index.
    ISBN 0-07-025134-7
    1. German language—Grammar—Outlines, syllabi, etc. I. Feuerle,
Lois M. II. Title. III. Title: German grammar. IV. Series.
PF3118.G8 1996
438.2'421—DC20   96-35002
                                                      CIP

McGraw-Hill

A Division of The McGraw-Hill Companies

Preface

Like the first and second editions of *Schaum's Outline of German Grammar*, the third edition has been developed as a study aid and reference tool to assist students in their acquisition of German.

This new edition has incorporated a number of changes designed to make it easier for the student to master the language. First, it has added a chapter on "The Sounds of German" to the grammatical chapters of the previous two editions. This new chapter, which guides the reader through the rules of German pronunciation, should prove invaluable to those who are using the Outline as a text for self-study. For those students who are using the Outline as a supplement to their class text, it will be a useful review and reinforcement of what they have learned in the classroom.

Each of the following nine chapters is devoted to an important aspect of German Grammar—Nouns and Articles; Prepositions; Pronouns; Adjectives and Adverbs; Numbers, Dates, Time; Verbs; Negative Words and Constructions; Interrogative Words and Constructions; and Word Order and Conjunctions.

Grammatical explanations have been tightened and in some cases expanded in order to make it easier for the student to grasp the point presented. A graphical presentation now follows the grammatical rule or explanation whenever possible, and it is boxed to stand out clearly from the text and practice exercises. This visual device will help students remember the essential patterns that provide the framework necessary for them to generate their own linguistic statements, which is ultimately the foundation of true language proficiency.

Each grammatical point is followed by illustrative examples. Read the explanation first and then study the examples carefully. Once you have done this, go on to the exercises that follow. Write out the answers to the exercises and then check them against the answer key at the back of the book. It is advisable to correct yourself immediately before proceeding to the next exercise.

One of the most difficult and burdensome tasks in acquiring a second language is mastering the many forms that exist in that language. In *Schaum's Outline of German Grammar* these forms have been grouped to make their acquisition as simple as possible and to minimize what at first might appear to be irregularities. The new presentation of the verb tenses permits the verbs to be presented in the order in which their principle parts are traditionally and invariably presented in dictionaries and reference lists.

Schaum's Outline of German Grammar can be used as a review text or as companion to any text, traditional or otherwise. Thus the addition of a comprehensive index makes this edition an even more useful tool.

I would like to express my gratitude to Helmut Leuffen for his careful review of my manuscript and his invaluable comments and suggestions, to Ursula Dievenich for her clear-sighted recommendations which set the course for this work in its initial phase, and to Arthur Biderman, Sponsoring Editor, whose interest and meticulous attention to detail have made this a better book.

LOIS M. FEUERLE

Contents

Chapter 1   THE SOUNDS OF GERMAN: A KEY TO PRONUNCIATION **1**

The German Alphabet 1

Avoiding Misunderstandings 2

Remember, there are differences 2

The Vowels 3
> Long vowels versus short vowels.

The Diphthongs 4

The Consonants 5
> Similarities. Differences. Other differences.

The Glottal Stop 8

Stress 8

Syllabification 9
> Single consonants and double consonants. Consonant clusters and groups of consonants.

Chapter 2   NOUNS AND ARTICLES **14**

Capitalization 14

Gender 14

Gender Identification by Noun Groups 14
> Nouns referring to people. Masculine nouns. Feminine nouns. Neuter nouns.

Gender Identification by Word Endings 18
> Masculine endings. Feminine endings. Neuter endings.

Words with Different Meanings in Masculine, Feminine, and Neuter Forms   21

Compound Nouns 22
> Formation. Gender.

Nouns Used Only in the Singular 24

Plural Forms of Nouns 25

Cases of Nouns 32
> Nominative case. Accusative case. Dative case. Genitive case.

Review of Case Endings for the "der" Words (der, dieser, jeder, jener, mancher, solcher, welcher) 47

Review of Case Endings for the "ein" Words (ein, kein, mein, dein, sein, ihr, unser, euer, Ihr) 48

Special Uses of the Definite Article 48

Omission of the Indefinite or Definite Article 50

Chapter 3   PREPOSITIONS **52**

Prepositions Governing the Accusative Case 52
> Contractions of prepositions governing the accusative.

Prepositions Governing the Dative Case 54
> Contractions of prepositions governing the dative.

CONTENTS

Prepositions Governing either the Accusative or the Dative Case 57
Contractions of the Two-Way Prepositions. Combinations with verbs of direction. Combinations with verbs of location. **Da-** Compounds with accusative and dative prepositions. **Wo-** Compounds with accusative and dative prepositions.
Prepositions Governing the Genitive Case 64
Word Order in Prepositional Phrases 66

Chapter 4 **PRONOUNS** **69**
Personal Pronouns 69
Nominative case. Accusative case. Dative case. Position of pronoun objects. Pronouns in idiomatic verb + preposition combinations (Phrasal verbs).
Reflexive Pronouns 76
Accusative case. Dative case. Position.
Possessive Pronouns 78
Demonstrative Pronouns 78
Indefinite Pronouns 79
Relative Pronouns 82
Nominative case. Accusative case. Dative case. Genitive case. Indefinite relative pronouns.

Chapter 5 **ADJECTIVES AND ADVERBS** **88**
Demonstrative Adjectives 88
Descriptive Adjectives 89
Predicate adjective. Attributive adjective—preceded by **"der"** words or definite articles. Attributive adjective—preceded by the indefinite article or other **"ein"** words (Preceded adjectives). Attributive adjective—not preceded by **"der"** or **"ein"** words (Unpreceded adjectives).
Adjectival Constructions: Adjectives Derived From Verbs 110
Present participle used as adjective. Past participle used as adjective.
Adjectives used as nouns 111
Neuter adjectives used as nouns: preceded by **etwas, nichts, viel, wenig.**
Possessive Adjectives 113
Comparison of Adjectives and Adverbs 115
Vowel change in monosyllabic adjectives. Irregular adjectives. Comparison of adjectives and adverbs.
Adverbs 122
Adverbs referring to time. Adverbs referring to manner. Adverbs referring to place. Position of adverbs. Idiomatic use of adverbs.

Chapter 6 **NUMBERS, DATES, TIME** **126**
Numbers 126
Cardinal numbers. Numbers over 1,000,000. Measurements, prices, and other decimal fractions. Ordinal numbers. Fractions.
Dates 129
Days of the week. Months. Seasons. Days of the month and year. Dating a letter. Reversal of numbers.
Time 131
Conversational German. Official time. The use of **um . . . Uhr.** Periods of the day. Customary action. Other adverbs of time. Time expressions in the accusative case. Time expressions in the dative case. Time expressions in the genitive case.

Chapter 7   **VERBS** **137**

Verb Overview 137
Transitive and intransitive verbs. Personal endings. Forms of address: formal versus informal. Verb tenses. Strong verbs and weak verbs.

Simple Present Tense 138
Weak and strong verbs. Irregular verbs. Special use of the present tense.

Simple Past Tense 148
Weak verbs. Irregular weak verbs. Strong verbs. Auxiliary verbs **sein, haben, werden.** Usage notes on the simple past tense.

Present Perfect Tense 157
Formation of the past participle. Regular weak verbs. Irregular weak verbs. Intransitive verbs. Strong verbs. Auxiliary verbs **sein, haben, werden.**

Past Perfect Tense 168
Weak and strong verbs. Uses of the past perfect tense.

Future Tense 169
Weak and strong verbs. Use of the future tense.

Future Perfect Tense 171
Weak and strong verbs. Use of the future perfect tense.

Verbs with Inseparable Prefixes 171

Verbs with Separable Prefixes 172
Position of the separable prefix. Separable prefix verbs in dependent clauses.

Case Following Verbs 176
Accusative and dative case for direct and indirect objects. Dative case. Prepositional objects.

Reflexive Verbs 178
Reflexive verbs governing the accusative case. Reflexive verbs with separable prefixes. Reflexive imperative forms. Reflexive versus nonreflexive use of verbs. Reflexive verbs governing the dative case.

Modal Auxiliary Verbs 184
Present tense. Simple past tense. Compound tenses.

Dependent Infinitives 189
Simple tenses—present and past. Compound tenses—present perfect and past perfect. Future tense. Dependent clauses. Infinitives preceded by **zu** (*to*).

Verbs as Other Parts of Speech 193
Infinitives used as nouns. Present participles used as adjectives and adverbs. Past participles used as adjectives and adverbs. Participles used as nouns.

Imperatives 195
Weak and strong verbs. Formal commands (singular and plural)—**Sie.** Familiar commands. Irregular imperative forms. First person command (Let's). Impersonal imperative.

The Conditional 198
Weak and strong verbs. Use of the conditional.

The Subjunctive 199
General subjunctive and special subjunctive. Present-time subjunctive. Past-time subjunctive. Indirect speech. Special subjunctive.

Passive Voice 212
Present tense. Past tense. Compound tenses. Substitute for the passive. Passive versus false (or apparent) passive.

Special Meanings of Certain Verbs 217

Chapter 8   **NEGATIVE WORDS AND CONSTRUCTIONS** **221**

Negation 221
Nicht in final position. **Nicht** preceding certain other elements in the sentence. **Nicht** in dependent clauses. **Nicht** with **sondern. Nicht** with interrogative.

CONTENTS

Answering Affirmative and Negative Questions—**Ja** and **doch** 224
The Negative Form of **brauchen** 224
Other Negative Words 225
  Negative article **kein-**. Pronouns **nichts, niemand.**

Chapter 9 **INTERROGATIVE WORDS AND CONSTRUCTIONS** **227**
General Questions 227
  Formation of questions by inversion. Simple tenses. Compound tenses and depen-
  dent infinitives. Use of **doch** in answer to negative questions.
Specific Questions 228
  Interrogative adverbs and adverbial expressions. Interrogative Pronouns.
  Interrogative Adjective.

Chapter 10 **WORD ORDER AND CONJUNCTIONS** **235**
Word Order 235
  Statements. Questions. Commands (V(+ S)). Exclamations.
Coordinating Conjunctions—Regular Word Order 240
Subordinating Conjunctions—Verb in Final Position 241
Words Functioning as Subordinating Conjunctions—Verb in Final Position 244
  Relative pronouns and interrogatives. **Haben** or **werden** with the double
  infinitive. Conditional sentences. Main clauses following dependent clauses.
Position of the Object 246
Position of the Adverb 247

ANSWERS **249**

VERB CHART **285**

INDEX **287**

Chapter 1

The Sounds of German: A Key to German Pronunciation

Since German pronunciation is to a large extent phonetic and regular, an understanding of the basic sounds and stress patterns of German will enable the student to pronounce most words easily and correctly.

THE GERMAN ALPHABET

The German alphabet has the 26 standard letters found in the English alphabet plus four letters that are specific to German.

Alphabet

Letter	German Name
a	ah
b	beh
c	tseh
d	deh
e	eh
f	eff
g	geh
h	hah
i	ih
j	yot
k	kah
l	ell
m	emm
n	enn
o	oh
p	peh
q	kuh
r	err
s	ess
t	teh
u	uh
v	fau
w	veh
x	iks
y	üppsilon
z	tsett
ä	äh (a-umlaut)
ö	öh (o-umlaut)
ü	üh (u-umlaut)
ß	ess-tsett (scharfes ess)

1

It is important to learn to pronounce the *German names* of the letters of the alphabet so that you will be able to spell names, addresses, and other essential information when needed during stays in German-speaking countries and over the telephone.

AVOIDING MISUNDERSTANDINGS

Sometimes a bad connection makes it particularly difficult to understand the spelling of a word over the telephone. For this reason the Federal Post Office in Germany has issued an alphabet of code words that will make it perfectly clear what letter is intended. The post office spelling chart is as follows.

A	Anton
Ä	Ärger
B	Berta
C	Cäsar
Ch	Charlotte
D	Dora
E	Emil
F	Friedrich
G	Gustav
H	Heinrich
I	Ida
J	Julius
K	Kaufmann
L	Ludwig
M	Martha
N	Nordpol
O	Otto
Ö	Ökonom
P	Paula
Q	Quelle
R	Richard
S	Samuel
Sch	Schule
T	Theodor
U	Ulrich
Ü	Übermut
V	Viktor
W	Wilhelm
X	Xantippe
Y	Ypsilon
Z	Zacharias

REMEMBER, THERE ARE DIFFERENCES

Even though both English and German employ the same basic alphabet, there are, of course, significant differences in the pronunciation of the individual German and English sounds represented by the standard letters. The most obvious of these differences will be noted in the pronunciation key below.

Please bear in mind, however, that the pronunciations given below are only approximations to aid the English-speaking reader. *They are not exact equivalents.* To perfect pronunciation, it is essential to avail oneself of every possible opportunity to hear and use spoken German, e.g., through audiotapes, videotapes, radio, television, movies, conversations with native speakers, and visits to German-speaking countries.

It might be helpful to remember that precisely those sounds that characterize a German accent in English are the sounds that will require the most work in order for you to overcome *your foreign accent in German*. Think of Dieter of "Sprockets" on the television show "Saturday Night Live."

THE VOWELS

Vowels in German are either long or short. In our pronunciation key long vowels are followed by a colon, e.g., **[a:]**, **[e:]**, **[i:]**, **[o:]**, **[u:]**; short vowels stand alone, e.g., **[a]**, **[e]**, **[i]**, **[o]**, **[u]**. Note that identical sounds can sometimes be represented by different letters or combinations of letters (i.e., different spellings).

Note that certain sounds are represented orthographically by the so-called umlauts **[ä]**, **[ö]**, **[ü]**. Both the long and the short umlauts are included in the vowel chart that follows.

Vowel Sound	Examples	Approximate English Sounds
[a]	wann, kalt, rasch, ab	w<u>a</u>nder
[a:]	ja, Haar, Jahr, kam, sagen	f<u>a</u>ther
[e]	Bett, Geld, Fenster, sechs, es	m<u>e</u>n
[e:]	See, Weh, Mehl, dem, Regen	m<u>ay</u>
[i]	immer, ist, ich, nicht, mit	<u>i</u>n
[i:]	ihm, mir, wider, wie, Liebe, antik, Musik	b<u>ee</u>t
[o]	offen, oft, morgen, Ochs	n<u>o</u>t
[o:]	Boot, ohne, Note, oben, wo	s<u>o</u>
[u]	Mutter, null, und, Sucht	f<u>oo</u>t
[u:]	Kuh, Stuhl, gut, Fuß, Juni	m<u>oo</u>t
[ä]	Männer, Hände, älter	m<u>e</u>n
[ä:]	Fähre, spät, Käse, Diät	m<u>ay</u>
[ö]	Hölle, Löffel, völlig, können	No close equivalent in English. However, one can approximate this sound by pronouncing the word *further*, but without the first *r*.
[ö:]	schön, böse, Möbel, Höhle, Söhne	No close equivalent in English. To approximate this sound, start to pronounce the [ö], but draw it out longer.
[ü]	müssen, küssen, hübsch, Id<u>y</u>lle, Hütte, fünf	No close equivalent in English. To approximate this sound, try to pronounce the [i], but with rounded lips. If you try to say the word **Kissen** with rounded lips, you will come close to the [ü] sound in **küssen**.

[ü:]	**Tür, Hüte, Bühne, kühl, Physik, Lyrik**	No close equivalent in English. To approximate this sound, try to pronounce the [i:], but with rounded lips. If you try to pronounce the word **Biene** with your lips rounded, you will come close to the pronounciation of the [ü:] in **Bühne**.

Long Vowels versus Short Vowels

There are a number of basic rules that help the student in determining whether a vowel is to be pronounced long or short.

(1)   A double vowel is *long*.
  Haar, Boot, Beet

(2)   A vowel followed by a silent **h** (the so-called **Dehnungs-hah** or *stretching H*) is *long*.
  Jahr, ihm, Stuhl, Stühle

(3)   A vowel followed by a single consonant is *usually long*. See also note (7).
  gut, dem, wen, Mode

(4)   An **i** followed by an **e** (that is, **ie**) is *long*.
  Liebe, wieder, sieben, die

(5)   A vowel followed by a double consonant is *short*.
  Bett, kommen, können, hell

(6)   A vowel followed by two or more consonants, including the combinations **ch** and **sch**, is usually *short*.
  ich, typisch, sicher, Fenster, Sack

(7)   A vowel in one-syllable prepositions and other common one-syllable words ending in a single consonant are often *short*.
  mit, im, um, es

(8)   An **e** not in combination with another vowel, standing at the end of a word, is *short*.
  Hase, gebe, bitte, Hilfe

THE DIPHTHONGS

A diphthong is a combination of two vowel sounds pronounced with a glide. There are three common diphthongs in German. Note that two of these diphthongs can be spelled in several different ways.

Diphthong	*Examples*	*Approximate English Sounds*
[au]	**auf, aus, Haus, Frau, brauchen**	*house*
[ei]	**ein, mein, Leid, Mai, Kaiser, Bayern, Meyer**	*site*
[eu]	**Feuer, Fräulein, heute, Häuser**	*noise*

Note: In German diphthongs are not drawn out as they are in English. They are pronounced short and clipped.
Note: The combination **ie** is not a diphthong but rather a spelling variant of the [i:] sound.

die, Sie, Lied, Knie, Brief, wieder, Spiegel

See the examples under [**i**:] above.

THE CONSONANTS

Similarities

Many of the German consonants are pronounced more or less as they are in English. Included in this group are **f, h, k, m, n, p, t, x**.

Consonants	Examples
f	**Freitag, Fisch, Neffe**
h	**Haus, haben, hastig**
k	**kaufen, küssen, Park**
m	**Montag, immer, dem**
n	**nicht, Biene, bin**
p	**Problem, Mappe, Lampe**
t	**Tag, Täter, tat**
x	**Taxi, Axt, boxen**

The consonants **b, d, g** are also pronounced more or less as they are in English when they are at the beginning of a word or a syllable. However, when **b, d, g** appear at the end of a word or syllable, or before **t** or **st**, they are pronounced as **p, t, k**.

	Consonants **b, d, g**, Initial or Medial Position	Pronounced as p, t, k, Final Position or before t or st
b	**Bett, Graben, beben**	**Grab, lieb, liebt, liebst, Obst**
d	**Danke, Dorf, wieder, Fremde,**	**Bad, fremd, abends, Schmidt**
g	**Tage, lügen, gehen, gegen**	**log, Tag, mag, liegt, liegst**

Note: When **g** appears in the suffix **-ig** at the end of a word, it is pronounced like **-ich**.
  hastig, billig, durstig, fertig, zwanzig, neunzig

Differences

*The **ich** sound and the **ach** sound*

The consonant cluster **ch** can represent two closely related, but different sounds that are present in German, but not in standard English. Both sounds are produced with the tongue and mouth in more or less the same position as for the **k** sound. However, the stream of breath is not cut off as when pronouncing a **k**, but rather it is forced through the narrow opening between the tongue and the roof of the mouth.

Whether the **ch** becomes an **ich** sound or an **ach** sound is determined by the immediately preceding vowel, that is, by the position of the mouth that is required to produce these vowel sounds.

When **ch** follows the vowels **a, o, u** and the diphthong **au**, it is pronounced toward the back in the throat and is very similar to the **ch** in the Scottish word *Loch*.

  ach, acht, nacht, doch, Woche, Tochter, Buch, Tuch, Kuchen, besuchen, Frucht, auch, rauchen, gebraucht

In other environments, that is, after the vowels **e, i, ä, ö, ü**, as well as after the diphthongs **ei (ai, ay, ey)** and **eu (äu)** and the consonants **l, n, r,** the stream of air is forced through a flatter but wider opening between the tongue and the roof of the mouth. The resulting **ich** sound is pronounced more toward the front of the mouth.

schlecht, ich, Sicht, lächeln, möchte, Bücher, schleichen, Eiche, euch, räuchern, welcher, München, Kirche

Other Differences

Other consonants that are pronounced differently in English and German include the letters **l, r, j, w, z, s, v, g, c.**

The letters [l] and [r]

Although both of these letters exist in both the English and the German alphabets, they are pronounced very differently in the two languages.

The English **l** is a dark sound that is pronounced rather far back in the mouth. By contrast, the German **l** is pronounced to the front of the mouth with the tongue flatter and touching the back of the front teeth. This produces a much lighter **l** sound.

Unlike English, German uses either the uvular **r** (the uvula is the small flap of skin hanging from the soft palate at the back of the mouth) or the tongue-trilled **r**. Of the two, the uvular **r**, which is probably more difficult for Americans to pronounce, is the more commonly used **r** in German.

Good listening skills and practice are required to master these sounds.

The letters [j], [w], and [z]

	German Examples	English Equivalents
j	**ja, Jahr, Jacke, Juli**	*yes*
w	**wild, Winter, Woche, wo**	*vest*
z	**Zimmer, duzen, schwarz, Arzt, Platz**	*cats*

The letter [s], alone and in combination

The pronunciation of the letter **s** depends on its position in the word. If it is in initial position preceding a vowel or stands between two vowels, it is pronounced like an English **z**. In other positions it is usually pronounced as a soft **s**.

The letter [s] alone

	German Examples	English Equivalents
Initial **s**	**Salz, sehr, Seife, Suppe, sagen, sicher, süß**	*zoo*
s between vowels	**lesen, Käse, Mäuse, Häuser, also, Eisen**	*zoo*
Final **s**	**Hals, Puls, das, Eis, Gans, Gas, mittags**	*bus*

Note: Both **ss** and **ß** are pronounced with a soft **s** as in English. It is a German spelling convention that the **ß** is used after long vowels (**Straße, groß, Fuß**), diphthongs (**Strauß, äußerst, weiß**), before the letter **t** (**faßte, ißt, mußt**), and at the end of words (**gewiß, Schloß, Schluß**), whereas the double **ss** is used after short vowels (**Wasser, Tasse, Messer, küssen**). The double **ss** is never found at the end of a word or syllable or before a consonant.

Note: The **ß** spelling convention is not followed in Swiss German, which uses a double **ss** instead.

Germany	*Switzerland*
die Straße	**die Strasse**
der Haß	**der Hass**
weiß	**weiss**

Consonant clusters with [s]

The letter **s** also occurs in combination with other letters.

s Combinations	German Examples	English Equivalents
sch	schön, Tisch, rasch, wischen, wünschen	*shine*
sp	spät, Spiel, sprechen, spazieren, Sprache	No equivalent—sounds like Yiddish *shpiel*
st	Stein, Stadt, still, entstehen, studieren	No equivalent—sounds like Yiddish *shtetl*

The letter [v]

The letter **v** is normally pronounced like an English **f** in German. However, in words of foreign origin it is often pronounced as a **v** unless it is at the end of the word.

	German Examples	English Equivalents
In German words	Vater, Vetter, von, viel	*father*
In foreign words	Vase, Revolution, Vanille	*vase*
In final position	brav, fiktiv, negativ	*relief*

The letter [q]

In German, as in English, the letter **q** is always followed by a **u**. However, in German this combination is pronounced as if it were written **kv**, like the Yiddish word *kvetch*.

	German Examples	English Equivalents
In German words	Qualität, quer, Quartett	*kvetch*

The letter [c]

As noted above, the letter **c** in German usually appears in combination with the letter **h** to form the **ich** and **ach** sounds. However, the letter **c** also appears in initial position in certain words of foreign origin used in German.

An initial [c] is pronounced as a **ts** if it comes before **e, i,** or **ä**. In other cases it is usually pronounced as a **k**.

	German Examples	English Equivalents
Before [ä], [e], [i]	Cäsar, Celsius, circa	*cats*
In other environments	Camping, Computer, Courage	*camping*

When the consonant cluster **ch** appears at the beginning of a number of words of foreign origin, it is pronounced in a variety of ways.

	German Examples	English Equivalents
Consonant cluster **ch** in initial position	Christ, christlich, Chor, Character, Chaos	*kitten*
	Champignon, charmant, Chance, Chef, Chauvi	*shine*
	Chemie, chinesisch, Chirurg	No equivalent—a very heavily aspirated version of the **h** in *Hugh*
	Check, checken, Chip	*chip*

Other consonant clusters

Consonant Cluster	German Examples	English Equivalents
gn	Gnade, Gnom	There is a light **g** sound pronounced just before the **n**
kn	Knie, knacken, Knochen	There is a light **k** sound pronounced just before the **n**
ng	singen, Finger, sang, länger, anfangen, jünger	*singer* (not *finger*)
pf	Pfanne, Pfeffer, Pfeife, Pfennig, Pfund	There is a light **p** sound pronounced just before the **f**
ph	Philosophie, Physiker, Phantasie, Phrase	The **f** sound in *philosophy*
ps	Pseudonym, psychologisch, psychotisch	There is a light **p** sound pronounced just before the **s**
th	Thomas, Theater, Theologie, Thema, Thron	The **h** is silent, pronounced like English *Thomas*
tsch	Deutsch, klatschen	*itch*
zw	zwingen, Zwang	ca*ts* + *v*

THE GLOTTAL STOP

The glottal stop is a brief closure of the vocal cords that is used to keep words and syllables from running together. It is used more frequently in German, a language in which words and syllables are pronounced clearly and distinctly, than in English, where there is more of a tendency of link sounds and syllables when they are spoken.

Observe the differences in pronunciation in the following phrases:

a nice house   *an ice house*

You will note that there is a distinct break or glottal stop before the word *ice* in the second phrase. In German a glottal stop occurs before all words and syllables that begin with a vowel.

jeden *A*bend
Sie kam *u*m *e*lf *U*hr.
Er hat seine *A*rbeit be*e*ndet.
Die Profession hat meine Frage be*a*ntwortet.

STRESS

As a general rule the stress is on the first syllable in native German words unless the first syllable is an unstressed prefix, e.g., an inseparable prefix.

In the case of words that have been borrowed from other languages, stress patterns are much less predictable. Often they follow the rules of the language from which the word has been borrowed.

There are, however, certain suffixes that have predictable stress patterns.

Suffix	German Example	Stress
-tät	Rarität, Majestät, Aktivität, Elektrizität, Sentimentalität	Last syllable
-ik	Kritik, Musik, Mathematik, Mosaik, Politik, Republik	Last syllable
-ie	Chemie, Poesie, Phantasie, Theorie	Last syllable
-erei	Malerei, Bücherei, Sklaverei, Zauberei, Konditorei	Last syllable
-eum	Museum, Mausoleum, Kolosseum	Next to last syllable
-ieren	datieren, servieren, studieren, argumentieren, demokratisieren	Next to last syllable

SYLLABIFICATION

Single Consonants and Double Consonants

Syllabification in German is relatively simple and highly predictable. Words are divided *before single consonants*

geben	ge-ben
liegen	lie-gen
spazieren	spa-zie-ren

and *between double consonants*

hoffen	hof-fen
Messer	Mes-ser
auffallen	auf-fal-len
donnern	don-nern

Consonant Clusters and Groups of Consonants

Consonant clusters **ch, sch, ph, ß,** as well as **z, x** are regarded as single consonants for purposes of syllabification.

blechen	ble-chen
Mädchen	Mäd-chen
wischen	wi-schen
wünschen	wün-schen
Philosophen	Phi-lo-so-phen
gräßlich	gräß-lich
Hexe	He-xe
kreuzen	kreu-zen

In the case of groups of consonants, the last one in the series usually starts the new syllable.

Punkte	Punk-te
Pünktchen	Pünkt-chen [remember, **ch** is treated as one consonant]
Schlendrian	Schlend-ri-an
Flüchtling	Flücht-ling

Note: Each syllable must contain a vowel or diphthong. However, words are never divided so that a single vowel stands alone—even when this vowel is pronounced separately. Thus although the word **Abend** is spoken as two syllables, it would never be divided into two syllables to accommodate a syllable break at the end of a line.

When dividing compound words into syllables, there is always a syllable break between the components of the compound in addition to the syllable breaks that normally occur within each component.

Hausfrau	Haus-frau
Eisenbahn	Ei-sen-bahn
Donnerstag	Don-ners-tag
Mittagessen	Mit-tag-es-sen
Lichtschalter	Licht-schal-ter
Radiergummi	Ra-dier-gum-mi

When the combination **ck** is divided into syllables, it is written **k-k**.

lecken	lek-ken
Becken	Bek-ken
anpacken	an-pak-ken
schicken	schik-ken
locken	lok-ken
verschlucken	ver-schluk-ken
frühstücken	früh-stük-ken

The combination **st** is never separated, and both consonants begin the next syllable.

ha-stig
be-ste
Li-ste
lieb-ste

An apparent exception to this rule occurs when an **s** and a **t** happen to be positioned next to each other in a compound word.

Don-ners-tag

Review

1. Spell your full name using the letters of the German alphabet. If necessary, refer back to the chart at the beginning of the chapter.

   _____

2. Now spell the name of the town and the state where you are living.

   _____

3. Spell your full name again, this time using the alphabet of code words developed by the German Post Office that appears on p. 2.

   _____

4. Study the list of words below, and in the order in which they appear, write each word that contains the short [a] sound. If necessary, review the vowel chart on p. 3.

Aal, wann, hastig, Vater, Wahnsinn, rasch, Stadt, Städte, Phase, Hand, lang, Bank, Ball, Haar, Hase, Gedanke, Handtasche

1. _____   6. _____
2. _____   7. _____
3. _____   8. _____
4. _____   9. _____
5. _____   10. _____

5. Study the list of words below, and in the order in which they appear, write each word that contains the long [e:] sound. If necessary, review the vowel chart on p. 3.

beten, bitten, Becken, Betten, Kopfweh, Vorlesung, dem, Regenwasser, fehlen, Eltern, Gebrauchtwagen, Mehlwurm, Seemann, mehr, Beet

1. _____   6. _____
2. _____   7. _____
3. _____   8. _____
4. _____   9. _____
5. _____   10. _____

6. Study the list of words below, and in the order in which they appear, write each word that contains the long [i:] sound. If necessary, review the vowel chart on p. 3.

Dienstag, immer, mir, Tischler, Lieder, ihm, wir, binden, leider, ihnen, Licht, Bier, Sonnenbrille, Briefträger, einmal, hier, antik

1. _____   6. _____
2. _____   7. _____
3. _____   8. _____
4. _____   9. _____
5. _____   10. _____

7. Study the list of words below, and in the order in which they appear, write each word that contains the short [o] sound. If necessary, review the vowel chart on p. 3.

Boot, Spott, schon, morgen, Segelsport, offen, sorgfältig, Bohne, Löffel, Norden, Ofen, Oktett, Stock, Topf, tot, Wochentag, Wohnung

1. _____   6. _____
2. _____   7. _____
3. _____   8. _____
4. _____   9. _____
5. _____   10. _____

8. Study the list of words below, and in the order in which they appear, write each word that contains the long [u:] sound. If necessary, review the vowel chart on p. 3.

Mutter, kühler, Fuß, Frühjahr, Strumpf, Stuhl, Pullover, lustig, Kuh, gut, Juli, Wurst, Natur, Bluse, Anzug, Mund, Butter, Ruhm, trug

1. _____   6. _____
2. _____   7. _____
3. _____   8. _____
4. _____   9. _____
5. _____   10. _____

9. Study the list of words below, and in the order in which they appear, write each word that contains the short [ä] sound. If necessary, review the vowel chart on p. 3.

Käse, älter, Eltern, Wände, Haar, Unterwäsche, ändern, anderes, Bett, fern, gefährlich, kalt, sauer, spät, kälter, beschäftigen, Ärzte

1. _____   6. _____
2. _____   7. _____
3. _____   8. _____
4. _____   9. _____
5. _____   10. _____

10. Study the list of words below, and in the order in which they appear, write each word that contains the long [ö:] sound. If necessary, review the vowel chart on p. 3.

blöd, Hölle, Möbel, öffnen, Löwe, Röcke, aushöhlen, Wölfe, öd, offen, völlig, Böhmen, Fön, Föhn, Gesöff, Löcher, Löffel, Öl, Vermögen

1. _____   6. _____
2. _____   7. _____
3. _____   8. _____
4. _____   9. _____
5. _____   10. _____

11. Study the list of words below, and in the order in which they appear, write each word that contains the short [ü] sound. If necessary, review the vowel chart on p. 3.

früh, Müller, müssen, Hüte, müde, Mütter, benützen, übel, Früchte, schüchtern, Züge, beglücken, prüfen, Lücke, Müll, Idyll

1. _____   6. _____
2. _____   7. _____
3. _____   8. _____
4. _____   9. _____
5. _____   10. _____

12. Study the list of words below, and in the order in which they appear, write each word that contains the [ich] sound. If necessary, review the material on the ich and ach sounds on p. 5.

Nacht, sich, nichts, rauchen, schlecht, besichtigen, wöchentlich, Tochter, Nichte, leichter, Frucht, Bauch, noch, Becher, Löcher, Bäuche, Buch

1. _____   6. _____
2. _____   7. _____
3. _____   8. _____
4. _____   9. _____
5. _____   10. _____

13. Study of list of words below, and in the order in which they appear, write each word that contains an [s] that is pronounced like an English **z** sound. If necessary, review the material on the letter **s** on p. 6.

heißen, messen, gewesen, Käsekuchen, Eiskaffee, Spaß, Nase, still, also, frischer, als, ansehen, Besuch, Pils, Eisen, sechzehn, so, Streß, Süden, das

1. _____   6. _____
2. _____   7. _____
3. _____   8. _____
4. _____   9. _____
5. _____   10. _____

14. Study the list of words below and in the order in which they appear, rewrite each word underlining the syllable that bears the primary accent. If necessary, review the material on stress on pp. 8–9.

Abend, Leute, Musik, sagen, Bäckerei, Phantasie, Suppe, Universität, beenden, studieren

1. _____   6. _____
2. _____   7. _____
3. _____   8. _____
4. _____   9. _____
5. _____   10. _____

15. Study the list of words and phrases below, and in the order in which they appear, rewrite each word or phrase containing a glottal stop. Mark each glottal stop. If necessary, review the material on the glottal stop on p. 8.

Telefonbeantworter, Postamt, eines Abends, eines Tages, in Aachen, also, Omnibus, was eßt ihr? auf Englisch, garstig, Ebbe und Flut, Verkehrsampel, Großmutter, beenden, der Start, die Eierkuchen

1. _____   6. _____
2. _____   7. _____
3. _____   8. _____
4. _____   9. _____
5. _____   10. _____

16. Study the list of words below, and in the order in which they appear, rewrite each word, dividing it into syllables (e.g., le-sen, brau-chen). If necessary, review the material on syllabification on pp. 9–10.

backen, Würstchen, Omnibus, Programme, Radiergummi, Restaurants, langweilig, Hase, außer, Waschlappen

1. _____   6. _____
2. _____   7. _____
3. _____   8. _____
4. _____   9. _____
5. _____   10. _____

Nouns and Articles

CAPITALIZATION

All German nouns and words used as nouns are capitalized, regardless of their position in the sentence: **der Herr, das Haus, die Alte, der Junge, der Reisende, die Bekannte, das Lesen, das Schreiben, das Singen**.

GENDER

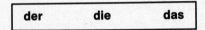

Unlike in English, where nouns almost always reflect natural gender (that is, the sex of the noun determines its gender, e.g., father, man, and boy are masculine; mother, woman, and girl are feminine; and hand, table, and friendship are neuter), all German nouns have a grammatical gender. A noun can be masculine, feminine, or neuter, regardless of its natural gender.

The definite article **der** (*the*) designates a masculine noun, **die** designates a feminine noun, and **das** a neuter noun.

Nouns that refer specifically to male beings, such as father or uncle, are usually masculine. Those that refer to female beings, such as mother or daughter, are usually feminine. However, nouns referring to things are not always neuter but can also be masculine or feminine. For this reason the gender of each noun must be memorized.

Although no definite rules for gender can be given, the following generalizations may be helpful in memorizing the gender of frequently used nouns.

GENDER IDENTIFICATION BY NOUN GROUPS

Nouns Referring to People

Nouns referring to male beings (people and animals) are usually masculine. Nouns referring to female beings are usually feminine.

Masculine		*Feminine*	
der Vater	*father*	die Mutter	*mother*
der Mann	*man*	die Frau	*Mrs., woman*
der Sohn	*son*	die Tochter	*daughter*
der Bruder	*brother*	die Schwester	*sister*
der Herr	*Mr., gentleman*	die Dame	*lady*
der Onkel	*uncle*	die Tante	*aunt*
der Sänger	*singer (male)*	die Sängerin	*singer (female)*
der Lehrer	*teacher (male)*	die Lehrerin	*teacher (female)*
der Kater	*cat*	die Katze	*cat (female or generic)*
der Hahn	*rooster*	die Henne	*chicken*
der Junge	*boy*	*But*: das Mädchen	*girl*

Nouns referring to young people and young animals are usually neuter. *Note:* All diminutives ending in **-chen** or **-lein** are neuter, regardless of the gender of the stem noun.

Neuter

das Mädchen	girl	das Kind	child
das Fräulein	Miss, young woman	das Kalb	calf
das Kätzchen	kitten	das Küken	chick
das Schwesterlein	little sister	das Fohlen	foal
das Bübchen	little boy	das Lamm	lamb
das Tischlein	little table	das Ferkel	piglet

1. Supply the appropriate definite articles.

1. _Der_ Lehrer kommt.
2. _Das_ Kalb ist klein.
3. _Die_ Dame ist freundlich.
4. _Der_ Mann ist alt.
5. _Das_ Kaninchen ist weiß.
6. _Die_ Tante bringt es.
7. _Das_ Büchlein liegt hier.
8. _Die_ Katze schläft.
9. _Der_ Sohn schreibt.
10. _Die_ Tochter ist hübsch.

11. _der_ Junge ist groß.
12. _Das_ Küken ist gelb.
13. _Die_ Lehrerin ist intelligent.
14. _Die_ Mutter kocht.
15. _Das_ Kind weint.
16. _Der_ Kater ist schwarz.
17. _Der_ Lehrer sitzt dort.
18. _Das_ Mädchen ist klein.
19. _Die_ Henne ist braun.
20. _Die_ Fräulein sieht uns.

Masculine Nouns

Names of all days of the week. **Note:** The gender of the word **Tag** is masculine.

der Montag	Monday	der Freitag	Friday
der Dienstag	Tuesday	der Samstag (Sonnabend)	Saturday
der Mittwoch	Wednesday	der Sonntag	Sunday
der Donnerstag	Thursday		

Names of all calendar months

der Januar	January	der Juli	July
der Februar	February	der August	August
der März	March	der September	September
der April	April	der Oktober	October
der Mai	May	der November	November
der Juni	June	der Dezember	December

Names of all seasons

der Frühling	spring	der Herbst	fall
der Sommer	summer	der Winter	winter

Names of all cardinal directions

der Süden	south	der Westen	west
der Norden	north	der Osten	east

2. Supply the appropriate definite articles.

1. _Der_ Sommer ist eine warme Jahreszeit.
2. _Der_ Süden Deutschlands ist malerisch.
3. _der_ Juli und _____ August sind Sommermonate.
4. _Der_ Frühling kommt bald.

5. _____*Der*_____ Sonntag ist ein Ruhetag.
6. _____ April ist regnerisch.
7. _____ Norden ist flach.
8. _____ Winter ist eine kalte Jahreszeit.
9. _____ November und _____ Dezember sind Wintermonate.
10. _____ Montag ist der erste Wochentag.

Feminine Nouns

Names of most trees			*Names of most fruits*	
die Tanne	*fir*		**die Banane**	*banana*
die Linde	*linden tree*		**die Pflaume**	*plum*
But: **der Ahorn**	*maple*		*But:* **der Apfel**	*apple*

Names of most flowers

die Orchidee	*orchid*
die Lilie	*lily*

3. Supply the appropriate definite articles.

1. _____*die*_____ Zitrone und _____*die*_____ Orange sind sauer.
2. _____ Geranie und _____ Begonie blühen.
3. _____ Birke ist ein Laubbaum.
4. _____ Banane ist süß.
5. _____ Orchidee ist teuer.
6. Wo ist _____*der*_____ Apfel?
7. _____ Lilie ist weiß.
8. _____ Tanne ist ein Nadelbaum.
9. _____ Pflaume ist sauer.
10. _____ Linde ist groß.

Neuter Nouns

Names of cities

das historische München	*historical Munich*
das übervölkerte Hongkong	*overpopulated Hong Kong*

Names of most countries

das neutrale Schweden	*neutral Sweden*
das moderne Deutschland	*modern Germany*

Note: The neuter article for cities and countries is used only if the noun is modified. Without a modifier one simply uses **München, Berlin, Italien**.

Exceptions:

Note, however, that the names of the following countries are not neuter but feminine:

die Schweiz	*Switzerland*
die Türkei	*Turkey*
die Tschechische Republik	*Czech Republic*

Still others are masculine:

der Iran   *Iran*
der Irak   *Iraq*

The following are used only in the plural:

die Niederlande   *Netherlands*
die Vereinigten Staaten   *United States*
die USA   *USA*

The above exceptions are always used with their articles, whether or not they are modified.

Wir besuchen die Schweiz.

4. Supply the appropriate definite articles when necessary.
1. Wir besuchen _____die_____ Türkei.
2. Wo liegt _____der_____ Iran?
3. _____das_____ Köln ist eine alte Stadt.
4. _____die_____ Vereinigten Staaten sind groß.
5. _____das_____ historische Wien ist malerisch.
6. _____die_____ Schweiz ist neutral.
7. _____die_____ Niederlande sind flach.
8. _____das_____ Deutschland ist modern.
9. Wir besuchen _____das_____ alte Heidelberg.
10. _____die_____ Tschechische Republik liegt im Osten.

Names of metals and chemical elements

das Gold   *gold*   **das Helium**   *helium*
das Kupfer   *copper*   *But:* **der Stahl**   *steel*

5. Supply the appropriate definite articles.
1. _____das_____ Aluminium ist ein leichtes Metall.
2. _____c_____ Chlor riecht scharf.
3. Wo wird _____der_____ Stahl produziert?
4. _____das_____ Silber glitzert in der Sonne.
5. _____c_____ Radium ist radioaktiv.
6. _____c_____ Neon ist ein Edelgas.
7. _____c_____ Kupfer ist rot.
8. _____c_____ Gold ist teuer.
9. _____c_____ Helium ist leicht.
10. _____c_____ Eisen ist ein Schwermetall.

Review

6. Complete the following with the appropriate definite articles.
1. _____die_____ Fräulein kauft nichts.
2. Wir besuchen _____das_____ sonnige Italien.

3. _der_ Apfel ist grün.
4. _der_ Sommer ist die schönste Jahreszeit.
5. _der_ Vater bringt etwas.
6. _der_ Februar ist der kürzeste Monat.
7. _der_ Junge spielt.
8. _den_ Dienstag ist der zweite Wochentag.
9. _das_ Gold ist ein Edelmetall.
10. _Der_ Lehrer fährt durch _die_ Niederlande.
11. _____ Rose blüht.
12. _Die_ Mädchen lacht.
13. Wo ist _die_ Katze?
14. _der_ Westen ist reich.
15. _der_ Januar ist ein Wintermonat.
16. _die_ Banane ist gelb.
17. _die_ Tanne ist groß.
18. _die_ Schweiz ist neutral.
19. _das_ historische München ist interessant.
20. _der_ Mai ist der schönste Monat.

GENDER IDENTIFICATION BY WORD ENDINGS

Masculine Endings

> **-el, -en, -er, -ig, -ich, -ling**

Nouns ending in **-el, -en, -er, -ig, -ich, -ling** are usually masculine.

der Schlüssel	*key*	der Eimer	*bucket*
der Löffel	*spoon*	der Zucker	*sugar*
der Wagen	*car, wagon*	der Honig	*honey*
der Boden	*floor*	der Pfennig	*penny*
der Teller	*plate*	der Teppich	*rug*
der Arbeiter	*worker*	der Lehrling	*apprentice*

Important exceptions to the above rule:

die Butter	*butter*	das Wasser	*water*
die Mutter	*mother*	das Fenster	*window*
die Tochter	*daughter*	das Wetter	*weather*
die Nummer	*number*	das Leder	*leather*
die Mauer	*wall*	das Kissen	*pillow*
das Messer	*knife*	die Gabel	*fork*
das Zimmer	*room*	die Kartoffel	*potato*

7. Supply the appropriate forms of the definite articles.

1. _der_ Mantel liegt hier.
2. Warum ist _das_ Fenster offen?
3. _der_ Sperling ist ein Vogel.
4. _die_ Gabel, _der_ Löffel und _das_ Messer sind aus Stahl.
5. _der_ Himmel ist blau.
6. _der_ Käfer fliegt durch _das_ Zimmer.
7. _der_ Rettich schmeckt scharf.

8. _____der_____ Essig ist sauer, aber _____der_____ Honig ist süß.
9. _____der_____ Teppich ist alt.
10. Wo ist _____der_____ Teller?
11. _____das_____ Wetter ist schön.
12. _____das_____ Wagen ist in der Garage.
13. _____der_____ Lehrling ist jung.
14. Wo ist _____die_____ Butter?
15. _____der_____ Zucker ist weiß.
16. _____die_____ Mutter und _____die_____ Tochter sind hübsch.
17. _____der_____ Leder ist weich.
18. Wo ist _____das_____ Kissen?

> **-and, -ant, -ar, -är, -ast, -ent, -eur, -ier, -ist, -ismus, -or, -us**

In addition nouns ending with the foreign suffixes **-and, -ant, -ar, -är, -ast, ent, -eur, -ier, -ist, -ismus, -or, -us** are usually masculine.

der Kommandant	**der Friseur**
der Kommissar	**der Offizier**
der Millionär	**der Optimist**
der Enthusiast	**der Idealismus**
der Student	**der Tenor**

8. Supply the appropriate forms of the definite articles.

1. _____der_____ Pianist spielt sehr gut.
2. _____der_____ Professor ist sehr beliebt.
3. _____der_____ Pessimist ist selten glücklich.
4. _____der_____ Pastor besucht die kranke Frau.
5. _____der_____ Präsident ist noch nicht hier.
6. _____der_____ Abiturient studiert nächstes Jahr an der Uni.
7. _____der_____ Visionär will die Welt verändern.
8. _____der_____ Emigrant ist nach Amerika ausgewandert.
9. _____der_____ Jazz-Enthusiast plant eine Reise nach New Orleans.
10. _____der_____ Redakteur arbeitet für einen Verlag.

Feminine Endings

> **-age, -e, -ei, -heit, -keit, -schaft, -ie, -ek, -eke, -ik, -in, -ion, -tät, -ung, -ur**

Nouns ending in **-age, -e, -ei, -heit, -keit, -schaft, -ie, -ek, -eke, -ik, -in, -ion, -tät, -ung, -ur** are almost always feminine. Nouns ending in **-e** are usually feminine.

die Courage	*courage*	**die Politik**	*politics*
die Liebe	*love*	**die Musik**	*music*
die Partei	*party (political)*	**die Fabrik**	*factory*
die Krankheit	*illness*	**die Köchin**	*cook (female)*
die Schönheit	*beauty*	**die Nation**	*nation*
die Freundlichkeit	*friendliness*	**die Rarität**	*rarity*
die Freundschaft	*friendship*	**die Universität**	*university*
die Melodie	*melody*	**die Wohnung**	*apartment*
die Familie	*family*	**die Rechnung**	*bill, invoice*
die Diskothek	*discotheque*	**die Diktatur**	*dictatorship*
die Apotheke	*pharmacy*	**die Literatur**	*literature*

Important exceptions to the above rule:

das Auge	*eye*
das Ende	*end*
der Buchstabe	*letter (of the alphabet)*
der Hase	*rabbit, hare*
der Käse	*cheese*
der Kunde	*customer*

Another whole group of nouns that end in **-e** but are not always feminine are those derived from adjectives and the present and past participles of verbs. Nouns formed in this way normally have both a masculine and a feminine form when they refer to persons, in addition to a neuter form when they refer to a neuter noun or an abstraction.

der Alte	*old man*
die Alte	*old woman*
der Kranke	*sick person (male)*
die Kranke	*sick person (female)*
der Jugendliche	*young person (male)*
die Jugendliche	*young person (female)*
der Angestellte	*employee (male)*
die Angestellte	*employee (female)*
der Studierende	*student (male)*
die Studierende	*student (female)*

9. Supply the appropriate definite articles.

1. _____ Pille ist bitter.
2. Er gibt _____ Hoffnung auf.
3. _____ Kultur dieses Volkes ist primitiv.
4. _____ Universität ist bekannt.
5. _____ Technik ist progressiv.
6. _____ Kopie ist unklar.
7. _____ Krankheit ist gefährlich.
8. _____ Bäckerei ist geschlossen.
9. Er sagt _____ Wahrheit.
10. _____ Schneiderin macht das Kleid.
11. _____ Fabrik ist im Zentrum.
12. _____ Wohnung ist modern.
13. _____ Familie ist zu Hause.
14. _____ Maschine ist neu.
15. _____ Bibliothek ist neu.
16. Wo ist _____ Rarität?
17. _____ Köchin kocht.
18. _____ Nation ist stark.
19. _____ Garage ist klein.
20. _____ moderne Musik ist interessant.

Neuter Endings

> **-tum, -ment, -eum, -ium, -um, -ett**

Nouns ending in **-tum, -ment, -eum, -ium, -um, -ett** are usually neuter.

das Christentum	*Christianity*	das Museum	*museum*
das Instrument	*instrument*	das Datum	*date*
das Gymnasium	*secondary school*	das Duett	*duet*

Infinitives used as nouns are always neuter.

| das Hören | *hearing* |
| das Sehen | *seeing* |

10. Supply the appropriate forms of the definite articles.

1. _____ Lachen des Kindes ist ansteckend.
2. Wir besuchen _____ Gymnasium.
3. _____ Medikament hat ihm geholfen.
4. Wo ist _____ Heiligtum?
5. _____ Aquarium ist hier.
6. _____ Instrument ist teuer.
7. Wo ist _____ Museum?
8. _____ Datum steht hier.
9. _____ Christentum ist eine Religion.
10. _____ Arbeiten macht müde.

11. Supply the appropriate definite articles.

1. _____ Explosion zerstört _____ Gymnasium.
2. _____ Gabel, _____ Messer und _____ Löffel liegen hier.
3. _____ Straße ist breit.
4. _____ Lehrling arbeitet.
5. _____ Konditorei ist geschlossen.
6. _____ Dokument ist gefälscht.
7. _____ Honig und _____ Zucker sind süß.
8. Wir hören _____ Melodie.
9. _____ ganze Familie hat _____ Krankheit.
10. _____ Wohnung ist teuer.
11. _____ Lesen und _____ Schreiben lernte er zu Hause.
12. _____ Vogel sitzt dort.
13. _____ Rakete umkreist _____ Erde.
14. Warum liegen _____ Hammer und _____ Nagel hier?
15. _____ Sinfonie ist lang.
16. _____ Zentrum ist modern.
17. _____ Apotheke ist um die Ecke.
18. _____ Fabrik produziert viel.
19. _____ Teller ist weiß.
20. _____ Schlüssel ist aus Metall.

WORDS WITH DIFFERENT MEANINGS IN MASCULINE, FEMININE, AND NEUTER FORMS

There are a small number of words that have different meanings for masculine, feminine, and neuter forms. Included in this group are:

| der Gehalt | *content* | das Gehalt | *salary* |
| der Golf | *gulf* | das Golf | *golf* |

der Leiter	leader, manager	die Leiter	ladder
die Mark	DM (German currency)	das Mark	marrow
der See	lake (inland)	die See	sea (ocean)
das Steuer	steering wheel	die Steuer	tax
der Tor	fool	das Tor	gate

There are even a few words that have different meanings for all three genders.

der Band	volume (book)
das Band	ribbon, tape, bond
die Band	band (musical group)

12. Supply the appropriate definite articles.

1. _____ Golf von Mexiko ist warm.
2. _____ Band spielt gut.
3. _____ Königssee liegt in Süddeutschland.
4. _____ neue Geschäftsleiter ist sympathisch.
5. _____ Golf ist ein Rasenspiel.
6. Wo wird _____ Knochenmark produziert?
7. _____ Deutsche Mark wird aufgewertet.
8. _____ Gehalt ist zu niedrig.
9. _____ Nordsee ist oft stürmisch.
10. _____ Mondsee ist in Österreich.
11. _____ Tor war offen.
12. _____ Tor tötete den Hund.
13. _____ Leiter ist kaputt.
14. _____ Steuer ist sehr hoch.
15. _____ Haarband ist gelb.

COMPOUND NOUNS

Formation

German is well-known for its ability to form compound nouns composed of two or more words. This can be of great help to the student of German, since knowing the meaning of the individual components often makes it possible to understand the meaning of a compound noun that has not been encountered previously.

Often two singular nouns are joined to form one compound noun.

das Hotel, das Zimmer	das Hotelzimmer	hotel room
der Motor, das Boot	das Motorboot	motorboat
der Winter, der Mantel	der Wintermantel	winter coat
das Auto, der Bus	der Autobus	bus
der Zahn, die Bürste	die Zahnbürste	toothbrush
das Wasser, die Farbe	die Wasserfarbe	watercolor

Another group of compound nouns is formed by joining a plural and singular noun.

die Tannen, der Baum	der Tannenbaum	*fir tree*
die Kranken, der Wagen	der Krankenwagen	*ambulance*
die Kinder, das Zimmer	das Kinderzimmer	*children's room*
die Tage, das Buch	das Tagebuch	*diary*
die Straßen, die Lampe	die Straßenlampe	*streetlamp*
die Blumen, die Vase	die Blumenvase	*vase*

Some compound nouns are formed by two singular nouns connected by **-s** or **-es**.

der Staat, das Examen	das Staatsexamen	*state exam*
der Sport, der Mann	der Sportsmann	*sportsman*
der Geburtstag, der Kuchen	der Geburtstagskuchen	*birthday cake*
das Mitglied, die Karte	die Mitgliedskarte	*membership card*
der Liebling, die Melodie	die Lieblingsmelodie	*favorite melody*
die Universität, der Professor	der Universitätsprofessor	*university professor*

Other compound nouns are formed by joining a verb and a noun.

schreiben, der Block	der Schreibblock	*(writing) pad*
schreiben, die Maschine	die Schreibmaschine	*typewriter*
schreiben, der Tisch	der Schreibtisch	*desk*
lesen, die Brille	die Lesebrille	*reading glasses*
Lesen, der Stoff	der Lesestoff	*reading material*
lesen, die Liste	die Leseliste	*reading list*

Note that in these verb-noun formations the verb preceding the noun drops its final **-en** or **-n**.

Still other compound nouns are formed by joining an adjective and a noun.

rot, der Kohl	der Rotkohl	*red cabbage*
blau, der Stift	der Blaustift	*blue pencil*
dumm, der Kopf	der Dummkopf	*fool*
nah, der Verkehr	der Nahverkehr	*local traffic*
frisch, das Gemüse	das Frischgemüse	*fresh vegetables*
hoch, das Haus	das Hochhaus	*high-rise*

Gender

The last component of the compound noun determines the gender of the noun.

der Stahl, <u>die Industrie</u>	<u>die</u> Stahlindustrie
die Suppen, <u>der Löffel</u>	<u>der</u> Suppenlöffel
der Lehrer, die Hand, <u>das Buch</u>	<u>das</u> Lehrerhand<u>buch</u>

13. Form compound nouns with the indicated nouns and fill in the blanks. Supply the appropriate definite articles.

1. _____ ist süß.   *Geburtstag, Kuchen*
2. _____ ist warm.   *Winter, Mantel*
3. _____ kommt.   *Auto, Bus*
4. _____ ist modern.   *Hotel, Zimmer*
5. _____ hat Courage.   *Sport, Mann*
6. _____ ist alt.   *Blume, Vase*
7. _____ ist klein.   *Kind, Zimmer*
8. _____ kommt.   *Kranke, Wagen*
9. _____ ist hell.   *Straße, Lampe*
10. _____ ist intelligent.   *Universität, Professorin*
11. _____ liegt hier.   *Tag, Buch*
12. _____ ist klein.   *Mitglied, Karte*
13. _____ ist dunkel.   *Wasser, Farbe*
14. _____ ist schwer.   *Staat, Examen*
15. _____ ist dort.   *Zahn, Bürste*
16. _____ liegt auf dem Schreibtisch.   *rot, Stift*
17. _____ war sehr interessant.   *rund, Fahrt*
18. _____ schmeckte gut.   *schnell, Imbiß*
19. _____ war bequem.   *sitzen, Platz*
20. _____ war nicht sehr groß.   *segeln, Boot*

NOUNS USED ONLY IN THE SINGULAR

Certain nouns are used only in the singular. This group includes the names of materials and substances, certain general and abstract nouns, nouns formed from the infinitive of the verb, as well as collective nouns and other words which, by definition, cannot be plural. The following nouns are normally used only in the singular.

das Gold	*gold*	**die Liebe**	*love*
das Eisen	*iron*	**der Mut**	*courage*
die Milch	*milk*	**die Ehrlichkeit**	*honesty*
die Butter	*butter*	**die Aufrichtigkeit**	*sincerity*
der Honig	*honey*		
		das Lesen	*reading*
das Gute	*good*	**das Singen**	*singing*
das Böse	*evil*		
		das Vieh	*cattle*
die Hitze	*heat*	**die Polizei**	*police*
die Kälte	*cold*	**das Obst**	*fruit*
die Musik	*music*	**das Fleisch**	*meat*

Note that plurals can be created by using compound forms.

Obstsorten   *kinds of fruit*

Note also that collective nouns are used with singular verbs.

Das Vieh ist auf der Weide.

14.   Form sentences from groups of words. Follow the model.

Polizei / sein / hier   **Die Polizei ist hier.**

1. Obst / sein / frisch   5. Honig / sein / süß
2. Musik / sein / modern   6. Milch / sein / sauer
3. Fleisch / sein / frisch   7. Vieh / sein / hungrig
4. Butter / sein / teuer   8. Gold / sein / kostbar

PLURAL FORMS OF NOUNS

Almost all English nouns form their plurals by adding -*s* or -*es* to the singular forms, such as *cat, cats; glass, glasses*. Only a few English nouns have irregular plural forms, such as *mouse, mice; woman women*. In German, nouns rarely form their plural forms by adding **-s**. Some plural forms are identical to the singular; others take only an umlaut. Many other nouns are made plural by adding various endings, with or without umlaut. Regardless of the gender of the noun, the nominative plural form of the definite article is always **die**. Although there are no definite rules, there are basic patterns for the formation of the plural noun forms.

Note that the abbreviations below are the ones normally used in standard German dictionaries to indicate the plural forms of nouns.

Group Number	Abbreviation	Description	EXAMPLES Singular	Plural
Group Ia	-	no change	das Fenster der Onkel	die Fenster die Onkel
Group Ib	¨	umlaut only	der Vogel die Mutter	die Vögel die Mütter
Group IIa	-e	-e ending	der Arm das Jahr	die Arme die Jahre
Group IIb	¨e	-e ending + umlaut	der Stuhl die Nacht	die Stühle die Nächte
Group IIIa	-er	-er ending	das Bild das Kind	die Bilder die Kinder
Group IIIb	¨er	-er ending + umlaut	der Mann das Buch	die Männer die Bücher
Group IVa	-n	-n ending	der Name die Farbe	die Namen die Farben
Group IVb	-en	-en ending	der Herr die Frau	die Herren die Frauen
Group V	-s	-s ending	das Auto das Restaurant	die Autos die Restaurants

Group I

The nominative plurals of nouns in Group I are either identical to the singular or they add an umlaut in the plural. They do not take a plural ending.

Masculine and neuter nouns ending in **-el, -en, -er** belong to Group I, as do neuter nouns ending in **-sel** and nouns with the diminutive endings **-chen** and **-lein**. Two very common feminine nouns belong to this group.

Masculine Nouns

Singular		Plural
der Bruder	brother	die Brüder
der Dichter	poet	die Dichter
der Finger	finger	die Finger
der Koffer	suitcase	die Koffer
der Lehrer	teacher	die Lehrer
der Schüler	student	die Schüler
der Teller	plate	die Teller
der Vater	father	die Väter
der Braten	roast	die Braten
der Wagen	car, wagon	die Wagen
der Apfel	apple	die Äpfel
der Löffel	spoon	die Löffel
der Mantel	coat	die Mäntel
der Onkel	uncle	die Onkel
der Schlüssel	key	die Schlüssel
der Morgen	morning	die Morgen

Neuter Nouns

Singular		Plural
das Rätsel	puzzle	die Rätsel
das Fenster	window	die Fenster
das Messer	knife	die Messer
das Theater	theater	die Theater
das Zimmer	room	die Zimmer
das Segel	sail	die Segel
das Becken	basin	die Becken
das Kissen	pillow	die Kissen
das Fräulein	Miss	die Fräulein
das Mädchen	girl	die Mädchen

Feminine Nouns

Singular		Plural
die Mutter	mother	die Mütter
die Tochter	daughter	die Töchter

15. Rewrite the following, changing all nouns to the plural. Make all necessary changes.

1. Das Kissen ist weich.
2. Der Onkel kommt.
3. Die Tochter ist klein.
4. Das Zimmer ist kalt.
5. Der Bruder raucht.
6. Der Mantel ist neu.
7. Das Fenster ist geschlossen.
8. Der Apfel ist rot.
9. Der Lehrer ist alt.
10. Der Koffer ist aus Leder.
11. Das Messer ist rostig.
12. Das Segel ist weiß.
13. Der Teller steht dort.
14. Der Schlüssel ist alt.
15. Das Fräulein ist hübsch.
16. Die Mutter wartet.
17. Der Wagen steht hier.
18. Das Theater ist modern.
19. Der Löffel ist teuer.
20. Der Schüler lernt.

Group II

These nouns add **-e** to the singular to form the plural. Some nouns also add an umlaut. Masculine, feminine, and neuter nouns belong to this group. Many of these nouns have only one syllable.

Masculine Nouns

Singular		Plural
der Arm	arm	die Arme
der Berg	mountain	die Berge
der Besuch	visit	die Besuche
der Brief	letter	die Briefe
der Freund	friend	die Freunde
der Hund	dog	die Hunde
der König	king	die Könige
der Krieg	war	die Kriege
der Monat	month	die Monate
der Schuh	shoe	die Schuhe
der Sohn	son	die Söhne
der Stuhl	chair	die Stühle
der Tag	day	die Tage
der Tisch	table	die Tische
der Zug	train	die Züge

Neuter Nouns

Singular		Plural
das Boot	boat	die Boote
das Brot	bread	die Brote
das Gedicht	poem	die Gedichte
das Heft	notebook	die Hefte
das Jahr	year	die Jahre
das Papier	paper	die Papiere
das Tier	animal	die Tiere

Feminine Nouns

Singular		Plural
die Frucht	fruit	die Früchte
die Hand	hand	die Hände
die Nacht	night	die Nächte
die Stadt	city, town	die Städte
die Wurst	sausage	die Würste

16. Rewrite the following, changing all nouns to the plural. Make all necessary changes.

1. Die Wurst schmeckt gut. *Die Würste*
2. Der Monat ist lang.
3. Die Hand ist naß.
4. Das Gedicht ist kurz.
5. Der Hund ist braun.
6. Der Zug kommt an.
7. Der Tisch ist aus Holz.
8. Die Stadt ist modern.
9. Der Berg ist hoch.
10. Das Tier ist verletzt.
11. Der Krieg ist brutal.
12. Der Sohn ist groß.
13. Der Brief ist interessant.
14. Der Schuh ist aus Leder.
15. Der Tag ist kurz.
16. Der Freund lacht.
17. Die Nacht ist kalt.
18. Das Jahr geht vorüber.

Group III

These nouns add **-er** to the singular to form the plural. All nouns containing **a, o, u, au** in the stem add also an umlaut. Most of these nouns are neuter. Some are masculine, none are feminine.

Masculine Nouns

Singular		Plural
der Geist	*spirit*	**die Geister**
der Gott	*god*	**die Götter**
der Irrtum	*mistake*	**die Irrtümer**
der Mann	*man*	**die Männer**
der Wald	*forest*	**die Wälder**
der Wurm	*worm*	**die Würmer**

Neuter Nouns

Singular		Plural
das Bild	*picture*	**die Bilder**
das Blatt	*leaf*	**die Blätter**
das Buch	*book*	**die Bücher**
das Ei	*egg*	**die Eier**
das Glas	*glass*	**die Gläser**
das Haus	*house*	**die Häuser**
das Kind	*child*	**die Kinder**
das Kleid	*dress*	**die Kleider**
das Land	*country*	**die Länder**
das Lied	*song*	**die Lieder**
das Volk	*people*	**die Völker**

17.   Rewrite the following, changing all nouns to the plural. Make all necessary changes.

1. Der Wurm ist lang.
2. Das Buch ist interessant.
3. Das Ei schmeckt gut.
4. Das Land ist neutral.
5. Das Glas ist kalt.
6. Das Blatt ist grün.
7. Der Mann raucht.
8. Das Haus ist teuer.
9. Das Kleid paßt nicht.
10. Das Kind weint.
11. Das Volk ist hungrig.
12. Das Bild ist billig.
13. Das Lied ist melodisch.
14. Der Gott ist alt.

Group IV

These nouns add **-n** or **-en** to the singular. Nouns belonging to this group never add an umlaut. Most of these nouns are feminine. Feminine nouns ending in **-in** add **-nen** in the plural, e.g. **die Lehrerin, die Lehrerinnen**.

Masculine Nouns

Singular		Plural
der Hase	*rabbit*	**die Hasen**
der Junge	*boy*	**die Jungen**
der Name	*name*	**die Namen**

der Held	hero	die Helden
der Herr	Mr., gentleman	die Herren
der Mensch	human being	die Menschen
der Präsident	president	die Präsidenten

Neuter Nouns

Singular		*Plural*
das Auge	eye	die Augen
das Herz	heart	die Herzen
das Ohr	ear	die Ohren

Feminine Nouns

Singular		*Plural*
die Blume	flower	die Blumen
die Dame	lady	die Damen
die Katze	cat	die Katzen
die Minute	minute	die Minuten
die Schule	school	die Schulen
die Straße	street	die Straßen
die Stunde	hour	die Stunden
die Tante	aunt	die Tanten
die Tasse	cup	die Tassen
die Woche	week	die Wochen
die Schwester	sister	die Schwestern
die Antwort	answer	die Antworten
die Fabrik	factory	die Fabriken
die Frau	woman	die Frauen
die Nation	nation	die Nationen
die Tür	door	die Türen
die Universität	university	die Universitäten
die Wohnung	apartment	die Wohnungen
die Zeitung	newspaper	die Zeitungen
die Freundin	girlfriend	die Freundinnen
die Studentin	female student	die Studentinnen

18. Rewrite the following, changing all nouns to the plural. Make all necessary changes.

1. Der Herr ist alt.
2. Die Dame ist freundlich.
3. Die Katze ist schwarz.
4. Die Nation ist progressiv.
5. Der Junge ist hier.
6. Die Studentin lernt.
7. Die Tür ist offen.
8. Die Straße ist breit.
9. Der Student ist arm.
10. Die Freundin ist krank.
11. Der Hase ist weiß.
12. Die Blume blüht.
13. Die Fabrik ist grau.
14. Die Tasse ist gelb.
15. Die Wohnung is kalt.
16. Der Präsident ist alt.
17. Der Name ist lang.
18. Die Antwort ist falsch.
19. Der Held ist stark.
20. Die Zeitung liegt hier.

Group V

These nouns add **-s** to the singular. This group consists mainly of nouns of foreign origin, particularly those ending in vowels. However, it also includes German words that end in a vowel and abbreviations.

Masculine Nouns

Singular		Plural
der Job	*job*	die Jobs
der Park	*park*	die Parks
der Vati	*daddy*	die Vatis
der VW	*VW*	die VWs

Feminine Nouns

Singular		Plural
die Bar	*bar*	die Bars
die Kamera	*camera*	die Kameras
die Lobby	*lobby*	die Lobbys
die Mutti	*mommy*	die Muttis
die Party	*party*	die Partys
die Talk-Show	*talk show*	die Talk-Shows

Neuter Nouns

Singular		Plural
das Auto	*car*	die Autos
das Baby	*baby*	die Babys
das Foto	*photo*	die Fotos
das Hobby	*hobby*	die Hobbys
das Hotel	*hotel*	die Hotels
das Kino	*movie theater*	die Kinos
das Radio	*radio*	die Radios
das Sofa	*sofa*	die Sofas

Note: Some words ending in **-y** can also be spelled with **-ies** in the plural, e.g., **die Parties**.

19. Rewrite the following, changing all nouns to the plural. Make all necessary changes.

1. Die Kamera ist teuer.
2. Die Bar ist geschlossen.
3. Das Radio ist kaputt.
4. Das Hotel ist teuer.
5. Das Sofa ist weich.
6. Der Park ist groß.
7. Der Job ist interessant.
8. Das Foto ist alt.

Irregular Plural Nouns

Masculine Nouns

Singular		Plural
der Bus	*bus*	die Busse

Feminine Nouns

Singular		Plural
die Firma	*firm, company*	**die Firmen**

Neuter Nouns

Singular		Plural
das Drama	*drama*	**die Dramen**
das Gymnasium	*secondary school*	**die Gymnasien**
das Museum	*museum*	**die Museen**
das Zentrum	*center*	**die Zentren**

A few nouns that have the same singular form have two plurals with different meanings.

Singular		Plural
die Bank	*bench*	**die Bänke**
die Bank	*bank*	**die Banken**
das Wort	*word*	**die Wörter** (disconnected words on a list)
das Wort	*word*	**die Worte** (connected words in a sentence)
die Mutter	*mother*	**die Mütter**
die Mutter	*nut*	**die Muttern** (technical)

Some nouns are used only in the plural in German.

die Eltern	*parents*
die Ferien	*vacation*
die Geschwister	*brothers and sisters*
die Leute	*people*

20. Rewrite the following in the plural. Make all necessary changes.

1. Die Firma ist bekannt.
2. Ist das Wort auf der Liste?
3. Die Bank ist im Park.
4. Das Drama ist interessant.
5. Das Museum ist modern.
6. Der Bus kommt.
7. Die Bank ist geschlossen.
8. Das Zentrum ist groß.

Remember: When learning new nouns in German, it is necessary to memorize both the gender of the noun and its plural form.

---

das Abendessen	*evening meal*	**die Abendessen**
der Bleistift	*pencil*	**die Bleistifte**
das Antibiotikum	*antibiotic*	**die Antibiotika**

Review

21. Rewrite the following, changing the nouns to the singular whenever possible. Make all the necessary changes.

1. Die Teller sind weiß.
2. Die Lehrerinnen sind hübsch.
3. Die Gläser sind leer.
4. Die Mäntel hängen hier.
4. Die Zimmer sind warm.
6. Die Studenten lernen.
7. Die Geschäfte sind geschlossen.
8. Die Nächte sind lang.
9. Die Helden sind bekannt.
10. Die Bars sind billig.
11. Die Gymnasien sind progressiv.
12. Die Sofas sind rot.
13. Die Mütter sind freundlich.
14. Die Segel sind weiß.
15. Die Städte sind übervölkert.
16. Die Radios sind kaputt.
17. Die Zeitungen sind alt.
18. Die Männer sind krank.
19. Die Hände sind schmutzig.
20. Die Theater sind modern.
21. Die Eltern sind zu Hause.
22. Die Leute sind im Zentrum.

22. Rewrite the following, changing the nouns to the plural whenever possible. Make all necessary changes.

1. Das Vieh ist im Stall.
2. Der Schuh ist schwarz.
3. Die Freundin ist nett.
4. Das Fleisch ist teuer.
5. Der Apfel ist sauer.
6. Der Schlüssel ist rostig.
7. Das Mädchen ist freundlich.
8. Der Bus ist rot.
9. Die Mutter schreibt.
10. Die Wurst ist lecker.
11. Das Auto ist neu.
12. Der Brief ist lang.
13. Die Hand ist naß.
14. Das Zimmer ist groß.
15. Das Tier ist wild.
16. Das Glas ist teuer.
17. Das Buch ist interessant.
18. Die Straße ist eng.
19. Der Freund ist reich.
20. Das Lied ist kurz.

CASES OF NOUNS

German has four cases. These cases signal how nouns (and pronouns, too) are used within a sentence, clause, or phrase. The cases are:

> **nominative**
> **accusative**
> **dative**
> **genitive**

The grammatical functions reflected by these four cases correspond more or less to the subject, direct object, indirect object, and possessive cases in English usage. Similarities and differences between German and English usage will be pointed out as each case is discussed.

Most German nouns do not change their endings for each of the various cases. However, the articles and/or adjectives preceding the nouns do change their forms to reflect the case. Thus it is often necessary to look to the article and/or adjective in order to be able to identify the case of a noun.

As in English, there are two types of article in German, the *definite article* and the *indefinite article*.

> *Definite Article*
> **der, das, die**

> *Indefinite Article*
> **ein, ein, eine**

The *definite article* (**der, das, die**) is used to refer to a *particular* or *specific* person, place, or thing.

Der **Arzt hat montags Sprechstunde.**   *The doctor has office hours on Mondays.*

Here we are speaking of a particular doctor.

The *indefinite article* (**ein, ein, eine**) is used to refer to an *unspecified* person, place, or thing.

| *Ein* **Arzt hat viele Patienten.** | *A doctor has many patients.* |

In this case we are not referring to a particular doctor.

As noted at the beginning of this chapter, it is the definite article (**der, das, die**) that most clearly indicates the *gender* of a noun. Due to the changes in the endings of the definite article, the definite article is also most useful in identifying the *case* of a noun. The group of words that take the same grammatical endings as the definite article are referred to as **"der"** words.

dieser	*this*	**mancher**	*many (a)*
jeder	*each, every*	**solcher**	*such*
jener	*that*	**welcher**	*which*

Similarly, the group of words that take the same grammatical endings as the indefinite article (**ein, ein, eine**) are referred to as **"ein"** words.

mein	*my*	**ihr**	*her* or *their*
dein	*your* (familiar, sing.)	**unser**	*our*
sein	*his* or *its*	**euer**	*your* (familiar, pl.)
		Ihr	*your* (formal)

These **"ein"** words are also referred to as *possessive adjectives*, since their function is to describe the nouns they modify by indicating possession or ownership.

Note that **kein**, *no, not any*, is also an **"ein"** word.

The case endings for the **"der"** words and the **"ein"** words follow slightly different patterns. These patterns are presented for each case, followed by an overview of all cases presented, in the Review Chart. (See p. 47.)

Note: The possessive adjective **euer** *usually contracts* by dropping the last (and unstressed) **e** of the stem when an adjective ending is added.

eu(e)re Kinder ⟶ eure Kinder
eu(e)re Hunde ⟶ eure Hunde

However, the possessive adjective **unser** *usually does not contract* but rather retains its unstressed **e**, even when it is followed by an adjective ending, particularly in written German.

uns(e)re Kinder ⟶ unsere Kinder
uns(e)re Hunde ⟶ unsere Hunde

(For additional exercises on the use of the possessive adjectives, see Chapter 5.)

Nominative Case

Singular and Plural

The nominative forms of the definite and indefinite articles and of the **"der"** and **"ein"** words are as follows.

| | SINGULAR | | | PLURAL |
	Masculine	Neuter	Feminine	All Genders
Definite article "der" words	der dieser jener welcher	das dieses jenes welches	die diese jene welche	die diese jene welche
Indefinite article "ein" words	ein mein ihr unser	ein mein ihr unser	eine meine ihre unsere	(no plural) meine ihre unsere
Negative article	kein	kein	keine	keine

The nominative case is used in German in several ways.

As the Subject of the Verb

Der Mann **spielt Golf.**	*The man is playing golf.*
Die Freundin **kommt.**	*The girlfriend is coming.*
Das Auto **ist neu.**	*The car is new.*
Die Kinder **weinen.**	*The children are crying.*
Dieser Apfel **ist sauer.**	*This apple is sour.*
Diese Stadt **ist bekannt.**	*This city is well known.*
Dieses Zimmer **ist groß.**	*This room is large.*
Diese Bücher **sind interessant.**	*These books are interesting.*
Ein Hund **bellt.**	*A dog is barking.*
Eine Kopie **ist hier.**	*A copy is here.*
Ein Mädchen **singt.**	*A girl is singing.*
Mein Bruder **ist krank.**	*My brother is ill.*
Meine Katze **ist weiß.**	*My cat is white.*
Mein Messer **ist rostig.**	*My knife is rusty.*
Meine Eltern **sind dort.**	*My parents are there.*
Kein Wagen **ist billig.**	*No car is inexpensive.*
Keine Fabrik **ist sauber.**	*No factory is clean.*
Kein Hotel **ist so modern.**	*No hotel is as modern.*
Keine Museen **sind geschlossen.**	*No museums are closed.*

As a Predicate Nominative

A predicate nominative is a noun (or pronoun) that follows a linking verb and refers back to and is equated with the subject of the sentence or clause. Common linking verbs include:

sein	*to be*
werden	*to become*
bleiben	*to remain*
heißen	*to be called*
scheinen	*to appear*

Martin ist *unser Freund.*	*Martin is our friend.*
Die Frau ist *seine Mutter.*	*The woman is his mother.*
Gisela wird *keine Lehrerin.*	*Gisela will not become a teacher.*
Dr. Meyer bleibt *unser Hausarzt.*	*Dr. Meyer remains our family doctor.*
Der Hund heißt *Waldi.*	*The dog is named Waldi.*
Das scheint mir *eine gute Idee.*	*That seems a good idea to me.*

As a Noun of Direct Address

Bitte, nehmen Sie es, *Frau Breu!*	*Please take it, Mrs. Breu.*
Herr Müller, **kommen Sie?**	*Mr. Müller, are you coming?*
Guten Tag, *mein Freund!*	*Good day, my friend!*

23. Complete the following with **der, das, die.**

1. _____ Universität ist alt.
2. _____ Mann schreibt.
3. Ist _____ Mädchen krank?
4. _____ Junge studiert.
5. _____Wohnung ist kalt.
6. _____ Wetter ist schön.
7. Warum schreit _____ Kind?
8. _____ Frau ist hübsch.
9. _____ Lehrer ist jung.
10. _____ Vogel singt.

24. Rewrite the previous sentences with **dieser, dieses, diese.**

25. Rewrite the following, changing the nouns to the plural. Make all necessary changes.

1. Dieses Land ist reich.
2. Welcher Mann kommt?
3. Jenes Haus ist alt.
4. Wo ist die Zeitung?
5. Welche Studentin ist hübsch?
6. Jene Frau ist krank.
7. Dort liegt der Apfel.
8. Dieses Mädchen lernt.
9. Diese Stadt ist modern.
10. Wo ist das Buch?

26. Complete the following with **ein, ein, eine.**

1. Dort ist _____ Junge.
2. _____ Gabel ist aus Silber.
3. Das ist _____ Käfer.
4. _____ Mädchen kommt.
5. Dort steht _____ Museum.
6. Ist das _____ Lilie?
7. Dort liegt _____ Pille.
8. _____ Wohnung ist teuer.
9. Das ist _____ Pfennig.
10. Dort liegt _____ Apfel.

27. Complete the previous sentences with **kein, kein, keine.**

28. Complete the following with the appropriate endings, when necessary.

1. Sein_____ Freundin ist hier.
2. Wo ist euer_____ Haus?
3. Mein_____ Vater ist alt.
4. Ihr_____ Tochter lacht.
5. Dein_____ Auto ist teuer.
6. Wo ist Ihr_____ Hotel?
7. Hier ist sein_____ Mantel.
8. Unser_____ Kind ist klein.
9. Wo ist mein_____ Mutter?
10. Unser _____Kopie liegt dort.

29. Rewrite the following, changing the definite articles to the possessive **sein**.

1. Ist das die Firma?
2. Der Job ist schwer.
3. Das Glas ist leer.
4. Der Hund bellt.
5. Wo ist die Frau?

6. Das Auto ist neu.
7. Der Bus kommt.
8. Das Drama ist lang.
9. Wo ist der Junge?
10. Die Freundin ist hübsch.

30. Rewrite the following, changing the nouns to the plural. Make all necessary changes.

1. Meine Freundin lacht.
2. Ihr Bruder ist krank.
3. Wo ist sein Lehrer?
4. Dein Messer liegt dort.
5. Wo ist unser Schlüssel?

6. Ist das euer Haus?
7. Wo ist Ihre Zeitung?
8. Dort ist mein Onkel.
9. Ist das dein Kind?
10. Wo ist eure Lehrerin?

31. Complete the following with the appropriate endings when necessary.

1. Dies_____ Frau ist ihr_____Mutter.
2. Das ist doch kein_____ Hund!
3. Solch_____ Menschen sind beliebt.
4. Wann kommt euer_____ Vater?
5. Jen_____ Museum ist bekannt.

6. Dies_____ Männer sind wichtig.
7. Welch_____ Junge ist dein_____ Bruder?
8. Er wird kein_____ Doktor.
9. Ist das dein_____ Pille?
10. Unser_____ Eltern sind dort.

Accusative Case
Singular and Plural

The accusative forms of the definite and indefinite articles and of the **"der"** and **"ein"** words are as follows.

	SINGULAR			PLURAL
	Masculine	*Neuter*	*Feminine*	*All Genders*
Definite article "der" words	den	das	die	die
	diesen	dieses	diese	diese
	welchen	welches	welche	welche
Indefinite article "ein" words	einen	ein	eine	(no plural)
	meinen	mein	meine	meine
	ihren	ihr	ihre	ihre
Negative article	keinen	kein	keine	keine

The accusative case is used in several ways.

As the Direct Object of the Verb

Wir kaufen *den Wagen.*	*We are buying the car.*
Ich nehme *die Zeitung.*	*I take the newspaper.*
Kennst du *das Drama?*	*Do you know the drama?*
Ich habe *die Bücher.*	*I have the books.*
Wir kennen *ihren Bruder.*	*We know her brother.*
Sie braucht *ihre Tasche.*	*She needs her purse.*
Sie verkaufen *ihr Auto.*	*They are selling their car.*
Sie hat *ihre Karten.*	*She has her tickets.*

Er hat *keinen Hund*.   *He doesn't have a dog.*
Sie hat *keine Zeit*.   *She has no time.*
Ich habe *kein Geld*.   *I have no money.*
Er kauft *keine Schuhe*.   *He is not buying shoes.*

With Expressions of Definite Time and Duration of Time

Er bleibt *eine Woche* **in Bonn.**   *He is staying one week in Bonn.*
Sie besucht mich *jeden Tag*.   *She visits me every day.*
Sie fährt *jedes Jahr* **nach Deutschland.** *She goes to Germany every year.*

The accusative form of **der** is used when dating a letter: **Köln,** *den* **13. 8. 1996**

With Prepositions

The accusative case is used as the object of certain prepositions, which are discussed in Chapter 3.

32. Complete the following with the appropriate forms of **der, das, die.**

1. Kaufst du _____ Mantel?   6. Er kennt _____ Mädchen.
2. Wir besuchen _____ Museum.   7. Hast du _____ Zeitung?
3. Kennst du _____ Frau?   8. Ich esse _____ Apfel.
4. Ich nehme _____ Banane.   9. Wir kaufen _____ Haus.
5. Brauchst du _____ Buch?   10. Sie sehen _____ Mann.

33. Complete the previous sentences with the appropriate forms of **dieser, dieses, diese.**

34. Rewrite the following sentences, changing the nouns to the plural. Make all necessary changes.

1. Wir kennen den Dichter.   6. Wir besuchen die Stadt.
2. Ich bekomme den Brief.   7. Ich kenne den Berg.
3. Er kauft die Wurst.   8. Er schreibt das Gedicht.
4. Ich sehe das Tier.   9. Ich kaufe die Blume.
5. Sie treffen den Freund.   10. Wir singen das Lied.

35. Complete the following with the appropriate forms of **ein, ein, eine.**

1. Ich habe _____ Koffer.   6. Er bringt _____ Vase.
2. Er besucht _____ Universität.   7. Sie brauchen _____ Tisch.
3. Wir kaufen _____ Bild.   8. Wir haben _____ Hund.
4. Ich nehme _____ Ei.   9. Schreibst du _____ Gedicht?
5. Wir besuchen _____ Freund.   10. Hast du _____ Freundin?

36. Complete the previous sentences with the appropriate forms of **kein.**

37. Rewrite the following sentences, changing the definite articles to the possessive adjective **unser.**

1. Kaufst du das Auto?   4. Er ruft den Lehrer.
2. Ich sehe die Katze.   5. Ich nehme den Schlüssel.
3. Wir besuchen das Kind.   6. Wir kennen die Lehrerin.

38. Complete the following with the appropriate endings when necessary.

1. Er nimmt mein_____ Wagen.   6. Habt ihr eur_____ Zeitung?
2. Er besucht sein_____ Mutter.   7. Er kennt unser_____ Stadt.
3. Besuchst du ihr_____ Bruder?   8. Sie verkaufen ihr_____ Haus.

4. Braucht ihr euer_____ Zimmer?   9. Ich brauche mein_____ Auto.
5. Ich kenne ihr_____ Schwester.   10. Kennst du sein_____ Tante?

39. Rewrite the following, changing the nouns to the plural. Make all necessary changes.

1. Hat er mein Bild?   6. Wir kennen ihr Kind.
2. Brauchst du dein Buch?   7. Ich habe ihren Schuh.
3. Seht ihr unsere Freundin?   8. Verkaufst du unseren Wagen?
4. Ich nehme seine Zeitung   9. Sie brauchen ihren Freund.
5. Hast du deinen Mantel?   10. Treffen Sie Ihren Lehrer?

Noun Endings in the Accusative Case

Singular

The accusative singular of most German nouns is identical with the nominative singular. There is, however, a small group of masculine nouns that add an **-n** or **-en** ending to the noun in the accusative singular (as well as in the dative and genitive singular). These nouns are often referred to as *weak nouns* or *n-nouns*.

Although many of these nouns must simply be memorized, it is helpful to remember that masculine nouns formed from adjectives and verb participles (**der Junge, der Alte, der Bekannte, der Reisende, der Verwandte**) fall into this category as well as masculine nouns ending in **-ent** and **-ist** (**der Student, der Tourist**).

Examples of other masculine nouns that belong to this group follow.

Nominative Singular		*Accusative Singular*
der Hase	*rabbit*	**den Hasen**
der Held	*hero*	**den Helden**
der Herr	*gentleman*	**den Herrn**
der Junge	*boy*	**den Jungen**
der Mensch	*human being*	**den Menschen**
der Präsident	*president*	**den Präsidenten**
der Student	*student*	**den Studenten**

Wir treffen *den Studenten.*	*We meet the student.*
Kennst du *einen Helden?*	*Do you know a hero?*
Wir haben *euren Nachbarn* **gesehen.**	*We saw your neighbor.*

40. Complete the following with the appropriate endings.

1. Sie liebt d_____ Student_____.   6. Wer sieht jen_____ Herr_____?
2. Wir sehen kein_____ Mensch_____.   7. Kennst du unser_____ Präsident_____?
3. Ich kenne d_____ Präsident_____.   8. Sie treffen kein_____ Held_____.
4. Er ruft mein_____ Junge_____.   9. Welch_____ Hase_____ kaufst du?
5. Ich kaufe kein_____ Hase_____.   10. Sie haben ein_____ Junge_____.

Review

41. Complete the following with the appropriate endings when necessary.

1. Sein_____ Frau fährt jed_____ Montag nach Köln.
2. Wann verkauft ihr euer_____ Haus?
3. Er füttert d_____ Has_____.

4. Welch_____ Junge_____ kennst du?
5. Dies_____ Herr_____ schreibt ein_____ Brief.
6. Unser_____ Mutter kauft kein_____ Mantel.
7. Jen_____ Student_____ besucht sein_____ Freundin.
8. D_____ Kind hat mein_____ Bücher.
9. Ihr_____ Freundin bleibt ein_____ Tag hier.
10. Welch_____ Mann hat Ihr_____ Auto?
11. Mein_____ Bruder kauft dies_____ Bild.
12. Mein_____ Schwester kennt d_____ Präsident_____.
13. Besucht ihr eur_____ Kinder jed_____ Tag?
14. Unser_____ Junge_____ kann solch_____ Romane lesen.
15. Dies_____ Katze trinkt kein_____ Milch.
16. Welch_____ Museen besucht er?
17. Manch_____ Eltern sind streng.
18. Kennen Sie dies_____ Herr_____?
19. Welch_____ Kleider kauft jen_____ Mädchen?
20. München, d_____ 6. 5. 1996.

Dative Case

Singular and Plural

The dative forms of the definite and indefinite articles and of the **"der"** and **"ein"** words are as follows.

	SINGULAR			PLURAL
	Masculine	Neuter	Feminine	All Genders
Definite article "der" words	dem diesem jenem	dem diesem jenem	der dieser jener	den diesen jenen
Indefinite article "ein" words	einem meinem ihrem	einem meinem ihrem	einer meiner ihrer	(no plural) meinem ihren
Negative article	keinem	keinem	keiner	keinen

The dative case is used in several ways.

As the Indirect Object of the Verb.

In English this relationship is often expressed by the prepositions *to* or *for*. The person or animal to whom something is given, shown, or told is in the dative case.

Ich hole *dem Hund* das Futter.	*I am getting the food for the dog.*
Er kauft *der Frau* die Karte.	*He is buying the ticket for the women.*
Wir zeigen *dem Kind* das Boot.	*We are showing the boat to the child.*
Wir geben *einem Mann* Geld.	*We are giving money to a man.*
Ich schicke *meiner Freundin* nichts.	*I am sending nothing to my girlfriend.*
Sie kauft *unserem Kind* Schokolade.	*She is buying chocolate for our child.*

The following verbs are frequently used with both a direct and an indirect object, that is, with an accusative and a dative object.

bringen	*to bring, take*	**Er bringt** *seiner Freundin* **Blumen.**
		He brings flowers to his girlfriend.
geben	*to give*	**Wir geben** *der Katze* **Milch.**
		We are giving milk to the cat.
holen	*to get*	**Ich hole** *meinem Bruder* **den Schlüssel.**
		I am getting the key for my brother.
kaufen	*to buy*	**Sie kauft** *ihrer Mutter* **ein Auto.**
		She is buying a car for her mother.
schicken	*to send*	**Sonja schickt** *ihrer Tante* **ein Geschenk.**
		Sonja is sending a gift to her aunt.
sagen	*to say, tell*	**Sie sagt** *ihrem Mann* **die Wahrheit.**
		She is telling her husband the truth.
zeigen	*to show*	**Er zeigt** *dem Mädchen* **das Museum.**
		He is showing the museum to the girl.

With Dative Verbs

A number of German verbs take only dative objects. The following commonly used verbs are always used with the dative case.

antworten	*to answer*	**Ich antworte** *dem Herrn.*
		I answer the gentleman.
danken	*to thank (for)*	**Wir danken** *unserem Lehrer.*
		We thank our teacher.
helfen	*to help*	**Ich helfe** *dem Kind.*
		I am helping the child.
gehören	*to belong*	**Dieses Buch gehört** *ihrem Sohn.*
		This book belongs to her son.
gefallen	*to like, be pleasing*	**Jener Hut gefällt** *seiner Frau.*
		His wife likes that hat.
folgen	*to follow*	**Der Hund folgt** *mir* **nach Hause.**
		The dog follows me home.

The verb **glauben** is used with the dative when followed by a person. The accusative is used when it is followed by a thing.

Ich glaube *dem Kind.*	*I believe the child*
Ich glaube *die Geschichte.*	*I believe the story.*

Note: Many impersonal constructions also require the dative case.

Es geht *mir* **gut.**	*I'm fine (doing well).*
Es geht *mir* **besser.**	*I'm feeling better.*
Es tut *mir* **leid.**	*I'm sorry.*
Es gefällt *mir* **nicht.**	*I don't like it. (Literally: It doesn't please me.)*
Es schmeckt *mir* **(gut).**	*It tastes good (to me).*

With Prepositions

The dative case is used with certain prepositions, which are presented in Chapter 3.

42. Complete the following sentences with the appropriate forms of **der, das, die.**

    1. Er holt _____ Lehrer Kaffee.
    2. Ich schreibe _____ Freundin.
    3. Wir helfen _____ Mann.
    4. Dankst du _____ Kind?
    5. Ich schicke _____ Studentin Geld.
    6. Er sagt _____ Mädchen alles.
    7. Wir kaufen _____ Onkel das Buch.
    8. Es gehört _____ Dame.
    9. Ich glaube _____ Fräulein.
    10. Ich gebe _____ Katze Wasser.

43. Complete the previous sentences with the appropriate forms of **jener.**

44. Complete the following sentences with the appropriate forms of **ein.**

    1. Wir danken _____ Frau.
    2. Ich kaufe _____ Studentin das Buch.
    3. Wir helfen _____ Tier.
    4. Sie geben es _____ Dame.
    5. Wir glauben _____ Mann.
    6. Ich helfe _____ Familie.
    7. Es gehört _____ Dichter.
    8. Ich schreibe _____ Freund.
    9. Sie schickt es _____ Kind.
    10. Er antwortet _____ Mädchen.

45. Complete the preceding sentences with the appropriate forms of **kein.**

46. Complete the following with the appropriate endings.

    1. Er gibt sein_____ Frau Blumen.
    2. Ich sage mein_____ Onkel nichts.
    3. Wir danken unser_____ Mutter.
    4. Sie hilft ihr_____ Mann.
    5. Es gehört dein_____ Freund.
    6. Zeigst du ihr_____ Tante den Brief?
    7. Ich glaube ihr_____ Bruder.
    8. Holen Sie Ihr_____ Sohn Milch?
    9. Zeigt ihr eur_____ Tochter das Geschenk?
    10. Es gehört unser_____ Vater.

47. Complete the following with the dative forms of the indicated words.

    1. Ich zeige _____ Lehrer dieses Buch. *kein*
    2. Wir geben _____ Vater ein Geschenk. *unser*
    3. Es gehört _____ Studentin. *dies_____*
    4. Sie gefällt _____ Bruder. *mein*
    5. Ich kaufe _____ Mutter etwas. *euer*
    6. Wir schreiben _____ Tante eine Karte. *unser*
    7. Er sagt _____ Mann die Neuigkeit. *jen_____*
    8. Ich bringe _____ Kind ein Bonbon. *jed_____*
    9. Er holt _____ Freundin Limonade. *sein*
    10. Helfen Sie _____ Frau? *Ihr*

Noun Endings in the Dative Case

Singular

The dative singular of most German nouns is identical with the nominative singular. The same nouns that add an **-n** or **-en** ending in the accusative singular add the **-n** or **-en** in the dative singular. (See section on accusative case.)

Ich gebe *dem Herrn* **die Zeitung.**	*I am giving the newspaper to the gentleman.*
Wir bringen *dem Studenten* **ein Buch.**	*We are bringing a book to the student.*
Er gibt *dem Touristen* **eine Landkarte.**	*He gives the tourist a map.*

Note: Masculine and neuter nouns of one syllable may take an optional **-e** ending in the dative singular. Although this ending was once a grammatical requirement, it has become increasingly infrequent. Today it is primarily limited to certain common idiomatic phrases and extremely formal and poetic utterances.

Some idiomatic phrases retaining the **-e** ending include:

zu Hause	*at home*
nach Hause	*(go/come) home*
auf dem Lande	*in the country*
am Tage	*during the day*

48. Complete the following with the appropriate endings.

1. Wir danken d_____ Held_____.
2. Es gehört jen_____ Student_____.
3. Sie glaubt unser_____ Präsident_____.
4. Es gefällt dies_____ Herr_____.
5. Er zeigt es sein_____ Junge_____.
6. Ich gebe ein_____ Hase_____ die Karotte.
7. Wir helfen kein_____ Mensch_____.
8. Welch_____ Junge_____ gehört das Auto?

Plural

The dative plural noun always adds **-n**, unless the nominative plural form already ends in **-n**.

Ich schicke *den Kindern* **Geschenke.**	*I am sending presents to the children.*
Wir geben *den Mädchen* **nichts.**	*We are giving nothing to the girls.*

Nouns ending in **-s** in the nominative plural retain the **-s** in the dative plural and do not add **-n**.

Er zeigt *den Babys* **das Tier.**	*He is showing the animal to the babies.*

49. Rewrite the following sentences, changing the dative nouns to the plural. Make all necessary changes.

1. Schreibst du deiner Freundin?
2. Er hilft jenem Kind.
3. Es gefällt seinem Lehrer.
4. Sie zeigt es ihrem Bruder.
5. Er antwortet dem Mann.
6. Ich hole dem Baby Milch.
7. Es gehört diesem Jungen.
8. Wir glauben der Frau.
9. Sie dankt ihrem Freund.
10. Es gehört eurem Studenten.

50. Complete the following with the appropriate forms of the dative of the indicated words.

1. Ich helfe _____ Frauen. *jen_____*
2. Ich danke _____ Vater. *mein*
3. Sie hilft _____ Kindern. *unser*
4. Wir kaufen es _____ Mann. *ihr.*

5. Gehört es _____ Freundinnen? *dein*
6. Er dankt _____ Frau. *dies_____*
7. _____ Kind gefällt es? *welch_____*
8. Sie antwortet _____ Herrn. *kein*
9. Ich bringe es _____ Baby. *ein*
10. Wir schicken _____ Studenten Geld. *jed_____*

Review

51. Complete the following with the correct endings when necessary.

1. Unser_____ Junge hilft sein_____ Freund.
2. Wer hat mein_____ Tante d_____ Wohnung gezeigt?
3. Man kann solch_____ Leuten nicht helfen.
4. Wer glaubt dies_____ Frau?
5. Jen_____ Auto gefällt mein_____ Tochter.
6. Welch_____ Kellnerin holt dies_____ Gast d_____ Braten?
7. Warum has du jed_____ Kind dies_____ Buch gekauft?
8. Wir danken unser_____ Eltern.
9. D_____ Enkel holt sein_____ Großvater d_____ Pfeife.
10. Kein_____ Mensch hat d_____ Invalidin geholfen.
11. Warum schreibt er sein_____ Geschwister_____ kein_____ Brief?
12. Jen_____ Hund gehört ihr_____ Bruder.
13. Antwortet ihr eur_____ Freundinnen_____?
14. Wann sagst du dein_____ Mann d_____ Wahrheit?
15. Wer hat d_____ Kinder_____ mein_____ Puppe gegeben?

Genitive Case

Singular and Plural

The genitive forms of the definite and indefinite articles and of the **"der"** and **"ein"** words are as follows.

| | SINGULAR | | | PLURAL |
	Masculine	Neuter	Feminine	All Genders
Definite article **"der"** words	des dieses jenes	des dieses jenes	der dieser jener	der dieser jener
Indefinite article **"ein"** words	eines meines ihres	eines meines ihres	einer meiner ihrer	(no plural) meiner ihrer
Negative article	keines	keines	keiner	keiner

The genitive case is used in several ways.

To Show Possession or Relationships Between Two Nouns

In English this is expressed by the preposition *of* or with *'s*. The apostrophe is not normally used in German. (See exception below.)

Dort liegt das Buch *des Lehrers*.	*There lies the teacher's book.*
Wo ist das Auto *der Frau*?	*Where is the woman's car?*
Der Griff *des Messers* **ist rostig.**	*The handle of the knife is rusty.*
Das ist die Frau *meines Sohnes*.	*That is my son's wife.*
Wo ist die Tasche *meiner Tochter*?	*Where is my daughter's purse?*
Hier ist ein Foto *unseres Hauses*.	*Here is a picture of our house.*
Frau Schnabels **Mann ist hier.**	*Mrs. Schnabel's husband is here.*
Die Eltern *dieser Kinder* **sind hier.**	*The parents of these children are here.*

Note: In German the genitive noun generally follows the noun that it modifies, whereas in English the possessive noun usually precedes the noun it modifies.

der Wagen *meines Onkels*	*my uncle's car*
das Buch *des Mädchens*	*the girl's book*
die Bluse *meiner Tante*	*my aunt's blouse*

However, when a proper name is put into the genitive in German, it usually precedes the noun it modifies.

Uwes **Wagen**	*Uwe's car*
Mariannes **Buch**	*Marianne's book*

With Expressions of Indefinite Time

In English these are expressed with *one day, some day* (*night, evening,* etc.).

Eines Tages **wird sie ihren Freund sehen.**	*Some day she'll see her friend.*
Eines Morgens **kam er zu Besuch.**	*One morning he came for a visit.*

By way of analogy the feminine noun **Nacht** also adds **-s** in such time expressions.

Eines Nachts **war er wieder gesund.**	*One night he was well again.*

With Prepositions

The genitive case is used with certain prepositions, which are presented in Chapter 3.

With Verbs

Note: A very small number of verbs take a genitive object. These constructions often sound rather formal and somewhat archaic.

Wir gedenken *unserer gefallenen Soldaten*.	*We remember our fallen soldiers.*
Er rühmt sich *seines Talentes*.	*He brags about his talent.*

Noun Endings in the Genitive Case

Singular

<u>*Masculine and Neuter*</u>

-s or **-es** endings

Most masculine and neuter nouns add **-s** or **-es** in the singular. No apostrophe is used. An **-s** is added if the masculine or neuter noun has more than one syllable, such as **meines Bruders, dieses Zimmers**.

An **-es** is added if the masculine or neuter noun has only one syllable, such as **des Buches**. If the last syllable is accented, the genitive ending is also **-es**, such as **des Gedíchtes**.

-n or -en endings

Those nouns that take **-n** or **-en** in the accusative and dative singular also add **-n** or **-en** in the genitive singular.

Die Frau *des Präsidenten* **ist krank.**   The wife of the president is ill.

-ns or -ens endings

Some nouns add **-ens** to form the genitive singular, such as **des Herzens**, **des Namens**, **des Friedens**.

Traurigen Herzens *zog er in den Krieg.*   *With a heavy heart he went to war.*

Feminine

No ending is added to feminine nouns in the genitive case.

Der Rand *der Tasse* **ist angeschlagen.**   *The rim of the cup was chipped.*

Proper names

An **-s** is added to proper names in the genitive case.

Luises **Bruder spielt Fußall.**   *Louise's brother plays soccer.*
Frau Bauers **Hut war teuer.**   *Mrs. Bauer's hat was expensive.*

When a masculine name ends in a sibilant (an *s* sound), the genitive can be formed by adding **-ens** or an apostrophe.

Maxens Geburtstag **ist am 11. Mai.**   *Max's birthday is May 11th.*
Max' Geburtstag **ist am 11. Mai.**   *Max's birthday is May 11th.*

However, the **von** construction is preferred in such cases.

Der Geburtstag *von Max* **ist am 11. Mai.**   *Max's birthday is May 11th.*

Plural

The genitive plural noun form is identical to the nominative plural noun form.

Die Kleider der *Frauen* **waren modisch.**   *The women's clothing was stylish.*

52. Complete the following with the appropriate forms of **der, das, die** and the appropriate noun endings when necessary.

   1. Die Fabrik _____ Familie_____ ist groß.
   2. Das Auto _____ Doktor_____ ist kaputt.
   3. Die Farbe _____ Wagen_____ ist schön.
   4. Der Bau _____ Haus_____ beginnt bald.
   5. Der Mantel _____ Frau_____ ist aus Leder.
   6. Der Preis _____ Bild_____ ist zu hoch.
   7. Die Buchstabierung _____ Name_____ ist schwer.
   8. Der Vater _____ Junge_____ ist hier.
   9. Der Titel _____ Gedicht_____ ist kurz.
  10. Die Freundin _____ Student_____ wartet.

53. Complete the previous sentences with the appropriate forms of **dieser**.

54. Complete the following sentences with the appropriate forms of **ein** and the appropriate noun endings when necessary.

1. Das Leben _____ Held_____ ist interessant.
2. Es ist die Geschichte _____ Junge_____.
3. Ich höre das Lachen _____ Kind_____.
4. Das ist die Wohnung _____ Student_____.
5. Die Frau _____ Arbeiter_____ ist krank.
6. Die Mutter _____ Mädchen_____ ist hier.
7. Die Politik _____ Nation_____ ist wichtig.
8. Ich esse die Hälfte _____ Apfel_____.
9. Wo ist das Bild _____ Herr_____?
10. Ich höre den Motor _____ Maschine_____.

55. Complete the following with the appropriate genitive forms of the indicated words. Supply the appropriate noun endings when necessary.

1. Das ist das Buch _____ Lehrer_____. *sein*
2. Ich nehme den Wagen _____ Mutter_____. *mein*
3. Wo ist die Frau _____ Präsident_____? *unser*
4. Dort ist das Zimmer _____ Junge_____. *euer*
5. Das Leben _____ Vater_____ ist schwer. *ihr*
6. Wo ist der Mantel _____ Tante_____? *dein*
7. Wir sehen das Gymnasium _____ Tochter_____. *ihr*
8. Dort hängt das Foto _____ Kind_____. *mein*
9. Die Freundin _____ Sohn_____ kommt. *sein*
10. Wo ist die Katze _____ Großmutter_____? *Ihr*

56. Rewrite the following, changing the genitive nouns to the plural. Make all necessary changes.

1. Die Kinder jener Frau sind krank.
2. Die Sitze seines Autos sind bequem.
3. Das sind die Fotos unserer Tochter.
4. Die Bücher jenes Studenten liegen hier.
5. Wann beginnt der Bau eures Hauses?
6. Die Museen dieser Stadt sind modern.
7. Die Kleider meiner Freundin sind neu.
8. Der Wagen des Herrn steht dort.
9. Die Betonung des Namens ist schwer.
10. Die Gemälde jenes Museums sind bekannt.

Substitute for the Genitive Case

In colloquial German the preposition **von** with the dative case is frequently used instead of the genitive construction.

Das Kleid *meiner Tochter* **war teuer.**	*My daughter's dress was expensive.*
Das Kleid *von meiner Tochter* **war teuer.**	*My daughter's dress was expensive.*
Das Auto *meines Bruders* **ist kaputt.**	*My brother's car is broken.*
Das Auto *von meinem Bruder* **ist kaputt.**	*My brother's car is broken.*

57. Rewrite the following. Substitute the **von** plus dative construction for the genitive. Make all necessary changes.

1. Die Schneide dieses Messers ist scharf.
2. Die Dokumente unseres Präsidenten sind im Museum.
3. Wir haben die Hälfte des Gedichtes gelesen.
4. Hier ist ein Bild meiner Freunde.
5. Der Preis des Autos ist zu hoch.

58. Rewrite the following. Substitute the genitive for the **von** plus dative construction.

1. Das Wasser von jenem See ist eiskalt.
2. Der Hund von Peter bellt.
3. Die Ohren von solchen Hasen sind sehr lang.
4. Die Mutter von dem Mädchen steht dort.
5. Die Produkte von dieser Fabrik sind teuer.

Review

59. Complete the following with the appropriate endings when necessary.

1. Wo ist d_____ Wohnung dein_____ Tante_____?
2. Das is d_____ Geschäft sein_____ Eltern_____.
3. D_____ Götter jen_____ Volk_____ waren nicht gütig.
4. Ein_____ Nachmittag_____ besuchten sie uns.
5. Ist d_____ Krankheit eur_____ Bruder_____ ansteckend?
6. D_____ Blätter dies_____ Baum_____ sind schon abgefallen.
7. Frau Schneider_____ Mann ist schon angekommen.
8. D_____ Titel dies_____ Roman_____ ist zu lang.
9. D_____ Freunde mein_____ Tochter_____ sind hier.
10. D_____ Mutter jen_____ Junge_____ ist krank.
11. D_____ Hand d_____ Frau_____ ist kalt.
12. Wo ist d_____ Foto dein_____ Haus_____?
13. D_____ Kinder ihr_____ Freundin_____ sind hier.
14. Ich kenne d_____ Professor jen_____ Student_____.
15. Sie kauft d_____ Wagen mein_____ Großvater_____.

REVIEW OF CASE ENDINGS FOR THE "der" WORDS
(der, dieser, jeder, jener, mancher, solcher, welcher)

	SINGULAR Masculine	SINGULAR Neuter	SINGULAR Feminine	PLURAL All genders
Nominative	-er	-(e)s	-e	-e
Accusative	-en	-(e)s	-e	-e
Dative	-em	-em	-er	-en
Genitive	-es	-es	-er	-er

REVIEW OF CASE ENDINGS FOR THE "ein" WORDS
(ein, kein, mein, dein, sein, ihr, unser, euer, Ihr)

	SINGULAR			PLURAL
	Masculine	*Neuter*	*Feminine*	*All genders*
Nominative	—	—	-e	-e
Accusative	-en	—	-e	-e
Dative	-em	-em	-er	-en
Genitive	-es	-es	-er	-er

SPECIAL USES OF THE DEFINITE ARTICLE

With General or Abstract Nouns

Die Katze ist ein Haustier.	*A cat is a domestic animal.*
Die Liebe ist eine Himmelsmacht.	*Love is a heavenly power.*
Das Leben ist kurz.	*Life is short.*

60. Complete the following with the appropriate definite articles.

1. _____ Panther ist eine Wildkatze.
2. _____ Technik ist progressiv.
3. _____ Leben ist kompliziert.
4. _____ Gravitation ist eine Kraft.
5. _____ Chemie ist eine Wissenschaft.
6. _____ Mensch ist sterblich.
7. _____ Hund ist ein Haustier.
8. _____Schule ist wichtig.

With Names of Streets, Lakes, Mountains, and Countries

Die Theatinerstraße ist in München.	*Theatiner Street is in Munich.*
Der Bodensee ist tief.	*Lake Constance is deep.*
Der Tafelberg ist in Südafrika.	*Table Mountain is in South Africa.*

The definite article is required with names of countries that are masculine, feminine, or plural. (See the section "Neuter Nouns" for gender of countries.)

Der Iran ist im Osten.	*Iran is in the east.*
Die Schweiz ist neutral.	*Switzerland is neutral.*
Die Vereinigten Staaten sind groß.	*The United States is large.*

The definite article is not used with countries that are neuter, unless the name of the country is modified.

Deutschland produziert viel.	*Germany produces much.*
Das moderne Deutschland ist progressive.	*Modern Germany is progressive.*

61. Complete the following with the appropriate definite articles when necessary.

1. _____ Vesuv ist ein Vulkan.
2. Wo ist _____ Bergstraße?
3. _____ Niederlande sind im Norden.
4. Hier liegt _____ Türkei.
5. _____ Tegernsee ist klein.
6. _____ Irak ist im Osten.
7. Wie hoch ist _____ Montblanc?
8. _____ historische Italien ist bekannt.
9. Dort ist _____ Alpenstraße.
10. _____ Vereinigten Staaten sind reich.
11. _____ Afrika ist groß.
12. _____ heutige Deutschland ist modern.

With Weights, Measures, and Expressions of Time

The accusative case of the definite article is used in German with expressions of weight, measure, and time. In English the indefinite article is used in the sense of *per*.

Das kostet 2 Mark *das Pfund*.	*That costs 2 marks a pound.*
Es kostet 50 Pfennig *das Meter*.	*It costs 50 pfennig a meter.*
Er kommt einmal *die Woche*.	*He comes once a week.*
Wir bezahlen zweimal *den Monat*.	*We pay twice a month.*

62. Complete the following with the appropriate definite articles.

1. Er kommt einmal _____ Jahr.
2. Es kostet 20 Pfennig _____ Pfund.
3. Ich sehe Peter einmal _____ Woche.
4. Sie schreit zweimal _____ Sekunde.
5. Das kostet 3 Mark _____ Meter.
6. Es klingelt fünfmal _____ Stunde.

With Parts of the Body or Articles of Clothing

The definite article is used in German to refer to parts of the body or articles of clothing, unless there is doubt as to the identity of the possessor. In English the possessive is used.

Er zieht sich *den Mantel* **an.**	*He is putting on his coat.*
Ich wasche mir *das Gesicht*.	*I am washing my face.*

63. Complete the following with the correct forms of the definite articles.

1. Er zieht sich _____ Hose an.
2. Sie waschen sich _____ Hände.
3. Wir putzen uns _____ Schuhe.
4. Ich ziehe mir _____ Mantel an.
5. Wäschst du dir _____ Gesicht?
6. Sie setzt sich _____ Hut auf.
7. Ich wasche mir _____ Kopf.
8. Putzt du dir _____ Zähne?

Review

64. Complete the following with the appropriate forms of the definite articles.

1. Ich fahre 100 Kilometer _____ Stunde.
2. Er wäscht sich _____ Hände.

3. _____ Vogesenstraße ist dort.
4. Das kostet 50 Pfennig _____ Pfund.
5. _____ Zugspitze ist in Deutschland.
6. _____ Ammersee ist malerisch.
7. Sie besucht uns zweimal _____ Monat.
8. _____ Vierwaldstättersee ist in der Schweiz.
9. Er putzt sich _____ Zähne.
10. _____ Niederlande sind flach.
11. Sie kommt einmal _____ Woche.
12. _____ Schweiz ist reich.
13. _____ Leben ist schön.
14. _____ Biologie ist wichtig.
15. _____ industrielle Österreich ist modern.
16. Wo ist _____ Schwanseestraße?
17. Wir ziehen uns _____ Schuhe an.
18. _____ Haupstraße ist breit.

OMISSION OF THE INDEFINITE OR DEFINITE ARTICLE

The indefinite or definite article is omitted in the following cases.

Before a Predicate Nominative

Sie ist *Russin.*   *She is a Russian.*
Er wird *Zahnarzt.*   *He will become a dentist.*

If the predicate nominative is modified, the article is expressed.

Er ist *ein bekannter Pianist.*   *He is a well-known pianist.*
Er ist *der beste Lehrer.*   *He is the best teacher.*

With Certain Set Phrases

Sie hat *Fieber.*   *She has a fever.*
Wir haben *Kopfweh.*   *We have a headache.*
Hast du *Zahnweh?* (*Halsweh,* etc.)   *Do you have a toothache? (a sore throat, etc.)*

After the conjunction **als,** *meaning "as a(n)"*

Er arbeitet dort als *Ingenieur.*   *He works there as an engineer.*
Sie ist als *Studentin* **in Bonn.**   *She is in Bonn as a student.*

65. Write the German for the following.

1. I have a fever.
2. He is a teacher.
3. She is a good teacher.
4. Does he have a toothache?
5. He is in Berlin as a student.
6. He is a professor.
7. She will become a pianist.
8. We have a sore throat.

Review

66. Complete the following with the appropriate endings when necessary.

1. D_____ Tochter mein_____ Freund_____ hat dies_____ Brief geschrieben.
2. Ein_____ Tag_____ kaufte er sein_____ Frau_____ ein_____ Pelzmantel.
3. D_____ Eltern dies_____ Mädchen_____ sind dort.
4. Unser_____ Sohn ist dies_____ Woche hier.
5. Welch_____ Blumen hat d_____ Junge sein_____ Mutter_____ gekauft?
6. Solch_____ Tiere fressen kein_____ Blätter.
7. Mein_____ Freundinnen geben unser_____ Eltern_____ kein_____ Geschenk.
8. D_____ Wagen jen_____ Herr_____ ist teuer.
9. Sie gibt ihr_____ Sohn jed_____ Tag ein_____ Apfel.
10. Welch_____ Auto gehört d_____ Frau d_____ Lehrer_____ ?

67. Rewrite the following sentences, changing all nouns to the plural. Make all necessary changes.

1. Wir haben kein Foto.
2. Wo ist sein Bruder?
3. Wer hat jenes Bild genommen?
4. Welches Lied soll ich singen?
5. Wer hilft dem Baby?
6. Das gefällt dem Mädchen.
7. Meine Freundin kommt.
8. Unser Auto ist rot.
9. Wann kommt Ihre Tochter?
10. Das Kind unseres Lehrers ist hier.
11. Wo ist unser Hotel?
12. Manches Land ist arm.
13. Wo ist das Museum?
14. Das Buch des Studenten liegt hier.
15. Wird diese Geschichte eurem Freund gefallen?

68. Complete the following with the appropriate articles when necessary.

1. _____ Deutschland ist modern.
2. Sie ist _____ Engländerin.
3. Hast du _____ Kopfweh?
4. Äpfel kosten 2 Mark _____ Pfund.
5. _____ Bergstraße ist im Zentrum.
6. _____ Tschechische Republik ist im Osten.
7. Er ist _____ reicher Amerikaner.
8. _____ Königssee ist malerisch.
9. Ich wasche mir _____ Hände.
10. _____ Löwe ist eine Wildkatze.
11. Er zieht sich _____ Mantel an.
12. Ich bin einmal _____ Woche hier.
13. _____ Vesuv ist bekannt.
14. _____ heutige China ist übervölkert.
15. Sie ist _____ beste Sängerin.
16. Sie arbeitet als _____ Sekretärin.

Chapter 3

Prepositions

Prepositions are words which in combination with a noun (or pronoun) show position, direction, time, or manner (such as *under* the table, *to* the store, *in* April, *without* a word).

In German, as in English, the noun (or pronoun) following a preposition is in a case other than the nominative. In English all prepositions are followed by the same case (such as, with *him*, without *him*, behind *him*, for *him*, by *him*, on *him*). In German, however, prepositions can be followed by the accusative, the dative, or the genitive case. In addition, certain prepositions can be followed by either the accusative or the dative case, depending on whether they are used with verbs that indicate motion or change of position, or with verbs that indicate location or position.

Consequently, when learning the prepositions in German, it is necessary to memorize which case each particular preposition requires.

It is also important to bear in mind that the use of prepositions within a language is highly idiomatic, and thus prepositional usage in German does not necessarily correspond to prepositional usage in English.

PREPOSITIONS GOVERNING THE ACCUSATIVE CASE

The following prepositions are always followed by the accusative case.

bis
durch
entlang
für
gegen
ohne
um
wider

bis—*by, until, up to* (*Note:* **bis** can be used alone or in combination with another preposition. When used alone, it is followed by the accusative case; when **bis** is followed by another preposition, the second preposition determines the case that follows.)

Wir müssen *bis* nächsten Montag fertig sein.	*We have to be finished* by *next Monday.*
Die Soldaten kämpften *bis auf* den letzten Mann.	*The soldiers fought* to *the last man.*
Ich laufe mit dir *bis zur* Ecke.	*I'll walk with you* up to *the corner.*

durch—*through, by* (*Note:* **durch** is used in a passive construction (see Chapter 7) to express the means by which something is done.)

Er läuft *durch* das Haus.	*He is running* through *the house.*
Wir gehen *durch* die Zimmer.	*We are walking* through *the rooms.*
Er wurde *durch* einen Schuß getötet.	*He was killed* by *a shot.*

entlang—*along* (*Note:* **entlang** *follows* the accusative object; when it *precedes* its object, it takes the dative.)

Wir gehen die Strasse *entlang*.	*We are walking* along *the street.*

für—*for*

Warum kaufte er nichts *für* **seinen Freund?**	*Why didn't he buy anything* for *his friend?*
Sie arbeitet *für* **meine Eltern.**	*She is working* for *my parents.*
Ich kaufte die Bluse *für* **zehn Mark.**	*I bought the blouse* for *10 marks.*

gegen—*against, toward, about*

Ich habe nichts *gegen* **den Lehrer.**	*I don't have anything* against *the teacher.*
Er kämpfte *gegen* **den Weltmeister.**	*He fought* against *the world champion.*
Haben Sie etwas *gegen* **Kopfschmerzen?**	*Do you have something* for *headaches?*

ohne—*without*

Ohne **seine Frau geht er nicht.**	*He is not going* without *his wife.*
Wir können *ohne* **unsere Kinder nicht kommen.**	*We can't come* without *our children.*

um—*around*

Warum fährst du *um* **das Haus?**	*Why are you driving* around *the house?*
Die Familie sitzt *um* **den Tisch.**	*The family is sitting* around *the table.*

wider—*against, contrary to* (used in elevated style and in certain idiomatic expressions)

Wider **alle Erwartungen hat der Kandidat den Wahlkampf gewonnen.**	*Contrary to all expectations the candidate won the election*
Er handelte *wider* **das Gesetz.**	*He acted* contrary to *the law.*

Contractions of Prepositions Governing the Accusative

> **durchs**
> **fürs**
> **ums**

When followed by the definite article **das,** the prepositions **durch, für, um** often contract to form **durchs, fürs, ums,** particularly in spoken German, but also in written German. If, however, the definite article functions as a demonstrative, that is, if it acts as a word that specifies or singles out the person, place, or thing referred to (see Chapter 5, p. 88), or if the noun is followed by a clause describing it, these contractions cannot be used.

durch das = durchs

Er läuft *durchs* **Geschäft.**	*He is running* through *the store.*

für das = fürs

Ich bringe es *fürs* **Baby.**	*I am bringing it* for *the baby.*

um das = ums

Wir stehen *ums* **Auto.**	*We are standing* around the *car.*

1. Complete with the appropriate accusative prepositions.

   1. Der Ball fliegt _____ die Luft.
   2. Das Auto fährt die Straße _____ .
   3. Sie laufen _____ die Ecke.
   4. Er stößt den Stuhl _____ die Wand.

5. Ich muß _____ meine Freundin gehen weil sie krank ist.
6. Die Arbeit muß _____ nächste Woche fertig sein.
7. Ich kaufe es _____ meinen Vater weil er Geburtstag hat.
8. Bringst du es _____ deinen Lehrer?
9. Sie wandern _____ die Museen dieser Stadt.
10. Der Blinde kann _____ seinen Hund nicht gehen.

2. Fill in the appropriate endings or contractions.

1. Das Fahrrad fährt gegen ein_____ Baum.
2. Ich schaue durch_____ Teleskop.
3. Wir fahren ein_____ Fluß entlang.
4. Kaufst du es für dein_____ Großmutter?
5. Wir sind um unser_____ Garten gelaufen.
6. Ohne mein_____ Töchter kann ich nicht kommen.
7. Warum stehen die Leute um_____ Auto?
8. Das Haus wurde durch ein_____ Bombe zerstört.
9. Warum läufst du gegen d_____ Wand?
10. Habt ihr etwas für_____ Kind mitgebracht?
11. Wir fahren um_____ Museum.
12. Ich komme ohne mein_____ Freundin.
13. Er wurde durch ein_____ Explosion getötet.
14. Wer macht es für d_____ Leher?
15. Wider all_____ Erwartungen hat unser Team gewonnen.
16. Warum geht ihr durch_____ Kaufhaus?
17. Die Kinder tanzen um ein_____ Linde.
18. Er geht d_____ Straße entlang.
19. Sie kämpfen gegen d_____ Diktatur.
20. Ich kaufe es für mein_____ Schwester.

3. Complete with the appropriate forms of the indicated words.

1. Ich komme ohne _____ Frau.   *mein*
2. Sie bauen einen Zaun um _____ Garten.   *ihr*
3. Wir haben den Brief für _____ Großmutter.   *unser*
4. Kurt wurde nicht durch _____ Schuß getötet.   *sein*
5. Geht nicht _____ Berg entlang!   *jen* _____
6. Viele waren gegen _____ Revolution.   *dies* _____
7. Sie kaufte es für _____ Jungen.   *ihr*
8. Der Wagen rollte gegen _____ Auto.   *euer*

PREPOSITIONS GOVERNING THE DATIVE CASE

The following prepositions are always followed by the dative case.

aus
außer
bei
mit
nach
seit
von
zu

aus—*out of, from* (point of origin; denotes coming from place of birth or domicile), *of* (usually without an article)

Das Mädchen kommt *aus* **dem Hotel.**	*The girl is coming* out of *the hotel.*
Kommen Sie auch *aus* **Deutschland?**	*Do you also come* from *Germany?*
Das Messer ist *aus* **Stahl.**	*The knife is (made)* of *steel.*

außer—*except (for), besides*

Außer **meiner Mutter waren wir alle da.**	*Except for my mother, we were all there.*
Außer **diesem Volkswagen besitze ich nichts.**	*I own nothing* besides *this Volkswagen.*

bei—*with* (at the home of), *near, at*

Ich bleibe *bei* **meinen Großeltern.**	*I am staying* with *my grandparents.*
Wohnst du *bei* **der Schule?**	*Do you live* near *school?*
Ich treffe dich *bei* **der Universität.**	*I'll meet you* at *the university.*

gegenüber—*across (from)* (usually follows the dative object)

Wir wohnen dem Park *gegenüber.*	*We live* across from *the park.*
Er sitzt seinen Eltern *gegenüber.*	*He sits* across from *his parents.*

mit—*with, by (means of)*

Er arbeitet *mit* **einem Hammer.**	*He is working* with *a hammer.*
Ich reise *mit* **diesen Leuten.**	*I am traveling* with *these people.*
Sie kommt *mit* **dem Zug.**	*She is coming* by *train.*

nach—*after, according to* (with this meaning, the preposition usually *follows* the noun), *to* (when used with neuter geographical names no article is expressed; Chapter 2, p. 16.)

Nach **dem Abendessen gehen wir aus.**	*We are going out* after *dinner.*
Der Geschichte *nach* **wurde er 100 Jahre alt.**	*According to the story, he lived to be 100 years old.*
Der Flug *nach* **Kanada war lang.**	*The flight* to *Canada was long.*
But: Sie reist *nach* **den USA**	*She is traveling* to *the USA.*

seit—*since, for* (with time expressions)

Seit **seiner Kindheit wohnt er in Ulm.**	*He has been living in Ulm* since *his childhood.*
Ich habe die Krankheit *seit* **einem Jahr.**	*I have had the illness* for *one year.*

von—*from, by, of*

Er weiß nichts *von* **seinen Töchtern.**	*He knows nothing* about *his daughters.*
Die Uhr ist *von* **meiner Schwester.**	*The watch is* from *my sister.*
Das Geschenk kommt *von* **meiner Großmutter.**	*The present is* from *my grandmother.*
Ist das ein Drama *von* **Goethe?**	*Is that a drama* by *Goethe?*

from (coming from a certain direction, as opposed to origin)

Das Flugzeug kommt *von* **Frankfurt.**	*The airplane is coming* from *Frankfurt.*

by (used in the passive construction (see Chapter 7, p. 212) to express the personal agent).

Das Essen wurde *von* meiner Mutter gekocht.   *The dinner was cooked* by *my mother.*

zu—*to* (direction toward people and places when no geographical name is used)

Wir gehen *zu* einem neuen Zahnarzt.   *We are going* to *a new dentist.*
Wir gehen *zu* der großen Buchmesse.   *We are going* to *the big book fair.*

Contractions of Prepositions Governing the Dative

> **beim**
> **vom**
> **zum**
> **zur**

The prepositions **bei, von, zu** contract with the dative definite articles **dem** and **der** unless these articles function as demonstratives or the noun is followed by a descriptive clause.

The following prepositions contract with the dative definite article, unless the article is stressed.

bei + dem = *beim*

Ich bin *beim* Doktor.   *I am at the doctor's office.*

von + dem = *vom*

Kommt er schon *vom* Kino?   *Is he already coming* from the *movies?*

zu + dem = *zum*

Wir gehen *zum* Museum.   *We are going* to the *museum.*

zu + der = *zur*

Warum fährt er *zur* Schule?   *Why is he driving* to *school?*

4. Complete with the appropriate prepositions or contractions.

1. Ich fahre _____ dem Auto _____ Hamburg.
2. Ich wohne _____ meinen Schwestern.
3. Er geht _____ Lehrer.
4. Wir wohnen _____ einem Jahr hier.
5. Die Universität ist dem Park _____.
6. _____ dem Frühstück gehe ich _____ Schule.
7. Dieser Brief kommt _____ meiner Freundin.
8. Gehst du _____ deinem Bruder ins Kino?
9. Der Zug kommt _____ Augsburg.
10. Das Fenster wurde _____ unserem Jungen zerschlagen.

5. Complete with the correct endings or contractions when necessary.

1. Der Arzt kommt aus d_____ Schlafzimmer.
2. Nach d_____ Schule besuche ich dich.
3. Ich kenne sie seit jen_____ Tag.
4. Bist du zu_____ Doktor gegangen?
5. Sie wurde von kein_____ Menschen gefragt.
6. Dies_____ Park gegenüber wohnt unser Onkel.
7. Er steht bei_____ Hotel.

8. Wann fahren wir nach _____ Österreich?
9. Kommt sie schon von d_____ Universität?
10. _____ Sage nach wurde er König.
11. Seit ein_____ Monat ist sie in der Schweiz.
12. Außer jen_____ Herrn war niemand da.
13. Ich fahre mit mein_____ Freunden nach _____ Bremen.
14. Sie ist seit ihr_____ Abreise dort.
15. Sie bekam von jed_____ Kind eine Orchidee.
16. Ich bleibe bei mein_____ Geschwistern.
17. Sie kommt von_____ Garten.
18. Sie wurde von dies_____ Hund gebissen.
19. Arbeitest du bei dies_____ Firma?
20. Das Paket kommt von mein_____ Eltern.

6. Complete the following with the appropriate forms of the indicated words.

1. Er läuft zu _____ Tante. *sein*
2. Sie werden von _____ Mädchen gefragt. *ein*
3. Er ist bei _____ Kaufhaus. *jen_____*
4. Ich wohne seit _____ Jahr hier. *ein*
5. _____ Geschichte nach ist er reich. *dies_____*
6. Sie sprechen mit _____ Lehrer. *unser*
7. Kommt ihr von _____ Haus? *euer*
8. Er wohnt _____ Park gegenüber. *der*
9. Nach _____ Vorlesung essen wir. *die*
10. Sie kommt aus _____ Museum. *das*
11. Ich wohne seit _____ Kindheit hier. *mein*
12. Er kam aus _____ Hotelzimmer. *sein*
13. Sie sitzt _____ Brüdern gegenüber. *ihr*
14. Was machst du mit _____ Mitgliedskarte? *dein*

PREPOSITIONS GOVERNING EITHER THE ACCUSATIVE OR THE DATIVE CASE

Another group of German prepositions can be used with either the accusative or the dative case. For this reason they are often referred to as *two-way* or *either-or* prepositions.

an
auf
hinter
in
neben
über
unter
vor
zwischen

Whether these prepositions are followed by the accusative or by the dative is determined by how they are used within the sentence.

The accusative case is used when the verb in combination with the preposition expresses *change of position* or *movement toward a place*. These prepositions answer the question "wohin?" (literally: "where to?"). (See Chapter 9, p. 230.)

The dative case is used when the verb in combination with the preposition expresses *position*, or *location*, or *motion within a fixed location*. These prepositions answer the question "wo?" ("where?" or "in what place?"). (See Chapter 9, p. 230.)

an (accusative)—*to, onto*

    Der Hund läuft *an die* **Tür.**   *The dog runs* to *the door.*
    Sie hängt das Bild *an die* **Wand.**   *She is hanging the picture* on *the wall.*

an (dative)—*at*

    Der Hund steht *an der* **Tür.**   *The dog is standing* at *the door.*
    Das Bild hängt *an der* **Wand.**   *The picture is hanging* on *the wall.*

---

auf (accusative)—*on, on top of, onto, upon*

    Er legt das Messer *auf den* **Tisch.**   *He puts the knife* on *the table.*
    Wir fahren *aufs* **Land.**   *We are going* to *the country.*

auf (dative)—*on, in*

    Das Messer liegt *auf dem* **Tisch.**   *The knife is lying* on *the table.*
    Wir wohnen *auf dem* **Lande.**   *We live* in *the country.*

---

hinter (accusative)—*behind*

    Die Kinder gehen *hinter das* **Haus.**   *The children go* behind *the house.*
    Er stellt die Schuhe *hinter die* **Tür.**   *He puts the shoes* behind *the door.*

hinter (dative)—*behind*

    Die Kinder spielen *hinter dem* **Haus.**   *The children are playing* behind *the house.*
    Die Schuhe stehen *hinter der* **Tür.**   *The shoes are (standing)* behind *the door.*

---

in (accusative)—*in, into, to*

    Die Kinder gehen *in die* **Schule.**   *The children go* to *school.*
    Er springt *in den* **Fluß.**   *He jumps* into *the river.*
    Fliegst du *in die* **Türkei?**   *Are you flying* to *Turkey.*

in (dative)—*in*

    Die Kinder sind *in der* **Schule.**   *The children are* in *school.*
    Er schwimmt *in dem* **Fluß.**   *He swims* in *the river.*
    Wohnst du *in der* **Türkei?**   *Are you living* in *Turkey?*

---

neben (accusative)—*beside, next to*

    Luise stellt den Stuhl *neben das* **Fenster**   *Louise places the chair* next to *the window.*
    Setze dich *neben diesen* **Herrn.**   *Sit down* beside *this gentleman.*

neben (dative)—*beside, next to*

    Der Stuhl steht *neben dem* **Fenster.**   *The chair is (standing)* next to *the window.*
    Ich sitze *neben diesem* **Herrn.**   *I am sitting* beside *this gentleman.*

über (accusative)—*over, above, across*

Ich hänge die Lampe *über den* **Tisch.**	*I am hanging the lamp* over (above) *the table.*
Der Junge klettert *über den* **Zaun.**	*The boy climbs* over *the fence.*
Das Kind läuft *über die* **Straße.**	*The child runs* across *the street.*

über (dative)—*over, above*

Die Lampe hängt *über dem* Tisch.	*The lamp is hanging* over (above) *the table.*
Das Handtuch hängt *über dem* **Zaun.**	*The towel is hanging* over *the fence.*
Die Ampel hängt *über der* **Straße.**	*The traffic light is hanging* over *the street.*

---

unter (accusative)—*under, below, among*

Der Ball rollte *unter den* **Sessel.**	*The ball rolled* under *the easy chair.*
Die Katze verschwindet *unter das* **Bett.**	*The cat disappears* under *the bed.*

unter (dative)—*under, below, beneath*

Der Ball ist *unter dem* **Sessel.**	*The ball is* under *the easy chair.*
Die Katze liegt *unter dem* **Bett.**	*The cat is lying* under *the bed.*

---

vor (accusative)—*in front of, before*

Ich habe mich *vor den* **Fernseher gesetzt.**	*I sat down* in front of *the TV.*
Der Zeitungsausträger legte die Zeitung *vor die* **Tür.**	*The newspaper carrier laid the newspaper* in front of *the door.*

vor (dative)—*in front of, before*

Ich sitze jeden Abend *vor dem* **Fernseher.**	*I sit* in front of *the TV every evening.*
Die Zeitung lag *vor der* **Tür.**	*The newspaper lay* in front of *the door.*

---

zwischen (accusative)—*between*

Sie hat den Brief *zwischen das* **Buch und die Zeitung gelegt.**	*She placed the letter* between *the book and the newspaper.*

zwischen (dative)—*between*

Der Brief liegt *zwischen dem* **Buch und der Zeitung.**	*The letter is lying* between *the book and the newspaper.*

Contractions of the Two-Way Prepositions

ans
am
aufs
ins
im
hinters
übers
unters
vors

The prepositions **an, auf, in, hinter, über, unter, vor** usually contract with the dative articles **das** and **dem** unless these articles function as demonstratives or the noun is followed by a descriptive clause.

an + das = *ans*

    Sie geht *ans* **Fenster.**   *She is going* to the *window.*

an + dem = *am*

    Er stand *am* **Bett.**   *He stood* at the *bed.*

auf + das = *aufs*

    Er setzt sich *aufs* **Sofa.**   *He is sitting down* on the *Sofa.*

in + das = *ins*

    Geht ihr *ins* **Kino?**   *Are you going* to the *movies?*

in + dem = *im*

    Sitzt sie *im* **Garten?**   *Is she sitting* in the *Garden?*

hinter + das = *hinters*

    Wir gehen *hinters* **Haus.**   *We are going* behind *the house.*

über + das = *übers*

    Es fliegt *übers* **Nest.**   *It is flying* over the *nest.*

unter + das = *unters*

    Leg es nicht *unters* **Bett!**   *Don't put it* under *the bed.*

vor + das = *vors*

    Stell dich *vors* **Mädchen!**   *Stand* in front of the *girl.*

Combinations with Verbs of Direction

The following verbs denote direction. When they are used in combination with one of the preceding prepositions, they require the accusative case.

legen—*to lay, to put, to place*

    Ich *lege* **die Zeitung** *aufs* **Sofa.**   *I am putting the newspaper on the sofa.*

setzen—*to place, to set, to sit down*

    Er *setzte* **sich** *neben das* **Fräulein.**   *He sat down beside the young woman.*

stellen—*to put, to place, to set*

    Stell **den Stuhl** *hinter den* **Tisch!**   *Place the chair behind the table.*

Combinations with Verbs of Location

The following verbs denote location. When they are used in combination with one of the preceding prepositions, they require the dative case.

liegen—to lie, to rest

> **Warum** *liegst du unter deinem* **Bett?**   *Why are you lying under your bed?*

sitzen—*to sit*

> **Du** *sitzt auf ihrem* **Mantel.**   *You are sitting on her coat.*

stehen—*to stand*

> **Warum** *steht er neben meinem* **Bruder?**   *Why is he standing next to my brother?*

7. Complete with the appropriate forms of the indicated words. Make contractions when possible.

1. Wir sitzen schon in _____ Auto. *das*
2. Er geht über _____ Straße. *die*
3. Stell die Schuhe unter _____ Bett! *das*
4. Wir sitzen vor _____ Kindern. *unser*
5. Wer kommt in _____ August? *der*
6. Sie wohnt in _____ Schweiz. *die*
7. An _____ Mittwoch fliege ich ab. *der*
8. Geh in _____ Haus! *das*
9. Schwimmt ihr immer in _____ Fluß? *dieser*
10. Wann fährst du in _____ Türkei? *die*
11. In _____ Sommer haben wir Ferien. *der*
12. Er besuchte uns vor _____ Monat. *ein*
13. Warum gehst du an _____ Küchenfenster? *das*
14. Ich legte den Löffel neben _____ Teller. *dein*
15. Er steht zwischen _____ Brüdern. *sein*
16. Sie steht hinter _____ Fabrik. *jene*
17. An _____ Abend bin ich müde. *der*
18. Dürfen wir in _____ Theater? *das*
19. Stell dich neben _____ Eltern! *dein*
20. Sein Kopf ist unter _____ Kissen. *das*
21. Warst du schon in _____ Irak? *der*
22. Setz dich nicht auf _____ Koffer! *mein*
23. Es liegt zwischen _____ Zeitungen. *ihr*
24. In _____ Mai wird es wieder warm. *der*
25. Warum geht er hinter _____ Museum? *das*
26. Er legte es auf _____ Tisch. *der*
27. Ich bin in _____ Kaufhaus. *ein*
28. Es liegt unter _____ Bett. *euer*
29. Sie sitzt auf _____ Mantel. *mein*
30. Setz dich hinter _____ Freundin! *dein*
31. Das Haus ist neben _____ Park. *jener*
32. Stell es vor _____ Garage! *unser*
33. Setzt euch in _____ Auto! *das*
34. Wir sind in _____ Vereinigten Staaten. *die*
35. Bist du in _____ Küche? *die*

Da- Compounds with Accusative and Dative Prepositions

Da- compounds are used when referring to inanimate objects or abstract ideas discussed in a previous sentence. They are used the same way as the English pronouns *it* and *them* with prepositions. In German the **da-** form is used regardless of whether the noun it replaces is masculine, feminine, neuter, singular, or plural. If the preposition starts with a vowel, **dar-** is prefixed (**darin, darüber, darauf**). Note that **da(r)-** compounds are *never used to refer to people*. (See Chapter 4, pp. 75–76.)

Bist du *gegen den Plan?*	*Are you against the plan?*
Ja, ich bin *dagegen.*	*Yes, I am against it.*
Denkst du *an die Ferien?*	*Are you thinking about your vacation?*
Nein, ich denke nicht *daran.*	*No, I am not thinking about it.*
Was macht ihr *mit den Bleistiften?*	*What are you doing with the pencils?*
Wir schreiben *damit.*	*We are writing with them.*
Steht sie *neben dem Bild?*	*Is she standing next to the picture?*
Ja, sie steht *daneben.*	*Yes, she is standing next to it.*

All accusative, dative, and accusative/dative prepositions can be prefixed by **da(r)-** with the exception of **entlang, ohne, außer, gegenüber, seit.**

8. Complete the answers with the appropriate **da-** compounds.

1. Sitzt ihr schon im Bus? Ja, wir sitzen schon _____.
2. Spielst du mit der Puppe? Ja, ich spiele _____.
3. Stellt ihr euch neben die Bank? Ja, wir stellen uns _____.
4. Bist du schon bei der Arbeit? Ja, ich bin schon _____.
5. Legt ihr euch unter die Bäume? Ja, wir legen uns _____.
6. Ist er hinter dem Geschäft? Ja, er ist _____.
7. Glaubst du an seine Schuld? Ja, ich glaube _____.
8. Setzt ihr euch aufs Sofa? Ja, wir setzen uns _____.
9. Unterhaltet ihr euch über den Roman? Ja, wir unterhalten uns _____.
10. Brauchst du Mehl zum Backen? Ja, ich brauche es _____.
11. Geht ihr nach der Arbeit spazieren? Ja, wir gehen _____ spazieren.
12. Hast du ihm von unserer Reise erzählt? Ja, ich habe ihm _____ erzählt.

When **dar-** Is Not Used

hinein, herein

When the preposition **in** expresses direction rather than location, it is not prefixed by **dar-** but has the following distinct forms.

Motion away from speaker

Gehst du schon ins Haus?	*Are you going into the house already?*
Ja, ich gehe schon *hinein.*	*Yes, I am already going in (into it).*

Motion toward speaker

Kommt sie ins Wohnzimmer?	*Is she coming into the living room?*
Ja, sie kommt *herein.*	*Yes, she is coming in (into it).*

hinaus, heraus

Similarly, the dative preposition **aus** has distinct forms.

Motion away from speaker

Steigt er aus dem Fenster?	*Is he climbing out of the window?*
Ja, er steigt *hinaus*.	*Yes, he is climbing out (of it).*

Motion toward speaker

Kommt sie aus der Garage?	*Is she coming out of the garage?*
Ja, sie kommt *heraus*.	*Yes, she is coming out (of it).*

9. Complete the following with **hinein, herein, hinaus,** or **heraus.**

1. Kommt sie ins Zimmer? Ja, sie kommt _____.
2. Geht sie aus der Küche? Ja, sie geht _____.
3. Läufst du ins Eßzimmer? Ja, ich laufe _____.
4. Kommt er ins Haus? Ja, er kommt _____.
5. Kommen sie aus dem Museum? Ja, sie kommen _____.
6. Kommt sie ins Hotel? Ja, sie kommt _____.
7. Geht sie in die Kirche? Ja, sie geht _____.
8. Gehen sie aus dem Haus? Ja, sie gehen _____.
9. Wandern sie in den Wald? Ja, sie wandern _____.
10. Läuft sie aus der Fabrik? Ja, sie läuft _____.

Wo- Compounds with Accusative and Dative Prepositions

In German the interrogative **was** (referring to things) is usually avoided after an accusative or dative preposition. Instead, **wo-** is prefixed to the preposition. If the preposition starts with a vowel, **wor-** is used.

Womit **kann ich helfen?**	*What can I help you with?*
Wovon **soll er denn leben?**	*What is he supposed to live off?*
Worüber **sprecht ihr?**	*What are you talking about?*
Worauf **wartest du?**	*What are you waiting for?*

These **wo-** compounds are used only in questions referring to things or ideas. *They cannot be used when referring to people.*

Wo- can be prefixed to accusative, dative, and accusative/dative prepositions, with the exception of **entlang, ohne, außer, gegenüber, seit, hinter, neben, zwischen.**

10. Complete the questions with the appropriate **wo-** compounds, following the cue provided in the answer.

1. _____ fährt er nach Köln? Mit dem Auto.
2. _____ sitzen sie? Auf dem Kissen.
3. _____ schwimmt sie? Im See.
4. _____ denkst du? An die Prüfung.
5. _____ kommt er? Aus dem Hotel.
6. _____ erzählt ihr? Von der Reise.

7. _____ handelt es sich? Um Geld.
8. _____ sprechen sie? Über Chemie.
9. _____ hat er Angst? Vor der Bombe.
10. _____ brauchst du den Bleistift? Zum Schreiben.
11. _____ liegt er? Auf dem Bett.
12. _____ ist er? Bei der Arbeit.
13. _____ ist sie? Gegen die Reise.
14. _____ schreibt er? Mit dem Kugelschreiber.
15. _____ interessierst du dich? Für Musik.

PREPOSITIONS GOVERNING THE GENITIVE CASE

The most commonly occurring genitive prepositions are:

> **(an)statt**
> **trotz**
> **während**
> **wegen**

(an)statt—*instead of*

(An)statt **seiner Schwester ist seine Tante gekommen.**	*His aunt came* instead of *his sister.*

trotz—*in spite of, despite*

Er kam *trotz* **seiner Krankheit zur Schule.**	*He came to school* in spite of *his illness.*

während—*during*

Während **unserer Ferien fahren wir nach Spanien.**	*We are going to Spain* during *our vacation.*

wegen—*because of*

Wir konnten *wegen* **ihrer Verspätung nicht gleich abfahren.**	*We could not depart immediately* because of *her delay.*

Note: In colloquial usage the dative rather than the genitive is often heard with **(an)statt, trotz, wegen,** particularly when these prepositions are followed by a pronoun.

Other useful genitive prepositions include:

> **außerhalb**
> **innerhalb**
> **oberhalb**
> **unterhalb**
> **diesseits**
> **jenseits**
> **um ... willen**

außerhalb—*outside of*

> **Die Kinder spielen** *außerhalb* **des Gartens.** *The children are playing* outside of *the garden.*

innerhalb—*inside of, within*

> ***Innerhalb* dieser Mauern stehen die Ruinen.** Inside of *these walls are the ruins.*
> **Er beendet sein Studium** *innerhalb* **eines** *He is finishing his studies* within *a year.*
> **Jahres.**

oberhalb—*on the upper side of, above*

> **Wir wohnen** *oberhalb* **jenes Dorfes.** *We live* above *that village.*

unterhalb—*on the lower side, below*

> *Unterhalb* **unseres Hauses ist ein See.** *Below our house there is a lake.*

diesseits—*on this side of*

> **Die Stadt ist** *diesseits* **der Berge.** *The city is* on this side of *the mountains.*

jenseits—*on the other side of*

> **Der Park ist** *jenseits* **dieses Sees.** *The park is* on the other side of *this lake.*

um ... willen—*for the sake of*

> *Um* **seiner Mutter** *willen* **hat er abgesagt.** *He canceled* for the sake of *his mother.*

11. Complete the following with the appropriate endings.

     1. Wir wohnen außerhalb d_____ Stadt.
     2. Er ist während d_____ Nacht angekommen.
     3. Innerhalb ein_____ Monats ist er wieder gesund.
     4. Trotz d_____ Kälte kommt er mit.
     5. Liegt das Haus innerhalb dies_____ Dorfes?
     6. Ich bleibe diesseits d_____ Grenze.
     7. Ich habe es um mein_____ Brüder willen getan.
     8. Was liegt jenseits dies_____ Berge?
     9. Statt ein_____ Autos hat er ein Pferd gekauft.
    10. Er blieb wegen jen_____ Warnung zu Hause.
    11. Das Haus steht oberhalb d_____ Kirche.
    12. Während d_____ Sommers gehen wir oft baden.
    13. Unterhalb d_____ Waldes liegt eine Wiese.
    14. Wegen mein_____ Erkältung darf ich nicht ausgehen.
    15. Statt ein_____ Zeitung habe ich diese Zeitschrift gekauft.
    16. Während d_____ Ferien bin ich in Kanada.
    17. Wir sind diesseits d_____ Berges.
    18. Ich arbeite trotz d_____ Hitze im Garten.
    19. Der See ist außerhalb d_____ Parks.
    20. Er kommt wegen sein_____ Krankheit nicht.

WORD ORDER IN PREPOSITIONAL PHRASES

As illustrated in the examples above, most German prepositions precede their objects. However, as also noted above **(entlang, gegenüber)**, a few prepositions more commonly, or even must, follow their objects. For example, **wegen** can either precede or follow its object.

Wegen des schlechten Wetters **blieb ich zu Hause.**	Because of the bad weather *I stayed home.*
Des schlechten Wetters wegen **blieb ich zu Hause.**	Because of the bad weather *I stayed home.*

Other prepositions, however, require that certain special features be kept in mind when they follow their object.

When ***nach*** follows its object, it is used in the sense of *according to*.

Der Geschichte nach **war er der Sohn eines Königs.**	According to the story *he was the son of a king.*

When **durch** follows its object, it is used in connection with a period of time. (*Note:* the longer form **hindurch** is often used in this sense.)

Die Kranke schlief *die Nacht (hin)durch.*	*The sick woman slept* through the night.

When **entlang** follows its object, it takes the accusative case. However, when it precedes its object, it takes either the dative or the genitive.

Entlang dem Fluß **sind viele reizende kleine Dörfer.**	Along the river *are many charming small villages.*
Den Fluß entlang **sind viele kleine Dörfer.**	Along the river *are many small villages.*

The preposition **gegenüber** usually follows its object when it is used with a noun: However, it *always* follows its object when its object is a personal pronoun.

Er wohnt dem Bahnhof *gegenüber.*	He lives across from *the train station.*
Er wohnt *gegenüber* **dem Bahnhof.**	He lives across from *the train station.*
Er sitzt mir *gegenüber.*	He is sitting across from *me.*

The object + preposition construction is found in a number of standard idiomatic phrases.

Meiner Meinung nach **ist er ein Narr.**	In my opinion *he is a fool.*
Meiner Ansicht nach **ist das ganz falsch.**	In my opinion *that is totally wrong.*
Tu es *deiner Mutter wegen.*	*Do it* for your mother's sake.

12.   Supply the appropriate forms of the indicated words.

1. _____ Meinung nach soll man das Rauchen verbieten.   *sein*
2. Um _____ Kindes willen mußten sie ihre Lebensweise ändern.   *das*
3. Wegen _____ kalten Wetters wollte er nach Süden fahren.   *das*
4. Lisa und Loisl gingen _____ Straße entlang.   *die*

5. Ich wohnte _____ Post gegenüber. *die*
6. Meine Schwester arbeitete _____ ganzen Sommer durch. *der*
7. Entlang _____ Mauer sah man viele Blumen. *die*
8. _____ Geschichte nach ist er nach Amerika ausgewandert. *die*
9. _____ schlechten Wetters wegen konnten wir euch nicht besuchen. *das*
10. Gegenüber _____ Bahnhof steht die Bank. *der*

Review

13. Complete the following with the appropriate endings, prepositions, or contractions when necessary.

1. Warum schaust du hinter d_____ Tür?
2. Wir fahren _____ Herbst _____ Deutschland.
3. Ich fahre zu mein_____ Eltern.
4. Innerhalb ein_____ Stunde hatte er kein Kopfweh mehr.
5. Die Tasse steht in jen_____ Küchenschrank.
6. Er hatte wegen d_____ Glatteises den Unfall.
7. Sie lief in ihr_____ Schlafzimmer.
8. Der Bus fährt unter d_____ Brücke.
9. Das Auto fährt um d_____ Stadt.
10. Sitzt du gern in d_____ Sonne?
11. Wir fahren d_____ Nordsee entlang.
12. Nach d_____ Essen gehen wir spazieren.
13. Während d_____ Krieges waren viele Leute arm.
14. Liegt das Buch schon auf mein_____ Schreibtisch?
15. Er wohnt bei sein_____ Schulfreund.
16. Hast du soviel für jed_____ Bild bezahlt?
17. Sie soll a_____ Mittwoch ankommen.
18. Wohnt ihr auch in dies_____ Straße?
19. Ich hänge das Bild an d_____ Wand.
20. Wir unterhalten uns mit d_____ Krankenpfleger.
21. Hat er etwas für sein_____ Kinder gekauft?
22. Warum bist du gegen unser_____ Freunde?
23. Er wollte trotz sein_____ Alters bergsteigen.
24. Sie tanzten um d_____ Goldene Lamm.
25. Sie sind ohne ihr_____ Sohn _____ Bonn geflogen.

14. Complete the following with the appropriate **wo-** compounds.

1. _____ liegt das Geld? In der Schachtel.
2. _____ brauchst du es? Zum Lesen.
3. _____ fährt er weg? Mit dem Zug.
4. _____ bist du? Gegen den Plan.
5. _____ unterhaltet ihr euch? Über seine Erfindungen.
6. _____ wartest du? Auf den Bus.
7. _____ fiel das Kind? Vom Pferd.
8. _____ hast du Angst? Vor dem Hund.

15. Complete the following with the appropriate **da-** compounds when necessary.

    1.   Liegt die Wäsche im Korb? Ja, sie liegt _____.

    2.   Ist das Ei neben dem Teller? Ja, es ist _____.

    3.   Steht ihr vor der Kamera? Ja, wir stehen _____.

    4.   Setzt du dich aufs Sofa? Ja, ich setze mich _____.

    5.   Liegt der Brief unter der Zeitung? Ja, er liegt _____.

Chapter 4

Pronouns

PERSONAL PRONOUNS

Nominative Case

Singular		Plural	
ich	*I*	**wir**	*we*
du	*you*	**ihr**	*you*
er	*he, it*	**sie**	*they*
es	*it*		
sie	*she, it*		
		Sie	*you*

First person

The first person (**ich, wir**) is used to indicate the speaker, writer, or narrator.

Second person

The second person is used to indicate the person or persons addressed or spoken to. In German there are three personal pronouns for *you*: a familiar singular (**du**), a familiar plural (**ihr**), and a formal form of address (**Sie**). The singular familiar pronoun **du** is used when addressing family members, close friends, children below the age of about sixteen, pets and other animals, and in prayer. The familiar plural **ihr** is used when addressing two or more members of these groups.

The familiar forms are also increasingly used among members of groups of equals, such as students, athletes, blue-collar workers, members of certain trades and occupations, soldiers, and criminals.

In situations where first names are used, it is customary to use the pronoun **du**.

The German pronoun of formal address **Sie** is used for acquaintances and other adults with whom the speaker is not on intimate terms, including anyone whom the speaker would address by last name or title. The **Sie** form is used for both the singular and the plural. **Sie** takes the same verb ending as the third person plural, **sie** (*they*). All forms of the pronoun **Sie** and its possessive adjective are always capitalized.

Karin, kannst *du* **mir helfen?**	*Karin, can* you *help me?*
Kinder, habt *ihr* **Zeit?**	*Children, do* you *have time?*
Frau Stifter, kommen *Sie* **auch?**	*Ms. Stifter, are* you *coming too?*

In a letter, personal note, or other correspondence, all forms of the personal pronouns **du** and **ihr** as well as the corresponding possessive adjectives are capitalized.

Liebe Inge, ich freue mich schon auf *Deinen* **Besuch. Wie nett, daß** *Deine* **Kinder mitkommen können. Wir werden viel mit** *Euch* **unternehmen, während** *Ihr* **bei uns seid.**

Third person

The third person indicates the person or persons spoken about or referred to. The gender of a third person pronoun is determined by its antecedent, that is, by the gender of the word the pronoun refers back to. Masculine, feminine, and neuter nouns are replaced by the masculine, feminine, and neuter pronouns corresponding to their grammatical genders. When the pronouns **er, sie, es** refer to inanimate objects, they are translated by the English word *it*. When they relate back to male or female beings, **er** and **sie** are translated as *he* and *she*.

The third person plural pronoun **sie** (*they*) refers to both things and people. The third person plural does not distinguish between masculine, feminine and the neuter.

Wo ist der Wagen?	*Er* **ist in der Garage.**
Where is the car?	*It is in the garage.*
Wo ist der Junge?	*Er* **ist im Haus.**
Where is the boy?	*He is in the house.*
Dort ist die Kirche.	*Sie* **ist sehr alt.**
There is the church.	*It is very old.*
Wann kommt Mutter?	*Sie* **kommt bald.**
When is mother coming?	*She is coming soon.*
Who sind die Bücher?	*Sie* **sind auf dem Schreibtisch.**
Where are the books?	*They are on the desk.*
Wann kommen die Gäste?	*Sie* **kommen um 20 Uhr.**
When are the guests coming?	*They are coming at 8 o'clock.*

The neuter noun **das Mädchen** is replaced by the personal pronoun **es**, unless the girl's name is stated. Then it is replaced by **sie**.

Wer ist das Mädchen?	*Es* **ist Roberts Schwester.**
Gabi ist nicht hier.	*Sie* **ist in der Stadt.**

The neuter noun **das Fräulein** is always replaced by **sie**.

Welches Fräulein hat dir geholfen?	**Dort steht** *sie*.

Note: **Fräulein**, as a form of address for unmarried women, is being replaced by **Frau**, which is now used as the preferred form of address for both married and unmarried women.

1. Complete the following with the correct personal pronouns.

1. Paul war in Deutschland. Jetzt spricht _____ gut Deutsch.
2. Petra, wohin hast _____ das Geld gelegt?
3. Meine Herren, was brauchen _____ noch?
4. Wo liegt die Zeitung? Dort liegt _____.
5. Rex, _____ bist ein guter Hund.
6. Liebe Kinder, hoffentlich habt _____ Eure Ferien gut verbracht.
7. Das Mädchen blutet. _____ hat sich verletzt.
8. Wo ist Frau Horstmann? _____ ist am Bodensee.
9. Toni und Georg, wo seid _____ denn?
10. Meine Kinder sind nicht hier. _____ sind in England.
11. Die Katze schläft. _____ ist müde.
12. Inge ist krank. _____ ist im Krankenhaus.
13. Frau Steinhagel, kommen _____ heute abend mit?
14. Die Blätter sind abgefallen. _____ liegen unter dem Baum.
15. Wo ist das Messer? Hier ist _____.
16. Gudrun and Ute, was habt _____ gemacht?

17. Meine Eltern machen Urlaub. _____ sind in der Schweiz.
18. Günther, hast _____ den Wagen?

Accusative Case

Singular		Plural	
mich	*me*	**uns**	*us*
dich	*you*	**euch**	*you*
ihn	*him, it*	**sie**	*them*
es	*it*		
sie	*her, it*		
		Sie	*you*

The accusative personal pronouns are used when they are the direct object of the verb or the object of a preposition requiring the accusative case.

Er hat *mich* **besucht.**	*He visited* me.
Wir gehen ohne *ihn*.	*We are going without* him.
Liebst du *sie*?	*Do you love* her?
Wir haben *sie* **gesehen.**	*We saw* them.

The third person singular and plural may refer to both things and people.

Kennst du nicht Herrn Krull? Doch, ich kenne *ihn*.
Hast du die Tasche? Ja, ich habe *sie*.

2. Complete the following with the correct pronouns.

1. Schreibt Karl den Brief? Ja, _____ schreibt _____.
2. Trifft Marlene ihre Freundinnen? Ja, _____ trifft _____.
3. Seht ihr Helga? Ja, _____ sehen _____.
4. Kocht Mutter das Abendessen? Ja, _____ kocht _____.
5. Will Ute die Blumen pflücken? Ja, _____ will _____ pflücken.
6. Kennt Konrad seine Großeltern? Ja, _____ kennt _____.
7. Siehst du den Beamten? Ja, _____ sehe _____.
8. Erinnerten sich die Kinder an ihre Tante? Ja, _____ erinnerten sich an _____.
9. Kennst du das Mädchen? Ja, _____ kenne _____.
10. Kauft ihr den Mantel? Ja, _____ kaufen _____.
11. Triffst du mich? Ja, _____ treffe _____.
12. Liebt Peter seine Freundin? Ja, _____ liebt _____.
13. Eßt ihr den Kuchen? Ja, _____ essen _____.
14. Nimmst du das Auto? Ja, _____ nehme _____.

3. Rewrite the following, substituting the italicized elements with pronouns.

1. Renate braucht *das Buch*.
2. Wir kaufen *den Apparat*.
3. Ich setzte mich neben *die Dame*.
4. Wir essen *die Bananen*.
5. Ich darf *den Roman* lesen.
6. Wer hat *den Hasen* gefüttert?

4. Answer the following questions in the affirmative using complete sentences.

1. Hat er mich erkannt? Ja, ...
2. Schreibt er euch? Ja, ...
3. Hast du es für mich gekauft? Ja, ...

4. Geht er ohne euch? Ja, ...
5. Könnt ihr uns dort besuchen? Ja, ...

Dative Case

Singular		Plural	
mir	*me*	**uns**	*us*
dir	*you*	**euch**	*you*
ihm	*him, it*	**ihnen**	*them*
ihm	*it*		
ihr	*her, it*		
		Ihnen	*you*

The dative personal pronouns are used as the indirect object of verbs, or as the object of prepositions requiring the dative case. *Note:* the accusative forms and the dative forms **uns, euch** are identical.

Kaufst du *ihr* **etwas?**   *Are you buying her something?*
Warum ist er neben *dir?*   *Why is he beside you?*
Ich sage *Ihnen* **die Wahrheit.**   *I'm telling you the truth.*

5. Rewrite the following, substituting the italicized nouns with personal pronouns.

1. Er gab es *seiner Freundin*.
2. Wir helfen *unserem Lehrer*.
3. Gibst du *dem Hund* das Futter?
4. Wir unterhielten uns mit *der Dame*.
5. Er erzählte von *dem Bekannten*.
6. Wohnst du bei *deinen Verwandten*?
7. Ich schrieb *meinen Freunden* Ansichtskarten.
8. Sie holte *dem Mädchen* Medizin.
9. Es gehört *meinen Eltern*.
10. Sie bringen *der Kranken* Essen.
11. Es gefällt *meinem Onkel*.
12. Ich kaufe *Ihrer Mutter* etwas.
13. Er kommt von *seinem Freund*.
14. Wir stehen hinter *dem Mann*.

6. Answer the following questions with complete sentences. Start with **Ja, ...**

1. Hat er dir etwas gebracht?
2. Zeigst du uns die Stadt?
3. Sagt ihr uns die Wahrheit?
4. Hat er dir geholfen?
5. Bringst du mir etwas mit?

6. Hat er dir dafür gedankt?
7. Hat sie euch geholfen?
8. Kaufen Sie ihm etwas?
9. Gefällt dir das Bild?
10. Kauft ihr mir den Wagen?

Position of Pronoun Objects

With both a noun object and a pronoun object

When a sentence contains both a noun object and a pronoun object, *the pronoun object precedes the noun object*, regardless of the cases of the noun and the pronoun.

Er hat *mir* das Problem erklärt.
Er hat *es* seinem Vater erklärt.

Er hat *sie* seinem Vater vorgestellt.
Er hat *ihm* seine Freundin vorgestellt.

7. Rewrite the following, substituting pronouns for the italicized elements. Make changes in the word order when necessary.

    1. Er gab seiner Mutter *das Geld.*
    2. Ich habe *meiner Freundin* ein Paket geschickt.
    3. Sie zeigte ihrem Kind *die Tiere.*
    4. Sie erzählen *ihren Freunden* die Neuigkeit.
    5. Sie bringen den Kranken *Blumen.*
    6. Er kauft seiner Tante *die Orchidee.*
    7. Ich schreibe *dem Lehrer* eine Karte.
    8. Sie glaubt *dem Jungen* die Geschichte.
    9. Ich gebe der Dame *die Karte.*
    10. Wir kaufen *den Kindern* Geschenke.

With two pronoun objects

When a sentence contains two pronoun objects, *the accusative pronoun always precedes the dative pronoun.*

Er hat *es* mir erklärt.
Er hat *sie* ihm vorgestellt.

Hat er *es* dir geschrieben?
Ich habe *ihn* ihm geschenkt.

8. Rewrite the following, changing the noun objects to pronouns.

    1. Wir bringen dem Verletzten Wasser.
    2. Ich hole meinem Freund den Fußball.
    3. Wir erzählten den Kindern die Geschichte.
    4. Er gibt dem Kind den Hund.
    5. Er hat seiner Freundin die Geschichte geglaubt.
    6. Johann zeigte den Ausländern das Rathaus.
    7. Der Professor erklärte den Studenten die Theorie.
    8. Ich kaufe meinen Eltern die Maschine.
    9. Er schreibt seinem Lehrer die Neuigkeit.
    10. Dieter holt dem Hund das Wasser.

9. Answer the following questions affirmatively with complete sentences. Change the noun objects to pronouns. Make all necessary changes.

    1. Hat er dir die Theaterkarten geschenkt?
    2. Hast du ihnen die Aufnahme gezeigt?

3. Hat er euch die Bücher gekauft?
4. Bringst du mir den Kaffee?
5. Hat sie euch den Wagen gegeben?

Pronouns in relation to the subject

<u>Following the subject</u>

If the subject (either a noun or a pronoun) is in first position in the sentence, the pronoun object (or objects) follows the subject. The subject and the object (or objects) are separated only by the verb.

Jörg **kennt** *ihn.*
Ich **zeige** *dir* **nichts.**
Max **hat** *ihn* **gesehen.**
Sie **bringen** *es uns*.

<u>Following or preceding the subject</u>

If the subject is a noun and is not in first position in the sentence or clause, the pronoun object (or objects) may either precede or follow the subject.

Kennt *ihn* **Jörg?**	or	**Kennt Jörg** *ihn?*	*Does Jörg know him?*
Kauft *dir* **Ute etwas?**	or	**Kauft Ute** *dir* **etwas?**	*Is Ute buying you something?*

However, if the subject is a pronoun, the pronoun object must always follow the subject.

Kennt er *ihn?*
Kauft sie *dir* **etwas?**
Gibt er *es uns?*

10. Rewrite the following, changing the italicized elements to pronouns. Have the pronoun objects precede the subjects when possible.

1. Hilft Ellen *ihren Brüdern?*
2. Ich glaube, daß Maria *das Kleid* gekauft hat.
3. Wir wissen nicht, ob er *die Kirche* besichtigt hat.
4. Ich habe Zeit, weil Norma *unseren* Onkel abholt.
5. Morgen kauft Susi *ihrer Freundin* den Pullover.

11. Rewrite the following, changing the italicized elements to personal pronouns. Have the pronoun objects follow the subjects.

1. Jeden Tag holt Pia *ihrem Vater* die Zeitung.
2. Ich weiß, wann Peter *Frau Müller* geholfen hat.
3. Bringt Gabriele *das Programm?*
4. Hat er *das Geld* genommen?
5. Weißt du, wo Dieter *die Leute* getroffen hat?

Pronouns in Idiomatic Verb + Preposition Combinations (Phrasal Verbs)

Pronouns following the prepositions in idiomatic expressions with verbs may be in either the accusative or the dative case. As expected, the accusative prepositions are followed by accusative pronouns and the dative prepositions are followed by dative pronouns. However, the cases following the *either-or* prepositions must be learned, since the movement/lack of movement distinction is not applicable to these idiomatic verb constructions.

Accusative case

Many verb phrases containing the prepositions **an, auf, über** are followed by the accusative case.

denken an	*to think of*	**Ich denke oft an** *dich.*
lachen über	*to laugh about*	**Wir lachten über** *ihn.*
sprechen über	*to talk about* (*in detail*)	**Sprecht ihr über** *sie?*
warten auf	*to wait for*	**Warten Sie auf** *uns?*

Dative case

The dative case is required after verb phrases containing the prepositions **von, zu, nach, vor.**

Angst haben vor	*to be afraid of*	**Er hat keine Angst vor** *Ihnen.*
einladen zu	*to invite to*	**Wir laden ihn zu** *uns* **ein.**
fragen nach	*to ask about*	**Hat er nach** *mir* **gefragt?**
hören von	*to hear from*	**Hast du von** *ihr* **gehört?**
sprechen von	*to talk of*	**Wir haben von** *ihm* **gesprochen.**
wissen von	*to know about*	**Was weißt du von** *ihnen?*

12. Replace the nouns with the appropriate pronouns.

1. Er lachte über die Geschichte.
2. Wir sprechen von den Leuten.
3. Er fragt nach meiner Schwester.
4. Was weißt du von dem Herrn?
5. Er denkt an seine Frau.
6. Warten Sie auf den Professor?
7. Warum hast du Angst vor dem Hund?
8. Wir sprechen über seinen Onkel.
9. Ich habe von meinem Bruder gehört.
10. Er lädt sie zu seinen Eltern ein.

13. Complete the following with the appropriate accusative or dative pronouns.

1. Sie haben von _____ (*du*) gesprochen.
2. Wer hat Angst vor _____ (*er*)?
3. Was weiß er von _____ (*wir*)?
4. Wir haben über _____ (*sie*) gelacht.
5. Haben Sie über _____ (*wir*) gesprochen?
6. Hast du etwas von _____ (*er*) gehört?
7. Er fragt immer nach _____ (*du*).
8. Er wartete auf _____ (*du*).
9. Ladet ihr mich zu _____ (*ihr*) ein?
10. Denkst du auch an _____ (*ich*)?
11. Wer lacht über _____ (*wir*)?
12. Wir sprechen von _____ (*du*).
13. Ich spreche über _____ (*sie*).
14. Er wartet auf _____ (*Sie*).

Da-*compounds*

When the third person pronouns are used with prepositions, they can refer only to people.

Sprecht ihr von Klaus?	**Ja, wir sprechen** *von ihm.*
	Yes, we are talking about him.
Wartet er auf seine Frau?	**Ja, er wartet** *auf sie.*
	Yes, he is waiting for her.
Bist du bei deinen Eltern?	**Ja, ich bin** *bei ihnen.*
	Yes, I am with them.

When the pronouns refer to things or ideas, the prepositions are prefixed by **da(r)-**. (See Chapter 3, p. 62.)

Sprecht ihr von dem Plan?   **Ja, wir sprechen** *davon*.
                                  Yes, we are talking about it.

Wartest du auf den Brief?   **Ja, ich warte** *darauf*.
                                  Yes, I am waiting for it.

14. Answer the following questions affirmatively, using the appropriate **da-** compounds or personal pronouns.

1. Denkst du an deine Reise?
2. Liegst du unter dem Auto?
3. Wartest du auf Anna?
4. Sprecht ihr über die Oper?
5. Sprichst du von Marlene?
6. Fährst du mit dem Zug?
7. Stehst du vor den Bildern?
8. Wartest du auf das Paket?

9. Steht ihr neben euren Eltern?
10. Denkt er an seine Frau?
11. Fragt sie nach deiner Schwester?
12. Sitzen Sie hinter dem Herrn?
13. Arbeitest du mit dem Hammer?
14. Fahrt ihr mit euren Freunden?
15. Weißt du etwas von dem Plan?
16. Hast du Angst vor dem Lehrer?

REFLEXIVE PRONOUNS

Reflexive pronouns are used when the action of the verb is both executed by and performed upon the subject. (For a complete review, see Chapter 7.)

Accusative Case

	Singular		*Plural*
mich	*myself*	**uns**	*ourselves*
dich	*yourself*	**euch**	*yourselves*
sich	*him-, her-, itself*	**sich**	*themselves, yourself, yourselves*

Accusative reflexive pronouns are identical with the accusative personal pronouns, except for the third person singular and plural. The reflexive pronoun for the formal **Sie** is **sich**. Note that this form is not capitalized in correspondence.

15. Complete the following with the correct reflexive pronouns.

1. Ich verletzte _____ beim Skilaufen.
2. Er rasiert _____ jeden Tag.
3. Wir müssen _____ waschen.
4. Stellt _____ vor!
5. Fürchten Sie _____ vor dem Hund?
6. Helga kann _____ nicht daran erinnern.
7. Warum hast du _____ verspätet?
8. Freust du _____ auf Weihnachten?
9. Ich lege _____ aufs Bett.
10. Die Kinder ziehen _____ um.

Dative Case

Singular		Plural	
mir	*myself*	**uns**	*ourselves*
dir	*yourself*	**euch**	*yourselves*
sich	*him-, her-, itself*	**sich**	*themselves, yourself, yourselves*

The dative reflexive pronouns are identical with the dative personal pronouns, except in the third person singular and plural. Here, as in the accusative, the reflexive pronoun is **sich**, and the reflexive form for the formal **Sie** is also **sich**. Here, too, this form is not capitalized in correspondence.

16. Complete the following with the correct reflexive pronouns.

1. Kauft ihr _____ das Pferd?
2. Ich habe _____ das Bier bestellt.
3. Er hat _____ weh getan.
4. Nimm _____ etwas!
5. Ich wasche _____ das Gesicht.
6. Kannst du _____ das vorstellen?
7. Die Kinder kauften _____ Schokolade.
8. Ich nehme _____ das Buch.
9. Kaufst du _____ das Auto?
10. Holen wir _____ die Möbel!

Position

Reflexive pronouns are placed as close to the subject as possible. The reflexive pronoun follows a pronoun subject. However, the reflexive pronoun never comes between the pronoun subject and the verb.

> **Er kauft** *sich* **einen Anzug.**
> **Erinnerst du** *dich* **an ihn?**

If the subject is a noun, the reflexive pronoun may precede or follow it. However, the noun subject cannot be in first position in the sentence or clause.

> **Gestern hat** *sich* **Erika verletzt.**   or   **Gestern hat Erika** *sich* **verletzt.**

17. Answer the following questions with complete sentences. Start each answer with the cue and place the reflexive pronoun in the same position as in the original sentence.

1. Wann haben sich die Kinder weh getan?   *heute morgen*
2. Worauf freut sich Max?   *auf die Ferien*
3. Warum hat sich der Beamte verspätet?   *wegen des Unfalls*
4. Wann hat Vater sich das Auto gekauft?   *vor einer Stunde*
5. Woran erinnert sich dein Freund?   *an seine Ferien*
6. Wann putzt Barbara sich die Zähne?   *am Abend*
7. Was kauft sich Herr Obermeyer?   *ein Motorrad*
8. Wann rasiert sich Vater?   *am Morgen*

POSSESSIVE PRONOUNS

mein-	*mine*	**unser-**	*ours*
dein-	*yours*	**eur-**	*yours*
sein-	*his, its*	**ihr-**	*theirs*
ihr-	*hers*		
		Ihr-	*yours*

The possessive pronoun receives the endings of **dieser, dieses, diese** in all cases. The gender of the possessive pronoun is determined by the gender of the noun it replaces.

Possessive used as adjective

Wann triffst du *deinen* **Freund?**
When are you meeting your friend?
Das ist *sein* **Mantel.**
That is his coat.
Eure **Kinder sind hier.**
Your children are here.

Possessive used as pronoun

Ich treffe *meinen* **um zwei Uhr.**
I am meeting mine at two o'clock.
Meiner **hängt im Schrank.**
Mine is hanging in the closet.
Wo sind *unsere?*
Where are ours?

18.   Complete the following with the correct forms of the possessive pronouns.

1. Ich habe meine Bücher. Hast du _____ ?
2. Wir sprechen von unserer Reise. Sprecht ihr von _____ ?
3. Habt ihr schon eure Freunde gesehen? Wir haben _____ noch nicht gesehen.
4. Er hat sein Geld bekommen. Ich habe _____ noch nicht bekommen.
5. Er schreibt seinen Freunden. Schreibst du _____ ?
6. Das ist nicht meine Schwester, sondern _____ (*his*).
7. Ich habe nicht deinen Mann gesehen, sondern _____ (*hers*).
8. Er wohnt nicht in seinem Haus, sondern in _____ (*ours*).
9. Ich war nicht bei deinen Eltern, sondern bei _____ (*mine*).
10. Ich schreibe nicht mit seinem Bleistift, sondern mit _____ (*hers*).

DEMONSTRATIVE PRONOUNS

	SINGULAR			PLURAL
	Masculine	*Neuter*	*Feminine*	*All Genders*
Nominative	**der**	**das**	**die**	**die**
	dieser	**dieses**	**diese**	**diese**
Accusative	**den**	**das**	**die**	**die**
	diesen	**dieses**	**diese**	**diese**
Dative	**dem**	**dem**	**der**	*denen*
	diesem	**diesem**	**dieser**	*diesen*

The demonstrative pronouns (**der, das, die** and **dieser, dieses, diese**) are used in place of the personal pronouns (**er, es, sie**) when the pronoun is to receive special emphasis. They follow the same pattern of case endings as the definite article, except for the form of the dative plural, which is **denen** instead of **den** (see p. 47). The gender and number of a demonstrative pronoun is determined from the noun it refers back to, and its case is determined by the pronoun's function in the sentence.

In spoken German the demonstrative pronouns receive greater vocal stress than the personal pronouns or the definite articles, and they are frequently expanded by the addition of **hier** (*this one/these*), **da, dort** (*that one/those*) to more clearly specify the object referred to.

Ich kaufe *den hier.*	*I'll buy this one.*
Wem gehört *dieser dort?*	*To whom does that one belong?*
Geben Sie mir *diese da!*	*Give me those.*
Bleib bei *denen hier!*	*Stay with these.*

19. Complete the following with the appropriate forms of the demonstrative pronoun **der**. Follow the model.

> **Der Mantel hier ist wärmer als _____.**
> **Der Mantel hier ist wärmer als der dort (da).**

1. Der Film hier ist länger als _____.
2. In dem Parkhaus dort sind mehr Autos als in _____.
3. Die Frau hier ist jünger als _____.
4. Er kam aus dem Haus da, nicht aus _____.
5. Ich kaufe die Maschine dort, nicht _____.
6. Wir sprechen von den Leuten hier, nicht von _____.

20. Complete the following with the correct demonstrative pronoun **dieser**.

1. Diese Brücke hier ist breiter als _____.
2. Wir fahren mit diesem Auto dort, nicht mit _____.
3. Er kauft nicht diese Bücher hier, sondern _____.
4. Dieser Ring da ist teurer als _____.
5. Ich möchte dieses Kleid dort, nicht _____.

INDEFINITE PRONOUNS

The indefinite pronouns refer to persons, things, and concepts that are not precisely defined.

Singular

The following indefinite pronouns refer to persons. They are used only in the nominative, accusative, and dative cases singular.

jeder
jemand
niemand
man (nominative only)

jeder—*everyone*

Jeder **muß mitmachen.**	*Everyone has to participate.*
Ich habe *jeden* **gefragt.**	*I asked everyone.*
Er bekommt von *jedem* **etwas.**	*He gets something from everyone.*

Note that the accusative and dative forms take the same endings as the definite articles **der, das, die.** The neuter form can be used to refer back to things.

jemand—*someone*

Ist *jemand* **da?**	*Is anyone there?*
Er hat *jemand*(en) **gehört.**	*He heard someone.*
Ich rede gerade mit *jemand*(em).	*I'm talking with someone at the moment.*

Note that the accusative and dative forms can take the same endings as the masculine definite article. However, these endings can also be omitted. The genitive is used rarely, but when it is used, it precedes the noun:

jemand(e)s Hilfe

niemand—*no one*

Niemand **war zu Hause.**	*No one was home.*
Ich kenne *niemand*(en) **hier.**	*I know no one here.*
Sie hat mit *niemand*(em) **geredet.**	*She spoke with no one.*

Note that like jemand, **niemand** takes the same endings as the masculine definite article in the accusative and dative. However, these endings can also be omitted. The genitive is used rarely, but when it is used, it precedes the noun:

niemand(e)s Hilfe

man—*one, you, we, they, people*

Man **kann nicht alles wissen.**	*One can't know everything.*
Er sieht *einen* **nicht, wenn er sich beeilt.**	*He doesn't see you when he's in a hurry.*
Er redet nicht mit *einem.*	*He doesn't talk to people.*

The indefinite pronoun **man** occurs only in the nominative case. It is used with the third person singular verb. If the accusative or dative cases are called for, the form **einen** and **einem** are used, respectively. There is no genitive form of **man**; the possessive adjective **sein** is used instead.

The following indefinite pronouns refer only to things. They do not take any endings.

alles
etwas
nichts
viel
wenig

alles—*everything*

Ich habe *alles* **gegessen.**	*I ate everything.*

etwas—*something*

Ja, er hat *etwas* **gesagt.**	*Yes, he said something.*

Note: the shortened form **was** is often used colloquially.

nichts—*nothing*

> **Sie hat uns *nichts* gebracht.**   *She brought us nothing.*

viel—*much*

> **Wir haben *viel* gelernt.**   *We learned much.*

wenig—*little*

> **Er weiß *wenig*.**   *He knows little.*

Plural

The following indefinite pronouns may refer to *things* or to *persons*. They take the plural endings of the definite article.

> **alle**
> **andere**
> **einige**
> **manche**
> **mehrere**
> **viele**
> **wenige**

alle—*everyone, all*

> **Es gehört *allen*.**   *It belongs to everyone.*

andere—*others* (*other ones*)

> **Wir haben auch *andere*.**   *We also have others.*

einige—*some, several*

> ***Einige* haben ihn im Park getroffen.**   *Some met him in the park.*

manche—*many*

> ***Manche* bleiben gern hier.**   *Many like to stay here.*

mehrere—*several*

> **Ich habe *mehrere* davon gekauft.**   *I bought several of them.*

viele—*many*

> **Er hat mit *vielen* gespielt.**   *He played with many.*

wenige—*few*

> ***Wenige* haben das Problem verstanden.**   *Few understood the problem.*

21. Complete the following with the correct forms of the German indefinite pronoun.

1. Ich habe _____ (*no one*) gesehen.
2. Er hat _____ (*something*) gesagt.
3. _____ (*Few*) haben ihn besucht.
4. Er hat sich mit _____ (*some*) unterhalten.
5. _____ (*Everyone*) war zu Hause.
6. Sie kann _____ (*nothing*).
7. _____ (*One*) sollte ihm danken.

8. _____ (*Many*) haben es gewußt.
9. Ich kenne _____ (*everyone*).
10. Sie gibt _____ (*one*) _____ (*nothing*).
11. Er weiß _____ (*much*).
12. Wir haben _____ (*little*) gesehen.
13. _____ (*Someone*) ist gekommen.
14. Ich habe dann _____ (*other ones*) gesucht.
15. Hast du _____ (*several*) gekauft?
16. _____ (*Many*) haben Talent.
17. Habt ihr _____ (*everything*) gemacht?
18. _____(*People*) hat ihn gern.

RELATIVE PRONOUNS

| | SINGULAR | | | PLURAL |
	Masculine	Neuter	Feminine	All Genders
Nominative	der	das	die	die
Accusative	den	das	die	die
Dative	dem	dem	der	denen
Genitive	dessen	dessen	deren	deren

   A relative pronoun both refers back to a previously mentioned noun or pronoun (often referred to as its antecedent) and introduces a dependent relative clause that modifies this antecedent. The most frequently used relative pronoun in German is a form of **der, das, die.**

   A relative pronoun must have the same number and gender as its antecedent. However, the grammatical case of a relative pronoun is determined by its function within the relative clause. Thus if the relative pronoun is the subject of the relative clause, it must be in the nominative case; if it is the direct object of the relative clause, it will usually be in the accusative case, etc. (See the Section *Cases of Nouns* in Chapter 2.) The endings of the relative pronouns are the same as those for the definite articles except for the dative plural **denen** and the genitive forms **dessen** and **deren.**

   Since the relative clause is a dependent (also called subordinate) clause, the conjugated verb moves to the final position in the clause (see Chapter 10, pp. 244–245). In this position separable prefixes remain joined to the verb. The relative clause is set off from the main clause by a comma (or commas).

   The relative pronoun **welcher, welches, welche** is used relatively infrequently. When it is used, it is used primarily in written German and usually either to clarify meanings or for stylistic considerations, such as to avoid repetitions of identical forms.

Nominative Case

| | SINGULAR | | | PLURAL |
	Masculine	Neuter	Feminine	All Genders
der	das	die	die
welcher	welches	welche	welche

   The relative pronouns in the following examples are in the nominative case because they function as the subject of the relative clause.

Kennst du den Mann, *der* **dort steht?**
Do you know the man who is standing there?

Otto kommt von der Lehrerin, *die* **ihm das Problem erklärt hat.**
Otto is coming from the teacher who explained the problem to him.

Das Mädchen, *das* **dort steht, ist seine Schwester.**
The girl who is standing there is his sister.

Siehst du die Vögel, *die* **dort auf dem Baum sitzen?**
Do you see the birds that are sitting there on the tree?

In the following sentence the appropriate form of the relative pronoun **welch-** is preferred to avoid repetition of **die.**

Die Dame, *welche* (*die*) **die Brosche gekauft hat, ist sehr reich.**
The lady who bought the brooch is very rich.

22.   Complete the following with the appropriate forms of the nominative relative pronoun **der.**

1. Wo ist das Buch, _____ dir gehört?
2. Der Junge, _____ dort steht, ist mein Bruder.
3. Wo sind die Bilder, _____ uns so gefallen?
4. Die Frau, _____ bei uns wohnt, ist keine Sängerin.
5. Wie heißt der Dichter, _____ dieses Gedicht geschrieben hat?
6. Kennst du das Mädchen, _____ dort sitzt?
7. Dort ist die Lehrerin, _____ uns geholfen hat.
8. Wir fahren mit dem Zug, _____ jetzt ankommt.

Accusative Case

| | SINGULAR | | PLURAL |
Masculine	Neuter	Feminine	All Genders
den **welchen**	**das** **welches**	**die** **welche**	**die** **welche**

The forms of the accusative relative pronouns are identical with the nominative forms, except in the masculine singular. The accusative case of the relative pronoun is used when it functions as the direct object of the verb or as the object of a preposition that is followed by the accusative. No contractions are possible.

Der Anzug, *den* **du trägst, ist altmodisch.**
The suit that you are wearing is old-fashioned.

Die Geschichte, *die* **wir gelesen haben, war sehr lang.**
The story that we read was very long.

Das Haus, in *das* **wir ziehen, ist hundert Jahre alt.**
The house into which we are moving is one hundred years old.

Das sind die Freunde, für *die* **ich es gekauft habe.**
Those are the friends for whom I bought it.

23. Complete the following with the appropriate accusative form of the relative pronoun **der**.

1. Wo sitzt der Junge, _____ du kennengelernt hast?
2. Die Frau, neben _____ ich mich gesetzt habe, ist Schauspielerin.
3. Der Mantel, _____ er angezogen hat, gehört mir.
4. Das Mädchen, auf _____ er wartete, ist meine Freundin.
5. Die Hunde, _____ ich füttern soll, sind ja wild.
6. Die Bluse, _____ du trägst, ist sehr hübsch.
7. Hier ist das Paket, _____ er mir geschickt hat.
8. Wir kennen den Lehrer, für _____ sie es macht.

24. Combine the sentences with a nominative or accusative relative pronoun. Follow the model.

Wie heißt das Mädchen? Wir haben es kennengelernt.
Wie heißt das Mädchen, das wir kennengelernt haben?

1. Liest du das Buch? Er hat es gebracht.
2. Brauchst du die Zeitung? Sie liegt auf dem Tisch.
3. Kennst du den Herrn? Wir haben ihn getroffen.
4. Heute kam der Junge. Er hatte uns damals geholfen.
5. Kennst du die Leute? Sie gehen dort spazieren.
6. Wo sind die Blumen? Ich habe sie gekauft.

Dative case

| | SINGULAR | | PLURAL |
Masculine	Neuter	Feminine	All Genders
dem	dem	der	denen
welchem	welchem	welcher	welchen

The dative relative pronouns are used when they function as the indirect object of the verb of the dependent clause, or when they are the object of verbs or prepositions requiring the dative case. The dative plural relative pronoun differs from the definite article. It adds **-en** to become **denen.** No contractions are possible.

Dort liegt der Hund, vor *dem* **ich Angst habe.**
There lies the dog of which I am afraid.

Heute besucht mich meine Freundin, von *der* **ich dir erzählt habe.**
My girlfriend, about whom I told you, is visiting me today.

Das Mädchen, *dem* **ich die Kette gegeben hatte, hat sie verloren.**
The girl to whom I had given the necklace lost it.

Die Studenten, neben *denen* **er sitzt, sind sehr intelligent.**
The students next to whom he is sitting are very intelligent.

25. Complete the following with the correct dative relative pronoun **der**.

1. Das Buch, nach _____ er fragte, gehört mir.
2. Der Deutsche, mit _____ er spricht, kommt aus Berlin.
3. Die Leute, _____ ich helfen wollte, sind weggefahren.
4. Das Haus, in _____ wir wohnen, ist modern.

5. Dort ist die Reisende, _____ ich den Weg gezeigt habe.
6. Die Dame, _____ ich es gebe, ist sehr intelligent.
7. Die Straßen, nach _____ er fragt, sind im Zentrum.
8. Das Hotel, aus _____ er kommt, ist sehr alt.

26. Combine the two sentences with the correct form of the dative relative pronoun **welcher.**

1. Dort sitzt der Tourist. Du sollst ihm das Essen bringen.
2. Kennst du meine Geschwister? Ich wohne bei ihnen.
3. Die Leiter ist kaputt. Er steht darauf.
4. Hier ist das Auto. Wir fahren damit spazieren.
5. Der Stuhl ist alt. Du sitzt darauf.

Genitive Case

	SINGULAR		PLURAL
Masculine	Neuter	Feminine	All Genders
dessen	dessen	deren	deren

All genitive relative pronouns differ from the definite article. The relative pronoun **welcher** has no genitive forms.

Ich treffe meinen Freund, *dessen* **Auto ich brauche.**
I'll meet my friend whose car I need.

Dort ist die Dame, *deren* **Geld ich gefunden habe.**
There is the lady whose money I found.

Das Haus, *dessen* **Baustil mir gefällt, wurde 1910 gebaut.**
The house, the style of which I like, was built in 1910.

Die Kinder, *deren* **Katze verletzt wurde, laufen zum Tierarzt.**
The children whose cat was injured are running to the veterinarian.

27. Complete the following with the correct genitive relative pronouns.

1. Die Frau, _____ Auto kaputt ist, sucht einen Mechaniker.
2. Der Dichter, _____ Roman wir gelesen haben, hält einen Vortrag.
3. Hier kommt das Kind, _____ Eltern ich gut kenne.
4. Die Künstler, _____ Werke wir besichtigen, sind weltbekannt.
5. Die Studentin, _____ Buch ich gefunden habe, ist nett.
6. Die Museen, _____ Sammlungen ich kenne, sind reich.
7. Dort ist der Junge, _____ Vater uns geholfen hat.
8. Wo ist das Mädchen, _____ Fahrrad dort liegt?

Indefinite Relative Pronouns

Wer, was

The indefinite relative pronouns **wer** (*whoever*) and **was** (*whatever*) are used when there is no antecedent.

The case of **wer** is determined by its function in the relative clause that it introduces. **Wer** takes the same endings as the **er** form of the relative pronoun. It is always singular.

Nominative	**wer**
Accusative	**wen**
Dative	**wem**
Genitive	**wessen**

Was does not change its form according to how it is used in the relative clause.

When either **wer** or **was** is used in combination with the adverbs **auch, immer, auch immer,** the already indefinite character of these indefinite pronouns is intensified.

> *Wer* **mitgehen will, muß um fünf Uhr hier sein.**
> *Whoever wants to come along has to be here at five o'clock.*

> *Was* **auch immer passiert, ich habe keine Angst.**
> *Whatever happens, I am not afraid.*

28. Complete the following with the correct indefinite relative pronouns.

1. _____ mir hilft, wird belohnt.
2. _____ er sagt, ist die Wahrheit.
3. _____ das Geld genommen hat, soll es zurückgeben.
4. _____ er auch will, bekommt er.
5. _____ das Problem löst, bekommt den Preis.

The relative pronoun **was** (*that, which*) must be used if the antecedent is an indefinite pronoun referring to things (**alles, nichts, etwas,** etc.).

> **Er erzählte mir etwas,** *was* **ich schon wußte.**
> *He told me something that I knew already.*

Was is also used when the antecedent is an entire clause.

> **Er hatte das Geld gewonnen,** *was* **mich sehr freute.**
> *He had won the money, which made me very happy.*

Wo

When the antecedent is the name of a country, city, or place, **wo** (*where, in which*) is substituted for the relative pronoun.

> **Er besucht London,** *wo* **er viele Freunde hat.**
> *He is visiting London, where he has many friends.*

29. Complete the following with the correct relative pronouns or pronoun substitutes.

1. Er hat nichts, _____ großen Wert hat.
2. Wir sind in Bayern, _____ es viele Barockkirchen gibt.
3. Wir fahren in die Alpen, _____ man gut skifahren kann.
4. Er is sehr krank, _____ mir große Sorgen macht.
5. Alles, _____ ich habe, hat Inge mir geschenkt.
6. Er weiß etwas, _____ sehr wichtig ist.
7. Wir landen in Frankfurt, _____ es den internationalen Flughafen gibt.
8. Er ist der beste Sportler, _____ mich sehr freut.

Wo- *compounds in relative clauses*

When relative pronouns are preceded by prepositions and when they refer to things or ideas, they may be replaced by **wo-** compounds.

Das Paket, *worauf (auf das)* **er wartet, soll heute ankommen.**
The package for which he is waiting is supposed to arrive today.

30. Rewrite the following, substituting the correct **wo-** compound for the preposition + relative pronoun.

   1. Der Stuhl, auf dem du sitzt, ist eine Rarität.
   2. Wir besuchen das Haus, in dem Goethe geboren wurde.
   3. Ist das das Spielzeug, mit dem sie sich so amüsiert?
   4. Dort ist die Kirche, nach der er fragte.
   5. Sind das die Bücher, für die du dich interessierst?
   6. Wo ist der Brief, auf den er wartet?
   7. Das Problem, über das ihr sprecht, ist schwer.
   8. Wo ist die Ruine, von der er erzählt?

Review

31. Complete the following with the correct relative pronouns **der, wer, was,** or the substitute **wo.**

   1. Sie gab uns alles, _____ sie hatte.
   2. Wo ist der Brief, _____ ich mitnehmen soll?
   3. _____ er auch ist, er muß warten.
   4. Dort ist der Klub, zu _____ ich gehöre.
   5. Die Kinder, _____ Eltern noch nicht gekommen sind, warten noch.
   6. Willst du das Auto, _____ dort steht?
   7. Ist das das Flugzeug, mit _____ du geflogen bist?
   8. Ich habe den Apparat, _____ er vergessen hat.
   9. Wir besuchen München, _____ das Bier so gut ist.
   10. Der Koffer, _____ dort steht, gehört seiner Freundin.
   11. Wo ist das Buch, _____ er vergessen hat?
   12. Es gab nichts, _____ er nicht machen konnte.
   13. Der Komponist, _____ Oper uns so gut gefallen hat, ist tot.
   14. _____ alles weiß, braucht keine Angst zu haben.
   15. Kennst du das Gedicht, _____ wir lernen mußten.
   16. Die Kranken, _____ dort sitzen, brauchen viel Ruhe.
   17. Wir fliegen nach Holland, _____ zur Zeit die Tulpen blühen.
   18. Die Kinder, _____ ich die Geschenke brachte, danken mir.
   19. Kennst du die Leute, _____ Auto ich parken mußte?
   20. Ich sehe etwas, _____ ich kaufen will.
   21. Wo ist die Kirche, _____ er besuchte?
   22. Die Tasche, _____ ich kaufte, ist aus Leder.
   23. Der Mann, neben _____ er steht, ist bekannt.
   24. Alles _____ du brauchst ist hier.
   25. Dort ist der Deutsche, _____ ich den Weg zeigte.

Chapter 5

Adjectives and Adverbs

DEMONSTRATIVE ADJECTIVES

der, das, die

Demonstrative adjectives are used to point out or give special emphasis to the nouns they modify. In German the definite article **der, das, die** can also function as a demonstrative adjective, corresponding to the English *this* (plural, *these*) and *that* (plural, *those*). The demonstrative adjective, like the definite article, agrees with the noun it modifies in gender, number, and case. Thus the demonstrative adjective has the same endings as the definite article. (See Chapter 2, p. 47.) When used as demonstrative adjectives, the various forms of **der, das, die** are stressed in spoken German.

When **hier** is used with the demonstrative adjective, it corresponds to the English *this* (*these*). When **da** or **dort** is used, it corresponds to *that* (*those*). The words **hier, da, dort** follow the noun that is modified by the demonstrative adjective.

Die **Jacke hier ist teuer.**	*This jacket is expensive.*
Sie kam aus *dem* **Haus dort.**	*She came out of that house.*
Helfen Sie *dem* **Jungen da!**	*Help that boy!*

1. Complete with the appropriate demonstrative adjective.

1. Ich kaufe _____ Auto hier.
2. Wieviel kostet _____ Teppich da?
3. Sie wohnten in _____ Straße dort.
4. Warum kaufst du nicht _____ Mantel hier?
5. Er will aus _____ Glas da trinken.
6. _____ Schuhe hier sind bequem.
7. Wie findest du _____ Wein hier?
8. Er ist gegen _____ Baum dort gefahren.
9. Ich wohne bei _____ Leuten da.
10. Kennt ihr _____ Studentin dort?

dieser, dieses, diese

Another demonstrative adjective is **dieser.** Like **der, das, die,** it agrees with the noun it modifies in gender, number, and case. Any form of **dieser** can be made to correspond to the English *this* by adding **hier. Da** and **dort** make it correspond to *that*. Note that these patterns are primarily for use in spoken rather than written German. **Dieser** takes the same endings as the definite article.

Diese **Häuser da sind sehr alt.**	*Those houses are very old.*
Willst du *diesen* **Pullover hier?**	*Do you want this sweater?*
Ich fahre mit *diesem* **Bus dort.**	*I am taking that Bus.*

2. Form sentences from the following. Supply the appropriate forms of the demonstrative adjective **dieser.**

1. Mantel / dort / gehören / mir /
2. Wir / holen / etwas / für / Mädchen / hier /
3. Ich / helfen / Mann / da /

    4. Es / liegen / unter / Bücher / da /
    5. Mit / Wagen / hier / fahren / wir / nicht /
    6. Ursula / haben / Kamera / da /
    7. Ich / schlafen / nicht / in / Bett / da /
    8. Kennen / du / Mann / dort / ? /
    9. Frauen / hier / kaufen / nichts /
   10. Er / kaufen / Blumen / hier /

DESCRIPTIVE ADJECTIVES

Descriptive adjectives are words that describe or provide additional information about the qualities of people and things, such as *thin, green, good*. In German, as well as English, descriptive adjectives can be used in various ways.

Predicate Adjective

When the adjective follows a noun or pronoun subject and is preceded by a form of **sein, werden, bleiben,** it is used as a predicate adjective.

Der Kaffee war *bitter*.	*The coffee was bitter.*
Seine Haare werden schon *grau*.	*His hair is already getting gray.*

The predicate adjective never takes an ending.
    The following are some common German adjectives.

alt	*old*	**interessant**	*interesting*
amerikanisch	*American*	**jung**	*young*
arm	*poor*	**kalt**	*cold*
bequem	*comfortable*	**klein**	*small, short*
billig	*inexpensive*	**klug**	*clever, smart*
bitter	*bitter*	**krank**	*ill*
blond	*blond*	**kurz**	*short*
böse	*bad*	**lang**	*long*
deutsch	*German*	**langsam**	*slow*
dick	*heavy, thick*	**leer**	*empty*
dunkel	*dark*	**leicht**	*easy*
dünn	*skinny, thin*	**nah**	*near*
eng	*narrow*	**nett**	*nice*
faul	*lazy*	**neu**	*new*
fleißig	*industrious*	**reich**	*rich*
fremd	*strange*	**sauber**	*clean*
frisch	*fresh*	**sauer**	*sour*
gesund	*healthy*	**scharf**	*sharp, pungent*
glücklich	*happy*	**schmutzig**	*dirty*
groß	*big, tall*	**schnell**	*fast*
gut	*good*	**schwach**	*weak*
häßlich	*ugly*	**süß**	*sweet*
heiß	*hot*	**teuer**	*expensive*
hübsch	*pretty*	**voll**	*full*
intelligent	*intelligent*	**weit**	*far*

3.   Complete the following sentences with the opposite predicate adjectives.

    1. Das Wetter ist nicht _____ , sondern kalt.

2. Der Tee ist nicht _____, sondern bitter.
3. Der Schüler is nicht _____, sondern fleißig.
4. Die Straße ist nicht _____, sondern kurz.
5. Meine Tochter ist nicht _____, sondern gesund.
6. Sein Bruder ist nicht _____, sondern arm.
7. Ihre Hände sind nicht _____, sondern sauber.
8. Diese Aufgabe ist nicht _____, sondern schwer.
9. Sein Mädchen ist nicht _____, sondern hübsch.
10. Dieser Mantel war nicht _____, sondern teuer.
11. Sie ist nicht _____, sondern dünn.
12. Er ist nicht _____, sondern schnell.
13. Es ist nicht _____, sondern gut.
14. Es ist nicht _____, sondern neu.
15. Sie ist nicht _____, sondern groß.

Attributive Adjective—Preceded by "der" Words or Definite Articles

When the adjective precedes the noun, it is used as an attributive adjective. An attributive adjective in German always takes an ending. The adjective ending is determined by the number (singular or plural), gender (masculine, feminine, neuter), and the case of the noun it modifies. Another important factor determining the ending of the adjective is the presence or absence of a **"der"** or **"ein"** word.

The following words take the same endings as the definite article. Therefore they are referred to as **"der"** words.

dieser	*this*
jeder	*each*, *every* (used only in the singular)
jener	*that*
mancher	*many* (a)
solcher	*such* (usually occurs only in the plural)
welcher	*which*
alle	*all* (used only in plural)

Adjectives preceded by the definite article or **"der"** word require a specific set of endings.

Nominative case, singular (following "der" words)

When the attributive adjective modifies a noun that is in the nominative case singular, and when the adjective is preceded by the definite article or a **"der"** word, it takes the following endings:

Masculine	*Neuter*	*Feminine*
der billige Koffer	**das hübsche Mädchen**	**die alte Tasche**

Der alte **Tisch ist kaputt.**	*The old table is broken.*
Das kleine **Kind schreit.**	*The small child is screaming.*
Die nette **Frau hilft uns.**	*The nice woman is helping us.*
Dieser deutsche **Wagen ist schnell.**	*This German car is fast.*
Jene große **Maschine ist teuer.**	*That large machine is expensive*
Welches leere **Glas gehört dir?**	*Which empty glass belongs to you?*

If the noun is modified by two or more adjectives in succession, they all take the same endings.

Wo ist die *kleine, schwarze* **Katze?**	*Where is the small, black cat?*

4. Complete with the appropriate endings.

　　1. Dies＿＿＿＿＿＿ breit＿＿＿＿＿＿ Fluß ist die Donau.
　　2. Wo ist d＿＿＿＿＿ neu＿＿＿＿＿, blau＿＿＿＿＿ Kleid?
　　3. Welch＿＿＿＿＿ deutsch＿＿＿＿＿ Lied ist das?
　　4. Wann ist d＿＿＿＿＿ hübsch＿＿＿＿＿ Studentin wieder zu Hause?
　　5. Wieviel kostet dies＿＿＿＿＿ warm＿＿＿＿＿ Mantel?
　　6. Welch＿＿＿＿＿ bekannt＿＿＿＿＿, amerikanisch＿＿＿＿＿ Dichter hat den Roman geschrieben?
　　7. Manch＿＿＿＿＿ fremd＿＿＿＿＿ Student hat Heimweh.
　　8. Dies＿＿＿＿＿ alt＿＿＿＿＿ Schlüssel ist rostig.

5. Complete with the appropriate forms of the indicated words.

　　1. ＿＿＿＿＿＿ ＿＿＿＿＿＿ Stadt ist das?　*welch, deutsch*
　　2. ＿＿＿＿＿＿ ＿＿＿＿＿＿ Kind weint.　*jenes, klein*
　　3. ＿＿＿＿＿＿ ＿＿＿＿＿＿ Gymnasium ist modern.　*jedes, neu*
　　4. Wo ist ＿＿＿＿＿＿ ＿＿＿＿＿＿ Lehrerin?　*die, jung*
　　5. Wieviel kostet ＿＿＿＿＿＿ ＿＿＿＿＿＿ Wagen?　*dieser, amerikanisch*
　　6. Wie heißt ＿＿＿＿＿＿ ＿＿＿＿＿＿ Student?　*jener, blond*
　　7. Wo ist ＿＿＿＿＿＿ ＿＿＿＿＿＿ ＿＿＿＿＿＿ Buch?　*das, dünn, rot*
　　8. Was macht ＿＿＿＿＿＿ ＿＿＿＿＿＿ Mensch?　*jeder, gesund*
　　9. Dort steht ＿＿＿＿＿＿ ＿＿＿＿＿＿ Glas.　*das, leer*
　　10. Wieviel kostet ＿＿＿＿＿＿ ＿＿＿＿＿＿ Lampe?　*jene, groß*
　　11. Wann kommt ＿＿＿＿＿＿ ＿＿＿＿＿＿ Professor?　*der, interessant*
　　12. ＿＿＿＿＿＿ ＿＿＿＿＿＿ Limonade schmeckt gut.　*diese, kalt*

6. Form sentences from the following.

　　1. Jen / französich / Dichter / ist / weltbekannt /
　　2. Der / rot / Bus / wartet /
　　3. Manch / deutsch / Drama / ist / lang /
　　4. Wieviel / kostet / jen / schnell / Auto / ? /
　　5. Jed / modern / Museum / braucht / Geld /
　　6. Welch / alt / Maschine / ist / kaputt. / ? /
　　7. Wo / ist / die / weiß / Katze / ? /
　　8. Wo / steht / die / frisch / Milch / ? /

Accusative case, singular (following **"der"** *words)*

　　When the attributive adjective modifies a noun that is in the accusative singular and when the adjective is preceded by the definite article or by a **"der"** word, it takes the following endings:

Masculine	Neuter	Feminine
den kleinen **Schlüssel**	**das volle Glas**	**die reiche Sängerin**

Ich kenne *den deutschen* **Studenten.**	*I know the German student.*
Er kauft *das schnelle* **Auto.**	*He is buying the fast car.*
Sie läuft in *die alte* **Fabrik.**	*She is running into the old factory.*
Brauchst du *diesen langen* **Stock?**	*Do you need this long stick?*
Welche billige **Uhr hat er?**	*Which cheap watch does he have?*
Wir nehmen *jenes dünne* **Papier.**	*We are taking that thin paper.*

Note: the accusative singular adjective endings are identical to the nominative singular for neuter and feminine nouns; the masculine, however, takes a different ending.

7. Complete with the correct endings.

1. Setzt euch auf dies_____ bequem_____ Sofa!
2. Er bleibt d_____ ganz_____ Woche in Bonn.
3. Wir sammeln für jen_____ krank_____ Jungen.
4. Er hat manch_____ interessant_____ Gedicht geschrieben.
5. Hast du d_____ weiß_____ Kater gesehen?
6. Wer hat dir jen_____ wunderbar_____, blau_____ Orchidee gekauft?
7. Welch_____ neu_____ Handschuh hast du verloren?
8. Er kämpft gegen d_____ bekannt_____ Weltmeister.

8. Complete with the appropriate forms of the indicated words.

1. Wir gehen _____ _____ Straße entlang. *die, lang*
2. Ich besuche _____ _____ Gymnasium. *jenes, modern*
3. Wir laufen um _____ _____ Park. *dieser, groß*
4. _____ _____ Roman liest du? *welcher, interessant*
5. Ich brauche _____ _____ Messer. *das, scharf*
6. Leg es auf _____ _____ Platte! *die, klein*
7. Kennst du _____ _____ _____ Mädchen? *jenes, fremd, jung*
8. Ich kaufe es für _____ _____ Kind. *jedes, krank*
9. Wir nehmen _____ _____ Wagen. *der, schmutzig*
10. Setz dich neben _____ _____ Ofen! *jener, heiß*
11. Sie stellte sich hinter _____ _____ _____ Mann. *der, groß, blond*
12. Er kennt _____ _____ Helden. *jener, klug*

9. Form sentences from the following.

1. Er / restaurierte / manch / historisch / Haus /
2. Wer / hat / der / alt / Lederkoffer / ? /
3. Bring / dies / schmutzig / Glas / in / die / Küche / ! /
4. Wir / kaufen / jen / schnell / Motorboot /
5. Welch / rot / Apfel / möchtest / du / ? /
6. Wir / wandern / durch / die / klein / Stadt /
7. Sie / bringt / Blumen / für / das / krank / Kind /
8. Ich / brauche / jed / neu / deutsch / Briefmarke /

Dative case, singular (following "der" words)

When the attributive adjective modifies a noun that is in the dative singular and when the adjective is preceded by a definite article or by a "der" word, it takes the following endings:

Masculine	Neuter	Feminine
dem alten Herrn	dem neuen Haus	der kranken Mutter

Wir helfen *diesem kranken* **Herrn.**   *We are helping this ill gentleman.*
Welchem kleinen Kind gibst du das Spielzeug?   *Which small child are you giving the toy?*
Er wohnt bei *jener netten* **Familie.**   *He is staying with that nice family.*

10. Complete with the correct endings.

    1. Ich habe mich mit d_____ scharf_____ Messer geschnitten.
    2. Er kam aus jen_____ eng_____ Straße.
    3. Sie hat uns von dies_____ hoh_____ Baum erzählt.
    4. Er dankt d_____ klein_____ , freundlich_____ Mädchen.
    5. Ich gebe jed_____ klug_____ Studentin ein Buch.
    6. Warum sitzt du in d_____ kalt_____ Zimmer?
    7. Ich helfe dies_____ krank_____ Frau.
    8. Wir wohnen d_____ groß_____ Park gegenüber.

11. Complete with the appropriate forms of the indicated words.

    1. Sie kam aus _____ _____ Hotel.   *jenes, international*
    2. Wir gehen zu _____ _____ Vorlesung.   *jede, interessant*
    3. Wohnst du bei _____ _____ Familie?   *diese, nett*
    4. Sie sitzt auf _____ _____ Boden.   *der, schmutzig*
    5. Schreib nicht mit _____ _____ Bleistift!   *jener, kurz*
    6. Sie sitzen in _____ _____ _____ Wagen.   *der, groß, amerikanisch*
    7. Aus _____ _____ Land kommt er?   *welches, fremd*
    8. Er spricht mit _____ _____ Studentin.   *die, hübsch*
    9. Sie erzählt von _____ _____ Mann.   *jener, reich*
    10. Der Ballon gefällt _____ _____ Kind.   *das, klein*
    11. Ich gebe _____ _____ Patientin eine Pille.   *jede, krank*
    12. Sie sitzt auf _____ _____ Teppich.   *der, häßlich*

12. Form sentences from the following.

    1. Wir / schlafen / in / der / modern / Schlafwagen /
    2. Mit / welch / neu / Schreibmaschine / soll / ich / schreiben / ? /
    3. Er / wohnt / bei / jen / nett / Dame /
    4. Der / Ball / liegt / unter / der / blau / Sessel /
    5. Trink / nicht / aus / jen / rot / Glas / ! /
    6. Wir / gehen / bei / dies / kalt / Wetter / nicht / aus /
    7. Wer / sitzt / auf / die / alt / rostig / Bank / ? /
    8. Wir / bekamen / von / manch / amerikanisch / Studenten / Post /

Genitive case, singular (following **"der"** *words)*

    When the attributive adjective modifies a noun that is in the genitive singular and when the adjective is preceded by a definite article or by a **"der"** word, it receives the following endings:

Masculine	Neuter	Feminine
des jung*en* Lehrers	des bös*en* Kindes	der dick*en* Katze

Er wohnt jenseits *dieses hohen* **Berges.**   *He lives on the other side of this high mountain.*

Dort ist die Mutter *des kleinen* **Kindes.**   *There is the mother of the small child.*
Wir wohnen außerhalb *jener großen* **Stadt.**   *We live outside of that large city.*

13. Complete with the appropriate endings.

    1. Wo ist die Tochter dies_____ arm_____ Mannes?
    2. Dort steht das Haus d_____ reich_____ Familie.
    3. Ich kenne die Melodie jen_____ deutsch_____ Liedes.
    4. Die Zimmer dies_____ neu_____ Hauses sind groß.
    5. Wir waren während jen_____ kalt_____ Nacht zu Hause.
    6. Jenseits dies_____ klein_____ Dorfes ist die Grenze.
    7. Sie kommen um d_____ interessant_____ Professors willen.
    8. Wir sind innerhalb jen_____ alt_____ Stadt.

14. Complete the following with the appropriate forms of the indicated words.

    1. Der Preis _____ _____ Mantels ist zu hoch.   *der, blau*
    2. Sie sind innerhalb _____ _____ Gartens.   *jener, exotisch*
    3. Die Frau _____ _____ Technikers ist hier.   *der, deutsch*
    4. Die Farbe _____ _____ Kleides ist häßlich.   *dieses, billig*
    5. Er kommt um _____ _____ Frau willen.   *die, krank*
    6. Die Kissen _____ _____ Sofas sind weich.   *dieses, bequem*
    7. Die Studenten _____ _____ Universität sind hier.   *jene, bekannt*
    8. Die Straßen _____ _____ Stadt sind eng.   *diese, klein*
    9. Der Mann _____ _____ Sängerin ist dort.   *die, dick*
    10. Das ist die Mutter _____ _____ Babys.   *das, gesund*
    11. Sie wohnt diesseits _____ _____ Sees.   *jener, groß*
    12. Dort ist der Besitzer _____ _____ Sammlung.   *jene, interessant*

15. Form sentences from the following.

    1. Wo / ist / der / Besitzer / dies / schmutzig / Mantel / ? /
    2. Die / Gedichte / manch / deutsch / Dichter / sind / kompliziert /
    3. Die / Mutter / jen / krank / Kind / ist / hier /
    4. Der / Park / ist / jenseits / das / groß / Monument /
    5. Trotz / dies / stark / Explosion / gab / es / kein / Verwundete /
    6. Die / Straßen / jen / alt / Stadt / sind / eng /
    7. Die / Zimmer / die / neu / Wohnung / sind / modern /

Plural, all cases, all genders (following **"der"** *words)*

    When the attributive adjective modifies a plural noun and is preceded by the plural forms of the definite article or of a **"der"** word, the adjective ending is **-en** for all cases. The plural form of **jeder** is **alle**. The plural form of **manche** is not followed by adjectives ending in **-en**. (See the Section "Attributive Adjectives—Not Preceded by **"der"** or **"ein"** Words" for a discussion of plurals.)

Nominative	**die deutsch***en* **Zeitungen**
Accusative	**die alt***en* **Männer**
Dative	**den gesund***en* **Kindern**
Genitive	**der hoh***en* **Berge**

Diese frischen **Eier kosten viel.**	*These fresh eggs are expensive.*
Ich habe *alle leeren* **Flaschen.**	*I have all empty bottles.*
Mit *solchen neuen Autos* **kann man** schnell fahren.	*One can drive fast with such new cars.*
Das Leben *jener alten Leute* **ist traurig.**	*The life of those old people is sad.*

16. Rewrite the following, changing the nouns to the plural. Make all necessary changes.

1. Welche deutsche Stadt hat er besucht?
2. Ohne dieses warme Kleid fahre ich nicht.
3. Wir steigen auf jenen bekannten Berg.
4. Es gehört jener interessanten, jungen Frau.
5. Er schenkt etwas in jedes leere Glas.
6. Ich liege unter dem schattigen Baum.
7. Er erzählt dem kleinen Mädchen eine Geschichte.
8. Ich komme um des kranken Lehrers willen.
9. Jeder gesunde Patient darf nach Hause.
10. Sie hat den grünen Apfel.

Special adjective forms

A few adjectives omit certain letters when they receive an attributive adjective ending. Study the following changes. Adjectives ending in **-el** always drop the **e** in the final syllable when an ending is added.

Das Zimmer ist *dunkel*.	*The room is dark.*
Wir sind in dem *dunklen* **Zimmer.**	*We are in the dark room.*

Adjectives ending in **-euer** or **-auer** can drop or retain the **-e** when the attributive adjective ending is added.

Das Haus ist *teuer*.	*The house is expensive.*
Ich ziehe in jenes *teure (teuere)* **Haus.**	*I am moving into that expensive house.*
Die Orange ist *sauer*.	*The orange is sour.*
Wer kauft diese *sauren (saueren)* **Orangen?**	*Who is buying these sour oranges?*

But note that other adjectives such as **bitter** retain the **-e.**

Der Kaffee ist *bitter*.	*The coffee is bitter.*
Warum trinkst du den *bitteren* **Kaffee?**	*Why are you drinking the bitter coffee?*

The adjective **hoch** drops the **c** when an attributive adjective ending is added.

Der Turm ist *hoch*.	*The tower is high.*
Er steigt auf jenen *hohen* **Turm.**	*He is climbing that high tower.*

A small number of descriptive adjectives do not take any adjective endings at all, whether they are preceded by a **"der"** word or an **"ein"** word or are unpreceded. Included in this group are certain foreign loan words ending in **-a.**

Das *rosa* **Kleid schmeichelte sie sehr.**   *The pink dress flattered her very much.*
Er ist ein *prima* **Kerl.**   *He's a first-rate fellow.*
Lila **Blumen sind schön.**   *Lavender flowers are beautiful.*

Another group of adjectives that do not take adjective endings are those formed from city names plus the suffix **-er.**

Sie wohnt an der *Kieler* **Förde.**   *She lives on the Kiel fjord.*
Ich traf ihn am *Münchner* **Hauptbahnhof.**   *I met him at the Munich main train station*
Er besuchte die *Frankfurter* **Buchmesse.**   *He visited the Frankfurt Book Fair.*

Note: this is one of the rare situations in which a German adjective is capitalized.

17. Complete the following with the appropriate forms of the indicated words.

1. Was machst du in _____ _____ Haus? *das, dunkel*
2. Sie nehmen _____ _____ Pille. *die, bitter*
3. Er kauft _____ _____ Mantel. *jener, teuer*
4. Wir wohnen jenseits _____ _____ Bergs. *dieser, hoch*
5. Wo ist _____ _____ Wäsche? *die, sauber*
6. Trink nicht _____ _____ Milch! *die, sauer*
7. Wo ist _____ _____ Zimmer? *das, sauber*
8. Warum kaufst du _____ _____ Spielzeug? *dieses, teuer*
9. Wo sind _____ _____ Äpfel? *der, sauer*
10. Wie heißt _____ _____ Berg? *dieser, hoch*
11. Ich esse gern _____ Lebkuchen. *Nürberg*
12. Wir besuchen die _____ Messe. *Frankfurt*
13. Das ist _____ Bier. *Dortmund*
14. Er trinkt eine _____ Weiße. *Berlin*
15. Wie hoch ist der _____ Dom? *Köln*

Review: Adjectives following "der" Words

There are only two different sets of endings for adjectives following the definite articles or a **"der"** word, namely, **-e** or **-en.** The **-en** ending predominates, except for the three nominative singular forms and the accusative singular, feminine and neuter.

	SINGULAR			PLURAL
	Masculine	*Neuter*	*Feminine*	*All Genders*
Nominative	-e	-e	-e	-en
Accusative	-en	-e	-e	-en
Dative	-en	-en	-en	-en
Genitive	-en	-en	-en	-en

18. Complete with the correct endings.

1. Hast du d_____ deutsch_____ Zeitungen auf jen_____ rund_____ Tisch gelegt?
2. Dies_____ gelb_____ Mantel habe ich in d_____ neu_____ Geschäft gekauft.

3. In d_____ eng_____ Straßen dies_____ alt_____ Stadt gibt es viel Verkehr.
4. Wer ist d_____ dick_____ Dame neben d_____ schlank_____ Herrn?
5. Wegen dies_____ schlecht_____ Wetters bleibe ich zu Hause.
6. D_____ amerikanisch_____ Studentin kam aus jen_____ modern_____, weiß_____ Haus.
7. All_____ dunkl_____ Straßen werden i_____ nächst_____ Monat beleuchtet.
8. Mit solch_____ schmutzig_____ Händen kannst du d_____ neu_____ Buch nicht anfassen.
9. D_____ freundlich_____ Kellnerin hat gleich jed_____ leer_____ Glas mit Bier gefüllt.
10. Hat jen_____ deutsch_____ Dichter auch dies_____ traurig_____ Gedicht geschrieben?

19. Complete with the appropriate forms of the indicated words.

1. _____ _____ Fräulein wohnt bei _____ _____ Familie. *dieses, deutsch; jene, nett*
2. _____ _____ Männer kaufen _____ _____ Mäntel. *alle, elegant; diese, kurz*
3. _____ _____ Student braucht _____ _____ Buch. *jener, blond; dieses, teuer*
4. _____ _____ Frau hilft _____ _____ Herrn. *die, hübsch; der, dick*
5. _____ _____ Besitzer _____ _____ Wagens ist hier. *der, neu; der, teuer*
6. Wir waschen _____ _____ Hände _____ _____ Kindes. *die, schmutzig; das, klein*
7. _____ _____ Tourist kauft _____ _____ Kamera. *jener, amerikanisch; diese, billig*
8. _____ _____ Hund liegt unter _____ _____ Tisch. *der, schwarz; der, rund*
9. _____ _____ Leute essen auf _____ _____ Terrasse. *die, jung; die, dunkel*
10. _____ _____ Dame kauft _____ _____ Kuchen. *die, hungrig; der, groß*

Attributive Adjective—Preceded by the Indefinite Article or other "ein" Words (Preceded Adjectives)

The negative article **kein** and all the possessives are called **"ein"** words, because they take the same endings as the indefinite article. (See the Section "Possessive Adjectives" and Chapter 2.)

Adjectives preceded by the indefinite article or an **"ein"** word require a different set of endings.

Nominative case, singular (following "ein" words)

When the attributive adjective modifies a noun that is in the nominative singular, and when the adjective is preceded by the indefinite article or an **"ein"** word, it takes the following endings:

Masculine	Neuter	Feminine
ein blau*er* Hut	ein bequem*es* Sofa	eine lang*e* Reise

Ein alter **Herr wartet.**	*An old gentleman is waiting.*
Ein kleines **Kind kommt.**	*A small child is coming.*
Das ist *eine billige* **Tasche.**	*That is a cheap purse.*
Wo ist *dein neuer* **Freund?**	*Where is your new friend.*
Hier ist *unser altes* **Radio.**	*Here is our old radio.*
Dort ist *seine hübsche* **Freundin.**	*There is his pretty girlfriend.*

20. Complete with the appropriate endings when necessary. Make all necessary changes.

1. Wo ist mein_____ weiß_____ Hase?
2. Ihr_____ alt_____, amerikanisch_____ Freundin kommt.
3. Dein_____ hell_____ Bluse ist doch schmutzig.

4. Er ist kein_____ gut_____ Freund.
5. Wann besucht euch eur_____ reich_____ Tante?
6. Der Löwe ist ein_____ wild_____ Tier.
7. Nur ein_____ rot_____ Apfel liegt im Korb.
8. Das ist kein_____ hübsch_____ Melodie.
9. Das ist ein_____ schön_____, weiß_____ Lilie.
10. Mein_____ deutsch_____ Buch liegt dort.
11. Wo ist dein_____ alt_____ Onkel?
12. Es ist sein_____ neu_____ Auto.
13. Das ist unser_____ teuer_____ Schmuck.
14. Wo ist mein_____ weich_____ Kissen?
15. Das ist kein_____ sauer_____ Milch.
16. Dort kommt ein_____ französisch_____ Tourist.

21. Rewrite the following, changing the definite articles to indefinite articles. Make all necessary changes.

1. Wo ist das weiche Kissen?
2. Der alte Freund ist hier.
3. Wann schläft das wilde Tier?
4. Die neue Maschine steht dort.
5. Hier ist der schmutzige Teller.
6. Wo ist das kleine Buch?
7. Hier liegt die deutsche Zeitung.
8. Wieviel kostet das schnelle Auto?

22. Form sentences from the following. Make all necessary changes.

1. Mein / alt / Radio / ist / kaputt /
2. Wo / wohnt / dein / nett / Freundin / ? /
3. Wieviel / kostet / Ihr / neu / Wagen / ? /
4. Wann / kommt / sein / reich / Onkel / ? /
5. Das / ist / kein / eng / Straße/
6. Ist / unser / deutsch / Foto / interessant / ? /
7. Wo / ist / euer / schmutzig / Wäsche / ? /
8. Hier / ist / ihr / alt / Wein /

Accusative case, singular (following **"ein"** *words)*

When the attributive adjective modifies a noun that is in the accusative singular, and when the adjective is preceded by the indefinite article or an **"ein"** word, it takes the following endings:

Masculine	*Neuter*	*Feminine*
einen alt*en* **Mann**	**ein süß***es* **Getränk**	**eine blau***e* **Jacke**

Er schreibt *einen langen* **Brief.**　　　　　*He is writing a long letter.*
Habt ihr *kein scharfes* **Messer?**　　　　*Don't you have a sharp knife?*
Wir besuchen *unsere gute* **Freundin.**　　*We are visiting our good friend.*

Note that the accusative singular adjective endings are identical with the nominative singular, except for the masculine.

23. Complete with the correct endings when necessary.

1. Möchtest du kein_____ heiß_____ Tee?

    2. Setz dich auf unser_____ weich_____ Sofa!

    3. Wir kaufen kein_____ teur_____ Kamera für unser_____ klein_____ Tochter.

    4. Er geht durch sein_____ schmutzig_____ Fabrik.

    5. Sucht ihr eur_____ klein_____, schwarz_____ Hund?

    6. Warum besucht sie nicht ihr_____ krank_____ Großmutter?

    7. Wer braucht ein_____ groß_____, modern_____ Wagen?

    8. Ich suche ein_____ rot_____ Auto.

    9. Er hat kein_____ hübsch_____ Freundin.

  10. Wir treffen unser_____ neu_____ Lehrerin.

  11. Nehmt euer_____ alt_____ Bild!

  12. Wir gehen ohne mein_____ klein_____ Kind.

24. Rewrite the following, changing the definite articles to indefinite articles. Make all necessary changes.

    1. Er kauft den häßlichen Teppich.
    2. Wann bekommst du den neuen Mantel?
    3. Wir besuchen die historische Stadt.
    4. Siehst du das rote Auto?

    5. Ich kaufe es für das kranke Kind.
    6. Er geht durch den langen Tunnel.
    7. Der Bus fuhr gegen die alte Mauer.
    8. Ich möchte das weiße Bonbon.

25. Form sentences from the following. Make all necessary changes.

    1. Sie / geht / in / ihr / dunkel / Wohnung /
    2. Wir / verkaufen / unser / blau / Sofa /
    3. Haben / Sie / ein / billig / Zimmer / ? /
    4. Ich / habe / ein / bequem / Stuhl /
    5. Braucht / er / sein / neu / Kamera / ? /
    6. Wir / gehen / durch / ein / lang / Tunnel /
    7. Ich / schreibe / ein / kurz / Brief /
    8. Kennst / du / kein / hübsch / Studentin / ? /

Dative case, singular (following "ein" words)

    When the attributive adjective modifies a noun that is in the dative singular, and when the adjective is preceded by the indefinite article or an "ein" word, it requires the following endings:

Masculine	Neuter	Feminine
einem scharf*en* Messer	einem dunkl*en* Zimmer	einer rot*en* Blume

Das Buch liegt auf *einem runden* **Tisch.**   *The book is lying on a round table.*
Wir wohnen in *keinem alten* **Haus.**   *We are not living in an old house.*
Er erzählt von *seiner langen* **Reise.**   *He is talking about his long trip.*

26. Complete with the correct endings.

    1. Sie schrieb ihr_____ lieb_____ Mann eine Karte.
    2. Warum sitzt du in dein_____ klein_____, kalt_____ Zimmer?
    3. Außer unser_____ reich_____ Tante kam niemand.

4. Wir fahren mit ein_____ schnell_____ Wagen.
5. Ich trinke aus ein_____ neu_____ , weiß_____ Tasse.
6. Seit sein_____ traurig_____ Kindheit ist er melancholisch.
7. Es gehört ihr_____ alt_____ Onkel.
8. Ich helfe mein_____ klein_____ Schwester.
9. Ich bleibe bei mein_____ krank_____ Mutter.
10. Sie wurde von ein_____ wild_____ Hund gebissen.
11. Er arbeitet bei kein_____ groß_____ Firma.
12. Sie geht zu ihr_____ weiß_____ Auto.

27. Rewrite the following, changing the definite articles to indefinite articles.

1. Er sitzt auf dem harten Stuhl.   5. Wir stehen neben dem großen Mann.
2. Sie wohnt in dem modernen Haus.   6. Ich liege auf dem weichen Bett.
3. Ich bin bei der netten Frau.   7. Hilfst du dem fremden Mann?
4. Sie spielt mit dem süßen Baby.   8. Sie kommt von der langen Reise zurück.

28. Form sentences from the following. Make all necessary changes.

1. Er / kam / mit / ein / interessant / Freund /
2. Wir / kennen / uns / seit / unser / glücklich / Kindheit /
3. Er / schnitt / das / Brot / mit / sein / scharf / Messer /
4. Warum / sitzt / du / auf / ein / unbequem / Stuhl / ? /
5. Die / Katze / liegt / auf / mein / schwarz / Mantel /
6. Sie / kommt / aus / ihr / dunkel / Zimmer /
7. Was / steht / in / sein / lang / Brief / ? /
8. Sie / sitzt / in / mein / neu / Auto /

Genitive case, singular (following **"ein"** *words)*

When the attributive adjective modifies a noun that is in the genitive singular, and when the adjective is preceded by the indefinite article or an **"ein"** word, it requires the following endings:

Masculine	*Neuter*	*Feminine*
eines nett*en* Mannes	**eines bitter*en* Getränks**	**einer alt*en* Dame**

Er liegt im Schatten *eines hohen* **Baumes.**   *He is lying in the shade of a tall tree.*
Wann beginnt der Bau *eures neuen* **Hauses?**   *When does the construction of your*
                                                              new house start?

Hier ist das Zentrum *unserer kleinen* **Stadt.**   *Here is the center of our small town.*

29. Complete the following with the appropriate forms of the indicated words.

1. Er ist während _____ _____ Nacht verunglückt.   *ein, dunkel*
2. Die Farbe _____ _____ Autos ist häßlich.   *mein, alt*
3. Wegen _____ _____ Krankheit kann er nicht kommen.   *sein, schlimm*
4. Sie ist die Tochter _____ _____ Arztes.   *ein, amerikanisch*
5. Trotz _____ _____ Arbeit macht sie Urlaub.   *ihr, wichtig*

6. Sie tat es um _____ _____ Jungen willen.   *euer, krank*
7. Wie hoch war der Preis _____ _____ Waschmaschine?   *dein, neu*
8. Statt _____ _____ Radios kaufte ich eine Kamera.   *ein, teuer*

30. Rewrite the following, changing the genitive definite articles to indefinite articles.

1. Das ist die Frau des bekannten Dichters.
2. Es ist die Geschichte des fremden Volkes.
3. Der Preis des antiken Perserteppichs ist hoch.
4. Ich singe die Melodie des deutschen Liedes.
5. Der Direktor der großen Fabrik kommt.

31. Form sentences from the following. Make all necessary changes.

1. Trotz / mein / lang / Reise / war / ich / nicht / müde /
2. Die / Farbe / dein / neu / Pullover / ist / hübsch /
3. Sie / ist / die / Frau / ein / amerikanisch / Präsident /
4. Hier / ist / das / Foto / sein / bekannt / Bruder /
5. Wo / ist / das / Haus / Ihr / reich / Onkel / ? /
6. Wir / konnten / wegen / sein / lang / Verspätung / nicht / essen /
7. Der / Bus / ist / jenseits / ein / hoch / Turm /

Plural, all cases, all genders (following "ein" words)

When the attributive adjective modifies a plural noun, and when it is preceded by the plural forms of "ein" words, the adjective ending is -en for all cases. There is no plural form of the indefinite article **ein.**

Nominative	**keine leeren Gläser**
Accusative	**keine leeren Gläser**
Dative	**keinen leeren Gläsern**
Genitive	**keiner leeren Gläser**

Ihre deutschen **Freundinnen fliegen ab.**	*Her German friends are departing.*
Hast du *keine amerikanischen* **Zigaretten?**	*Don't you have American cigarettes?*
Wir trinken aus *keinen schmutzigen* **Tassen.**	*We don't drink out of dirty cups.*
Die Lehrerin *unserer kleinen* **Kinder ist hier.**	*The teacher of our small children is here.*

32. Rewrite the following, changing the nouns to the plural. Make all necessary changes.

1. Er hat keinen teuren Ring gekauft.
2. Er glaubt seinem kleinen Sohn.
3. Ich telefonierte mit meiner deutschen Freundin.
4. Unsere neue Nähmaschine war teuer.
5. Wer hat meinen roten Bleistift?
6. Wegen seines faulen Bruders darf er nicht kommen.
7. Wir trinken kein kaltes Getränk.
8. Wo ist ihre warme Jacke?

9   Willst du deinen alten Lehrer besuchen?
10.   Wo ist euer progressives Gymnasium?

Review: Adjectives Following "ein" Words

The **-en** adjective ending predominates after the indefinite article or **"ein"** words. As was the case with adjectives following **"der"** words, the exceptions to the **-en** endings occur in the nominative singular masculine, feminine, and neuter, and in the accusative singular, feminine, and neuter.

Compare the two sets of endings:

After **"der"** words

	SINGULAR Masculine	Neuter	Feminine	PLURAL All Genders
Nominative	-e	-e	-e	-en
Accusative	-en	-e	-e	-en
Dative	-en	-en	-en	-en
Genitive	-en	-en	-en	-en

After **"ein"** words

	SINGULAR Masculine	Neuter	Feminine	PLURAL All Genders
Nominative	-er	-es	-e	-en
Accusative	-en	-es	-e	-en
Dative	-en	-en	-en	-en
Genitive	-en	-en	-en	-en

33.   Complete the following with the correct endings when necessary.

1.   Mein_____ amerikanisch_____ Freund hat dies_____ herrlich_____ Sinfonie komponiert.
2.   In unser_____ neu_____ Wohnung ist auch ein_____ elektrisch_____ Ofen.
3.   D_____ kaputt_____ Maschine wurde mit ein_____ leicht_____ Metall repariert.
4.   Sie war wegen ihr_____ exotisch_____ Schönheit bekannt, nicht wegen ihr_____ groß_____ Talents.
5.   In d_____ eng_____ Straßen d_____ historisch_____ Innenstadt können kein_____ groß_____ Wagen fahren.
6.   Ein_____ melancholisch_____ Melodie kam aus d_____ offen_____ Fenster.
7.   Er brachte mir ein_____ rot_____ Rose in jen_____ klein_____ Glasvase.
8.   D_____ nagelneu_____ Auto fuhr gegen unser_____ rostig_____ Gartentür.
9.   Er hat kein_____ einzig_____ Geschenk von sein_____ bekannt_____ Geschwistern bekommen.
10.   Mit dies_____ schmutzig_____ Schuhen könnt ihr nicht in d_____ sauber_____ Küche kommen.

11. Machen dein_____ reich_____ Eltern schon wieder ein_____ lang_____ Reise?
12. In jen_____ rund_____ Korb sind d_____ frisch_____ Eier.

34. Complete the following with the appropriate form of the indicated word.

1. Er gibt _____ _____ Studentin _____ _____ Job. *die, jung; ein, interessant*
2. _____ _____ Onkel liegt auf _____ _____ Sofa. *mein, krank; unser, gut*
3. Sie fährt mit _____ _____ Volkswagen durch _____ _____ Stadt. *ihr, klein; die, leer*
4. Wo hat _____ _____ Tante _____ _____ Bild gekauft? *dein, reich; dieses, teuer*
5. Wegen _____ _____ Vorlesung konnte ich _____ _____ Freunde nicht treffen. *jene, lang; ihr, neu*
6. Wo ist _____ _____ Foto _____ _____ Sängers? *das, neu; der, bekannt*
7. _____ _____ Gäste trinken _____ _____ Kaffee. *mein, amerikanisch; kein, bitter*
8. Er fährt _____ _____ Auto in _____ _____ Garage. *sein, kaputt; die, dunkel*
9. Sie macht mit _____ _____ Geschwistern _____ _____ Reise. *ihr, nett; eine, kurz*
10. _____ _____ Leute sitzen in _____ _____ Wohnung. *die, arm; ihr, kalt*

Attributive Adjective—Not Preceded by "der" or "ein" Words (Unpreceded Adjectives)

When the attributive adjective is not preceded by a **"der"** or **"ein"** word, the adjective requires an ending to indicate the number, gender, and case of the noun it modifies. The adjective endings coincide with the endings of the definite article except in the genitive singular, masculine and neuter.

Note: When attributive adjectives follow the uninflected forms of certain adjectives (*that is, forms of the adjective that have no endings showing gender, number, and case*), they take the same endings as the unpreceded adjective. When used as adjectives, **viel** and **wenig** usually take no endings in the singular; in the plural, however, they take the regular adjective endings. The uninflected forms of **manch, solch,** and **welch** *are encountered relatively seldom in colloquial usage and can sound a bit old-fashioned or poetic.*

viel	*much, a lot*	**manch**	*many a*
wenig	*little*	**solch**	*such (a)*
		welch	*what*

Sie hat noch *viel* **deutsches Geld.**	*She still has a lot of German money.*
Er ißt sehr *wenig* **frisches Obst.**	*He eats very little fresh fruit.*
Manch **armer Seemann fand ein nasses Grab.**	*Many a poor seaman found a watery grave.*
Solch **schönes Wetter!**	*Such nice weather!*
Welch **liebes Kind!**	*What a dear child!*

35. Fill in the appropriate German words.

1. _____ schönes Wetter! *what*
2. Er hat _____ amerikanisches Geld. *much*
3. Wir haben _____ guten Wein. *little*
4. Er trank _____ kaltes Bier. *much*
5. _____ gute Idee! *such*
6. Sie hat _____ musikalisches Talent. *much*
7. Ich habe _____ großen Hunger. *such*
8. _____ neuer Schnee ist gefallen. *little*

Nominative case, singular (unpreceded)

When the attributive adjective modifies a nominative singular noun, and when it is not preceded by a **"der"** or **"ein"** word, it takes the following endings:

Masculine	*Neuter*	*Feminine*
schwarz*er* Kaffee	**schön*es* Wetter**	**frisch*e* Milch**

Alter **Wein ist teuer.**	*Old wine is expensive.*
Das ist *deutsches* **Geld.**	*That is German money.*
Frische **Luft ist gesund.**	*Fresh air is healthy.*
Hier ist *viel moderne* **Kunst.**	*Here is much modern art.*

The nominative adjective endings are frequently used in forms of address.

Lieber **Onkel Franz!**	*Dear uncle Franz,*
Liebe **Tante!**	*Dear aunt,*
Du *armes* **Kind!**	*You poor child!*

36. Complete the following with the appropriate forms of the indicated words.

1. Du _____ Mädchen!   *arm*
2. Das ist _____ Arznei!   *bitter*
3. _____ Tante Anni!   *lieb*
4. Dort liegt _____ _____ Wäsche.   *viel, schmutzig*
5. _____ Großvater!   *lieb*
6. Dort liegt _____ _____ Geld.   *wenig, deutsch*
7. _____ _____ Wein ist teuer.   *gut, alt*
8. Du _____ Kind!   *gut*
9. Hier ist Ursulas _____ Kleid.   *neu*
10. Zuviel _____ Bier ist schlecht für den Magen.   *kalt*
11. _____ Onkel Herbert.   *lieb*
12. Du _____ Hund!   *arm*
13. Das ist _____ Bier.   *teuer*
14. Sie ist _____ Berlinerin.   *typisch*

37. Form sentences from the following. Make all necessary changes.

1. Welch / interessant / Gedicht / ! /
2. Das / ist / teuer / Leder /
3. Frisch / Butter / schmeckt / gut /
4. Modern / Musik / ist / schnell /
5. Ist / das / billig / Schmuck / ? /
6. Kalt / Limonade / ist / erfrischend /
7. Du / süß / Baby / ! /

Accusative case, singular (unpreceded)

When the attributive adjective modifies a noun in the accusative singular, and when it is not preceded by a **"der"** or **"ein"** word, it takes the following endings:

Masculine	Neuter	Feminine
weiß*en* Flieder	gelb*es* Papier	bitter*e* Schokolade

Trinkt ihr *viel schwarzen* **Kaffee?** Do you drink much black coffee?
Ich brauche *wenig deutsches* **Geld.** I need little German money.
Er bestellt *kalte* **Milch.** He orders cold milk
Wir trinken *heißen* **Tee.** We drink hot tea.
Er ißt *viel weißes* **Brot.** He eats much white bread.
Hast du *saubere* **Wäsche?** Do you have clean laundry?

Salutations are in the accusative case.

Guten Morgen! *Guten* **Tag!** *Guten* **Abend!** Good morning! Hello! Good evening!
Gute Nacht! Good night!

38. Complete the following with the appropriate forms of the indicated words.
1. Ich trinke _____ _____ Limonade. *viel, sauer*
2. Wir essen _____ _____ Brot. *wenig, schwarz*
3. _____ Abend! _____ Nacht! _____ Tag! *gut*
4. Er hat _____ Hoffnung. *groß*
5. Was hast du gegen _____ Zucker? *weiß*
6. Ich trinke _____ _____ Tee. *wenig, süß*
7. Hattet ihr _____ Wetter? *schön*
8. Sie bestellt _____ Kaffee. *schwarz*
9. Ich kaufe _____ Papier. *dünn*
10. _____ _____ Butter esse ich gern. *frisch, holländisch*
11. Wo finde ich _____ _____ Käse? *pikant, französisch*
12. Wir geben uns _____ Mühe. *groß*
13. Er hat _____ _____ Geld. *viel, amerikanisch*
14. Ich brauche _____ _____ Wasser. *viel, heiß*

39. Form sentences from the following. Make all necessary changes.
1. Was / hast / du / gegen / klassisch / Musik / ? /
2. Leg / es / in / kalt / Wasser / ! /
3. Ich / esse / frisch / Brot /
4. Wir / brauchen / deutsch / Geld /
5. Er / hat / groß / Hunger /
6. Warum / trinkst / du / kalt / Kaffee / ? /
7. Sie / nimmt / braun / Zucker /
8. Sie / hat / viel / teuer / Schmuck /

Dative case, singular (unpreceded)

When the attributive adjective modifies a dative singular noun, and when it is not preceded by a **"der"** or **"ein"** word, it takes the following endings:

Masculine	Neuter	Feminine
rostfrei*em* Stahl	kalt*em* Wasser	heiß*er* Milch

Bei *starkem* **Wind gehen wir nicht segeln.**	*We don't go sailing in strong wind.*
Nach *langem* **Leiden ist sie gestorben.**	*She passed away after long suffering.*
Ich bin in *großer* **Not.**	*I am in great need.*
Ausser *viel heißem* **Tee trinkt er nichts.**	*He drinks nothing besides much hot tea.*
Sie helfen *manch armem* **Kind.**	*They help many a poor child.*

40. Complete the following with the appropriate forms of the indicated words.

1. Das Auto fährt mit _____ Geschwindigkeit. *groß*
2. Nach _____ Zeit kam er wieder. *lang*
3. Sie kommt aus _____ Familie. *gut*
4. Ich trinke Tee mit _____ _____ Milch. *viel, warm*
5. Er lebte auf _____ Fuß. *groß*
6. Bei _____ _____ Wetter gehen wir aus. *schön, sonnig*
7. Es ist aus _____ Stahl. *rostfrei*
8. Ich mache es mit _____ Freude. *groß*
9. Es ist aus _____ _____ Gold. *wenig, weiß*
10. Er wäscht sich mit _____ _____ Wasser. *viel, heiß*
11. Bei _____ _____ Wetter bleiben wir drinnen. *bitter, kalt*
12. Der Turm ist aus _____ Metall. *hart*

41. Form sentences from the following. Make all necessary changes.

1. Bei / schlecht / Wetter / fliege / ich / nicht /
2. Wer / schreibt / mit / grün / Kreide / ? /
3. Nach / kurz / Zeit / wurde / es / still /
4. Das / Messer / ist / aus / rostfrei / Stahl /
5. Warum / schwimmst / du / in / eiskalt / Wasser / ? /
6. Der / Dieb / kam / bei / hellicht / Tag /
7. Ich / kenne / ihn / seit / lang / Zeit /
8. Er / trank / nichts / außer / viel / stark / Kaffee /

Genitive case, singular (*unpreceded*)

When the attributive adjective modifies a noun in the genitive singular, and when it is not preceded by a **"der"** or **"ein"** word, it receives the following endings:

Masculine	*Neuter*	*Feminine*
starke**n Windes**	**schlechten Wetters**	**guter Qualität**

Trotz *starken* **Regens ging er spazieren.**	*He took a walk despite heavy rain.*
Schweren **Herzens nahm er Abschied.**	*He took leave with a heavy heart.*
Sie war wegen viel *anstrengender* **Arbeit müde.**	*She was tired because of much taxing work.*

42. Complete the following with the appropriate forms of the indicated words.

1. Er ist Kenner _____ Kunst. *klassisch*
2. Wegen _____ Nebels konnte er uns nicht finden. *dicht*
3. Trotz _____ Hilfe war sie einsam. *freundlich*
4. _____ Herzens reiste sie ab. *traurig*

5. Die Lagerung _____ Weines ist riskant. *alt*
6. Es ist eine Geschichte _____ Liebe. *wahr*
7. Trotz _____ Krankheit war sie lebensfroh. *lang*
8. Er hat eine Menge _____ Materials gekauft. *neu*
9. Trotz _____ Mühe kann sie es nicht. *groß*
10. Innerhalb _____ Zeit kam sie heraus. *kurz*

43. Form sentences from the following. Make all necessary changes.

1. Trotz / bitter / Kälte / spielten / die / Kinder / im / Schnee /
2. Er / ist / Liebhaber / modern / Musik /
3. Der / Preis / gut / alt / Wein / ist / hoch /
4. Wegen / schlecht / Wetter / hat / er / Verspätung /
5. Trotz / gut / Ausbildung / fand / er / keine / Stelle /
6. Trotz / nett / Hilfe / kam / sie / nicht / vorwärts /

Review

44. Complete the following with the correct endings.

1. Wir haben nun wieder schön_____ , sonnig_____ Wetter.
2. Bei grün_____ Licht darf man fahren.
3. Ich werde dich in nächst_____ Zeit besuchen.
4. Billig_____ Wein schmeckt mir nicht.
5. Persönlich_____ Freiheit ist für den modernen Menschen sehr wichtig.
6. Lieb_____ Maria! Lieb_____ Johann!
7. Der Schrank ist aus teur_____ Holz.
8. Weiß_____ Papier, bitte!
9. Hast du etwas gegen warm_____ Bier?
10. Trotz groß_____ Müdigkeit kann sie nicht schlafen.
11. Ihm gefällt wenig modern_____ Musik.
12. Trinkst du viel stark_____ Kaffee?
13. Gut_____ Nacht! Gut_____ Tag! Gut_____ Abend!
14. Es ist eine gelbe Schachtel mit braun_____ Deckel.
15. Ich brauche viel kalt_____ Wasser.

Plural (unpreceded)

When the attributive adjective modifies a plural noun, and when it is not preceded by a **"der"** or **"ein"** word, it has the same endings as the plural definite article. One of the following indefinite adjectives may precede the attributive adjective. In that case, they both have the endings of the plural definite article.

andere	*other*	**mehrere**	*several*
einige	*some, several*	**viele**	*many*
manche	*many*	**wenige**	*few*

Mehrere **Leute waren krank.**   *Several people were ill.*
Viele **Metalle sind teuer.**   *Many metals are expensive.*

45. Complete the following with the appropriate German words.

  1. Dort sind _____ Studenten. *some*
  2. _____ Leute machen das nicht. *other*
  3. _____ Kinder hatten Angst. *several*
  4. Dort stehen _____ Menschen. *many*
  5. _____ Hunde sind wild. *few*
  6. _____ Bücher sind interessant. *many*

Nominative and accusative case, all genders (unpreceded plural)

   The plural attributive adjective that may or may not be preceded by an indefinite adjective takes the following endings in the nominative and accusative plural, when it is not preceded by a **"der"** or **"ein"** word:

Nominative	**große Hunde**	Accusative	**große Hunde**

Alte Perserteppiche sind teuer.	*Old Persian rugs are expensive.*
Ich fahre gern durch *historische* **Städte.**	*I like to travel through historical cities.*
Mehrere alte **Leute warten dort.**	*Several old people are waiting there.*
Ich habe *viele deutsche* **Briefmarken.**	*I have many German stamps.*

46. Complete with the appropriate forms of the indicated words.

  1. Unser Eßzimmer hat _____ Wände. *gelb*
  2. Sie hat _____ _____ Freunde. *viele, gut*
  3. Wir besuchen _____ _____ Museen. *einige, bekannt*
  4. Ich esse gern _____ Eier. *braun*
  5. Jetzt sind _____ _____ Wolken am Himmel. *einige, grau*
  6. _____ _____ Lastwagen bringen _____ Äpfel. *mehrere, groß; frisch*
  7. Sie kauft noch _____ _____ Kleider. *andere, neu*
  8. _____ Menschen sind oft traurig. *alt*
  9. Ich brauche _____ _____ Sachen. *wenige, teuer*
 10. _____ _____ Kinder freuen sich über _____ Spielsachen. *manche, klein; bunt*

Dative case, all genders (unpreceded plural)

   When the attributive adjective modifies a dative plural noun, and when it is not preceded by a **"der"** or **"ein"** word, it takes the following ending:

Dative	**hohen Bäumen**

Sie wird mit *roten* **Rosen empfangen.**	*She is welcomed with red roses.*
Sie spricht mit *einigen alten* **Freunden.**	*She is talking with several old friends.*
Ich sitze auf *mehreren weichen* **Kissen.**	*I am sitting on several soft pillows.*

47. Complete the following with the appropriate forms of the indicated words.

  1. Er fand die Antwort in _____ Büchern. *alt*
  2. Das Buch hat _____ _____ Lesern nicht gefallen. *einige, deutsch*

3. Ich wohne jetzt bei _____ Leuten. *nett*
4. Sie unterhält sich mit _____ _____ Studenten. *einige, amerikanisch*
5. Sie waren in _____ _____ Käfigen. *mehrere, klein*
6. Komm nicht mit _____ Schuhen ins Haus! *schmutzig*
7. Wir sitzen neben _____ Männern. *dick*
8. Sie hilft _____ _____ Studentinnen. *viele, intelligent*
9. Es liegt unter _____ _____ Zeitungen. *andere, alt*
10. Sie kommt mit _____ _____ Menschen zusammen. *wenige, fremd*

Genitive case, all genders (unpreceded plural)

When the attributive adjective modifies a genitive plural noun, and when it is not preceded by a **"der"** or **"ein"** word, it takes the following ending:

Genitive	**klein*er* Kinder**

Trotz *guter* Freunde war sie einsam.   *Despite good friends she was lonely.*
Der Preis *mehrerer amerikanischer*   *The price of several American cars is*
   Wagen ist hoch.   *high.*
Die Qualität *vieler billiger* Sachen ist   *The quality of many cheap things is*
   schlecht.   *poor.*

48. Complete the following with the appropriate forms of the indicated words.

1. Die Blätter _____ _____ Bäume sind abgefallen. *einige, hoch*
2. Das Aussterben _____ _____ Tiere ist ein Problem. *mehrere, wild*
3. Der Wert _____ Münzen steigt. *alt*
4. Innerhalb _____ _____ Städte gibt es historische Funde. *viele, alt*
5. Die Häuser _____ _____ Leute sind wie Paläste. *einige, reich*
6. Die Götter _____ _____ Völker sind furchterregend. *manche, primitiv*
7. Das Dorf liegt jenseits _____ Berge. *hoch*
8. Das Leben _____ Studenten ist schwer. *arm*
9. Die Farben _____ Blätter sind schön. *herbstlich*
10. Die Titel _____ _____ Romane sind interessant. *einige, modern*

Review: Unpreceded Adjectives

The following is a summary of the endings of attributive adjectives not preceded by a **"der"** or **"ein"** word.

	SINGULAR			*PLURAL*
	Masculine	*Neuter*	*Feminine*	*All Genders*
Nominative	**-er**	**-es**	**-e**	**-e**
Accusative	**-en**	**-es**	**-e**	**-e**
Dative	**-em**	**-em**	**-er**	**-en**
Genitive	**-en**	**-en**	**-er**	**-er**

49. Complete the following with the correct endings.

1. Trotz schnell_____ Hilfe wurde sie nicht gerettet.
2. Ich kenne mehrer_____ bekannt_____ Schauspieler.
3. Das Messer ist aus rostfrei_____ Stahl.
4. Lieb_____ Vater! Lieb_____ Frau Binder! Lieb_____ Großmutter!
5. Krank_____ Leute brauchen frisch_____ Luft.
6. Gut_____ Morgen! Gut_____ Tag! Gut_____ Nacht!
7. Er will es mit rot_____ Farbe anmalen.
8. Es sind hoh_____ Berge.
9. Wir sind schon seit lang_____ Zeit gut_____ Freunde.
10. Warum trinkst du kalt_____ Wasser?
11. Er erzählt von alt_____ Ruinen.
12. Ich brauche stark_____, schwarz_____ Kaffee.
13. Bei schlecht_____ Wetter spiele ich nicht Golf.
14. Der Preis französisch_____ Weines ist sehr hoch.
15. Ich kaufte viel_____ halbreif_____ Bananen.
16. Einig_____ deutsch_____ Studenten fuhren nach England.
17. Sie fragte nach weiß_____ Brot.
18. Die Sprachkenntnisse viel_____ ausländisch_____ Arbeiter sind beeindruckend.
19. Mit schnell_____ Autos muß man aufpassen.
20. Er schickte rot_____ Rosen.

ADJECTIVAL CONSTRUCTIONS: ADJECTIVES DERIVED FROM VERBS

Present Participle Used as Adjective

In both English and German the present participle can be used as an attributive adjective. In English the present participle ends in *-ing*. In German the present participle is formed by the infinitive plus **-d**: **lachend** (*laughing*), **singend** (*singing*). When used attributively, the appropriate adjective endings are added in German.

Das *weinende* **Kind** tut mir leid.	*I feel sorry for the crying child.*
Er ist in der *brennenden* **Fabrik.**	*He is in the burning factory.*
Wie heißt der *regierende* **König?**	*What is the name of the reigning king?*

50. Complete with the appropriate forms of the indicated words.

1. Wirf die Nudeln ins _____ Wasser! *kochend*
2. Hört ihr den _____ Hund? *bellend*
3. Viel Glück im _____ Jahr! *kommend*
4. Wo ist das _____ Baby? *weinend*
5. Der _____ Holländer ist eine Oper. *Fliegend*
6. Ich brauche ein Zimmer mit _____ Wasser. *fließend*
7. Sie hilft der _____ Frau. *sterbend*
8. Er ist im _____ Haus. *brennend*
9. Er sieht die _____ Katze. *leidend*
10. Wir suchen jene _____ Frau. *schreiend*

Past Participle Used as Adjective

The past participles of both weak and strong verbs can be used as adjectives. (See Chapter 7 on the formation of past participles.) When used attributively, adjective endings are added to the **-(e)t** suffix of weak verbs and to the **-(e)n** suffix of strong verbs.

Gib das *gestohlene* **Geld zurück!**	*Return the stolen money.*
Ich nehme ein *weichgekochtes* **Ei.**	*I'll take a soft-boiled egg.*
Wir stehen vor der *geschlossenen*	*We are standing in front of the closed*
Tür.	*door.*

51.   Complete with the appropriate forms of the indicated words.

    1. Wo ist die _____ Suppe? *gekocht*
    2. Sie ist am _____ Fenster. *geöffnet*
    3. Wo ist der _____ Brief? *geschrieben*
    4. Er steht auf dem _____ Wasser. *gefroren*
    5. Dort steht der _____ Wagen. *repariert*
    6. Wo sind die _____ Blumen? *geschnitten*
    7. Wir sind in den _____ Staaten. *Vereinigt*
    8. Ich rieche die _____ Wurst. *angebrannt*
    9. Hast du die _____ Rechnung? *bezahlt*
    10. Wo ist die _____ Tasse? *zerbrochen*

ADJECTIVES USED AS NOUNS

In German many adjectives can also function as nouns. When used in this way, the adjective is capitalized and given a definite article that corresponds to natural gender. The endings of nouns created in this way follow the same patterns as the adjective endings described above; that is, the ending taken by an adjectival noun is determined by its gender, number, and case as well as by whether it follows a **"der"** word or an **"ein"** word, or is unpreceded.

der/die Kranke	*the sick person (masculine/feminine)*
ein Kranker/eine Kranke	*a sick person (masculine/feminine)*
Kranke	*sick persons*

The use of adjectival nouns is much more widespread in German than it is in English, where it is usually confined to a general, plural sense, such as, *the rich* should help *the poor; the strong* often do not help *the weak.* In German, however, an adjectival noun can be used to refer to a specific individual or group of individuals as well as to a more generalized group. Many adjectival nouns are created from simple, descriptive adjectives.

Ein *Toter* **lag auf der Straße.**	*A dead (man) lay in the street.*
Sie erzählte von dem *Alten*.	*She was telling about the old one (man).*
Wer hilft der *Kleinen?*	*Who is helping the little one (female)?*
Die *Kranken* **sind im Krankenhaus.**	*The sick are in the hospital.*

52.   Complete with the appropriate forms of the indicated words.

    1. Er spricht mit der _____ . *Klein_____*
    2. Wo ist die _____ ? *Blond_____*
    3. Der _____ ist besser. *Schnell_____*
    4. Die _____ warten. *Alt_____*
    5. Der Akzent des _____ ist melodisch. *Fremd_____*
    6. Er bekommt es von den _____ . *Reich_____*
    7. Sie bringt es für jene _____ . *Arm_____*
    8. Wir helfen einem _____ . *Krank_____*
    9. Die _____ singt. *Hübsch_____*
    10. Wo sind die _____ ? *Glücklich_____*

Adjectival nouns are also created from adjectives that have been derived from the present participle and the past participle of verbs. The endings taken by these adjectival nouns also reflect gender, number, and case and are determined by whether they follow a "der" word or an "ein" word or are unpreceded.

der/die Reisende	traveler
der/die Genesende	convalescent
der/die Studierende	student
der/die Auszubildende	traineee, apprentice
der/die Bekannte	acquaintance
der/die Verletzte	injured/wounded person
der/die Verwandte	relative
der/die Verlobte	fiancé, financée
der/die Gefangene	prisoner
der/die Verschollene	missing person

Note: the word **der Beamte** (*civil servant, official*) follows this pattern in the masculine; the feminine form, however, is **die Beamt*in*** by analogy to words such as **Ärzt*in*, Lehrer*in*, Künstler*in*, Leser*in*, Schweizer*in*.**

Der/die Deutsche is the only noun of nationality that takes an adjectival ending.

Ist das *eine Deutsche?*	*Is that a German (woman)?*
Der Deutsche **lacht.**	*The German (man) is laughing.*
Er spricht mit *einer Deutschen*.	*He is talking with a German (woman).*
Das ist *mein Verwandter.*	*That is my relative (male).*
Wir fragen *den Beamten.*	*We are asking the official (male).*
Die Angestellten **waren unzufrieden.**	*The employees were dissatisfied.*

53. Complete the following with the appropriate endings.

1. Warum ist der Gefangen_____ nicht hier?
2. Er spricht zum Beamt_____.
3. Meine Verlobt_____ ist hier.
4. Ich sehe viele Reisend_____ im Zug.
5. Dort steht ein Deutsch_____.
6. Meine Verwandt_____ ist krank.
7. Dort ist das Auto meiner Bekannt_____.
8. Die Deutsch_____ spricht schnell.
9. Der Beamt_____ ist nett.
10. Ich besuche meinen Verwandt_____.
11. Es liegt unter der Illustriert_____.
12. Ist das deine Bekannt_____?
13. Der Reisend_____ sitzt im Bus.
14. Dort ist eine Gefangen_____.
15. Unsere Bekannt_____ kommen.
16. Wir besuchen die armen Genesend_____.

Neuter Adjectives Used as Nouns: Preceded by etwas, nichts, viel, wenig

Adjectives following **etwas** (*something*), **nichts** (*nothing*), **viel** (*much*), **wenig** (*little*) are neuter and are capitalized.

Er macht viel *Gutes*.

Weißt du etwas *Interessantes?*

Ich habe nichts *Neues* **gehört.**

He does much good.

Do you know something interesting?

I haven't heard anything new.

54. Complete the following with the appropriate German words.

1. Ich kaufe nichts _____. *cheap*
2. Wir erfahren wenig _____. *new*
3. Ich esse gern etwas _____. *sweet*
4. Ich las nichts _____. *interesting*
5. Sie kocht etwas _____. *good*
6. Er schreibt nichts _____. *personal*
7. Sie bringt etwas _____. *old*
8. Ich habe viel _____. *modern*
9. Er trinkt etwas _____. *cold*
10. Sie hat wenig _____ erfahren. *important*

POSSESSIVE ADJECTIVES

Possessive adjectives are used to denote ownership or possession. The German possessive adjectives are as follows:

	Singular		Plural
mein	*my*	**unser**	*our*
dein	*your (familiar)*	**euer**	*your (familiar)*
sein	*his*		
sein	*its*		
ihr	*her*	**ihr**	*their*
Ihr	*your (formal)*	**Ihr**	*your (formal)*

Note: the possessive adjective **Ihr** (*your*, singular and plural forms relating to persons for whom formal address is appropriate) is always capitalized. However, **dein** and **euer** are capitalized only when written as a form of address in a letter or other correspondence.

Lieber Hans, vielen Dank für *Deinen*
Brief.

Dear Hans, thank you very much for
your letter.

The possessive adjectives are "**ein**" words and thus take the same set of endings as the indefinite article (see Chapter 2). These endings are determined by the gender, number, and case of the noun that the possessive adjective modifies. The choice of which possessive adjective to use in a given situation, however, is determined by who or what possesses the noun in question.

Wo ist *ihr* **Bruder?**

Where is her brother?

The ending of the possessive adjective **ihr** (*her*) is masculine, singular, nominative because the word **Bruder** *as used in this sentence* is masculine, singular, nominative. The choice of the third person, singular, feminine possessive **ihr** is determined by whose brother it is.

Ist das *seine* **Mutter?**

Is that his mother?

Here the ending of the possessive adjective **seine** (*his*) is feminine, singular, nominative because the word **Mutter** is feminine, singular, nominative. In this case, the third person singular masculine possessive adjective **sein** was selected because it is a male whose mother is referred to.

Note also that although the possessive **unser** is sometimes contracted to **unsr-** when the adjective endings are added to the stem, this occurs primarily in colloquial speech and literary writings. In normal usage **unser** is not contracted.

Unsere (Unsre) **Nachbarn sind hier.**   *Our neighbors are here.*

The possessive **euer,** however, is normally contracted to **eur-** when an adjective ending is added.

Wo ist *eure* **Schwester?**   *Where is your sister?*

55. Complete the following with the appropriate forms.

1. (*His*) _____ Mutter ist krank.
2. (*Our*) _____ Bücher liegen dort.
3. (*Her*) _____ Bruder ist klug.
4. Das ist (*my*) _____ Kätzchen.
5. Wo ist (*your*, familiar singular) _____ Freund?
6. Herr Walter, (*your*) _____ Wagen steht dort.
7. (*Their*) _____ Eltern sind reich.
8. Wo sind (*your*, familiar plural) _____ Schuhe?
9. (*Our*) _____ Haus ist sehr alt.
10. Herr und Frau Müller, (*your*) _____ Tochter steht dort.

56. Complete the following with the appropriate forms of the indicated words.

1. Er läuft durch _____ Garten.   *unser*
2. Sie kennt _____ Freundin.   *mein*
3. Hast du _____ Buch?   *dein*
4. Ich habe _____ Mäntel.   *euer*
5. Gehen Sie ohne _____ Frau?   *Ihr*
6. Das ist für _____ Onkel.   *ihr*
7. Kaufst du _____ Haus?   *sein*
8. Kennen Sie _____ Großmutter?   *mein*
9. Er setzt sich in _____ Auto.   *unser*
10. Ich nehme _____ Kamera.   *euer*

57. Complete the following with the appropriate endings.

1. Er kommt von sein_____ Freundin.
2. Ich wohne bei ihr_____ Tante.
3. Sie kommen aus unser_____ Haus.
4. Ich gehe mit mein_____ Eltern.
5. Sie steht hinter dein_____ Wagen.
6. Wir gehen zu eur_____ Lehrer.
7. Es liegt unter Ihr_____ Zeitung.
8. Außer sein_____ Freundinnen war niemand da.
9. Sie ist in mein_____ Zimmer.
10. Er ist bei sein_____ Professor.

58. Complete the following with the appropriate genitive forms of the indicated words.

1. Die Farbe _____ Autos ist häßlich. *sein*
2. Die Haare _____ Mutter sind grau. *ihr*
3. Die Frau _____ Lehrers ist hier. *unser*
4. Während _____ Ferien fahre ich nach Berlin. *mein*
5. Trotz _____ Alters spielt sie Tennis. *ihr*
6. Warst du wegen _____ Bruders dort? *dein*
7. Wo ist die Brille _____ Vaters? *euer*
8. Wo wohnt die Tochter _____ Schwester? *Ihr*
9. Der Fluß ist jenseits _____ Gartens. *unser*
10. Die Geschwister _____ Eltern sind dort. *ihr*

59. Complete the following with the appropriate forms of the possessive.

1. Wer hat (*his*) _____ Frau gesehen?
2. Dort steht (*my*) _____ Lehrer.
3. Gerda, (*your*) _____ Freunde warten.
4. (*Her*) _____ Geschwister kommen auch.
5. Wo sind (*our*) _____ Bücher?
6. Dort ist das Haus (*of her*) _____ Tante.
7. Er spielt mit (*his*) _____ Bruder.
8. Was bringt ihr für (*your*) _____ Kinder?
9. Herr Fischer, wer ist in (*your*) _____ Haus?
10. Kinder, sind das (*your*) _____ Hunde?
11. (*My*) _____ Familie wohnt hier.
12. Wo ist das Auto (*of his*) _____ Eltern.

COMPARISON OF ADJECTIVES AND ADVERBS

In German, as in English, adjectives have three degrees of comparison:

Positive	**klein**	*small, short*
Comparative	**kleiner**	*smaller, shorter*
Superlative	**kleinst-**	*smallest, shortest*
	am kleinsten	*the smallest*

The comparative of an adjective is formed by adding **-er** to the base form of the adjective. Many common one-syllable adjectives take an umlaut in the comparative and the superlative.

Helga ist *kleiner* **als Gisela.**   *Helga is shorter than Gisela.*
Hans ist *älter* **als Loisl.**   *Hans is older than Loisl.*

The superlative is formed by adding **-st** to the adjective. Note that **-est** is added to adjectives ending in **-d, -t, -s, -ß, -st, -x, -z, -sch.** The superlative form always requires an ending. The superlative form **am _____ (e)sten** is used with a predicate adjective.

Gertrud ist *am kleinsten*.   *Gertrud is the shortest.*
Die Geschichte ist *am interessantesten*.   *The story is the most interesting.*

Unlike in English, in German it is not possible to create compound comparative or superlative forms by adding the German equivalent for the words *more* or *most* to an adjective or adverb. Compare the German and English comparatives and superlatives below.

modern	*modern*
moderner	*more modern*
am modernsten	*most modern*

In German, unlike in English, an uninflected adjective (that is, an adjective in its base form without any grammatical endings) can be used as an adverb without making any changes to it. In English the suffix *-ly* is usually added to an adjective in order to make it an adverb.

The comparative and superlative of the adverb is formed in the same way as the comparative and superlative of the adjective, that is, by adding **-er** and **am** _____ **-(e)sten** to the adverb.

Er fährt *schnell*.	*He drives fast.*
Er fährt *schneller*.	*He drives faster.*
Er fährt *am schnellsten*.	*He drives fastest.*
Sie singt *schön*.	*She sings beautifully.*
Sie singt *schöner*.	*She sings more beautifully.*
Sie singt *am schönsten*.	*She sings most beautifully.*

As a general rule, there are no comparative or superlative forms for those adverbs that have not been derived from adjectives, such as **heute, zuerst, gerade, dort, nicht, doch, sehr, nur, deinetwegen**.

Vowel Change in Monosyllabic Adjectives

The stem vowels of the following monosyllabic adjectives add an umlaut in the comparatives and superlatives. Remember, only **a, o,** and **u** take an umlaut in German.

Adjective/adverb		*Comparative*	*Superlative*	
alt	*old*	**älter**	**ältest-**	**am ältesten**
arm	*poor*	**ärmer**	**ärmst-**	**am ärmsten**
hart	*hard*	**härter**	**härtest-**	**am härtesten**
jung	*young*	**jünger**	**jüngst-**	**am jüngsten**
kalt	*cold*	**kälter**	**kältest-**	**am kältesten**
klug	*smart*	**klüger**	**klügst-**	**am klügsten**
krank	*sick*	**kränker**	**kränkst-**	**am kränksten**
kurz	*short*	**kürzer**	**kürzest-**	**am kürzesten**
lang	*long*	**länger**	**längst-**	**am längsten**
oft	*often*	**öfter**	**öftest-**	**am öftesten**
scharf	*sharp*	**schärfer**	**schärfst-**	**am schärfsten**
schwach	*weak*	**schwächer**	**schwächst-**	**am schwächsten**
stark	*strong*	**stärker**	**stärkst-**	**am stärksten**
warm	*warm*	**wärmer**	**wärmst-**	**am wärmsten**

Irregular Adjectives

Adjectives ending in **-el** always drop the **e** in the comparative; certain adjectives ending in **-er** may drop the **e**.

teuer	*expensive*	**teurer**	**teuerst-**	**am teuersten**
dunkel	*dark*	**dunkler**	**dunkelst-**	**am dunkelsten**

The adjective **hoch** drops the **c** in the comparative.

| **hoch** | high | **höher** | **höchst-** | **am höchsten** |

The adjective **nah** adds the **c** in the superlative.

| **nah** | *near* | **näher** | **nächst-** | **am nächsten** |

Other irregular adjectives and adverbs are as follows.

gern	*(to) like (to)*	**lieber**	**liebst-**	**am liebsten**
groß	*big, tall*	**größer**	**größt-**	**am größten**
gut	*good*	**besser**	**best-**	**am besten**
viel	*much*	**mehr**	**meist-**	**am meisten**

60.   Follow the model.

> **Die Bluse ist billig. Das Hemd ist _____ . Der Schal ist _____ .**
> **Die Bluse ist billig. Das Hemd ist billiger. Der Schal ist am billigsten.**

1. Der Bleistift is lang. Das Lineal ist _____ . Der Stock ist _____ .
2. Das Brot ist teuer. Die Butter ist _____ . Der Käse ist _____ .
3. Das Zimmer ist groß. Die Wohnung ist _____ . Das Haus ist _____ .
4. Ute spricht schnell. Maria spricht _____ . Frau Weber spricht _____ .
5. Die Uhr kostet viel. Der Ring kostet _____ . Die Brosche kostet _____ .
6. Der Stein ist hart. Der Marmor ist _____ . Das Metall ist _____ .
7. Ich sehe Rolf oft. Ich sehe Heinz _____ . Ich sehe Paul _____ .
8. Der Käse riecht scharf. Das Gas riecht _____ . Die Säure riecht _____ .
9. Er trinkt Wasser gern. Er trinkt Milch _____ . Er trinkt Limonade _____ .
10. Das Gebäude is hoch. Der Turm ist _____ . Der Berg ist _____ .

Comparison of Adjectives and Adverbs

Comparison of inequality

Comparisons implying inequality are expressed with the comparative followed by **als** (*than*).

Erich ist *größer als* **ich.**	*Erich is taller than I.*
Der Ring ist *teurer als* **die Kette.**	*The ring is more expensive than the necklace.*
Er ißt *mehr als* **sein Vater.**	*He eats more than his father.*

61.   Follow the model.

> **Moritz ist intelligent, aber Thomas ist _____ Moritz.**
> **Moritz ist intelligent, aber Thomas ist intelligenter als Moritz.**

1. Inge spricht viel, aber ich spreche _____ Inge.
2. Sie ist dick, aber er ist _____ sie.
3. Köln ist groß, aber Frankfurt ist _____ Köln.
4. Der BMW ist teuer, aber der Mercedes ist _____ der BMW.
5. Ich trinke Tee gern, aber ich trinke Milch _____ Tee.
6. Der Brocken ist hoch, aber die Zugspitze ist _____ der Brocken.
7. Christian ist nett, aber du bist _____ Christian.
8. Du bist jung, aber ich bin _____ du.
9. Gestern war es dunkel, aber heute ist es _____ gestern.
10. Eisen ist hart, aber Stahl ist _____ Eisen.

62. Follow the model.

> **Der Brief ist interessant.   der Artikel.**
> **Der Brief ist interessanter als der Artikel.**

1. Der Februar is kurz.   *der Januar*
2. Das Kleid ist teuer.   *die Bluse*
3. Der Vater ißt viel.   *das Baby*
4. Ute kann gut Spanisch.   *Marianne*
5. Im Haus ist es warm.   *im Garten*
6. Das Auto fährt schnell.   *das Motorrad*
7. Robert ist arm.   *Manfred*
8. Mein Vater ist stark.   *mein Bruder*
9. Die Lilie ist schön.   *die Geranie*
10. Die Limonade ist kalt.   *das Wasser*
11. Der Kaffee ist heiß.   *der Tee*
12. Die Schule ist nah.   *die Kirche*

Immer *plus comparative form*

Immer followed by the comparative form expresses an increase in degree.

> **Es wird** *immer kälter*.   *It is getting colder and colder.*
> **Sie werden** *immer reicher*.   *They are getting richer and richer.*
> **Er spricht** *immer schneller*.   *He is talking faster and faster.*

63. Write the German.

1. It is getting darker and darker.
2. She is getting older and older.
3. He is driving faster and faster.
4. The days are getting longer and longer
5. It is coming closer and closer.

The superlative

The superlative form **am _____ -(e)sten** is always used as the superlative of adverbs. It is also used with predicate adjectives.

> **Dieses Auto ist** *am teuersten*.   *This car is the most expensive.*
> **Ich laufe** *am schnellsten*.   *I am running fastest.*
> **Dieses Messer schneidet** *am besten*.   *This knife cuts best.*

64. Follow the model.

> **Karl und Hans sind stark.   Gustav**
> **Gustav ist am stärksten.**

1. Inge und Pia springen hoch.   *ich*
2. Peter und Josef sind groß.   *Karl*
3. Ursel und Bärbel singen gut.   *wir*
4. Laura und Christl sprechen schnell.   *meine Mutter*
5. Renate und Rosa sind krank.   *Sabine*
6. Jochen und Rolf sparen viel.   *mein Bruder*
7. Das Rathaus und das Museum sind nah.   *die Kirche*
8. Gerda und Georg gehen langsam.   *Klaus und ich*

9. Meine Eltern sind reich.   *unsere Nachbarn*
10. Der Mantel und das Kleid sind kurz.   *der Rock*

65. Follow the model.

> **Das Fahrrad, das Motorrad, das Auto, fährt schnell.**
> **Das Fahrrad fährt schnell. Das Motorrad fährt schneller. Das Auto fährt am schnellsten.**

1. Der Brocken, das Matterhorn, die Zugspitze, ist hoch.
2. Wasser, Limonade, Bier, Ich trinke _____ gern.
3. Das Gedicht, die Geschichte, der Roman, ist lang.
4. Der Vogel, der Hubschrauber, das Düsenflugzeug, fliegt schnell.
5. Der Apfel, die Orange, die Zitrone, ist sauer.
6. Das Brot, der Kuchen, die Torte, schmeckt gut.
7. Hans, Josef, Franz, arbeitet viel.
8. Das Wollkleid, die Jacke, der Wintermantel, ist warm.

Comparison of equality

Comparisons implying equality are expressed by **so ... wie** (*as ... as*).

Karl ist *so groß wie* **Gerhard.**	*Karl is as tall as Gerhard.*
Der Mantel kostet *so viel wie* **das Kleid.**	*The coat costs as much as the dress.*
Sie fahren *so schnell wie* **wir.**	*They are driving as fast as we are.*

66. Follow the model.

> **Die Bank ist hoch.   Stuhl**
> **Die Bank is so hoch wie der Stuhl.**

1. Deine Nägel sind lang.   *Katzenkrallen*
2. Pia ist groß.   *Inge*
3. Die Jacke ist nicht warm.   *Mantel*
4. Deine Augen sind blau.   *Himmel*
5. Heute ist es kalt.   *Im Winter*
6. Peter ist stark.   *Max*
7. Die Hose ist teuer.   *Pullover*
8. Großmutter ist alt.   *Großvater*
9. Renate schreit laut.   *ich*
10. Mein Bruder schreibt viel.   *sein Freund*

Comparative and superlative forms as attributive adjectives

The comparative and superlative forms of adjectives take the same endings as the positive or base forms of the adjectives.

Dort ist der billigere Mantel.	*There is the cheaper coat.*
Ist das die teuerste Kamera?	*Is that the most expensive camera?*
Das ist ein größerer Wagen.	*That is a larger car.*
Ich kaufe den größeren Koffer.	*I'll buy the larger suitcase.*
Sie hat das größte Zimmer.	*She has the largest room.*
Sie nehmen meine beste Jacke.	*They are taking my best jacket.*
Wir sind in dem modernsten Theater.	*We are in the most modern theater.*
Er hilft einer jüngeren Frau.	*He is helping a younger woman.*
Das ist der Mann meiner jüngsten Schwester.	*That's the husband of my youngest sister.*

mehr *and* **weniger**

The comparative forms of **mehr** and **weniger** do not add adjective endings in the singular or plural.

Sie hat *mehr* **Bücher** *als* **du.**   *She has more books than you.*
Hast du *weniger* **Geld?**   *Do you have less money?*

67.   Complete with the comparative forms of the indicated adjectives.

    1.   Das ist der _____ Mantel.   *schön*
    2.   Dort liegt die _____ Tasche.   *teuer*
    3.   Hier ist das _____ Messer.   *scharf*
    4.   Das ist eine _____ Frau.   *arm*
    5.   Sein _____ Freund kommt.   *jung*
    6.   Ihr _____ Kind spielt.   *klein*
    7.   Wo ist euer _____ Teppich?   *gut*
    8.   Wann kommt _____ Wetter?   *kalt*

68.   Complete with the appropriate German forms of the adjectives.

    1.   Ich kaufe den _____ Mantel.   *warmer*
    2.   Wir brauchen einen _____ Wind.   *stronger*
    3.   Hast du ein _____ Messer?   *sharper*
    4.   Ich kaufe eine _____ Tasche.   *larger*
    5.   Er hat die _____ Kamera.   *better*
    6.   Ich brauche _____ Geld.   *more*
    7.   Wir gehen ins _____ Zimmer.   *smaller*
    8.   Das ist für _____ Leute.   *older*

69.   Rewrite in German changing the definite articles to the indefinite articles.

    1.   Wir sind in der kleineren Wohnung.
    2.   Er kommt aus dem bekannteren Museum.
    3.   Er fährt mit dem schnelleren Wagen.
    4.   Wir helfen dem kränkeren Patienten.
    5.   Sie erzählt von der besseren Zeit.
    6.   Er spricht mit der kleineren Frau.

70.   Complete the following with the appropriate comparative forms of the indicated words.

    1.   Es liegt jenseits des _____ Berges.   *hoch*
    2.   Sie konnte wegen ihres _____ Bruders nicht gehen.   *jung*
    3.   Er kam um der _____ Frau willen.   *alt*
    4.   Trotz des _____ Windes segeln wir nicht.   *stark*
    5.   Es ist innerhalb des _____ Parks.   *klein*
    6.   Wir tragen wegen des _____ Wetters Mäntel.   *kalt*

71.   Complete the following with the appropriate superlative forms of the indicated adjectives.

    1.   Das ist der _____ Weg.   *nah*
    2.   Wie heißt der _____ Berg?   *hoch*
    3.   Das ist meine _____ Jacke.   *warm*
    4.   Wo ist dein _____ Bild?   *teuer*

5. Hier ist das _____ Papier. *dünn*
6. Wie heißt das _____ Metall? *hart*
7. Das ist ihr _____ Freund. *gut*
8. Wo ist unsere _____ Tochter? *alt*

72. Complete the following with the appropriate German words.

1. Ich kenne seinen (*youngest*) _____ Sohn.
2. Wir gehen in das (*most modern*) _____ Theater.
3. Er kämpft gegen den (*strongest*) _____ Mann.
4. Ich habe die (*most expensive*) _____ Kette.
5. Er nimmt seine (*best*) _____ Maschine.
6. Sie haben die (*most*) _____ Kinder.
7. Das ist für den (*most intelligent*) _____ Studenten.
8. Ich setze mich neben das (*smallest*) _____ Kind.

73. Complete with the appropriate superlative forms of the indicated words.

1. Er wohnt in der _____ Wohnung. *teuer*
2. Sie schreibt mit ihrem _____ Bleistift. *kurz*
3. Wir helfen dem _____ Fräulein. *arm*
4. Ich sitze im _____ Zimmer. *warm*
5. Sie glaubt der _____ Frau. *jung*
6. Er arbeitet mit seiner _____ Maschine. *neu*
7. Wir sind im _____ Hotel. *teuer*
8. Sie segeln bei _____ Wind. *stark*

74. Complete with the appropriate German words.

1. Die Frau meines (*best*) _____ Freundes ist hier.
2. Was ist der Preis des (*most expensive*) _____ Instruments?
3. Wir sind innerhalb der (*oldest*) _____ Stadt.
4. Er macht es um des (*youngest*) _____ Kindes willen.
5. Was war das Thema des (*longest*) _____ Romans?
6. Der Freund ihrer (*prettiest*) _____ Tochter kommt.

Review

75. Complete with the appropriate endings when necessary.

1. Kennst du seine älter_____ Schwester?
2. Dort steht das größt_____ Kaufhaus.
3. Wir sind im billigst_____ Zimmer.
4. Ich habe mehr_____ Zeit.
5. Zieh deinen wärmer_____ Mantel an!
6. Ist das der best_____ Wein?
7. Habt ihr weniger_____ Bücher?
8. Ich brauche das schärfer_____ Messer.
9. Ich trinke keinen heiß_____ Kaffee.
10. Es ist jenseits des höher_____ Berges.

11. Das war der schönst_____ Tag meines Lebens.
12. Wie heißt der Mann seiner älter_____ Schwester?
13. Sie spricht mit der ärmer_____ Frau.
14. Ich fahre mit dem teurer_____ Auto.
15. Das war die dunkelst_____ Nacht.
16. Die größer_____ Jungen bleiben hier.
17. Wir sehen den kürzest_____ Film.
18. Trag das länger_____ Kleid!
19. Nimm den nächst_____ Weg!
20. Das war der kältest_____ Winter.

ADVERBS

The adverb **sehr** (*very*) precedes an adjective or adverb to express a high degree of a certain quality.

Dieses Auto fährt *sehr* **schnell**	*This car goes very fast.*
Im Sommer ist es *sehr* **heiß.**	*It is very hot in summer.*
Sie ist eine *sehr* **hübsche Frau.**	*She is a very pretty woman.*
Hier gibt es *sehr* **hohe Berge.**	*There are very high mountains here.*

76. Write the German.

1. He is very old.
2. They have very good teachers.
3. He is a very intelligent man.
4. It is very cold.
5. She sings very beautifully.

Many German adverbs do not have a corresponding adjective form. Such adverbs can refer to time, manner, or place. A few of these adverbs are listed as follows.

Adverbs Referring to Time

abends	*in the evening*	**morgens**	*in the morning*
bald	*soon*	**nachts**	*at night*
damals	*at that time*	**nie**	*never*
gestern	*yesterday*	**nun**	*now*
heute	*today*	**oft**	*often*
immer	*always*	**selten**	*seldom, rarely*
jetzt	*now*	**spät**	*late*
manchmal	*at times, sometimes*	**täglich**	*daily, every day*

77. Complete with the appropriate German words.

1. Wo ist er _____ ? *now*
2. Er ist _____ in der Schule. *today*
3. Wir sind _____ zu Hause. *rarely*
4. Was war _____ ? *yesterday*
5. Sie sind _____ krank. *never*
6. Ich bin _____ müde. *in the evening*
7. Wo waren Sie _____ ? *at that time*
8. Wir besuchen ihn _____ . *every day*
9. Kommen Sie _____ ? *soon*
10. Sie ist _____ beschäftigt. *always*

11. Er hilft uns _____ .   *sometimes*
12. Er fährt _____ ins Büro.   *in the morning*

Adverbs Referring to Manner

gern	*gladly, like to*	**sicherlich**	*certainly*
hoffentlich	*hopefully*	**so**	*so*
leider	*unfortunately*	**vielleicht**	*perhaps, maybe*
natürlich	*naturally*	**wirklich**	*really*
nicht	*not*	**ziemlich**	*rather*
schon	*already*	**zu**	*to*

78. Complete with the appropriate German words.

1. Er ist _____ reich.   *naturally*
2. Ich lese _____ .   *like to*
3. Wir können _____ nicht kommen.   *unfortunately*
4. Sie ist _____ hier.   *not*
5. Warum trinkst du _____ viel.   *so*
6. Es ist _____ heiß.   *really*
7. Du bist _____ klein.   *too*
8. Er ist _____ alt.   *rather*
9. War er _____ hier?   *already*
10. _____ hat sie Kopfweh.   *perhaps*

Adverbs Referring to Place

da	*there*	**links**	*(on to the) left*
dort	*there*	**oben**	*above, upstairs*
draußen	*outside*	**rechts**	*(on to the) right*
drinnen	*inside*	**überall**	*everywhere*
hier	*here*	**weg**	*away*
hinten	*in the back*		

79. Complete with the appropriate German words.

1. Was macht er _____ ?   *there*
2. Sie arbeitet _____ .   *upstairs*
3. Wir sind _____ .   *inside*
4. Ich war _____ .   *outside*
5. War er _____ ?   *here*
6. Sie sind _____ .   *away*
7. Müssen wir uns _____ halten?   *to the left*
8. Wir bleiben _____ .   *in the back*
9. Geht immer _____ !   *to the right*
10. Es gab _____ Blumen.   *everywhere*

Position of Adverbs

In German the adverb usually follows the verb and pronoun (if one is present). If more than one adverb occurs in a series, the following word order is observed: time, manner, place. **Nicht** precedes an adverb of place.

Wir sind *immer* **krank.**   *We are always ill.*
Er sagt mir *nie* **die Wahrheit.**   *He never tells me the truth.*
Sie ist *jetzt leider* **draußen.**   *She is unfortunately outside now.*
Er ist *heute wirklich nicht* **hier.**   *He is really not here today.*

80.   Form sentences from the following.

1. hier / er / natürlich / bleibt
2. Maria / wohnt / unten / nicht
3. uns / Karl / sieht / täglich
4. drinnen / gestern / waren / wir / wirklich
5. nicht / arbeite / ich / abends / draußen

6. Vater / suchte / überall / dich / damals
7. sitzen / gern / wir / dort / manchmal
8. Hunger / ich / wirklich / morgens / habe / großen
9. dick / ziemlich / sie / ist / jetzt
10. heute / weg / sie / leider / sind

81.   Write the German.

1. We never drink wine.
2. She was already here today.
3. I am not there in the evening.
4. They are unfortunately upstairs now.
5. She is always inside in the morning.

6. He was here at that time.
7. I always sit outside.
8. He is perhaps in the back.
9. I am rarely away.
10. She is certainly everywhere.

Idiomatic Use of Adverbs

German makes frequent use of a number of adverbs such as **denn, doch, ja, noch** to convey the attitude or feelings of the speaker toward a situation or event. Sometimes called *flavoring particles* and *intensifiers*, these adverbs are used in German to indicate the surprise, irritation, emphasis, certainty, uncertainty, doubt, etc., that we in English would express through voice clues such as emphasis and intonation. Consequently, there are no directly equivalent translations for these adverbs.

denn

Denn usually expresses impatience, curiosity, or interest. It is used in questions.

Wo ist er *denn?*   *Well, where is he?*

doch

This adverb occurs both stressed and unstressed. When it is stressed, it expresses that something happened despite expectations to the contrary. It is also used instead of **ja** (*yes*) as an answer to a negative question.

Ich habe es *doch* **verkauft.**   *I sold it after all.*
Trinkst du nichts? *Doch,* **ich trinke**   *Aren't you drinking anything? Yes (sure),*
   Tee   *I am drinking tea.*

When **doch** is unstressed, it expresses that the opposite is not expected to be true. In an imperative construction, **doch** corresponds to the English "*why don't you ...*" The word **doch** can also be used for emphasis.

Sie ist *doch* **nicht in Köln!**   *She isn't in Cologne, is she!*
Kauf ihm *doch* **etwas!**   *Why don't you buy him something?*
Das hast du *doch* **schon gesehen.**   *After all you've seen that before.*

ja

This adverb reinforces an idea, observation, or fact.

Sie ist *ja* **verrückt.**	*Why, she is crazy.*
Wir sind *ja* **schon zu Hause.**	*We are already home, you know.*
Ich war *ja* **krank.**	*After all, I was ill.*

noch

Noch corresponds to the English *still, yet*. It indicates that an action is still continuing.

Sie ist *noch* **im Krankenhaus.**	*She is still in the hospital.*
Das Kind kann *noch* **nicht sprechen.**	*The child can't talk yet.*

Noch ein frequently means *another*.

Sie wollen *noch ein* **Kind.**	*They want another child.*
Möchtest du *noch eine* **Tasse Tee?**	*Would you like another cup of tea?*

82. Complete the following with the correct German adverbs.

1. Wir haben (*still*) _____ Zeit.
2. Was habt ihr _____ bekommen?
3. Schreib uns _____ bald!
4. Wir sind (*after all*) _____ nicht dumm.
5. Hat sie keine Eltern? _____, sie sind aber verreist.
6. Habt ihr (*another*) _____ Bleistift?
7. Wir wissen es _____ schon. (*you know*)
8. Sie hat uns (*after all*) _____ besucht.

Chapter 6

Numbers, Dates, Time

NUMBERS

Cardinal Numbers

The cardinal numbers in German are as follows.

0	null	16	sechzehn	100	hundert
1	eins	17	siebzehn	101	hunderteins
2	zwei	18	achtzehn	102	hundertzwei
3	drei	19	neunzehn	120	hundertzwanzig
4	vier	20	zwanzig	123	hundertdreiundzwanzig
5	fünf	21	einundzwanzig	143	hundertdreiundvierzig
6	sechs	22	zweiundzwanzig	200	zweihundert
7	sieben	30	dreißig	300	dreihundert
8	acht	31	einunddreißig	400	vierhundert
9	neun	35	fünfunddreißig	999	neunhundertneunundneunzig
10	zehn	40	vierzig	1000	tausend
11	elf	50	fünfzig	1001	tausendeins
12	zwölf	60	sechzig	1110	tausendeinhundertzehn
13	dreizehn	70	siebzig	1996	tausendneunhundertsechsundneunzig
14	vierzehn	80	achtzig	in dates:	neunzehnhundertsechsundneunzig
15	fünfzehn	90	neunzig		

The final **-s** is dropped from **sechs** and the final **-en** from **sieben** in 16 (**sechzehn**), 60 (**sechzig**), 17 (**siebzehn**), and 70 (**siebzig**). **Eins** drops the final **-s** when followed by **und**, e.g., **einundvierzig**. However, when the word **eins** occurs at the end of a number, the final **-s** is always retained: **hunderteins, tausendeins.**

The word **ein** is not usually expressed before **hundert** and **tausend**. When it occurs within a numeral, it is expressed, e.g., **tausendeinhundert.** Numbers from 1 to 999 999 are written as one word:

345 890   (**dreihundertfünfundvierzigtausendachthundertneunzig**)

Numbers over 1,000,000

1 000 000	eine Million
2 000 000	zwei Millionen
1 000 000 000	eine Milliarde
1 000 000 000 000	eine Billion

Eine Million, eine Milliarde, and **eine Billion** are capitalized and have plural forms because they are nouns. There is a difference between the German **Billion** and the American *billion*. The German

Billion is equivalent to 1,000,000 millions, i.e., 10^{12}. The American *billion* is equivalent to 1000 millions, i.e., 10^9.

For convenience in reading large numbers, German uses a period or a space where English would use a comma. For example, *one hundred thousand*, which would normally be written *100,000* in English, is written **100.000** or **100 000** in German. Note that in Swiss usage this number is written **100′000.**

Measurements, Prices, and Other Decimal Fractions

Decimal fractions used in prices and measurements of various kinds, which would be expressed with a decimal point or period in English, are represented in German by a comma.

	German	English
2,3	zwei komma drei	2.3
4,45	vier komma fünfundvierzig	4.45
1,00 DM	eine Mark	DM 1.00
6,01 DM	sechs Mark eins	DM 6.01

The numeral **eins** is treated as an adjective when it is followed by a noun. It takes the ending of the indefinite article: **eine Mark.** When the German noun **Mark** refers to the German currency, it does not have a plural form; e.g., **Es kostet nur 10,00 DM (zehn Mark).** The abbreviation **DM (Deutsche Mark)** usually follows the amount in nonofficial use.

1. Write the following numbers in German.

1. 8	6. 56	11. 101	16. 10 million
2. 16	7. 70	12. 936	17. 8.9
3. 21	8. 89	13. 1274	18. 17.61
4. 34	9. 91	14. 1980 (date)	19. 20.30 DM
5. 51	10. 100	15. 2031	20. 191.67 DM

Ordinal Numbers

Ordinal numbers *up to nineteenth* are formed by adding **-t** plus adjective endings to the cardinal numbers. Ordinals from *twentieth upward* add **-st** plus adjective endings to the cardinals. Note that the German words for *first*, *third*, and *eighth* are irregular. In German a period following a number indicates that it is an ordinal number.

1. der, die, das erste	19. der, die, das neunzehnte
2. der, die, das zweite	20. der, die, das zwanzigste
3. der, die, das dritte	25. der, die, das einundzwanzigste
4. der, die, das vierte	40. der, die, das vierzigste
7. der, die, das siebente (or siebte)	100. der, die, das hundertste
8. der, die, das achte	1000. der, die, das tausendste
11. der, die, das elfte	

Ordinal numbers are adjectives in German. Therefore they require adjective endings. Ordinal numbers are used in titles of rulers.

Nominative: **Wilhelm I., Wilhelm der Erste**

Wilhelm I (der Erste) **wohnte hier.**   *Wilhelm I lived here.*

Accusative: **Wilhelm I., Wilhelm den Ersten**

Er kämpfte gegen *Wilhelm I.* (*den Ersten*)   *He fought against Wilhelm I.*

Dative: **Wilhelm I., Wilhelm dem Ersten**

Das Schloß gehörte *Wilhelm I.* (*dem Ersten*)   *The castle belonged to Wilhelm I.*

Genitive: **Wilhelm I., Wilhelms des Ersten**

Wo ist die Krone *Wilhelms I.?* (*des Ersten*)   *Where is the crown of Wilhelm I?*

2. Complete the following with the correct forms of the ordinal numbers.

1. Wir wohnen im (8.) _____ Stock.
2. Ich habe ein (2.) _____ Haus gekauft.
3. Das ist sein (4.) _____ Frau.
4. Ich bin der (1.) _____ .
5. Er wohnt in der (3.) _____ Straße links.
6. Heinrich (*VIII.*) _____ _____ hatte viele Frauen.
7. Sie kommen jede (5.) _____ Woche.
8. Wann regierte Friedrich (*I.*) _____ _____ ?
9. Er lebte in der Zeit Ludwigs (*XV.*) _____ _____ .
10. Wir besuchen ein Schloß von Ludwig (*II.*) _____ _____ .

Fractions

Fractions are formed by adding **-el** to the ordinal numbers. Fractions can be used as neuter nouns or as adjectives. No adjective endings are required for fractions. When $\frac{3}{4}$ is used as an adjective, the numerator and denominator are frequently written as one word. The same is true for fractions following whole numbers.

Fraction	Noun	Adjective
$\frac{1}{3}$	ein (das) Drittel	ein drittel
$\frac{1}{4}$	ein (das) Viertel	ein viertel
$\frac{1}{5}$	ein (das) Fünftel	ein fünftel
$\frac{3}{4}$	drei Viertel	dreiviertel
$\frac{5}{6}$	fünf Sechstel	fünf sechstel
$10\frac{1}{3}$		zehn eindrittel

Ein Viertel **der Klasse ist abwesend.**   *One-quarter of the class is absent.*

Er hat *ein Drittel* **des Kuchens**   *He ate one-third of the cake.*
   gegessen.

Ich habe *drei Viertel* **des Schatzes.**   *I have three-quarters of the treasure.*

Wir brauchen *ein viertel* **Pfund Butter.**   *We need one-quarter pound of butter.*

Es wiegt *dreiviertel* **Pfund.**   *It weighs three-quarter pounds.*

Wir müssen noch *fünf einzehntel*   *We still have to walk five and*
   Kilometer gehen.   *one-tenth kilometers.*

Forms of "Half"

The fraction ½ has the following forms in German, depending on how it is used.

Fraction	Noun	Adjective
$\frac{1}{2}$	**die (eine) Hälfte**	**halb**

The adjectival form **halb** requires adjective endings.

Er hat *eine halbe* **Stunde gewartet.**	*He waited for a half-hour.*
Ich trinke nur *ein halbes* **Glas.**	*I only drink half a glass.*
Sie gibt dir *eine Hälfte.*	*She is giving you one-half.*

Special forms of $1\frac{1}{2}$

The fraction $1\frac{1}{2}$ can be written the following ways:

eineinhalb **Pfund**
anderthalb **Kilo**
ein und ein halbes **Gramm**

3. Write the German for the following.

1. Who has my half?
2. $\frac{3}{4}$ pound
3. $\frac{1}{2}$ glass
4. $\frac{1}{3}$ of the work
5. $2\frac{1}{4}$ hours
6. $\frac{5}{8}$ of the population
7. $1\frac{1}{2}$ pounds
8. $\frac{1}{20}$
9. $\frac{1}{4}$ of the bread
10. $\frac{1}{2}$ pound

DATES

Days of the Week

The days of the week are always masculine. They are as follows.

der Montag	*Monday*
der Dienstag	*Tuesday*
der Mittwoch	*Wednesday*
der Donnerstag	*Thursday*
der Freitag	*Friday*
der Samstag or **Sonnabend**	*Saturday*
der Sonntag	*Sunday*

The contraction **am**

In German time expressions, the contraction **am (an dem)** is used with the names of the days. **Am** corresponds to the English *on*. The contraction **am** precedes the name of the day, unless a particular day is to be emphasized. In that case, **an dem** (*on that*) is used.

Am **Sonntag haben wir keine Schule.**	*We don't have school on Sunday.*
Er kommt *am* **Dienstag.**	*He arrives on Tuesday.*
Sie war *an dem* **Montag hier.**	*She was here on that Monday.*

Months

All months are masculine in gender. They are as follows.

der Januar	*January*	**der Juli**	*July*
der Februar	*February*	**der August**	*August*
der März	*March*	**der September**	*September*
der April	*April*	**der Oktober**	*October*
der Mai	*May*	**der November**	*November*
der Juni	*June*	**der Dezember**	*December*

Seasons

All seasons are masculine. They are as follows.

der Frühling	*spring*	**der Herbst**	*fall*
der Sommer	*summer*	**der Winter**	*winter*

The contraction **im**

In German time expressions, the contraction **im (in dem)** precedes the name of the month or the season, corresponding to the English *in*. When referring to a particular month or season, **in dem** (*in that*) is used.

Ich habe *im Juli* **Geburtstag.**	*My birthday is in July.*
Im **August haben wir Sommerferien.**	*We have our summer vacation in August.*
Im **Winter ist es sehr kalt.**	*It is very cold in winter.*
Er kam *in dem* **Herbst.**	*He came (in) that fall.*

4. Write the German for the following.

1. on Wednesday	7. on that Thursday	12. in summer
2. in fall	8. on Friday	13. in July
3. in August	9. in spring	14. in that September
4. on Tuesday	10. on Monday	15. on that Monday
5. in winter	11. on Saturday	16. on Sunday
6. in May		

Days of the Month and Year

The definite article is used with dates in German. A period following the date indicates that the number is an ordinal number. Note that ordinal numbers take adjective endings.

Welches Datum haben wir heute?	*What is today's date?*
Der wievielte ist heute?	*What is today's date?*
Heute ist *der 1. (erste)* **Mai 1996.**	*Today is May 1, 1996.*
Den wievielten haben wir heute?	*What is today's date?*
Heute haben wir *den 5. (fünften)* **Juni 1997.**	*Today is June 5, 1997.*
Wann hast du Geburtstag?	*When is your birthday?*
Ich habe *am 4. (vierten)* **Juli Geburtstag.**	*My birthday is July 4.*
Wann kommst du an?	*When are you arriving?*
Ich komme *am 6. (sechsten)* **März an.**	*I'll arrive March 6.*
Ich komme *am Montag, den 10. (zehnten)* **August an.**	*I'll arrive on Monday, August 10.*

Omission of in

The preposition **in** is not expressed in German when referring to a certain year, unless the numeral is preceded by the word **Jahr(e)** (*year*). In that case, the dative contraction **im** precedes **Jahr(e).**

Der Krieg war *1918* **vorbei.**	*The war was over in 1918.*
Er schrieb es *im Jahre* **1935.**	*He wrote it in the year 1935.*

Dating a Letter

Dates in the headings of letters, notes, etc., are preceded by the accusative form of the masculine definite article, **den.** In German the name of the place of origin of the writing may precede the date.

München, *den 14. (vierzehnten) Juni 1996*	*June 14, 1996*
Bonn, *den 20. November 1996.*	*November 20, 1996*

Reversal of Numbers

In German, unlike in English, the first number in a date refers to the day, the second to the month. This is easy to remember since the German pattern progresses from the smallest unit of time to the largest.

Köln, *den 9.3.1998.*	*3/9/1998.*
Sie starb am *22.12.1994.*	*She died 12/22/1994.*
Wir kommen am *13.8.1996 an.*	*We'll arrive 8/13/1996.*

5.   Write the German for the following.

1. His birthday is January 20.
2. Today is October 13, 1996.
3. I'll arrive Friday, March 9.
4. He died in 1970.
5. My birthday is December 10.
6. In the year 1980.
7. 5/30/1998.
8. Her birthday is August 10.
9. I'll arrive February 2.
10. Today is March 3, 1996.
11. He died in 1975.

TIME

The following expressions answer the questions: **Wieviel Uhr ist es?** or **Wie spät ist es?** (*What time is it?*)

Conversational German

1:00	**Es ist eins (ein Uhr).**	1.00
3:00	**Es ist drei Uhr (nachmittags, nachts).**	3.00
3:05	**Es ist fünf (Minuten) nach drei.**	3.05
3:15	**Es ist (ein) Viertel nach drei.**	3.15
3:20	**Es ist zwanzig (Minuten) nach drei.**	3.20
	Es ist zehn vor halb vier.	
3:25	**Es ist fünfundzwanzig (Minuten) nach drei.**	3.25
	Es ist fünf vor halb vier.	
3:30	**Es ist halb vier.**	3.30
3:35	**Es ist fünf nach halb vier.**	3.35
3:45	**Es ist (ein) Viertel vor vier.**	3.45
	Es ist drei Viertel vier.	
3:50	**Es ist zehn (Minuten) vor vier.**	3.50
12:00 (noon)	**Es ist zwölf Uhr (mittags).**	12.00
12:00 (midnight)	**Es ist zwölf Uhr (mitternachts).**	12.00
9:00	**Es ist neun Uhr (vormittags, abends).**	9.00

Note: German uses a period instead of a colon between hours and minutes.

In colloquial speech, the words **Uhr** and **Minuten** do not have to be expressed: **Es ist eins (zwei, sechs, neun).** Note that the **-s** of **eins** is dropped when **Uhr** is expressed: **Es ist ein Uhr.** In colloquial speech, adverbs of time are used to clarify a.m. and p.m. when necessary.

Der Zug kommt *um zwei Uhr* (*nachts, nachmittags*) **an.**
Er kommt um *6 Uhr* (*morgens, abends*).

The half hour is expressed by **halb** plus the next hour.

Es ist *halb zehn.*   *It is 9:30.*

Fifteen minutes before the hour are expressed by **drei Viertel** or **ein Viertel vor** plus the next hour.

Es ist *drei Viertel zehn.*   *It is 9:45.*
Es ist *ein Viertel vor zehn.*   *It is 9:45.*

Twenty and twenty-five minutes before or after the hour can be expressed by referring to 10 (5) minutes before or after the half-hour:

Es ist *fünf vor halb acht.*   *It is 7:25.*
Es ist *zehn nach halb sechs.*   *It is 5:40.*

6.   Write the German.

1. It is 8:00 p.m.
2. It is 10:30 a.m.
3. It is 5:15.
4. It is 7:35.
5. It is 6:25.
6. It is 4:45.
7. It is 11:20.
8. It is 3:10.
9. It is 1:00 p.m.
10. It is 12:00 noon.

Official Time

Official time in Germany is based on the 24-hour system. The word **Uhr** is always expressed. However, **Minuten** is omitted. Official time is used at railroad stations, at airports, and in public media.

Midnight	**vierundzwanzig Uhr**	**24.00**
12:20 a.m.	**null Uhr zwanzig**	**0.20**
1:00 a.m.	**ein Uhr**	**1.00**
3:30 a.m.	**drei Uhr dreißig**	**3.30**
11:15 a.m.	**elf Uhr fünfzehn**	**11.15**
12:20 p.m.	**zwölf Uhr zwanzig**	**12.20**
1:00 p.m.	**dreizehn Uhr**	**13.00**
2:40 p.m.	**vierzehn Uhr vierzig**	**14.40**
8:00 p.m.	**zwanzig Uhr**	**20.00**

7. Write the German, expressing the times officially.

1. It is 8:30 p.m.
2. 1:00 p.m.
3. 1:00 a.m.
4. Midnight
5. 12:35 a.m.

6. 9:25 p.m.
7. 12:40 p.m.
8. 10:45 a.m.
9. 2:00 p.m.
10. 11:00 p.m.

The Use of um ... Uhr

The idiom *um* **. . . Uhr** corresponds to the English *at . . . o'clock.*

Um wieviel Uhr **bist du dort?**   *At what time will you be there?*
Ich bin *um 10 Uhr* **dort.**   *I will be there at 10 o'clock.*

8. Write the German, expressing the times colloquially.

1. At 5 o'clock.
2. At 2 o'clock.
3. At 3:30.

4. At 7 o'clock.
5. At 11:00.

Periods of the Day

The periods of the day are preceded by the contraction **am,** corresponding to the English *in* or *at.*

am Morgen	*in the morning*
am Vormittag	*in the morning*
am Mittag	*at noon*
am Nachmittag	*in the afternoon*
am Abend	*in the evening*
But: **in der Nacht**	*at night*

ich gehe *am Nachmittag* **gern spazieren.**   *I like to take a walk in the afternoon.*
Wir besuchen dich *am Abend*.   *We'll visit you in the evening.*
Wo bist du *in der* **Nacht?**   *Where are you at night?*

9. Complete the following with the appropriate German phrases.

1. Er kommt _____ _____ . *in the morning*
2. _____ _____ trinken wir Tee. *in the afternoon.*
3. _____ _____ _____ schlafen wir. *at night*
4. Wir treffen ihn _____ _____ . *at noon*
5. Ich mache es _____ _____ . *in the evening*

Customary Action

When the adverb of time denotes customary or habitual action, the days of the week and the periods of the day add **-s** and are not capitalized.

Wir gehen *dienstags* **zum Kegeln.** *We go bowling on Tuesdays.*
Ich bin *vormittags* **zu Hause.** *I am home in the mornings.*

10. Express habitual action. Follow the model.

Kommst du am Montag an?
Ja, ich komme immer montags an.

1. Bist du am Abend hier?
2. Hast du am Sonntag Zeit?
3. Gehst du am Mittwoch mit?
4. Schreibst du am Nachmittag?
5. Fährst du am Morgen zur Schule?

Other Adverbs of Time

The following adverbs of time are not capitalized when used singly or in combination.

heute *today*
morgen *tomorrow*
übermorgen *the day after tomorrow*
gestern *yesterday*
vorgestern *the day before yesterday*
heute morgen *this morning*
gestern abend *last night*
morgen nachmittag *tomorrow afternoon*

Wir haben *gestern nachmittag* **Tennis gepielt.** *We played tennis yesterday afternoon.*

11. Write the German.

1. He is coming tomorrow evening.
2. He was home yesterday afternoon.
3. Otto, did you sleep last night?
4. They are coming the day after tomorrow.
5. She departed this morning.
6. He is coming tomorrow afternoon.

Time Expressions in the Accusative Case

Time expressions referring to a definite time or a duration of time require the accusative case.

Ich gehe *jeden Tag* **zur Arbeit.** *I go to work every day.*
Letzten Sommer **war ich in Spanien.** *I was in Spain last summer.*
Diesen Monat **ist er zu Hause.** *He is home this month.*
Wir bleiben *ein ganzes Jahr.* *We'll stay one entire year.*

12. Complete with the appropriate endings.

1. Ich bleibe ein_____ Tag dort.
2. Letzt_____ Herbst war ich in Deutschland.
3. Dies_____ Woche bleibe ich dort.
4. Er arbeitet d_____ ganz_____ Abend.
5. Er trinkt jed_____ Stunde Kaffee.
6. Wir singen ein_____ ganz_____ Stunde lang.

Time Expressions in the Dative Case

Time expressions using the prepositions **an, in, vor** require the dative case. The prepositions **an** and **in** are usually contracted to **am** and **im** when they precede the names of days, months, seasons, and periods of the day, unless a certain day, month, etc., is to be emphasized. *Ago* is expressed by the preposition **vor.** Unlike in English, the preposition **vor** (*ago*) precedes the time expression.

Wir gehen *am Morgen.*	*We are going in the morning.*
Warst du *an jenem Abend* **dort?**	*Were you there on that evening?*
Sie fahren *am Montag* **ab.**	*They'll leave on Monday.*
Im Sommer **gehen wir schwimmen.**	*We go swimming in the summer.*
Er hat *im Dezember* **Geburtsag.**	*His birthday is in December.*
Sie kommt heute *in vierzehn Tagen.*	*She'll come two weeks from today.*
In acht Tagen **bist du wieder gesund.**	*You'll be well again in one week.*
Er war *vor einer Woche* **in Afrika.**	*A week ago he was in Africa.*
Sie war *vor acht Tagen* **hier.**	*She was here eight days ago.*

13. Complete the following with the appropriate endings.

1. Er war vor ein_____ Woche in Kanada.
2. Er war an jen_____ Tag krank.
3. Ich war vor ein_____ Jahr dort.
4. Ich erwarte sie in acht Tag_____ .
5. Wir haben euch an jen_____ Abend gesehen.
6. Wo war er in jen_____ Nacht?
7. Sie besuchte uns vor vierzehn Tag_____ .
8. Wir spielten an jen_____ Samstag Golf.
9. Sie schrieb es vor ein_____ Jahr.
10. Sie heirateten in jen_____ Mai.

Time Expressions in the Genitive Case

Expressions of indefinite time require the genitive case in German. In English *someday* (night, morning, etc.) is used to refer to future time, and *one day* (night, etc.) is used for past time.

Eines Tages **erzählte sie die Geschichte.**	*One day she told the story.*
Ich zeige es dir *eines Tages.*	*I'll show it to you someday.*
Eines Abends **brachte er das Auto.**	*He brought the car one evening.*

By way of analogy, the feminine noun **Nacht** also adds **-s** in such indefinite time expressions.

Ich traf ihn *eines Nachts* **im Park.**	*I met him in the park one night.*

14. Complete the following with the appropriate German expressions.

   1. Ich werde dich _____ _____ besuchen. *someday*
   2. Sie wird _____ _____ mitgehen. *some night*
   3. Er brachte es _____ _____ . *one evening*
   4. Ich besuchte sie _____ _____ . *one afternoon*
   5. Sie wird es _____ _____ lesen. *one morning*

Review

15. Complete the following with the appropriate endings, prepositions, or time expressions.

   1. Wir fahren jed_____ Winter nach Italien.
   2. Ein_____ Abend_____ wurde er krank.
   3. Der Lehrer kommt _____ acht Uhr.
   4. Ich bleibe (*this evening*) _____ _____ zu Hause.
   5. Ich gehe _____ Sommer gerne baden.
   6. Warum arbeitest du d_____ ganz_____ Nacht?
   7. Ich kaufe es _____ Dienstag.
   8. Er besucht uns nächst_____ Jahr.
   9. (*At night*) _____ _____ _____ scheint der Mond.
  10. (*Tomorrow afternoon*) _____ _____ fliege ich ab.
  11. Kommen Sie doch heute _____ _____ _____ ! (*in one month*)
  12. _____ wieviel Uhr essen wir?
  13. (*In the morning*) _____ _____ war ich in der Schule.
  14. Er war _____ _____ _____ (*a week ago*) in der Schweiz.
  15. Ich gehe _____ (*Sundays*) nicht zur Arbeit.
  16. Du bist ja _____ _____ (*at noon*) im Büro!
  17. (*In two weeks*) _____ _____ _____ haben wir Ferien.
  18. Wir kaufen _____ _____ (*someday*) ein Auto.
  19. Ich warte schon ein_____ ganz_____ Stunde auf dich.
  20. Sie war (*this morning*) _____ _____ in der Stadt.

Chapter 7

Verbs

VERB OVERVIEW

In German, as in English, verbs are words that express an action, a process, or a state of being, for example, *to read, to redden, to become.*

Transitive and Intransitive Verbs

Also, as in English, in German verbs are divided into two basic grammatical categories—*transitive verbs* and *intransitive verbs.* A transitive verb is a verb that requires a direct object. Take, for example, the verb *to describe. He describes* is an incomplete statement; it is necessary to specify *what* he describes. An intransitive verb is one that does not require a direct object. An example of an intransitive verb is *to live.* The utterance *he lives* can by itself be a complete sentence and thus can stand alone. Some verbs may be used either as transitive verbs or as intransitive verbs, e.g., *he whistled as he worked* and *he whistled a tune.*

Personal Endings

However, unlike most English verb forms, German verbs normally take *personal endings*, which indicate both the person and the number of the subject of that verb. German, like English, distinguishes between the *first person*, the *second person*, and the *third person*. Moreover, each person can be either singular or plural. The present tense personal endings are introduced on p. 139, and the past tense personal endings are found on pp. 148 and 150.

Certain forms of the verb, such as the infinitive, the present participle, and the past participle, do not take personal endings. However, if the participles are used as adjectives, they take adjective endings (see Chapter 5).

Forms of Address: Formal versus Informal

There are three ways to express the pronoun *you* in German—the familiar singular **du,** the familiar plural **ihr,** and the formal **Sie.** The **du** form is used when addressing a close friend, relative, child, animal, or God. The familiar plural **ihr** is used to address two or more friends, relatives, children, animals, or deities. When addressing an acquaintance or a stranger, or persons whom one would address with **Herr** or **Frau,** the formal pronoun **Sie** is used. **Sie** is used for both the formal singular and the formal plural and is always capitalized. There is a distinctive personal ending for the verb for each form of address (see Chapter 4).

Verb Tenses

In German, as in other languages, verbs have *tense*; that is, different forms of the verb indicate the time when the action of the verb takes place, e.g. present, past, or future tense. Tense can be indicated by the personal ending on the verb as well as by the choice of the auxilliary, or helping verb used to form the compound tenses.

Strong Verbs and Weak Verbs

There are two basic types of verbs in German—*strong verbs* and *weak verbs.* Weak verbs keep the same stem vowel throughout all their forms, and strong verbs have stem vowel changes in their past tenses. As a *general* rule, the weak verbs have regular and predictable forms, whereas the strong verbs are irregular. Since, however, there are irregular weak verbs and certain predictable patterns for the strong verbs, we will not use the terms regular and irregular verbs, but will instead refer to verbs as *weak, strong,* or *mixed.*

> Since the patterns for the strong verbs and the irregular weak verbs are not fully
> predictable, it is essential to learn all the principal parts of such verbs when they
> are first introduced.

The three principal parts of a verb that must be learned are the *infinitive,* the *past tense,* and the *past participle.* In some cases a fourth form of the German verb must also be memorized—the second or third person singular of the present tense, since a small group of strong verbs also have vowel changes in these forms. (The most common strong and mixed German verbs are summarized in the Verb Chart on pp. 285–286.)

Speakers of English are already familiar with the phenomenon that some verbs have no vowel changes in their various forms while others do. Compare, for example, regular verbs such as *play, played, played* or *paint, painted, painted* with irregular verbs such as *sing, sang, sung* or *think, thought, thought.*

Study the principal parts of strong and weak verbs as illustrated by the verbs **spielen** (*to play*) and **singen** (*to sing*).

Weak Verb	
Infinitive	**spielen**
Past tense	**spielte**
Past participle	**gespielt**

Strong Verb	
Infinitive	**singen**
Past tense	**sang**
Past participle	**gesungen**

SIMPLE PRESENT TENSE

Weak and Strong Verbs

The simple present tense of both the weak and the strong verbs is formed by adding the personal endings for the present tense to the infinitive stem.

> *Simple Present = Infinitive Stem + Present Tense Personal Ending*

In German the infinitive is the dictionary form of the verb. Typically the infinitive ends in **-en.** A few end in **-eln, -ern, -n.** The *infinitive stem* is derived by dropping the **-en** or **-n** from the infinitive.

Infinitive	Infinitive Stem
denken	**denk-**
singen	**sing-**
handeln	**handel-**
wandern	**wander-**
tun	**tu-**

The present tense personal endings that must be added to the infinitive stem are:

	Singular	Plural
First person	-e	-en
Second person	-st	-t
Third person	-t	-en

Thus the fully conjugated present tense of **denken** is:

ich denke	wir denken
du denkst	ihr denkt
er	
sie }denkt	sie denken
es	
	Sie denken

Note: Since the same personal ending is used for **er, sie,** and **es,** all conjugations presented in this book will list only **er** (third person singular masculine). Similarly, **Sie** (the form for "you" formal) will not be listed separately since it takes the same personal ending as **sie** (they).

Note on personal endings

In informal conversational German the **-e** ending of the first person is often dropped.

Ich tu' das nie.	*I never do that.*
Ich glaub' nicht.	*I don't think so*
Ich geh' nach Hause.	*I'm going home.*

Note: There is only one present tense form in German. Thus the three forms of the present tense in English, *I think, I do think,* and *I am thinking,* are all translated with **ich denke.**

Below are some examples of present tense verbs used in sentences.

Wir *kaufen* **einen Wagen.**	*We are buying a car.*
Er *singt* **zu laut.**	*He is singing too loudly.*
Ich *kenne* **den Mann.**	*I know the man.*
Sagst **du die Wahrheit?**	*Are you telling the truth?*
Sie *studieren* **Englisch.**	*They study English.*
Trinkt **ihr nichts?**	*Aren't you drinking anything?*
Suchen **Sie den Hund?**	*Are you looking for the dog?*

The following is a list of a number of weak and strong verbs whose infinitives end in **-en.** They form their present tense according to the pattern just described. Note that the weak verbs ending in **-ieren** also belong to this group.

bauen	*to build*	**brennen**	*to burn*
beginnen	*to begin*	**bringen**	*to bring*
bellen	*to bark*	**buchstabieren**	*to spell*
besichtigen	*to view*	**danken**	*to thank*
bestellen	*to order*	**denken**	*to think*
besuchen	*to visit*	**drehen**	*to turn*
bezahlen	*to pay*	**empfangen**	*to receive*
bleiben	*to stay*	**empfehlen**	*to recommend*
brauchen	*to need*	**entdecken**	*to discover*

erklären	to explain	rufen	to call
erzählen	to tell	sagen	to say, tell
fliegen	to fly	schauen	to look
fragen	to ask	schenken	to give
gehen	to go, walk	schicken	to send
gehören	to belong to	schreiben	to write
glauben	to believe	schreien	to scream
holen	to get	schwimmen	to swim
hören	to hear	senden	to send
kämmen	to comb	singen	to sing
kauen	to chew	springen	to jump
kaufen	to buy	stehen	to stand
kennen	to know (be acquainted with)	steigen	to climb
klettern	to climb	stellen	to place, put
kommen	to come	stören	to disturb
leben	to live	studieren	to study
legen	to place, lay	suchen	to look for
lernen	to learn	tanzen	to dance
lieben	to love	telefonieren	to telephone
liegen	to lie	träumen	to dream
machen	to do	trinken	to drink
malen	to paint	vergessen	to forget
nennen	to call, name	verkaufen	to sell
operieren	to operate	wandern	to wander, hike
parken	to park	weinen	to cry
probieren	to try	wissen	to know (a fact)
rauchen	to smoke	wohnen	to live
reisen	to travel	zahlen	to pay
rennen	to run	zählen	to count
reparieren	to repair	zeigen	to show
riechen	to smell	zerstören	to destroy
		ziehen	to pull

1. Complete the following with the appropriate forms of the present tense of the indicated verbs.

1. _____ du Musik? *hören*
2. Wir _____ nichts. *trinken*
3. Wann _____ er? *kommen*
4. Ich _____ etwas. *schicken*
5. Die Sängerin _____. *singen*
6. Die Fabrik _____. *brennen*
7. Ich _____ nach Amerika. *fliegen*
8. Dieser Hund _____. *bellen*
9. Das Baby _____ hier. *bleiben*
10. _____ du an sie? *denken*
11. Warum _____ ihr? *weinen*
12. Die Touristen _____ vor der Kirche. *stehen*
13. Wann _____ die Vorstellung? *beginnen*
14. Man _____ Bier. *bringen*
15. Ich _____ schnell. *rennen*
16. Peter _____ das Auto. *parken*
17. Warum _____ ihr so? *schreien*
18. _____ Sie schon wieder? *rauchen*
19. _____ ihr seine Schwester? *kennen*
20. _____ du Richard? *lieben*
21. Pia _____ immer. *studierern*
22. Seine Eltern _____ Ihn. *besuchen*
23. Wann _____ ihr das Buch? *holen*
24. Der Sportler _____ hoch. *springen*
25. Man _____ uns. *rufen*
26. Es _____ scharf. *riechen*
27. Wir _____ den Brief. *schreiben*
28. _____ ihr aufs Dach? *steigen*
29. Man _____ ihm. *glauben*
30. Ich _____ die Suppe. *probieren*
31. Das Kind _____ nicht. *telefonieren*
32. Ich _____ etwas. *hören*

33. Die Kinder _____ nichts. *brauchen*   35. Wir _____ es. *holen*
34. Wo _____ er? *wohnen*   36. Die Leute _____ nach Hause. *gehen*

Variations in Personal Endings

Additional e

When the infinitive stem ends in **-d, -t, -m, -n** preceded by a consonant other than **-l, -r**, the endings in the second and third person singular and the second person plural are expanded by adding an **-e** before the personal endings. The pattern for the personal endings of such verbs is:

	Singular	*Plural*
First person	-e	-en
Second person	-est	-et
Third person	-et	-en

Thus the fully conjugated present tense for **arbeiten** is:

ich arbeite	**wir arbeiten**
du arbeitest	**ihr arbeitet**
er arbeitet	**sie arbeiten**

Sie *badet* **das Kind.**	*She is bathing the child.*
Er *blutet* **sehr stark.**	*He is bleeding severely.*
Ordnest **du die Karten?**	*Are you putting the cards in order?*
Er *atmet* **langsam.**	*He is breathing slowly.*
Zeichnet **ihr oft?**	*Do you draw often?*
Warum *öffnest* **du die Tür?**	*Why are you opening the door?*
Sie *begegnet* **Peter.**	*She meets Peter.*

The following verbs receive this additional **e.**

antworten	*to answer*	**ordnen**	*to put in order*
arbeiten	*to work*	**rechnen**	*to figure* (arithmetic)
atmen	*to breathe*	**reden**	*to talk*
baden	*to bathe*	**reiten**	*to ride*
begegnen	*to meet*	**retten**	*to save*
beobachten	*to observe*	**schneiden**	*to cut*
bitten	*to ask for*	**senden**	*to send*
bluten	*to bleed*	**warten**	*to wait*
finden	*to find*	**wenden**	*to turn*
öffnen	*to open*	**zeichnen**	*to draw*

2. Complete the following with the appropriate forms of the present tense of the indicated verbs.

1. Cornelia _____ auf den Bus. *warten*
2. _____ du in das Brot? *schneiden*
3. Man _____ auch sonntags hier. *arbeiten*
4. Worum _____ du? *bitten*

5. _____ du Inge oft? *begegnen*
6. Ute _____ gut. *reiten*
7. _____ ihr alles? *finden*
8. _____ ihr gerne? *rechnen*
9. Du _____ zu viel. *reden*
10. Warum _____ ihr die Katze nicht? *retten*
11. Er _____ das Fenster. *öffen*
12. _____ der Spion das Haus? *beobachten*
13. Warum _____ du so schnell? *atmen*
14. Er _____ die Briefmarken. *ordnen*
15. Es _____ stark. *bluten*
16. _____ du alles? *senden*
17. Warum _____ du nicht? *antworten*
18. Paula _____ das Blatt. *wenden*
19. _____ du? *arbeiten*
20. _____ du das Baby? *baden*

No additional s sound

When the stem of the infinitive ends in **-s, -ß, -x, -z**, the personal ending for the second person singular is **-t** (rather than **-st**). No additional **s** sound is required. Thus the forms of the second and third person singular are identical. All other endings are regular.

Warum *haßt* **du ihn?**	*Why do you hate him?*
Tanzt **du gern?**	*Do you like to dance?*

The following verbs belong to this group.

beißen	*to bite*	**reisen**	*to travel*
grüßen	*to greet*	**setzen**	*to set, place*
hassen	*to hate*	**sitzen**	*to sit*
heißen	*to be called*	**tanzen**	*to dance*
mixen	*to mix*		

3. Form sentences from the following, using the present tense of the verbs.

1. Wie / heißen / du?
2. Was / mixen / du?
3. Du / tanzen / gut
4. Warum / grüßen / du / mich / nicht?
5. Wohin / reisen / du?
6. Was / hassen / du?
7. Wo / sitzen / du?
8. Beißen / du / in den Apfel?

Infinitives ending in -eln, -ern

When the infinitive ends in **-eln,** the **e** preceding the **-ln** is dropped in the first person singular. All other forms retain the **e.**

Ich *klingle.*	*I am ringing. I ring.*

When the infinitive ends in **-eln** or **-ern** the ending in the first and third person plural is **-n.** Thus these forms are identical to the infinitive.

Wir *füttern* **den Hund.**	*We are feeding the dog.*
Sie *klettern* **auf den Baum.**	*They are climbing the tree.*

ich klingle	wir klingeln
du klingelst	ihr klingelt
er klingelt	sie klingeln

ich füttere	wir füttern
du fütterst	ihr füttert
er füttert	sie füttern

The following infinitives end in **-eln** or **-ern.**

behandeln	*to treat*	**ändern**	*to change*
klingeln	*to ring*	**bewundern**	*to admire*
lächeln	*to smile*	**füttern**	*to feed*
sammeln	*to collect*	**klettern**	*to climb*
		wandern	*to hike*

4. Complete the following with the appropriate forms of the present tense.

1. Das Kind _____ auf den Tisch.   *klettern*
2. Wohin _____ wir? *wandern*
3. Ich _____ seine Courage.   *bewundern*
4. Man _____ Sie sofort.   *behandeln*
5. Wann _____ du die Katze? *füttern*
6. Wir _____ nichts.   *ändern*
7. Ich _____ doch nicht.   *lächeln*
8. Die Ärzte _____ sie schon.   *behandeln*
9. Das Telefon _____ .   *klingeln*
10. Wir _____ alles.   *sammeln*
11. Ich _____ den Patienten.   *behandeln*
12. Die Kinder _____ den Hund.   *füttern*
13. Ich _____ nichts.   *sammeln*
14. Wir _____ auf den Berg.   *klettern*

Stem Vowel Changes in Strong Verbs in the Present Tense

Many German strong verbs have a vowel change in the stem of the present tense in the second and third person singular. Most strong verbs containing **a, au, e** undergo this vowel change. They can be grouped according to the changes that take place.

Changes from **a, au** *to* **ä, äu**

Verbs with the stem vowels **a** and **au** change to **ä** and **äu** respectively, in the second and third person singular.

ich fahre	wir fahren
du fährst	ihr fahrt
er fährt	sie fahren

ich laufe	wir laufen
du läufst	ihr lauft
er läuft	sie laufen

The following verbs follow the same pattern as **fahren.**

backen	*to bake*	**lassen**	*to allow, let*
blasen	*to blow*	**schlafen**	*to sleep*
empfangen	*to receive*	**schlagen**	*to hit, beat*
fallen	*to fall*	**tragen**	*to wear, carry*
fangen	*to catch*	**wachsen**	*to grow*
graben	*to dig*	**waschen**	*to wash*
halten	*to hold, stop*		

The following verbs change **au** to **äu**.

laufen   *to run*
saufen   *to drink* (of animals, people in excess)

5.   Rewrite the following, changing the plural to the singular.

1. Schlaft ihr die ganze Nacht?
2. Sie wachsen schnell.
3. Wascht ihr die Wäsche?
4. Wir halten die Ballons.
5. Was tragen sie zum Ball?
6. Laßt ihr mich gehen?
7. Wir backen Brot.
8. Warum graben sie ein Loch?

9. Sie schlagen das Kind.
10. Die Tiere saufen Wasser.
11. Sie blasen ins Feuer.
12. Wohin lauft ihr?
13. Sie fallen.
14. Fangt ihr den Ball?
15. Wir schlafen schon.
16. Was tragt ihr?

Changes from **e** *to* **i, ie**

Most strong verbs with an **e** in the infinitive stem change their stem vowels to **i** or **ie** in the second and third person singular. Study the following forms:

ich breche	**wir brechen**		**ich lese**	**wir lesen**
du brichst	**ihr brecht**		**du liest**	**ihr lest**
er bricht	**sie brechen**		**er liest**	**sie lesen**

The following verbs follow the same pattern as **brechen**.

erschrecken	*to frighten*		**sprechen**	*to speak, talk*
essen	*to eat*		**stechen**	*to sting*
fressen	*to eat* (of animals, people in excess)		**sterben**	*to die*
			treffen	*to meet*
geben	*to give*		**vergessen**	*to forget*
helfen	*to help*		**werfen**	*to throw*

The following verbs follow the same pattern as **lesen**.

empfehlen	*to recommend*		**sehen**	*to see*
geschehen	*to happen*		**stehlen**	*to steal*

Important exceptions

gehen and stehen

Although **gehen** and **stehen** are strong verbs containing **e** in their stems, they do not have the changes in the present tense described above (**du gehst, er geht; du stehst, er steht**).

nehmen

Note that the verb **nehmen** (*to take*) has an irregular spelling pattern. Study the following forms:

ich nehme	**wir nehmen**
du nimmst	**ihr nehmt**
er nimmt	**sie nehmen**

6. Rewrite the following, changing the plural to the singular.

1. Helft ihr mir?
2. Sie sterben bald.
3. Seht ihr uns?
4. Wir essen Suppe.
5. Die Hunde fressen.
6. Was gebt ihr ihm?
7. Wir sprechen gern.
8. Sie sehen uns.
9. Sie stehen beim Haus.
10. Geht ihr auch?
11. Was nehmt ihr?
12. Wann trefft ihr uns?
13. Was lesen sie?
14. Warum erschreckt ihr?
15. Was brechen sie?
16. Was stehlt ihr?
17. Was werfen sie?
18. Warum helfen sie nicht?
19. Was vergessen sie?
20. Empfehlt ihr dieses Hotel?

Irregular Verbs

The present tense of **sein** (*to be*), **haben** (*to have*), **werden** (*to get, become*), **wissen** (*to know*), and **tun** (*to do*) is irregular. Study the following:

sein	haben	werden	wissen	tun
ich bin	ich habe	ich werde	ich weiß	ich tue
du bist	du hast	du wirst	du weißt	du tust
er ist	er hat	er wird	er weiß	er tut
wir sind	wir haben	wir werden	wir wissen	wir tun
ihr seid	ihr habt	ihr werdet	ihr wißt	ihr tut
sie sind	sie haben	sie werden	sie wissen	sie tun

7. Complete the following with the correct forms of the present tense of **sein.**

1. Ich _____ zwanzig Jahre alt.
2. Er _____ in Afrika.
3. Wir _____ jetzt in der Schule.
4. Die Kinder _____ hungrig.
5. Ihr _____ freundlich.
6. _____ Sie auch Schauspielerin?
7. Meine Tante _____ leider krank.
8. _____ du denn glücklich?

8. Complete the following with the present tense of **haben.**

1. Meine Eltern _____ kein Auto.
2. Ich _____ keine Angst.
3. _____ du Kopfweh?
4. Die Studenten _____ jetzt Ferien.
5. _____ ihr Durst?
6. Er _____ ja Geld.
7. Wir _____ Besuch.
8. Wann _____ du denn Zeit?

9. Complete the following. Supply the correct forms of the present tense of **werden.** Follow the model.

Wir werden schon wieder gesund.

1. Ich ...
2. Ihr ...
3. Du ...
4. Barbara ...
5. Frau Sommer, Sie ...
6. Die Kinder ...
7. Er ...
8. Wir ...

10. Complete the following with the appropriate forms of **wissen.**

1. Wir _____ ja die Antwort.
2. Die Mädchen _____ es nicht.
3. _____ ihr es?
4. Ich _____, daß er hier ist.
5. Man _____ es schon.
6. _____ du es vielleicht?
7. Er _____ alles.
8. Die Leute _____ es.

11. Supply the correct forms of the present tense of **tun.**

1. Was _____ du?
2. Ich _____ immer alles.
3. Wir _____ nichts.
4. Er _____ viel.
5. _____ ihr etwas?
6. _____ Sie nichts?
7. Peter und Sonja _____ wenig.
8. Brigitte _____ etwas.

Special Use of Present Tense

Future meaning

As in English, the present tense in German can be used to indicate that an event will take place in the future. The future meaning is conveyed by the context or by an adverbial expression indicating future time.

Ich *gehe* **morgen in die Stadt.**   *I am going downtown tomorrow.*
***Fährst* du nächste Woche nach Boston?**   *Are you driving to Boston next week?*

12. Answer the following questions affirmatively. Write complete sentences, using the present tense.

1. Kommst du morgen?
2. Hat er übermorgen Geburtstag?
3. Geht ihr morgen abend ins Theater?
4. Fliegen Sie im Juli nach Frankfurt?
5. Fährst du nächstes Jahr nach Regensburg?
6. Besuchst du mich heute in acht Tagen?
7. Sind Sie nächsten Monat in Deutschland?
8. Bist du morgen abend zu Hause?
9. Habt ihr nächste Woche Zeit?
10. Spielt sie nächsten Samstag Golf?

Continued action

The present tense is used in German to express the fact that an action has been started in the past and continues into the present. In English one of the past tenses is used to express continued action. In German the time element is usually introduced by **schon** or **seit,** corresponding to the English *for.*

Ich *wohne schon* **zwei Monate hier.**   *I have been living here for two months.*
Er *ist seit* **einer Woche in Paris.**   *He has been in Paris for one week.*

13. Complete the following with the appropriate forms of the indicated verbs.

1. Ich _____ schon seit einem Monat.   *warten*
2. Ute _____ seit zehn Jahren hier.   *wohnen*
3. Er _____ schon eine Stunde dort.   *sein*

4. Wir _____ schon den ganzen Tag.   *arbeiten*
5. _____ du schon seit einer Stunde?   *singen*
6. Ich _____ Robert seit einem Jahr.   *kennen*
7. Wir _____ seit zehn Minuten hier.   *sein*
8. Der Pilot _____ schon drei Stunden.   *fliegen*
9. Es _____ schon zwei Tage.   *regnen*
10. _____ ihr schon eine Stunde?   *schreiben*

14. Answer the following questions with complete sentences, using the cues.

1. Seit wann liest du schon?   *eine Stunde*
2. Wie lange studiert er schon?   *zehn Tage*
3. Seit wann bist du hier?   *fünf Minuten*
4. Wie lange kennst du ihn schon?   *sechs Jahre*
5. Wie lange telefonierst du schon?   *zwanzig Minuten*

Review

15. Complete the following with the correct forms of the present tense of the indicated verbs.

1. Warum _____ du ein Loch?   *graben*
2. Ich _____ sofort.   *kommen*
3. Man _____ hier nicht.   *laufen*
4. Was _____ du daran?   *ändern*
5. Wir _____ die Vögel.   *füttern*
6. _____ ihr auch krank?   *sein*
7. Georg _____ Beamter.   *werden*
8. Wohin _____ du?   *reisen*
9. Hilde _____ schon den ganzen Tag.   *arbeiten*
10. _____ du die Zeitung?   *lesen*
11. Wir _____ sehr leise.   *atmen*
12. Das Tier _____.   *fressen*
13. Wohin _____ ihr?   *fahren*
14. Das Kind _____ den Ball.   *fangen*
15. Ich _____ das Auto.   *waschen*
16. Wir _____ ihn nicht.   *grüßen*
17. _____ Sie hungrig?   *sein*
18. Meine Geschwister _____ die Antwort.   *wissen*
19. Warum _____ du so lange?   *schlafen*
20. Es _____ schon wieder kalt.   *werden*
21. Helga _____ dort.   *stehen*
22. Was _____ die Studenten?   *studieren*
23. Wo _____ du?   *bluten*
24. Ich _____.   *klingeln*
25. Wie _____ du?   *heißen*
26. Was _____ er?   *essen*
27. Wann _____ du Franz das Auto?   *geben*
28. Manfred _____ seine Freundin.   *sehen*
29. Wir _____ den Kranken.   *behandeln*
30. Wo _____ du?   *sitzen*

SIMPLE PAST TENSE

In German the simple past tense (which is sometimes also referred to as the imperfect or preterit) is used to describe a completed action or a chain of events that took place in the past. This tense is generally not used in conversation, but is the customary tense used in written narratives. For this reason it is sometimes referred to as the *narrative* past. (See usage note at pp. 155–156.)

Weak Verbs

The simple past tense of the weak verbs is formed by adding the past tense marker **-te** plus the personal endings for weak verbs to the infinitive stems. Note that there are no changes in the stem vowels in the simple past tense of weak verbs.

> *Simple Past of Weak Verbs =*
> *Infinitive Stem + Past Tense Marker* **-te** *+ Weak Past Tense Personal Ending*

The full pattern for all persons is as follows:

	Singular	*Plural*
First person	**-te**-∅	**-te**-*n*
Second person	**-te**-*st*	**-te**-*t*
Third person	**-te**-∅	**-te**-*n*

Note that the first and third person singular takes no personal ending in the past tense. This no-ending pattern is represented in the chart above by the symbol "∅". The full conjugation of the simple past tense of **bestellen** is as follows:

> **ich bestellte   wir bestellten**
> **du bestelltest   ihr bestelltet**
> **sie bestellte   sie bestellten**

Study the past tense forms in the following sentences:

Wir *tanzten* **den ganzen Abend.**	*We danced the whole night.*
Ich *machte* **damals eine Reise.**	*I made a trip at that time.*
Sie *fragten* **den Lehrer.**	*They asked the teacher.*
Er *bestellte* **Schweinebraten.**	*He ordered pork roast.*

16. Rewrite the following in the simple past tense.

1. Sie spielen.
2. Er wohnt in Köln.
3. Wir glauben daran.
4. Ich studiere gern.
5. Der Hund bellt.
6. Ich bezahle die Rechnung.
7. Man gratuliert ihm.
8. Wir brauchen Milch.
9. Meine Eltern bauen es.
10. Das Telefon klingelt.

17. Complete the following with the correct simple past forms of the indicated verbs.

1. Du _____ damals ein Bild. *malen*
2. Wir _____ das Rathaus. *besichtigen*
3. Die Mädchen _____ ihn. *fragen*
4. Ich _____ ihm etwas. *schenken*
5. Wir _____ damals Französisch. *lernen*
6. Konrad _____ den Wagen. *reparieren*
7. Die Herren _____ mir den Weg. *zeigen*
8. Ihr _____ uns damals. *besuchen*
9. Unsere Eltern _____ eine Kamera. *kaufen*
10. Man _____ sie. *stören*

Variations in Personal Endings

Additional e

When the infinitive stem ends in **-d**, **-t**, or in **-m**, **-n** preceded by a consonant other than **-l**, **-r**, an additional **-e-** is inserted before the past tense personal endings. The addition of this **-e-** ensures that the tense marker will be heard clearly. The pattern for such verbs is:

	Singular	Plural
First person	*e-***te***-∅*	*e-***te***-n*
Second person	*e-***te***-st*	*e-***te***-t*
Third person	*e-***te***-∅*	*e-***te***-n*

Study the full conjugation and sentences below:

ich arbeitete	**wir arbeiteten**
du arbeitetest	**ihr arbeitetet**
er arbeitete	**sie arbeiteten**

Er *öffnete* **die Tür.**	*He opened the door.*
Wir *badeten* **das Kind.**	*We bathed the child.*
Sie *ordneten* **Briefmarken.**	*They put stamps in order.*
Ich *begegnete* **dem Mädchen.**	*I met the girl.*

18. Rewrite the following in the simple past tense.

1. Ich atme ganz regelmäßig.
2. Man tötet ihn.
3. Wir retten den Verunglückten.
4. Du öffnest die Tür.
5. Sie begegnen ihren Eltern.
6. Paul beobachtet den Vogel.
7. Ich arbeite gern.
8. Er ordnet die Bücher.
9. Sie antwortet nicht.
10. Sie bluten stark.

Irregular Weak Verbs

The following weak verbs are irregular in that they have stem vowel changes in the simple past. Study the forms below:

Infinitive	Simple Past		Infinitive	Simple Past
brennen	brannte		senden	sandte
kennen	kannte		bringen	brachte
nennen	nannte		denken	dachte
rennen	rannte		wissen	wußte

Er *brachte* **mir Blumen.**   *He brought me flowers.*
Wir *rannten* **ins Haus.**   *We ran into the house.*
Ich *kannte* **den Künstler.**   *I knew the artist.*

19. Rewrite the following in the simple past tense.

1. Er weiß das nicht.
2. Ich sende ihm einen Brief.
3. Es brennt dort.
4. Wir bringen Geschenke.
5. Sie denken daran.
6. Die Kinder rennen.
7. Man nennt es.
8. Ich kenne ihn auch.
9. Sie wissen die Antwort.
10. Du kennst uns.

Strong Verbs

In strong verbs the past tense is marked by a stem vowel change rather than the tense marker **-te** used to show the past tense in the weak verbs. The simple past tense of the strong verbs is formed by adding the past tense personal endings for strong verbs to the past tense stem.

> **Simple Past of Strong Verbs = Past Tense Stem + Strong Past Tense Personal Ending**

The full pattern for the past tense personal endings of strong verbs is as follows:

	Singular	Plural
First person	-∅	-en
Second person	-st	-t
Third person	-∅	-en

Note that the first and third person singular of both weak and strong verbs takes no personal endings in the simple past tense. Note also that the only difference between the personal endings in the past tense of the weak and the strong verbs is that the first and third person plural ending is **-n** for weak verbs and **-en** for strong verbs.

The full conjugation of the simple past tense of the strong verb **bleiben** is as follows:

ich blieb	wir blieben
du bliebst	ihr bliebt
sie blieb	sie blieben

Vowel Changes in Stem

To help remember the different patterns of vowel changes found in the past tense stems of strong verbs, the following groupings can be made.

Changes from **a, au, ei** *to* **ie, i**

The following verbs change to **ie** or **i** in the simple past tense.

Infinitive		Simple Past	Past Participle
a		*ie*	
fallen	*to fall*	**fiel**	gefallen
halten	*to stop, hold*	**hielt**	gehalten
lassen	*to let*	**ließ**	gelassen
schlafen	*to sleep*	**schlief**	geschlafen
au		*ie*	
laufen	*to run*	**lief**	gelaufen
ei		*ie*	
bleiben	*to stay*	**blieb**	geblieben
leihen	*to loan*	**lieh**	geliehen
scheinen	*to shine*	**schien**	geschienen
schreiben	*to write*	**schrieb**	geschrieben
schreien	*to scream*	**schrie**	geschrie(e)n
schweigen	*to be silent*	**schwieg**	geschwiegen
steigen	*to climb*	**stieg**	gestiegen
ei		*i*	
beißen	*to bite*	**biß**	gebissen
leiden	*to suffer*	**litt**	gelitten
reiten	*to ride*	**ritt**	geritten
schneiden	*to cut*	**schnitt**	geschnitten
e		*i*	
gehen	*to go, walk*	**ging**	gegangen
a		*i*	
fangen	*to catch*	**fing**	gefangen

Variations in personal endings

When the past stem ends in **-d, -t, -ss(ß), -chs,** an **-e-** is added between the stem and the personal endings of the second person singular and plural. However, these forms as well as the second person singular and plural of other verbs in the simple past are rarely used. For example, **du schnittest, ihr schnittet.**

When the past stem ends in **-ie,** the endings of the first and third person plural are **-n** instead of **-en.**

Wir *schrien* **sehr laut.**	*We screamed very loudly.*
Warum *schrien* **sie nicht?**	*Why didn't they scream?*

20. Rewrite in the simple past tense.

1. Sie leidet.
2. Er schläft schon.
3. Sie schreiben Briefe.
4. Wir reiten gerne.
5. Ich schreie laut.
6. Das Buch fällt auf den Boden.
7. Der Zug hält dort.
8. Ludwig bleibt dort.
9. Sie schweigen immer.
10. Wir leiden sehr.
11. Er schreibt die Aufgabe.
12. Sie schweigt nicht.
13. Ihr schneidet ins Papier.
14. Die Sonne scheint.
15. Man leiht dem Kind das Buch.
16. Der Hund beißt das Mädchen.

21. Write sentences from the following, using the simple past tense.

1. Ich / lassen / Gudrun / gehen.
2. Das Pferd / laufen / am schnellsten.
3. Hubert / reiten / den ganzen Tag.
4. Wir / leihen / Gisela / das Buch.
5. Der Rattenfänger / fangen / Ratten.
6. Ich / schneiden / ins Fleisch.
7. Meine Eltern / schreiben / den Brief.
8. Wir / schreien / nicht.

Changes from **e, ie, au** *to* **o**

The following verbs change to **o** in the simple past tense.

Infinitive		Simple Past	Past Participle
ie		*o*	
biegen	*to bend*	**bog**	gebogen
fliegen	*to fly*	**flog**	geflogen
fliehen	*to flee*	**floh**	geflohen
fließen	*to flow*	**floß**	geflossen
frieren	*to freeze*	**fror**	gefroren
riechen	*to smell*	**roch**	gerochen
schießen	*to shoot*	**schoß**	geschossen
schließen	*to shut*	**schloß**	geschlossen
verlieren	*to lose*	**verlor**	verloren
wiegen	*to weigh*	**wog**	gewogen
ziehen	*to pull*	**zog**	gezogen
au		*o*	
saufen	*to drink* (of animals)	**soff**	gesoffen
e		*o*	
heben	*to lift*	**hob**	gehoben

22. Complete the following with the appropriate simple past forms.

1. Er _____ nach Spanien. *fliegen*
2. Ich _____ mein Gepäck. *verlieren*
3. Es _____ stark. *riechen*
4. Wir _____ die Fensterläden. *schließen*
5. Der Jäger _____ auf das Reh. *schießen*
6. Du _____ an den Händen. *frieren*
7. Man _____ das Gold. *wiegen*
8. Die Kinder _____ das Spielzeug. *ziehen*
9. Wohin _____ das Wasser? *fließen*
10. Ihr _____ damals nach Frankreich. *fliehen*
11. Die Tiere _____ Wasser. *saufen*
12. Ich _____ in die Schweiz. *fliegen*
13. Er _____ den Sack vom Wagen. *heben*
14. Die Männer _____ das Metall. *biegen*

Changes from **e, i, ie, o, u** *to* **a**

The following verbs change to **a** in the simple past tense.

Infinitive		Simple Past	Past Participle
e		*a*	
brechen	*to break*	**brach**	gebrochen
empfehlen	*to recommend*	**empfahl**	empfohlen
essen	*to eat*	**aß**	gegessen
fressen	*to eat* (of animals)	**fraß**	gefressen
geben	*to give*	**gab**	gegeben
helfen	*to help*	**half**	geholfen
lesen	*to read*	**las**	gelesen
messen	*to measure*	**maß**	gemessen
nehmen	*to take*	**nahm**	genommen
sehen	*to see*	**sah**	gesehen
sprechen	*to speak*	**sprach**	gesprochen
stehen	*to stand*	**stand**	gestanden
stehlen	*to steal*	**stahl**	gestohlen
sterben	*to die*	**starb**	gestorben
treffen	*to meet*	**traf**	getroffen
treten	*to step*	**trat**	getreten
vergessen	*to forget*	**vergaß**	vergessen
werfen	*to throw*	**warf**	geworfen
i		*a*	
beginnen	*to begin*	**begann**	begonnen
binden	*to bind*	**band**	gebunden
bitten	*to ask*	**bat**	gebeten
finden	*to find*	**fand**	gefunden
gewinnen	*to win*	**gewann**	gewonnen
schwimmen	*to swim*	**schwamm**	geschwommen
singen	*to sing*	**sang**	gesungen
sinken	*to sink*	**sank**	gesunken
sitzen	*to sit*	**saß**	gesessen
springen	*to jump*	**sprang**	gesprungen
stinken	*to stink*	**stank**	gestunken
trinken	*to drink*	**trank**	getrunken
ie		*a*	
liegen	*to lie*	**lag**	gelegen
o		*a*	
kommen	*to come*	**kam**	gekommen
u		*a*	
tun	*to do*	**tat**	getan

23. Complete the following with the appropriate simple past forms of the indicated verbs.

1. Wir _____ Schokolade. *essen*
2. Ich _____ viel Geld. *gewinnen*
3. Er _____ über die Hürde. *springen*
4. Wir _____ das Haus. *sehen*
5. Er _____ am Abend. *kommen*
6. Ich _____ das Gedicht. *lesen*

7. Er _____ die Zeitung. *nehmen*

8. Die Hunde _____ ins Wasser. *springen*

9. Ich _____ nichts. *tun*

10. Das Schiff _____ schnell. *sinken*

11. Der Bandit _____ uns die Hände. *binden*

12. Die Frau _____ an Krebs. *sterben*

13. Meine Tanten_____ mir nichts. *geben*

14. Wir _____ auf dem Sofa. *sitzen*

15. Ich _____ die Bilder. *sehen*

16. Er _____ die Lektüre. *beginnen*

17. Die Leute _____ im Bodensee. *schwimmen*

18. Es _____ nach faulen Eiern. *stinken*

19. Ihr _____ uns im Zentrum. *treffen*

20. Ich _____ Ursel. *bitten*

21. Das Kind _____ den Ball. *werfen*

22. Du _____ darüber. *sprechen*

23. Wir _____ den Film. *sehen*

24. Otto _____ das Geld. *stehlen*

25. Ich _____ deine Schwester. *treffen*

26. Wir _____ dem Kranken. *helfen*

27. Die Leute _____ dort. *stehen*

28. Herr Kraus _____ seine Aktentasche. *vergessen*

29. Der Ingenieur _____ den Wasserstand. *messen*

30. Wir _____ nicht auf den Teppich. *treten*

24. Form sentences from the following, using the simple past tense.

1. Der Hund / fressen / das Futter.
2. Die Bücher / liegen / auf dem Tisch.
3. Wir / springen / aus dem Fenster.
4. Ich / sitzen / auf einem Stuhl.
5. Die Sängerin / singen / die Arie.
6. Die Kinder / trinken / keinen Wein.
7. Er / finden / die Diamantbrosche.
8. Wir / kommen / um acht Uhr.
9. Ich / sehen / Monika / im Kino.
10. Er / tun / alles.

Changes from **a** *to* **u**

The following verbs change to **u** in the simple past tense.

Infinitive		Simple Past	Past Participle
a		*u*	
fahren	*to drive, go*	**fuhr**	gefahren
graben	*to dig*	**grub**	gegraben
schlagen	*to hit*	**schlug**	geschlagen
tragen	*to carry, wear*	**trug**	getragen
wachsen	*to grow*	**wuchs**	gewachsen
waschen	*to wash*	**wusch**	gewaschen

25. Rewrite the following in the simple past tense.

1. Die Lehrerinnen fahren in die Stadt.
2. Ich schlage ihn nicht.
3. Die Arbeiterin gräbt ein Loch.
4. Wir tragen Lederhosen.
5. Das Baby wächst schnell.
6. Tante Ida wäscht die Bettwäsche.
7. Er trägt etwas.
8. Ich fahre mit dem Zug.

Auxiliary Verbs sein, haben, werden

The use of the simple past tense of the auxiliary verbs **sein, haben, werden** is not restricted to narration as is true with other verbs. All simple past forms of **sein, haben,** and **werden** are freely used in conversation. The simple past forms of these verbs are irregular. Study the following:

ich war	ich hatte	ich wurde
du warst	du hattest	du wurdest
er war	er hatte	er wurde
wir waren	wir hatten	wir wurden
ihr wart	ihr hattet	ihr wurdet
sie waren	sie hatten	sie wurden

26. Complete with the correct simple past forms of **sein.**

    1. Wie _____ die Oper?
    2. Wo _____ du?
    3. Ich _____ in Regensburg.
    4. _____ du krank?
    5. Wir _____ sehr müde.
    6. _____ ihr zu Hause?
    7. Herr Breu, _____ Sie nervös?
    8. Meine Geschwister _____ schon fertig.
    9. _____ ihr auch dort?
    10. Mutter _____ sehr böse.

27. Complete with the correct simple past forms of **haben.**

    1. _____ du Angst?
    2. Die Jungen _____ Hunger.
    3. Wir _____ Geld.
    4. Ich _____ nichts.
    5. _____ du keine Zeit?
    6. _____ ihr Durst?
    7. _____ du Glück?
    8. Gisela _____ keinen Freund.
    9. _____ ihr auch Kameras?
    10. _____ Sie ein Auto?

28. Complete with the correct simple past forms of **werden.**

    1. Unsere Eltern _____ immer älter.
    2. Wir _____ schnell wieder gesund.
    3. Es _____ sehr heiß.
    4. Klaus _____ Doktor.
    5. Ich _____ böse.
    6. Frau Eber _____ nervös.
    7. Wann _____ du krank?
    8. _____ ihr auch hungrig?
    9. _____ er böse?
    10. Wann _____ ihr müde?

Usage Notes on the Simple Past Tense

Narative past

In German the simple past tense (narative past) is used mainly in written materials to narrate or report a chain of events that took place in the past. The simple past is not interchangeable with the present perfect tense (conversational past), which is used when the speaker talks or asks about single past events. The following exemplifies the different uses of these two past tenses. Note that the simple past of **sein, haben, werden** is used in narration as well as in conversation.

Narration

„Ich **war** letzten Sonntag mit Bärbel in Garmisch. Wir **trafen** dort ihren Bruder und **machten** zusammen eine Radtour. Ich **wurde** schon nach einer Stunde müde. Endlich **kamen** wir zu einem Rasthaus, wo wir uns ein gutes Essen **bestellten.**"

Conversation

„Was **hast** du letzten Sonntag **gemacht**?"
„Ich **war** mit Bärbel in Garmisch."
„**Habt** ihr jemand **getroffen**?"
„Ja, wir **haben** ihren Bruder **getroffen** und **haben** zusammen eine Radtour **gemacht.**"
„**Seid** ihr weit **gefahren**?"
„Ja, aber ich **wurde** schon nach einer Stunde müde."
„**Habt** ihr nicht **gerastet**?"
„Doch, endlich **sind** wir zu einem Rasthaus **gekommen**, wo wir uns ein gutes Essen **bestellt haben** . . ."

29. Rewrite the following in paragraph form, using the narrative past (simple past).

1. Peter hat mich gestern besucht.
2. Wir haben Limonade getrunken.
3. Er hat auch ein Stück Schokoladenkuchen gegessen.
4. Wir sind ins Zentrum gefahren.
5. Wir haben dort seine Freunde getroffen und wir sind ins Kino gegangen.
6. Der Film war prima. Er hat mir sehr gefallen.
7. Wir sind um acht Uhr nach Hause gekommen.
8. Wir haben eine Stunde CDs gespielt und haben über Musik gesprochen.
9. Meine Mutter hat noch Wurstbrote gemacht.
10. Peter ist danach nach Hause gegangen.

Expression of simultaneous past events

The simple past is used to express that two actions took place at the same time. The dependent clauses are often introduced by **während** (*while, during the time which*) or **als** (*when*). Note that the verb is in last position in clauses introduced by **während** and **als** (i.e., the normal word order for dependent clauses).

Sie *trank* **Kaffee,** *als* **er ins Zimmer** *kam*.	*She was drinking coffee when he came into the room.*
Ich *arbeitete* **nicht,** *als* **ich krank** *war*.	*I did not work when I was ill.*
Er *las* **einen Roman,** *während* **ich** *studierte*.	*He was reading a novel while I was studying.*

30. Complete the following with the appropriate simple past tense forms of the indicated verbs.

1. Ich _____, während er _____.   *schlafen, lesen*
2. Er _____, während Karin _____.   *lächeln, singen*
3. Wir _____, während die Leute _____.   *essen, tanzen*
4. Ich _____, als das Telefon _____.   *schreiben, klingeln*
5. Er _____ Wein, als er mich _____.   *kaufen, treffen*
6. Wir _____ nach Hause, als es kalt _____.   *gehen, werden*
7. Er _____, als ich die Geschichte _____.   *lachen, erzählen*
8. Wir _____ draußen, als du _____.   *sein, kommen*

9. Ich _____ Klaus, als er im Garten _____ . *helfen, arbeiten*
10. Wir _____ , während er das Gras _____ . *schwimmen, schneiden*

Customary past occurrence

The German simple past tense is used to express habitual past action. Words like **gewöhnlich** (*usually*) and **immer** (*always*) occur in such sentences. In English the usual action is expressed by *used to*.

Wir *besuchten* **sie** *immer*.   We always used to visit her.
Er *schlief gewöhnlich* **die ganze Nacht**.   He usually slept the whole night.

31. Form sentences from the following, using the simple past tense to show customary occurrence.

1. Wir / fahren / gewöhnlich / in die Schweiz.
2. Ich / sein / immer / krank.
3. Die Damen / trinken / gewöhnlich / Tee.
4. Die Schauspielerin / werden / immer / nervös.
5. Wir / gehen / sonntags / gewöhnlich / zur Kirche.
6. Er / arbeiten / immer.
7. Karin / trinken / gewöhnlich / Limonade.
8. Wir / geben / den Kindern / immer / Geld.
9. Ich / helfen / Renate / immer.
10. Wir / spielen / gewöhnlich / moderne Musik.

Review

32. Complete the following with the appropriate simple past tense forms of the indicated verbs.

1. Wann _____ du krank? *werden*
2. Inge _____ an einer schlimmen Krankheit. *leiden*
3. Ich _____ dort ein ganzes Jahr. *arbeiten*
4. Er _____ das Autofenster. *öffnen*
5. Der Mechaniker _____ es. *reparieren*
6. Die Touristen _____ das Schloß. *besichtigen*
7. _____ ihr böse? *sein*
8. Ich _____ den Film. *sehen*
9. Er _____ , als ich _____ . *schlafen, kommen*
10. _____ du keine Zeit? *haben*
11. Herr Wimmer, _____ Sie auch dort? *sein*
12. Thomas _____ das Geld. *nehmen*
13. Ich _____ viel Wasser, während ich krank _____ . *trinken, sein*
14. Wir _____ ihm das Bild. *zeigen*
15. Man _____ immer. *klingeln*
16. Das Kind _____ durch den Garten. *laufen*
17. Die Haushälterin _____ die Wäsche. *waschen*
18. Ich _____ seine Adresse. *vergessen*
19. Wir _____ gewöhnlich um zehn Uhr dort. *sein*
20. Ich _____ ein Buch, während Ulrich _____ . *lesen, studieren*

PRESENT PERFECT TENSE

The present perfect tense of German verbs consists of the present tense inflected forms of the auxiliary **haben** or **sein** plus the past participle of the main verb.

The verbs that take **haben** as their auxiliary include the transitive verbs (those that take a direct object), the reflexive verbs, and the modal auxiliaries. The verbs that take **sein** as their auxiliary include the intransitive verbs (those without a direct object) indicating a change of condition or a change in location.

Note: When used as part of the verb (rather than as an adjective), the past participle never takes any endings, and in independent clauses the past participle is in last position (see Chapter 10).

The German present perfect tense can refer to completed actions in the past as well as to actions that have begun in the past and continue into the present (as is the case for the present perfect tense in English). In German the present perfect tense, also called the *conversational past,* is the past tense that is most frequently used for past events in normal conversation. In this situation it is best translated by the simple past tense in English.

> *Present Perfect Tense = Present Tense of* **sein** *or* **haben** *+ Past Participle*

Formation of the Past Participle

Past Participle of weak verbs

The past participle of most weak verbs is formed by placing the prefix **ge-** in front of the infinitive stem and adding **-t** or **-et** at the end of the stem.

> *Past Participle (Weak Verbs) =* **ge-** *+ Infinitive Stem + -t or -et*

spielen   *ge* + **spiel** + *t* = **gespielt**
lachen   *ge* + **lach** + *t* = **gelacht**

Past participle of strong verbs

The past participle of most strong verbs is formed by placing the prefix **ge-** in front of the past participle stem and adding **-en** at the end of the stem.

> *Past Participle (Strong Verbs) =* **ge-** *+ Past Participle Stem + -en*

singen   *ge* + **sung** + *en* = **gesungen**

As we learned in the section on the past tense, strong verbs are characterized by a stem vowel change in the past tense. This characteristic is also reflected in the past participle. However, the stem vowel of the past participle is not always the same as the vowel in the simple past tense form of a strong verb. **The stem vowel of the past participle can be the same as the stem vowel in the simple past, the same as the stem vowel in the infinitive, or a different vowel altogether.** Thus although there are some basic sound patterns that help predict the stem vowel of a past participle, it is necessary to learn the principal parts for each new strong verb.

Regular Weak Verbs

The present perfect tense of most regular weak verbs is formed with the present tense of **haben** or **sein** and the past participle of the main verb. Study the following forms:

Verb	*Third Person Singular*	*Past Participle*
arbeiten	**er arbeitet**	**gearbeitet**
lieben	**er liebt**	**geliebt**
machen	**er macht**	**gemacht**
öffnen	**er öffnet**	**geöffnet**

Study the following conjugation:

ich habe gemacht	wir haben gemacht
du hast gemacht	ihr habt gemacht
er hat gemacht	sie haben gemacht

Wir *haben* **einen Wagen** *gekauft.*	*We bought a car.*
Er *hat* **die Wahrheit** *gesagt.*	*He told the truth.*
Ich *habe* **den Lehrer** *gefragt.*	*I asked the teacher.*
Habt **ihr auch** *gearbeitet?*	*Did you also work?*
Er weiß, daß ich den Brief *geschickt habe.*	*He knows that I sent the letter.*

Weak Verbs without the -ge *Prefix*

Verbs ending in -ieren

The past participle of weak verbs ending in **-ieren** does not take the **ge-** prefix.

Infinitive	*Past Participle*
probieren	**probiert**
studieren	**studiert**
telefonieren	**telefoniert**

Additional verbs without ge- *prefix*

Verbs with the following inseparable prefixes do not take the additional **ge-** prefix in the past participle: **be-, emp-, ent-, er-, ge-, ver-, zer-** (see section on inseparable prefix verbs).

Note: Inseparable prefix verbs can be either weak or strong.

Weak Verbs		**Strong Verbs**	
Infinitive	*Past Participle*	*Infinitive*	*Past Participle*
bestellen	**bestellt**	**bestehen**	**bestanden**
entdecken	**entdeckt**	**entnehmen**	**entnommen**
erklären	**erklärt**	**erfahren**	**erfahren**
gehören	**gehört**	**gefallen**	**gefallen**
verkaufen	**verkauft**	**verbergen**	**verborgen**

Study the following conjugations:

ich habe zerstört	wir haben zerstört	ich habe zerbrochen	wir haben zerbrochen
du hast zerstört	ihr habt zerstört	du hast zerbrochen	ihr habt zerbrochen
er hat zerstört	sie haben zerstört	er hat zerbrochen	sie haben zerbrochen

33. Complete the following with the appropriate present perfect forms of the indicated verbs.

1. Wir _____ den Kellner _____ . *fragen*
2. Wo _____ Sie _____ ? *wohnen*
3. Wir _____ alles _____ . *glauben*
4. _____ du den Mantel _____ ? *kaufen*
5. Gisela _____ ihren Freund _____ . *lieben*
6. Die Leute _____ die Geschichte _____ . *hören*
7. Ich _____ den Hund _____ . *suchen*
8. Die Männer _____ viel _____ . *rauchen*
9. Wo _____ ihr das Auto _____ ? *parken*

10. Warum _____ du _____ ?   *weinen*
11. _____ du es auf den Tisch _____ ?   *legen*
12. Was _____ er dir _____ ?   *schenken*
13. Ich _____ das Baby _____ .   *kämmen*
14. Was _____ ihr _____ ?   *lernen*
15. Was _____ Sie _____ ?   *sagen*

34. Complete the following with the appropriate present perfect forms of the indicated verbs.

1. Warum _____ ihr _____ ?   *bezahlen*
2. _____ du die Maschine _____ ?   *verkaufen*
3. Die Jungen _____ das Auto _____ .   *reparieren*
4. Unsere Lehrerin _____ alles _____ .   *erzählen*
5. Ich _____ die ganze Nacht _____ .   *studieren*
6. Wir _____ die Suppe _____ .   *probieren*
7. Wer _____ die Stadt _____ ?   *zerstören*
8. _____ dir der Fußball _____ ?   *gehören*
9. _____ du _____ ?   *telefonieren*
10. Meine Eltern _____ schon _____ .   *bestellen*
11. Er _____ uns _____ .   *besuchen*
12. Wann _____ Kolumbus Amerika _____ ?   *entdecken*
13. Wer _____ das Problem _____ ?   *erklären*
14. Warum _____ du es _____ ?   *zerstören*
15. Inge _____ sich schon _____ .   *entschuldigen*

35. Rewrite in the present perfect.

1. Wir studieren viel.
2. Brauchst du Geld?
3. Warum bellt der Hund?
4. Er arbeitet viel.
5. Man zerstört das Haus.
6. Suchen Sie den Jungen?
7. Träumt ihr oft?
8. Sie atmet sehr laut.
9. Ich blute stark.
10. Die Kinder baden gerne.
11. Wo wohnt ihr?
12. Ich hole Papier.
13. Wir legen die Bücher auf den Tisch.
14. Sie telefoniert oft.
15. Die Katze gehört dem Mädchen.
16. Wer bezahlt dafür?

Irregular Weak Verbs

Some weak verbs have a vowel change in the past stem. The past participles of these irregular weak verbs also have a stem vowel change.

Infinitive		Simple Past	Past Participle
brennen	*to burn*	brannte	**gebrannt**
bringen	*to bring*	brachte	**gebracht**
denken	*to think*	dachte	**gedacht**
kennen	*to know (a person)*	kannte	**gekannt**
nennen	*to name*	nannte	**genannt**
senden	*to send*	sandte	**gesandt**
wenden	*to turn*	wandte	**gewandt**
wissen	*to know (a fact)*	wußte	**gewußt**

36.　Write sentences from the following, using the present perfect tense.

1. Er / kennen / meine Schwester.
2. Die Kinder / wissen / die Antwort.
3. Ich / bringen / Blumen.
4. Denken / du / daran?
5. Die Häuser / brennen.
6. Wir / senden / das Paket.
7. Nennen / ihr / den höchsten Berg?
8. Ich / wenden / das Blatt.

Intransitive Verbs

The present perfect tense of some German verbs is formed with the present tense of the auxiliary verb **sein** instead of **haben**. Such verbs are referred to as intransitive verbs (verbs that do not take a direct object). Such verbs usually denote a change of location or condition. The following weak verbs are conjugated with **sein.**

Infinitive		*Past Participle*
begegnen	*to meet*	**ist begegnet**
klettern	*to climb*	**ist geklettert**
reisen	*to travel*	**ist gereist**
rennen	*to run*	**ist gerannt**
wandern	*to wander*	**ist gewandert**

Note that the irregular weak verb **rennen** has a vowel change in the past participle. Intransitive verbs are conjugated as follows:

ich bin gereist	**wir sind gereist**
du bist gereist	**ihr seid gereist**
er ist gereist	**sie sind gereist**

Wir *sind* **auf den Baum** *geklettert.*	*We climbed the tree.*
Ich *bin* **nach Deutschland** *gereist.*	*I traveled to Germany.*
Bist **du deinem Freund** *begegnet?*	*Did you meet your friend?*

37.　Complete the following with the appropriate present perfect forms of the indicated verbs.

1. Wir _____ sehr schnell _____. *rennen*
2. Wohin _____ ihr _____? *reisen*
3. Ich _____ auf den Berg _____. *klettern*
4. _____ er durch die Schweiz _____? *reisen*
5. _____ ihr ins Dorf _____? *wandern*
6. Ich _____ nicht _____. *rennen*
7. Die Kinder _____ ihrem Lehrer _____. *begegnen*
8. Meine Mutter _____ nach München _____. *reisen*
9. _____ du auch auf den Baum _____? *klettern*
10. Ich _____ ihrem Freund _____. *begegnen*

Strong Verbs

The present perfect tense of most strong verbs is formed with the present tense of **haben** and the past participle of the main verb. Note that some are conjugated with **sein**. Remember also that the past participle of the strong verbs may have the same stem vowel as the infinitive, the same vowel as the simple past tense, or a completely different stem vowel.

Study the following forms:

sehen, sah, gesehen	*beißen, biß, gebissen*	*finden, fand, gefunden*
ich habe gesehen	**ich habe gebissen**	**ich habe gefunden**
du hast gesehen	**du hast gebissen**	**du hast gefunden**
er hat gesehen	**er hat gebissen**	**er hat gefunden**
wir haben gesehen	**wir haben gebissen**	**wir haben gefunden**
ihr habt gesehen	**ihr habt gebissen**	**ihr habt gefunden**
sie haben gesehen	**sie haben gebissen**	**sie haben gefunden**

Remember also that the past participles of verbs beginning with one of the inseparable prefixes (**be-, emp-, ent-, er-, ge-, ver-, zer-**) do not take the **ge-** prefix.

Past Participles With No Vowel Change

The past participle of the following strong verbs consist of the prefix **ge-** and the infinitive stem plus **-en.** Note the extra **g** in **gegessen.**

Infinitive		*Simple Past*	*Past Participle*
backen	*to bake*	backte (*old:* buk)	**gebacken**
essen	*to eat*	aß	**gegessen**
fahren	*to drive, go*	fuhr	**(ist) gefahren**
fallen	*to fall*	fiel	**(ist) gefallen**
fangen	*to catch*	fing	**gefangen**
fressen	*to eat* (of animals)	fraß	**gefressen**
geben	*to give*	gab	**gegeben**
graben	*to dig*	grub	**gegraben**
halten	*to hold*	hielt	**gehalten**
kommen	*to come*	kam	**(ist) gekommen**
lassen	*to let*	ließ	**gelassen**
laufen	*to run*	lief	**(ist) gelaufen**
lesen	*to read*	las	**gelesen**
messen	*to measure*	maß	**gemessen**
schlafen	*to sleep*	schlief	**geschlafen**
schlagen	*to hit*	schlug	**geschlagen**
sehen	*to see*	sah	**gesehen**
tragen	*to carry, wear*	trug	**getragen**
treten	*to step*	trat	**(ist) getreten**
vergessen	*to forget*	vergaß	**vergessen**
wachsen	*to grow*	wuchs	**(ist) gewachsen**
waschen	*to wash*	wusch	**gewaschen**

Note that the past participles preceded by **ist** take **sein** as their auxiliary verbs in the present perfect tense.

ich bin gewachsen	**wir sind gewachsen**
du bist gewachsen	**ihr seid gewachsen**
er ist gewachsen	**sie sind gewachsen**

Er *ist* **nach Hamburg** *gefahren*.   *He went (by car or train) to Hamburg.*
Ich *bin* **ins Zimmer** *getreten*.   *I stepped into the room.*
Sie *sind* **schnell** *gewachsen*.   *They grew fast.*

38. Complete with the appropriate present forms of the indicated verbs.

1. _____ du den Roman _____ ? *lesen*
2. Er _____ den Jungen _____ . *schlagen*
3. Ich _____ es meinem Lehrer _____ . *geben*
4. Wann _____ ihr den Film _____ ? *sehen*
5. Wir _____ einen Kuchen _____ . *backen*
6. Ich _____ die Strecke _____ . *messen*
7. Was _____ das Tier _____ ? *fressen*
8. Die Männer _____ nach Gold _____ . *graben*
9. Die Frau _____ keinen Hut _____ . *tragen*
10. Ich _____ mir die Hände _____ . *waschen*
11. _____ ihr den Tiger _____ ? *fangen*
12. Wer _____ die Bananen _____ ? *essen*
13. _____ du den Mantel zu Hause _____ ? *lassen*
14. Warum _____ ihr nicht _____ ? *schlafen*

39. Write sentences from the following using the present perfect tense.

1. Mein Bruder / fahren / schnell.
2. Treten / du / ins Haus?
3. Wir / wachsen / schon wieder.
4. Fahren / ihr / nach Bremen?
5. Die Kinder / wachsen / immer.
6. Ich / fahren / gestern.
7. Laufen / ihr / in Haus?
8. Wann / du / kommen?
9. Die Leute / laufen / schnell.
10. Ich / ins Wasser / fallen.

Past Participles with Vowel Change

Many strong verbs change their stem vowels in the past participle. The participles of such verbs can be grouped according to the vowel changes taking place. The following groups may facilitate learning these past participles.

Changes from **ei** *to* **(i)e**

The **ei** of the infinitive stems is changed to **(i)e** in the past participles of the following verbs.

Infinitive		*Simple Past*	*Past Participle*
ei		*ie*	*ie*
bleiben	*to stay*	blieb	**(ist) geblieben**
leihen	*to loan*	lieh	**geliehen**
scheinen	*to shine, seem*	schien	**geschienen**
schreiben	*to write*	schrieb	**geschrieben**
schreien	*to scream*	schrie	**geschrien**
schweigen	*to be silent*	schwieg	**geschwiegen**
steigen	*to climb*	stieg	**(ist) gestiegen**
ei		*i*	*i*
beißen	*to bite*	biß	**gebissen**
leiden	*to suffer*	litt	**gelitten**
reiten	*to ride*	ritt	**(ist) geritten**
schneiden	*to cut*	schnitt	**geschnitten**

Note: The stem vowels in the past participles in the above group of verbs are the same as in the simple past tense.

40. Rewrite the following in the present perfect tense.

1. Reitest du oft?
2. Wir schreien laut.
3. Warum schreibt ihr nicht?
4. Die Sonne scheint.
5. Warum beißt er?
6. Bleibt ihr lange?
7. Die Kranken leiden.
8. Warum schweigt ihr?
9. Steigst du auf die Leiter?
10. Ich leihe dir Geld.
11. Er schneidet dem Kind die Haare.
12. Leidet ihr nicht?
13. Ich schreie nicht.
14. Schreibst du den Brief?

Changes from **ie, au** *to* **o, e**

The **ie, au** of the infinitive stems is changed to **o** or **e** in the past participles of the following verbs.

Infinitive		Simple Past	Past Participle
ie		*o*	*o*
biegen	*to bend*	bog	**gebogen**
fliegen	*to fly*	flog	**(ist) geflogen**
fliehen	*to flee*	floh	**(ist) geflohen**
fließen	*to flow*	floß	**(ist) geflossen**
frieren	*to freeze*	fror	**gefroren**
riechen	*to smell*	roch	**gerochen**
schießen	*to shoot*	schoß	**geschossen**
schließen	*to shut*	schloß	**geschlossen**
verlieren	*to lose*	verlor	**verloren**
wiegen	*to weigh*	wog	**gewogen**
ziehen	*to pull*	zog	**gezogen**
au		*o*	*o*
saufen	*to drink* (of animals)	soff	**gesoffen**

Note: The stem vowels in the past participle in the above groups of verbs are the same as in the simple past tense.

ie		*a*	*e*
liegen	*to lie*	lag	**gelegen**

Note: The stem vowel in the past participle of **liegen** is different from both the infinitive and the simple past.

41. Complete the following with the correct present perfect forms of the indicated verbs.

1. _____ du den Schlüssel _____ ? *verlieren*
2. Er _____ den Braten _____ . *riechen*
3. _____ ihr nach Nürnberg _____ ? *fliegen*
4. Ein Beamter _____ den Koffer _____ . *wiegen*
5. Warum _____ du auf den Hasen _____ ? *schießen*

6. Er _____ sie an den Haaren _____. *ziehen*
7. Ein Gefangener _____ gestern _____. *fliehen*
8. Wohin _____ das Wasser _____? *fließen*
9. Warum _____ du die Augen _____? *schließen*
10. Wir _____ an den Beinen _____. *frieren*
11. Der Wind _____ die Bäume _____. *biegen*
12. Er _____ im Schatten _____. *liegen*
13. Der Hund _____ das Wasser _____. *saufen*
14. Ich _____ das Geld _____. *verlieren*

Changes from i to u, o, e

The **i** of the infinitive stems is changed to **u, o,** or **e** in the past participles of the following verbs.

Infinitive		Simple Past	Past Participle
i		*a*	*u*
binden	*to bind*	band	**gebunden**
finden	*to find*	fand	**gefunden**
singen	*to sing*	sang	**gesungen**
sinken	*to sink*	sank	**(ist) gesunken**
springen	*to jump*	sprang	**(ist) gesprungen**
stinken	*to stink*	stank	**gestunken**
trinken	*to drink*	trank	**getrunken**
i			*o*
beginnen	*to begin*	begann	**begonnen**
gewinnen	*to win*	gewann	**gewonnen**
schwimmen	*to swim*	schwamm	**(ist) geschwommen**
i			*e*
bitten	*to ask*	bat	**gebeten**
sitzen	*to sit*	saß	**gesessen**

Note: The stem vowels in the past participles of the above groups of verbs are different from the stem vowels in both the infinitive and the simple past.

42. Form sentences from the following, using the present perfect tense.

1. Die Sonne / sinken / ins Meer.
2. Die Vorlesung / beginnen.
3. Springen / ihr / von der Brücke?
4. Ich / singen / das Lied.
5. Schwimmen / du / über die Nordsee?
6. Er / gewinnen / den Preis.
7. Das Gas / stinken.
8. Binden / du / den Hund / an den Baum?
9. Die Männer / springen / über die Hürde.
10. Singen / ihr / oft?
11. Ich / trinken / Wasser.
12. Wir / beginnen / gestern.
13. Er / sitzen / auf dem Sofa.
14. Bitten / ihr / die Frau?
15. Wer / finden / den Schmuck?
16. Er / trinken / kaltes Bier.

Changes from e, u to o, a

The **e** or **u** of the infinitive stems are changed to **o** or **a** in the past participles of the following verbs.

Infinitive		Simple Past	Past Participle
e		*a*	*o*
brechen	*to break*	brach	**gebrochen**
empfehlen	*to recommend*	empfahl	**empfohlen**
helfen	*to help*	half	**geholfen**
nehmen	*to take*	nahm	**genommen**
sprechen	*to talk, speak*	sprach	**gesprochen**
stehlen	*to steal*	stahl	**gestohlen**
sterben	*to die*	starb	**(ist) gestorben**
treffen	*to meet*	traf	**getroffen**
werfen	*to throw*	warf	**geworfen**
e		*i*	*a*
gehen	*to go*	ging	**(ist) gegangen**

Note: The stem vowels in the past participles of the above group of verbs are different from the stem vowels in both the infinitive and the simple past.

e		*a*	*a*
stehen	*to stand*	stand	**(ist or hat) gestanden**
u		*a*	*a*
tun	*to do*	tat	**getan**

43. Rewrite the following in the present perfect tense.

1. Trefft ihr sie?
2. Sie werfen den Ball.
3. Warum brichst du es in Stücke?
4. Ich helfe ihr.
5. Das Kind nimmt nichts.
6. Der Verletzte stirbt.
7. Warum stiehlst du?
8. Frau Knauer, Sie sprechen zu schnell.
9. Wir helfen dem Kranken.
10. Sprichst du viel?
11. Gehst du ins Kino?
12. Ich stehe hier.
13. Wir empfehlen die Suppe.
14. Der Kran hebt das Auto.
15. Was tust du?

Auxiliary Verbs sein, haben, werden

The present perfect tense of these verbs **sein, haben, werden** is as follows:

sein	*haben*	*werden*
ich bin gewesen	**ich habe gehabt**	**ich bin geworden**
du bist gewesen	**du hast gehabt**	**du bist geworden**
er ist gewesen	**er hat gehabt**	**er ist geworden**
wir sind gewesen	**wir haben gehabt**	**wir sind geworden**
ihr seid gewesen	**ihr habt gehabt**	**ihr seid geworden**
sie sind gewesen	**sie haben gehabt**	**sie sind geworden**

Wir *sind* **in Japan** *gewesen*.   *We were in Japan.*
Ich *bin* **müde** *geworden*.   *I became tired.*
Hast **du Geld** *gehabt?*   *Did you have money?*
Seid **ihr krank** *geworden?*   *Did you become ill?*
Er *ist* **in der Schule** *gewesen*.   *He was in school.*

44. Rewrite the following, changing the verbs to the present perfect.

1. Hast du Hunger?
2. Ich bin krank.
3. Wir haben Hunger.
4. Sie werden immer dicker.
5. Er wird wieder gesund.
6. Wann sind Sie dort?
7. Ich habe Kopfweh.
8. Wir werden naß.
9. Bist du auch müde?
10. Ich werde böse.
11. Habt ihr Geld?
12. Ich habe Sorgen.
13. Sie ist unglücklich.
14. Die Pferde sind unruhig.
15. Wirst du nervös?
16. Seid ihr krank?

Review

45. Complete the following with the appropriate forms of the present perfect tense.

1. _____ Sie den Turm _____? *besichtigen*
2. Er _____ mir nichts _____. *geben*
3. Wie lange _____ du dort _____? *wohnen*
4. Otto _____ etwas _____. *kaufen*
5. Die Leute _____ mich _____. *kennen*
6. Was _____ du _____? *backen*
7. _____ ihr ihn _____? *sehen*
8. Die Kinder _____ laut _____. *schreien*
9. Er _____ vor einer Stunde _____. *telefonieren*
10. Ich _____ den ganzen Tag _____. *arbeiten*
11. _____ ihr schon _____? *bestellen*
12. Wem _____ du _____? *begegnen*
13. Warum _____ er _____? *schweigen*
14. Wir _____ nichts _____. *verloren*
15. Die Katze _____ es _____. *fressen*
16. Du _____ aber _____! *wachsen*
17. _____ ihr auch ins Wasser _____? *springen*
18. Ich _____ von dir _____. *träumen*
19. Man _____ es ganz _____. *zerstören*
20. _____ du schon _____? *studieren*
21. Wann _____ du _____? *kommen*
22. Ich _____ alles _____. *erzählen*
23. _____ ihr den Kuchen _____? *essen*
24. _____ Sie lange _____? *warten*
25. Die Kinder _____ Limonade _____. *trinken*
26. Wir _____ das Haus _____. *verkaufen*
27. _____ du stark _____? *bluten*
28. Ich _____ auf die Leiter _____. *steigen*
29. Er _____ alles _____. *sagen*

30. Der Mechaniker _____ den Wagen _____ .   *reparieren*
31. _____ du die Suppe _____ ?   *empfehlen*
32. Warum _____ das Boot _____ ?   *sinken*
33. Wen _____ ihr nach der Arbeit _____ ?   *treffen*
34. Wie lange _____ du _____ ?   *schlafen*
35. Die Kinder _____ die Tür _____ .   *schließen*

PAST PERFECT TENSE

Weak and Strong Verbs

The past perfect tense of both the weak and the strong verbs is formed with the simple past tense form of the auxiliary **haben** or **sein** plus the past participle. The past perfect tense is sometimes referred to as the *pluperfect* tense.

> *Past Perfect Tense = Simple Past Tense of* **sein** *or* **haben** *+ Past Participle*

Study the following forms:

ich hatte gesucht	ich war gegangen
du hattest gesucht	du warst gegangen
er hatte gesucht	er war gegangen
wir hatten gesucht	wir waren gegangen
ihr hattet gesucht	ihr wart gegangen
sie hatten gesucht	sie waren gegangen

Ich *hatte* **die Geschichte** *gehört*	*I had heard the story.*
Wir *waren* **zu Hause** *geblieben*.	*We had stayed at home.*
Er *war* **schon dort** *gewesen*.	*He had already been there.*
Sie *hatten* **den Hund** *gefüttert*.	*They had fed the dog.*

46. Rewrite the following in the past perfect tense.

1. Wir haben getanzt.
2. Hast du gesungen?
3. Sie sind gefahren
4. Habt ihr gefragt?
5. Man hat es genommen.
6. Sie haben viel getrunken.
7. Hast du studiert?
8. Ich habe es repariert.
9. Wann ist er gekommen?
10. Er hat mich besucht.
11. Hast du den Wagen gewaschen?
12. Konrad ist dort geblieben.
13. Ich habe die Jacke getragen.
14. Sie ist in Rom gewesen.
15. Hat er dem Kranken geholfen?
16. Wir haben gearbeitet.

Use of Past Perfect Tense

In German, as in English, the past perfect tense is used to report events that took place prior to another event in the past. Note that the conjunction **denn** (*for*) does not affect the word order of the clause that contains the past perfect form of the verb. The simple past tense is used in the main clause. Study the following examples.

Ich war müde, denn ich *hatte* den ganzen   *I was tired for I had worked the*
   Tag *gearbeitet*.   *entire day.*
Er hatte Hunger, denn er *hatte* nichts   *He was hungry for he had not eaten*
   gegessen.   *anything.*

47. Follow the model.

> **Ich bin glücklich. Ich habe Geld gewonnen.**
> **Ich war glücklich, denn ich hatte Geld gewonnen.**

1. Wir sind arm. Wir haben alles verloren.
2. Sie hat Angst. Sie ist schon oft im Krankenhaus gewesen.
3. Ich weiß alles. Ich habe viel studiert.
4. Sie bestellen viel. Sie haben den ganzen Tag nichts gegessen.
5. Laura ist traurig. Ihr Freund hat sie nicht besucht.
6. Sie sind schwach. Sie waren krank.
7. Ich bin müde. Ich habe schlecht geschlafen.
8. Wir haben Durst. Wir haben nichts getrunken.
9. Es riecht nach Wein. Er hat die Flasche zerbrochen.
10. Ich habe kein Geld. Ich habe viel gekauft.

FUTURE TENSE

Weak and Strong Verbs

The future tense of both weak and strong verbs is formed with the auxiliary verb **werden** and the infinitive. The infinitive is in last position, unless it occurs in a dependent clause.

> *Future Tense = Present Tense of* **werden** *+ Infinitive*

Study the following conjugation:

ich werde suchen	**wir werden suchen**
du wirst suchen	**ihr werdet suchen**
er wird suchen	**sie werden suchen**

Ich *werde* **dich nicht** *vergessen*.   *I shall not forget you.*
Werdet **ihr auch** *kommen?*   *Will you also come?*
Wir *werden* **einen Hund** *kaufen*.   *We are going to buy a dog.*
Ich weiß, daß du *kommen wirst*.   *I know that you will come.*

48. Complete the following with the correct future forms of the indicated verbs.

1. _____ ihr hier _____ ? *bleiben*
2. _____ du _____ ? *telefonieren*
3. Die Leute _____ es nicht _____ . *glauben*
4. Ich _____ die Rechnung _____ . *bezahlen*
5. Er _____ es _____ . *lesen*
6. Wir _____ es _____ . *machen*
7. _____ ihr uns _____ ? *helfen*
8. Die Kinder _____ den Brief _____ . *schreiben*
9. Ich _____ die Tür _____ . *öffnen*

10. _____ du den Mantel _____ ? *kaufen*
11. Was _____ ihr _____ ? *bestellen*
12. Warum _____ er nicht _____ ? *kommen*
13. Ich _____ es nicht _____ . *vergessen*
14. Wir _____ das Metall _____ . *biegen*
15. Die Leute _____ laut _____ . *schreien*
16. Du _____ in der Kälte _____ . *frieren*

Use of the Future Tense

The future tense is of course used to indicate actions that will take place entirely in the future. If an adverb or adverbial phrase indicating future time is not expressed, the future using **werden** is commonly used. If the adverbial indicator is present or if it is obvious from the context that the future is clearly intended, the present tense (with a future meaning) is frequently encountered, particularly in spoken German.

Wir *werden* **unsere Freunde** *besuchen*.   *We will visit our friends.*
Ich *fahre morgen* **nach Stuttgart.**   *I am going to Stuttgart tomorrow.*

49. Rewrite the following in the future tense, omitting the adverbs of time.

1. Wir bringen morgen das Auto.
2. Ich fahre nächste Woche nach Berlin.
3. Kommst du übermorgen?
4. Er schreibt das Gedicht morgen abend.
5. Zeigt ihr euren Eltern das Haus nächsten Monat?
6. Sie arbeiten heute abend.
7. Ich esse morgen bei Inge.
8. Kaufst du es morgen nachmittag?

Probability

In German the future tense may also indicate present or future probability or likelihood, particularly when used in conjunction with adverbs such as **sicher, schon, vielleicht, wohl.**

Die Wolken sind sehr dunkel. Es *wird* **wohl bald** *regnen*.
    The clouds are very dark. It will probably rain soon.

Ingo ist nicht zur Schule gekommen. Er *wird sicher* **krank** *sein*.
    Ingo didn't come to school. He's probably sick.

Du hast schwer gearbeitet. Du *wirst wohl* **müde** *sein*.
    You've worked hard. You're probably tired.

The future tense in German can also be used to show determination. When used in this way, the verb **werden** is usually stressed.

Sag was du willst. Ich *werde* **das Buch zu Ende** *schreiben*.
    Say what you want. I will finish my book.

50. Write the German.

1. Perhaps she is ill.
2. We are probably coming.
3. Perhaps they are crying.

4. Children, you are probably hungry.   *Hunger haben*
5. Peter, you probably know it.
6. I am probably going.
7. He is probably working.
8. Perhaps they are helping.

FUTURE PERFECT TENSE

Weak and Strong Verbs

The future perfect tense is formed with the present tense of **werden** plus the past participle plus the auxiliary verb **haben** or **sein**.

> *Future Perfect Tense = Present Tense of **werden** + Past Participle + Infinitive of **haben** or **sein***

Study the following forms:

ich werde gemacht haben	ich werde gefahren sein
du wirst gemacht haben	du wirst gefahren sein
er wird gemacht haben	er wird gefahren sein
wir werden gemacht haben	wir werden gefahren sein
ihr werdet gemacht haben	ihr werdet gefahren sein
sie werden gemacht haben	sie werden gefahren sein

Use of the Future Perfect Tense

The future perfect tense is used to indicate an action that will end at or prior to a specified time in the future. It is most frequently used to express past probability or likelihood. When used in this way, adverbs such as **sicher, vielleicht, wahrscheinlich, wohl** often occur in the same sentence. Otherwise this tense is rarely used.

Er *wird wohl* **lange** *geschlafen haben.*   *He probably slept late.*
Sie *werden vielleicht* **dort** *geblieben sein.*   *They probably stayed there.*

51. Rewrite the following in the future perfect tense. Add **wohl** to the sentences.

1. Ihr habt getanzt.
2. Sie sind gekommen.
3. Maria hat geschlafen.
4. Wir haben es nicht gesehen.
5. Du hast nicht gefragt.
6. Er hat das Gedicht geschrieben.
7. Sie hat sich gefreut.
8. Du hast lange gewartet.

VERBS WITH INSEPARABLE PREFIXES

Verbs beginning with the prefixes **be-, emp-, ent-, er-, ge-, ver-, zer-** are called *inseparable prefix verbs* because these prefixes are never separated from the verb stem. The inseparable prefixes do not have an independent meaning by themselves and they cannot stand alone. They do, however, change the meaning of the stem verb to which they are prefixed.

The inseparable prefix verbs can be either strong or weak, following the same conjugational patterns of the verb stem, except that they do not take the characteristic **ge-** prefix in the past participle. Therefore, those verbs beginning with the inseparable prefix **ge-** have the same past participle form as the stem verb from which they are derived.

fallen	*to fall*	**fiel**	**gefallen**
gefallen	*to please*	**gefiel**	**gefallen**
langen	*to be sufficient, suffice*	**langte**	**gelangt**
gelangen	*to reach, attain*	**gelangte**	**gelangt**

In spoken German the inseparable prefixes do not receive any stress. The primary stress is given to the first syllable of the verb stem.

Only the prefix **zer-** has a constant meaning. It denotes destruction or reduction to small parts or components: **drücken** (*to squeeze*), **zerdrücken** (*to squash*). The prefix **be-** makes a verb transitive. (The verb can be followed by a direct object and is conjugated with **haben**.)

Er *ist gekommen.*　　　But: **Er** *hat* **Geld** *bekommen.*

Note how the different prefixes alter the meanings of the verbs.

stehen—*to stand*

bestehen	*to pass, persist*	**Ich** *habe* **das Examen** *bestanden.*
entstehen	*to originate*	**Wie** *entsteht* **das Gas?**
gestehen	*to confess*	**Er** *gestand* **alles.**
verstehen	*to understand*	**Sie** *werden* **das Problem** *verstehen.*

fallen—*to fall*

entfallen	*to fall out of, slip*	**Sein Name** *ist mir* **entfallen.**
gefallen	*to be pleasing*	**Das Kleid** *hat ihr* **gefallen.**
verfallen	*to decline*	*Verfällt* **das Zentrum?**
zerfallen	*to fall apart*	**Der Kuchen** *ist zerfallen.*

52. Complete the following with the appropriate present tense forms of the indicated verbs.

1. Ute _____ ein Klavier.　*bekommen*
2. Ich _____ alles.　*zerbrechen*
3. Er _____ das Bild.　*verkaufen*
4. Wir _____ die Antwort.　*verstehen*
5. Ich _____ die Gäste.　*empfangen*
6. Er _____ Kuchen.　*bestellen*
7. _____ dir das Motorrad?　*gefallen*
8. _____ ihr eure Eltern.　*besuchen*
9. Ich _____ das Problem.　*erklären*
10. _____ du alles?　*erzählen*
11. Wir _____ das Hotel.　*empfehlen*
12. Du _____ alles.　*vergessen*

53. Rewrite the following in the present perfect tense.

1. Wir verstehen das Wort.
2. Es gefällt mir nicht.
3. Sie gestehen die Wahrheit.
4. Warum zerfällt es?
5. Ich bestehe das Examen.
6. Wer besucht dich?
7. Verkauft ihr das Haus?
8. Er empfängt den Brief.
9. Warum erzählst du alles?
10. Was entdeckt er?

VERBS WITH SEPARABLE PREFIXES

Another group of verbs are known as the *separable prefix verbs* because the prefix is separated from the verb stem under certain conditions, which will be explained below. Many separable prefixes are prepositions (**an, auf, nach**) or adverbs (**zurück, heim, vorbei**); others are verbs (**kennen, spazieren, stehen**). Occasionally adjectives (**frei, kalt, wach**) and nouns (**Rad, Schlittschuh**) also function as separable prefixes. The separable prefixes have definite meanings, very often denoting direction.

Like the inseparable prefix verbs, the separable prefix verbs can be either strong or weak, following the same conjugational patterns of the verb stems. However, unlike the inseparable prefix verbs, they take the past participle prefix **ge-** in addition to the separable prefix.

Unlike the inseparable prefix verbs, the separable prefix verbs always have their main stress on the prefix.

Study the following list of common separable prefixes with their basic meanings. Note that is is also possible for the added prefix to change the meaning of the stem verb in very subtle ways.

ab	*off, down*	**abfliegen** (*to take off*), **abschreiben** (*to copy down*)
an	*at, on*	**anschauen** (*to look at*), **anziehen** (*to put on*)
auf	*up, open*	**aufstehen** (*to get up*), **aufmachen** (*to open up*)
aus	*out*	**ausbrechen** (*to break out*), **ausbrennen** (*to burn out*)
ein	*into, in*	**eintreten** (*to step into*), **einsteigen** (*to get into*)
fort	*away*	**fortgehen** (*to go away*), **fortbleiben** (*to stay away*)
heim	*home*	**heimkommen** (*to come home*), **heimgehen** (*to go home*)
her	*toward the speaker, hither*	**hersehen** (*to look toward*), **herkommen** (*to come toward*)
hin	*away from the speaker, there*	**hingehen** (*to go there*), **hinwerfen** (*to throw there*)
mit	*with, along*	**mitfahren** (*to ride along*), **mitlachen** (*to laugh along*)
nach	*after*	**nachschauen** (*to look after*), **nachkommen** (*to come after*)
nieder	*down*	**niederlegen** (*to lie down*), **niedersetzen** (*to sit down, set down*)
vor	*before*	**vorsetzen** (*to set before*), **vorlegen** (*to put before*)
weg	*away*	**weglaufen** (*to run away*), **wegnehmen** (*to take away*)
zu	*to, close*	**zuhören** (*to listen to*), **zumachen** (*to close*)
zurück	*back*	**zurücknehmen** (*to take back*), **zurückgeben** (*to give back*)
zusammen	*together*	**zusammenkommen** (*to come together*), **zusammennähen** (*to stitch together*)

Not all German prefixes can be translated into idiomatic English by using these equivalents:

ausbessern	*to repair, mend*	**nachmachen**	*to imitate*
aussehen	*to look like*	**zusammenlegen**	*to fold*

Three commonly used verbs with separable prefixes are as follows:

kennenlernen	*to become acquainted with, meet*
spazierengehen	*to take a walk*
spazierenfahren	*to go for a ride*

Position of the Separable Prefix

A separable prefix is always the final element of the sentence or main clause when the verb is in the present tense, the simple past tense, or the imperative. Study the following examples.

Present tense

Ich *gehe* **oft** *aus*.
Kommst **du auch** *heim?*
Geht **ihr morgen** *mit?*

54. Complete the following with the correct present tense of the indicated verbs.

    1. Er _____ in den Zug _____ .   *einsteigen*
    2. Wir _____ oft _____ .   *zusammenkommen*
    3. Ich _____ auch _____ .   *mitfahren*
    4. Warum _____ du den warmen Mantel _____ ?   *anziehen*
    5. _____ ihr euch schon _____ ?   *niederlegen*
    6. Wann _____ ihn deine Eltern _____ ?   *kennenlernen*
    7. Wann _____ du _____ ?   *zurückkommen*
    8. Ich _____ nicht gern _____ .   *hingehen*
    9. Wann _____ ihr _____ ?   *aufstehen*
  10. Deine Freunde _____ mit uns _____ .   *spazierenfahren*

Simple past tense

Sie *ging* **abends** *spazieren*.
Warum *schaute* **sie es** *an?*

55. Form sentences from the following, using the simple past tense.

    1. Er / aufessen / alles.   5. Kinder / nachmachen / alles.
    2. Ich / abschreiben / das Lied.   6. Wer / zumachen / das Fenster?
    3. Wir / kennenlernen / ihn.   7. Wie / zusammennähen / er / das Leder?
    4. Arnim / einsammeln / für die Armen.   8. Wann / heimgehen / die Studenten?

Imperative

See the section on the imperative at pp. 194–197.

Geh **mit uns** *spazieren!*
Kommt **bald** *zurück!*
Lernen **Sie Arnold** *kennen!*

56. Write the imperative. Follow the model.

    Irmgard / herkommen / schnell.
    Irmgard, komm schnell her!

    1. Gisela / weglaufen / nicht.   5. Frau Breuer / aufstehen / langsam.
    2. Frau Bayer / zumachen / schnell.   6. Helga / herkommen / doch.
    3. Konrad / mitfahren / bitte.   7. Mutter / zumachen / die Schachtel.
    4. Ursula und Theo / eintreten / leise.   8. Arno / anschauen / es / nicht.

Infinitive

The separable prefix does not separate from the verb stem in the infinitive. However, in infinitive clauses with **zu,** the **zu** comes between the separable prefix and the verb stem.

Ich bin nicht bereit *anzufangen*.   *I'm not ready to start.*

Compound tenses

Future tense

Er *wird* **wohl** *mitessen*.
Ich *werde* **nicht** *ausgehen*.

57.   Rewrite in the future tense.

    1. Wir gehen fort.   4. Sie nehmen nichts weg.
    2. Ich gehe hinaus.   5. Gehst du aus?
    3. Er bringt es zurück.   6. Ich schaue das Album an.

Present perfect tense

Note that the separable prefix verbs, unlike the inseparable prefix verbs, take the **ge-** prefix. However, it is placed between the separable prefix and the past participle stem. For this reason the **-ge-** in this position is sometimes referred to as an *infix*.

Strong Verbs	*Weak Verbs*
an**ge**kommen	ein**ge**kauft
aus**ge**laufen	an**ge**macht

Der Zug *ist* **endlich** *angekommen*.
Mutter *hat* **schon** *eingekauft*.
Sie *sind* **schon** *angekommen*.

58.   Rewrite in the present perfect tense.

    1. Sie lachten auch mit.   5. Wir gingen spazieren.
    2. Wir schauten bei ihr nach.   6. Ich fuhr mit ihm heim.
    3. Ich lernte ihn kennen.   7. Gudrun stand dann auf.
    4. Der Zug kam bald an.   8. Sie schauten bald nach.

Past perfect tense

Ich *hatte* **es schon** *aufgemacht*.
Der Vorrat *war ausgelaufen*.
Der Lehrer *hatte* **das Licht** *angemacht*.

59. Fill in the correct past perfect forms of the indicated verbs.

1. Er _____ sofort _____ . *einsteigen*
2. Ich _____ das Licht _____ . *ausmachen*
3. Wir _____ es _____ . *abschreiben*
4. Die Kinder _____ die Bücher _____ . *niederlegen*
5. _____ ihr _____ ? *zusammenkommen*
6. Ich _____ ihn _____ . *kennenlernen*
7. Unsere Eltern _____ lange _____ . *fortbleiben*
8. Wer _____ uns _____ ? *zuhören*

Separable Prefix Verbs in Dependent Clauses

The separable prefix is never separated from the verb when the separable prefix verb occurs in a dependent clause. Study the following:

Present	**Ich weiß, daß er bald** *ankommt.*
Simple past	**Er lachte, als ich** *hinfiel.*
Future	**Sie weiß, warum ich** *mitgehen werde.*
Present perfect	**Ich freue, mich, daß du** *heimgekommen bist.*
Past perfect	**Er weiß, daß er** *abgeschrieben hatte.*

60. Rewrite the following, introducing each sentence with **Ich weiß, daß. . .**

1. Er ist fortgegangen.
2. Sie wird herkommen.
3. Wir fliegen morgen ab.
4. Ihr habt Peter kennengelernt.
5. Der Zug war angekommen.
6. Ich komme nach.
7. Er ging aus.
8. Wir werden heimkommen.
9. Du fährst mit.
10. Er hatte nachgeschaut.

CASE FOLLOWING VERBS

Accusative and Dative Case for Direct and Indirect Objects

Many transitive verbs can take an indirect object in addition to a direct object. The direct object can be identified by asking the question, *who* or *what* receives the action of the verb, i.e., who or what is given, shown, brought, etc. Normally in German the answer to this question will be the direct object in the accusative case. The indirect object can be identified by asking the question, *to or for whom*, or *to or for what* was the action of the verb undertaken, i.e., to or for whom/what is something being given, shown, brought, etc. In German the indirect object is the dative case.

The following verbs are common examples of verbs that can take both a direct object in the accusative and an indirect object in the dative.

bringen	*to bring, take*	**Sie bringt** *dem Kranken Suppe.*
geben	*to give*	**Er gibt** *seiner Tochter das Gold.*
holen	*to get*	**Wir holen** *dem Hasen eine Karotte.*
kaufen	*to buy*	**Ich kaufte** *den Kindern das Spielzeug.*
sagen	*to say, tell*	**Sie sagen** *ihren Eltern die Wahrheit.*
schenken	*to give, present*	**Ich habe** *meinem Vater eine Krawatte* **geschenkt.**
schicken	*to send*	**Wer hat** *dir das Paket* **geschickt?**
schreiben	*to write*	**Er hat** *seiner Freundin einen Brief* **geschrieben.**
zeigen	*to show*	**Sie zeigten** *den Touristen den Hafen.*

Dative Case

A small number of German verbs take objects in the dative rather than the accusative case. The dative verbs must be memorized. The following are common examples of dative verbs.

antworten	*to answer*	**Wir antworten** *dem Lehrer.*
danken	*to thank*	**Er dankte** *seiner Tante.*
folgen	*to follow, obey*	**Folgst du** *deiner Mutter?*
gefallen	*to like, be pleasing to*	**Der Film hat** *den Kindern* **gefallen.**
gehören	*to belong to*	**Das gehört** *seiner Freundin.*
glauben	*to believe*	**Ich glaube** *meinem Freund.*
gratulieren	*to congratulate*	**Wir gratulieren** *ihr* **zum Geburtstag.**
helfen	*to help*	**Er hilft** *seiner Mutter.*
schmecken	*to taste, taste good*	**Dieses Fleisch schmeckt** *mir.*

61. Write sentences from the following, using the present tense of the verbs.

　　1. Ich / zeigen / das Kind / das Buch.
　　2. Er / schicken / deine Mutter / eine Karte.
　　3. Wir / glauben / der Mann.
　　4. Ich / bringen / die Studentin / der Roman.
　　5. Danken / du / dein Lehrer?
　　6. Wir / helfen / unsere Großmutter.
　　7. Das Haus / gehören / meine Eltern.
　　8. Antworten / ihr / die Lehrerin?
　　9. Maria / kaufen / ihre Freundin / eine Kette.
　　10. Der Wagen / gehören / mein Bruder.
　　11. Wer / holen / der Kranke / eine Pille?
　　12. Die Blumen / gefallen / unsere Tante.
　　13. Warum / gratulieren / du / deine Schwester?
　　14. Er / schenken / das Baby / eine Puppe.
　　15. Wir / schicken / der Präsident / ein Protest.
　　16. Die Kinder / folgen / der Großvater.

Prepositional Objects

Many German verbs plus prepositions are followed by either the dative or the accusative case. Often the German prepositions do not correspond to the prepositions used with the English verbs.

Accusative objects after **an, auf, über**

When verbs are followed by the prepositions **an, auf, über,** these prepositions take the accusative case. Study the following examples.

antworten auf	*to reply to something*	**Wir** *antworten auf* **seine Frage.**
denken an	*to think of*	**Ich** *denke* **oft** *an* **meine Freundin.**
glauben an	*to believe in*	**Wir** *glaubten an* **seine Unschuld.**
hoffen auf	*to hope for*	**Er hat** *auf* **gutes Wetter** *gehofft.*
lachen über	*to laugh about*	**Sie** *hat* **nicht** *über* **das Thema** *gelacht.*
sprechen über	*to talk about in detail*	*Sprecht* **ihr** *über* **das Instrument?**
warten auf	*to wait for*	**Warum** *hast* **du nicht** *auf* **deine Eltern** *gewartet?*

Dative objects after **von, zu, nach, vor**

The dative case is used after the following verbs plus prepositions.

fragen nach	*to ask about*	**Er** *fragte nach* **meiner Mutter.**
gehören zu	*to be a part or member of*	**Otto** *gehört* **auch zum Klub.**
halten von	*to think of something, somebody*	**Was** *hältst* **du** *von* **dem Programm?**
hören von	*to hear from*	**Ich** *habe* **heute** *von* **meiner Schwester** *gehört*.
sprechen von	*to talk of*	**Er** *hat von* **seiner Reise** *gesprochen*.
suchen nach	*look for*	**Ich** *suche nach* **meinen Eltern.**
träumen von	*dream about*	**Sie** *träumte von* **ihrem Hund.**
wissen von	*to know about*	**Er** *weiß* **nichts** *von* **diesem Thema.**

62. Complete the following with the correct case endings.

1. Er fragte nach mein_____ Adresse.
2. Er weiß nichts von d_____ Thema.
3. Sie lachte über d_____ Frage.
4. Sie brachte ihr_____ Mann ein_____ Krawatte.
5. Wir glauben d_____ Kind.
6. Was hältst du von sein_____ Frau?
7. Das Buch gehört zu dies_____ Sammlung.
8. Hast du dein_____ Freund geholfen?
9. Warum dankst du nicht sein_____ Mutter?
10. Ich habe mein_____ Bruder nicht geantwortet.
11. Dieses Bild gefällt mein_____ Freundin.
12. Wer wartet auf d_____ Zug?
13. Sucht ihr nach d_____ Schule?
14. Ich träume von mein_____ Reise.
15. Wir antworten auf sein_____ Brief.
16. Ich schenke mein_____ Großmutter ein_____ Orchidee.
17. Hast du d_____ Geburtstagskind gratuliert?
18. Die Torte schmeckte mein_____ Mutter.

REFLEXIVE VERBS

A reflexive verb is one that expresses that the action of the verb is both performed and received by the subject, i.e., the object of the verb is identical with the subject of the verb. *He amuses himself easily.* The object pronoun used to show this relationship is called a *reflexive pronoun* because it refers or reflects back to the subject of the sentence or clause.

In English this relationship is often implied rather than being stated expressly. *He is shaving (himself).* Many verbs and verb idioms in German require a reflexive pronoun (**Er erholt sich.** *He is getting better; he is recovering.*) There are other verbs, however, that may be used both reflexively (**Er amüsiert sich leicht.** *He amuses himself easily.*) and nonreflexively (**Er amüsiert sein Enkelkind.** *He amuses his grandchild.*)

In German reflexive pronouns may be in either the accusative or the dative case, depending on the verb in question and how the reflexive pronoun functions within the sentence. When the reflexive pronoun functions as a direct object, the accusative is generally used.

Reflexive Verbs Governing the Accusative Case

The following is a partial list of common reflexive verbs followed by accusative reflexive pronouns.

sich amüsieren	*to enjoy, amuse oneself*
sich anziehen	*to dress*
sich aufregen	*to get excited*
sich ausziehen	*to undress*
sich benehmen	*to behave*
sich bewegen	*to move*
sich entscheiden	*to decide*
sich entschuldigen	*to apologize, excuse oneself*
sich erinnern an	*to remember*
sich erkälten	*to catch a cold*
sich freuen	*to be glad*
sich freuen auf	*to look forward to*
sich freuen über	*to be glad about*
sich fürchten vor	*to be afraid of*
sich gewöhnen an	*to get used to*
sich interessieren für	*to be interested in*
sich legen	*to lie down*
sich rasieren	*to shave*
sich setzen	*to sit down*
sich stellen	*to place oneself*
sich umziehen	*to change (clothing)*
sich unterhalten	*to converse, enjoy oneself*
sich verletzen	*to hurt oneself*
sich verspäten	*to be late*
sich vorstellen	*to introduce oneself*
sich waschen	*to wash oneself*
sich wundern über	*to be surprised at*
sich zuwenden	*to turn to*

Accusative reflexive pronouns

The accusative reflexive pronouns are identical with the accusative personal pronouns, except in the third person singular and plural and for the formal form of address **Sie.**

	ACCUSATIVE CASE		
	Personal Pronouns	*Reflexive Pronouns*	
ich	mich	mich	*myself*
du	dich	dich	*yourself*
er	ihn	sich	*himself*
sie	sie	sich	*herself*
es	es	sich	*itself*
wir	uns	uns	*ourselves*
ihr	euch	euch	*yourselves*
sie	sie	sich	*themselves*
Sie	Sie	sich	*yourselves*

Note that **sich,** the reflexive pronoun used with the formal form of address **Sie,** is not capitalized. Study the following forms:

ich wasche mich	wir waschen uns
du wäschst dich	ihr wascht euch
er wäscht sich	sie waschen sich

Er *interessiert sich* **für klassische Musik.**
Ich *fürchte mich* **vor großen Hunden.**
Sie *werden sich* **wohl an ihn** *erinnern.*
Ich *habe mich* **schon** *rasiert.*
Sie *legte sich* **aufs Sofa.**
Warum *hast du* **dich nicht** *entschuldigt?*

The reflexive pronoun is placed as close as possible to the subject. However, it never comes between pronoun subject and verb.

Rasierst du *dich* **jeden Tag?**
Ich habe *mich* **darüber gewundert.**

Reflexive Verbs with Separable Prefixes

The separable prefixes of reflexive verbs act like the separable prefixes of verbs used nonreflexively. (See section on separable prefix verbs.)

Ich *ziehe mich* **nicht** *aus.*
Er *zog sich* **an.**
Sie *werden sich* **wohl** *umziehen.*
Warum *hast du* **dich** *aufgeregt?*

63. Complete the following with the correct reflexive verbs and pronouns. Use the present tense.

1. Ich _____ _____ für Chemie.   *sich interessieren*
2. Wir _____ _____ über Politik.   *sich unterhalten*
3. Du _____ _____ so _____.   *sich aufregen*
4. Wohin _____ ihr _____?   *sich setzen*
5. Ich _____ _____ sehr oft.   *sich erkälten*
6. Wann _____ du _____ _____?   *sich vorstellen*
7. Die Eltern _____ _____ _____.   *sich umziehen*
8. Er _____ _____.   *sich freuen*
9. Ursula _____ _____ aufs Sofa.   *sich legen*
10. Wir _____ _____ über das Geschenk.   *sich freuen*
11. Unser Vater _____ _____.   *sich rasieren*
12. Ich _____ _____ immer.   *sich amüsieren*
13. Das Tier _____ _____ schnell.   *sich bewegen*
14. _____ du _____ auf die Ferien?   *sich freuen*
15. _____ ihr _____?   *sich waschen*
16. Er _____ _____ nicht.   *sich entscheiden*
17. Ich _____ _____ oft.   *sich verspäten*
18. _____ Sie _____ an meinen Onkel?   *sich erinnern*
19. Der Junge _____ _____ schon _____.   *sich anziehen*
20. _____ du _____ immer?   *sich entschuldigen*

64. Rewrite in the present perfect tense.

1. Er fürchtet sich vor Pferden.
2. Wir interessieren uns für die Sammlung.
3. Sie benehmen sich ganz nett.
4. Freut ihr euch über das Geschenk?
5. Ich ziehe mich schon um.

6. Wir stellen uns heute vor.
7. Erkältest du dich oft?
8. Sie wäscht sich schon.
9. Die Männer rasieren sich.
10. Verspätet ihr euch?

65. Answer the following questions, using the cues.

1. Worauf hast du dich gefreut?   *auf seine Ankunft*
2. Wohin legt ihr euch denn?   *aufs Bett*
3. Wann hast du dich verletzt?   *am Freitag*
4. Wofür interessierst du dich?   *für Briefmarken*
5. Woran hast du dich schon gewöhnt?   *an die Arbeit*
6. Wann hat er sich erkältet?   *im Winter*
7. Worüber wundern Sie sich?   *über die Explosion*
8. Wovor fürchten sich die Kinder?   *vor dem Gewitter*

Reflexive Imperative Forms

The reflexive pronouns are always expressed in commands. The reflexive pronoun follows the imperative form of the verb. (See section on imperatives.)

Setz *dich!*
Zieht *euch* **um!**
Fürchten Sie *sich* **nicht!**
Waschen wir *uns!*

66. Write the German.

1. Don't get excited.
2. Children, don't be late.
3. Peter, don't catch a cold.
4. Mr. Ziegler, introduce yourself.
5. Let's sit down.

6. Gisela, wash yourself.
7. Girls, excuse yourselves.
8. Mrs. Klein, hurry up.
9. Ute, don't be afraid of the dog.
10. Father, shave.

Reflexive versus Nonreflexive Use of Verbs

As mentioned above, some German reflexive verbs can be used nonreflexively as well. The reflexive pronoun is used only when the action refers back to the subject.

Reflexive use	**Ich amüsiere mich.**	*I am amusing myself.*
Nonreflexive use	**Ich amüsiere das Baby.**	*I am amusing the baby.*

67. Complete the following with the correct reflexive pronouns when necessary.

1. Leg _____ den Mantel auf den Stuhl!
2. Er stellt _____ meiner Mutter vor.
3. Ich unterhalte _____ mit ihm.
4. Sie haben _____ verletzt.
5. Er zieht _____ aus.
6. Die Mutter wäscht _____ das Kind.
7. Wir waschen _____.
8. Sie haben _____ das Tier verletzt.
9. Ich ziehe _____ das Baby an.
10. Sie setzt _____ hin.

Reflexive Verbs Governing the Dative Case

When the verb has a direct object in the accusative case, the reflexive pronoun is in the dative case. Note that in such cases the reflexive functions like an indirect object. Study the difference between the following two constructions:

Accusative reflexive pronoun	**Ich wasche** *mich*.	*I wash (myself).*
Dative reflexive pronoun	**Ich wasche** *mir die Hände*.	*I wash my hands.*

Dative reflexives are also used when a verb can only take a dative object.

Dative reflexive pronoun	**Ich konnte** *mir* **nicht helfen.**	*I couldn't help myself.*
Dative object after dative verb.	**Ich helfe** *meiner* **Mutter.**	*I help my mother.*

The dative case is required after the following reflexive verbs:

sich einbilden	*to imagine*
sich etwas vorstellen	*to imagine something*
sich weh tun	*to hurt oneself*

Dative reflexive pronouns

The dative reflexive pronouns are identical with the dative personal pronouns, except in the third person singular and plural and for the formal form of address **Sie.** Here, as in the accusative, the reflexive pronoun is **sich.**

	DATIVE CASE		
	Personal Pronouns	*Reflexive Pronouns*	
Ich	mir	mir	*myself*
du	dir	dir	*yourself*
er	ihm	sich	*himself*
sie	ihr	sich	*herself*
es	ihm	sich	*itself*
wir	uns	uns	*ourselves*
ihr	euch	euch	*yourselves*
sie	sie	sich	*themselves*
Sie	Sie	sich	*yourselves*

Note that **sich,** the reflexive pronoun used with the formal form of address, **Sie,** is not capitalized. Study the following forms:

ich tue mir weh	wir tun uns weh
du tust dir weh	ihr tut euch weh
er tut sich weh	sie tun sich weh

The dative reflexive pronoun is also frequently used with such verbs as **kaufen, holen, bestellen, machen, nehmen.** Such constructions are rendered in English with *for myself* (*yourself*, etc.).

| **Ich** *kaufe mir* **ein Auto.** | *I am buying a car for myself.* |
| **Er** *holte sich* **etwas.** | *He got something for himself.* |

Dative reflexive pronouns with parts of body

To show possession when referring to parts of the body or articles of clothing, German often uses the definite article coupled with a dative reflexive in place of the possessive adjective. In English the possessive adjective is used in such situations.

Ich *habe mir* **die Zähne geputzt.**	*I brushed my teeth.*
Ich *ziehe mir* **die Schuhe** an.	*I am putting on my shoes.*
Wäschst du dir **den Kopf?**	*Are you washing your hair?*

68. Complete the following with the appropriate reflexive forms of the indicated verbs. Use the present tense.

1. Du _____ _____ bestimmt _____. *sich weh tun*
2. Wir _____ _____ die Schuhe. *putzen*
3. Ich _____ _____ die Uhr. *kaufen*
4. Warum _____ ihr _____ nicht die Hände? *waschen*
5. Das Mädchen _____ _____ so viel _____. *sich einbilden*
6. Die Dame _____ _____ den Hut _____. *aufsetzen*
7. Er _____ _____ Bier. *bestellen*
8. Ich _____ _____ die Reise _____. *sich vorstellen*
9. Wir _____ _____ das Motorrad. *kaufen*
10. Er _____ _____ Kaffee. *holen*
11. Die Kinder _____ _____ _____. *sich weh tun*
12. Ihr _____ _____ viel _____. *sich einbilden*
13. Ich _____ _____ den Kopf. *waschen*
14. _____ ihr _____ etwas? *nehmen*
15. Wann _____ du _____ das Kleid? *machen*

69. Answer the following questions, using the cues.

1. Was stellst du dir vor? *das Haus*
2. Was haben Sie sich geholt? *das Papier*
3. Wann bestellt ihr euch das Essen? *bald*
4. Wo hast du dir weh getan? *am Fuß*
5. Wo ziehen sich die Gäste an? *im Schlafzimmer*
6. Wer bildet sich etwas ein? *Gisela*

70. Form the imperative. Follow the model.

Inge / waschen / Gesicht.
Inge, wasch dir das Gesicht!

1. Herr Müller / bestellen / Buch.
2. Kinder / putzen / Zähne.
3. Peter und Heinz / kaufen / etwas.

4. Marlene / weh tun / nicht.
5. Kinder / waschen / Hände.
6. Frau Wimmer / nehmen / etwas.

MODAL AUXILIARY VERBS

Unlike most other verbs in German, the modal auxiliaries do not by themselves express an action, process, or change in condition, but instead affect the meaning of the main verb. It is often said that they indicate an attitude toward the main verb.

The modal auxiliaries are usually used with a dependent infinitive. The six modal auxiliaries and their basic meanings are as follows:

dürfen	permission	*may, to be allowed to*
	negative—prohibition	*must NOT*
müssen	necessity, obligation	*must, to have to, be obliged to*
können	ability	*can, to be able to, know how to*
mögen	inclination, desire, liking	*to like to, care for, want to*
	negative—not liking	*NOT to like to, care for, want to*
wollen	desire, intention	*to want to*
sollen	obligation	*should, ought, to be supposed to*

Present Tense

The present tense of the modal auxiliary verbs is irregular. Study the following forms:

dürfen		*müssen*	
ich darf	wir dürfen	ich muß	wir müssen
du darfst	ihr dürft	du mußt	ihr müßt
er darf	sie dürfen	er muß	sie müssen

können		*mögen*	
ich kann	wir können	ich mag	wir mögen
du kannst	ihr könnt	du magst	ihr mögt
er kann	sie können	er mag	sie mögen

wollen		*sollen*	
ich will	wir wollen	ich soll	wir sollen
du willst	ihr wollt	du sollst	ihr sollt
er will	sie wollen	er soll	sie sollen

Note that all modals except **sollen** use different stem vowels for the singular and the plural in the present tense. The plural stem agrees with the infinitive. The first and third person singular forms have no personal endings in the present tense.

The modal auxiliary verbs are used with the infinitive. The infinitive occurs in last position of the sentence, unless the modal plus infinitive is used in a dependent clause. In a negative sentence, **nicht** usually precedes the infinitive.

Wir *dürfen* **dem Techniker** *helfen.*	*We may help the technician.*
Darfst **du** *rauchen?*	*Are you allowed to smoke?*
Ich *darf* **mir eine Zeitung** *nehmen.*	*I am allowed to take a newspaper.*
Ihr *dürft nicht bleiben.*	*You must not stay.*
Mußt **du noch** *studieren?*	*Do you still have to study?*
Ich *muß* **nach Hause** *gehen.*	*I have to go home.*
Werner *kann* **gut** *singen.*	*Werner can sing well.*
Du *kannst nicht mitkommen.*	*You cannot come along.*
Wir *mögen* **es nicht** *sehen.*	*We don't want to see it.*
Ich *mag* **es auch** *hören.*	*I like to hear it also.*
Wollt **ihr bei uns** *bleiben?*	*Do you want to stay with us?*
Ich *will es nicht machen.*	*I don't want to do it.*
Wir *sollen* **etwas** *mitbringen.*	*We are supposed to bring something.*
Du *sollst* **die Wahrheit** *sagen.*	*You ought to tell the truth.*

71. Complete the following with the appropriate present tense forms of **dürfen.**

1. Wir _____ nicht bleiben.
2. Die Kinder _____ gehen.
3. Dieter, du _____ nicht rauchen.
4. _____ ich das Geschenk aufmachen?
5. Er _____ die Geschichte erzählen.
6. Anna, du _____ heute helfen.
7. _____ ihr das Radio kaufen?
8. Du _____ nicht gehen.

72. Rewrite the following, supplying the appropriate forms of the present tense of **müssen.**

1. Er arbeitet schwer.
2. Sie holen Brot.
3. Studierst du?
4. Singen Sie heute?
5. Wir stehen auf.
6. Wann seid ihr im Büro?
7. Die Kinder bleiben zu Hause.
8. Ich bestelle das Essen.

73. Form sentences from the following, using the present tense.

1. Ich / können / glauben / die Geschichte / nicht.
2. Können / ihr / mitkommen / morgen?
3. Wir / helfen / können / unserem Freund / nicht.
4. Max / können / gut / tanzen.
5. Können / du / langsamer / sprechen?
6. Ich / können / alles / hören.

74. Complete the following with the appropriate present tense forms of **mögen.**

1. Ich _____ nicht studieren.
2. Er _____ nicht helfen.
3. Wir _____ nicht arbeiten.
4. _____ du nicht helfen?
5. _____ ihr das Auto sehen?
6. Inge _____ alles essen.
7. _____ Sie nichts anschauen?
8. Die Kinder _____ nicht schlafen.

75. Write the German, using the modal **wollen** in all instances.

1. We want to help.
2. I don't want to see it.
3. He wants to come.
4. Do they want to sleep?
5. Ursel, do you want to go?
6. She wants to study.
7. Erika and Franz, do you want to work?
8. I want to visit the museum.

76. Rewrite the following, supplying the appropriate forms of the present tense of **sollen.**

1. Ich kaufe dem Kind etwas.
2. Er kommt schnell.
3. Sagst du die Wahrheit?
4. Die Studenten lernen.

5. Man stiehlt nicht.
6. Wir kommen nicht.
7. Bleibt ihr?
8. Ich repariere das Auto.

Omission of the dependent infinitive with modal auxiliaries

In colloquial German the dependent infinitive is often omitted when the meaning of the sentence is clear from the context. This occurs most frequently with verbs such as **machen, tun** and with verbs indicating motion, such as **fahren, gehen.**

Er *muß* nach Hause.	*He has to go home.*
Wir *müssen* in die Stadt.	*We have to go downtown.*
***Mußt* du zur Arbeit? (zur Schule)**	*Do you have to go to work? (to school)*
Gerda *kann* Deutsch.	*Gerda knows German.*
***Kannst* du Französisch?**	*Do you know French?*
Wir *wollen* ins Kino. (nach Hause)	*We want to go to the movies. (home)*
Das *darfst* du (machen).	*You may (do it).*

77. Write the German. Do not express the infinitive.

1. We know English.
2. I don't want any soup.
3. They have to go home.

4. Does he know German?
5. She has to go downtown.
6. He doesn't want any milk.

Simple Past Tense

The simple past tense of the modals is formed by taking the infinitive stem, dropping the umlaut if there is one, and then adding the past tense marker **-te** plus the past tense personal verb endings for weak verbs (see p. 148). Study the following simple past tense forms:

dürfen		*müssen*	
ich durfte	wir durften	ich mußte	wir mußten
du durftest	ihr durftet	du mußtest	ihr mußtet
er durfte	sie durften	er mußte	sie mußten

können		*mögen*	
ich konnte	wir konnten	ich mochte	wir mochten
du konntest	ihr konntet	du mochtest	ihr mochtet
er konnte	sie konnten	er mochte	sie mochten

wollen		*sollen*	
ich wollte	wir wollten	ich sollte	wir sollten
du wolltest	ihr wolltet	du solltest	ihr solltet
er wollte	sie wollten	er sollte	sie sollten

Note that **dürfen, müssen, können, mögen** drop their umlauts in the past tense. In addition, **mögen** also has a consonant change; in the past tense **mögen** becomes **mochten.**

Wir *konnten* die Geschichte nicht verstehen.
Er *durfte* nicht kommen.
Sie *wollte* nicht aufmachen.
Ich *mußte* ihn tragen.

78. Rewrite the following in the simple past tense.

1. Wir wollen mitmachen.
2. Ich mag keinen Reis.
3. Kannst du bleiben?
4. Dürft ihr denn rauchen?
5. Du kannst nicht heimgehen.

6. Luise will bezahlen.
7. Warum wollen Sie helfen?
8. Mußt du studieren?
9. Ich will es sehen.
10. Könnt ihr das machen?

79. Write sentences from the following. Use the simple past tense.

1. können / ihr / ihm / helfen?
2. ich / wollen / etwas / kaufen.
3. sollen / er / auch / mitmachen?

4. wir / müssen / ihn / anrufen.
5. die Kinder / mögen / kein / Gemüse.
6. dürfen / du / nicht / gehen?

Use of simple past tense

The simple past tense of the modals is not restricted to narration, but is used freely in conversation and posing questions.

80. Form questions from the following. Use the simple past tense. Follow the model.

du abfahren?   müssen
Mußtest du abfahren?

1. Herr Maier, Sie schlafen?   *wollen*
2. ihr rauchen?   *dürfen*
3. du ausgehen?   *können*
4. ihr Bananen?   *mögen*
5. Frau Lang, Sie daran glauben?   *sollen*
6. ihr helfen?   *müssen*
7. du es kaufen?   *sollen*

8. ihr fragen?   *wollen*
9. du mitmachen?   *dürfen*
10. ihr es sehen?   *können*
11. Sie alles nehmen?   *müssen*
12. ihr Bier bestellen?   *sollen*
13. du keine Milch?   *mögen*
14. Sie Konrad kennenlernen?   *wollen*

Compound Tenses

Present Perfect Tense

Past participles of modals

The modal auxiliary verbs are unique because they have two different past participles. One is formed the conventional way with the **ge-** prefix, the other is identical to the infinitive. In either case the perfect tenses are formed with **haben.**

*Past participles formed with **ge-** prefix*

When no dependent infinitive is needed to convey the meaning in context, the following past participles of the modals are used.

dürfen	gedurft	müssen	gemußt
können	gekonnt	sollen	gesollt
mögen	gemocht	wollen	gewollt

Ich *habe* **Französisch** *gekonnt.*	*I knew French.*
Er *hat* **nach Hause** *gemußt.*	*He had to go home.*
Wir *haben* **keinen Spinat** *gemocht.*	*We didn't like any spinach.*

81.   Rewrite the following. Use the present perfect tense.

1. Ich mag ihn nicht.
2. Sie will nach Köln.
3. Darfst du das?
4. Wir müssen zur Schule.
5. Kann er das?
6. Die Leute mögen nicht.

7. Ihr könnt doch Deutsch.
8. Sie können Englisch.
9. Ich muß zur Arbeit.
10. Wir dürfen es.
11. Magst du keine Limonade?
12. Ich soll in die Stadt.

Double infinitive construction

When the modal is followed by the infinitive of another verb, the present perfect is then formed with a form of **haben** plus the infinitive of the verb plus the infinitive of the modal. This construction is called double infinitive construction, because the two infinitives occur together in last position in the sentence.

Sie *haben* **es nicht** *sehen dürfen.*	*They weren't allowed to see it.*
Ich *habe* **nicht** *arbeiten können.*	*I was not able to work.*
Hast **du den Roman** *lesen müssen?*	*Did you have to read the novel?*
Er *hat* **Gisela** *kennenlernen wollen.*	*He wanted to get acquainted with Gisela.*

82.   Rewrite the following in the present perfect tense.

1. Wir sollten nicht mitfahren.
2. Ich konnte nicht schreiben.
3. Mußtet ihr hier bleiben?
4. Warum wollte er anrufen?
5. Ich durfte es bringen.
6. Man konnte Musik hören.
7. Sie mochten nicht aufstehen.
8. Warum wolltest du es zerstören?

9. Er durfte es sehen.
10. Wolltet ihr dort parken?
11. Ich wollte heimgehen.
12. Mußtest du zu Hause bleiben?
13. Sie konnten gut lesen.
14. Hubert mußte studieren.
15. Wir wollten Maria helfen.
16. Konnten Sie schwimmen?

Past Perfect Tense

As in the formation of the present perfect tense, the past perfect of modal auxiliaries can be formed with two different past participles. Compare the following:

Er *hatte* **Deutsch** *gekonnt.*	*He had known German.*
Wir *hatten* **es** *machen dürfen.*	*We had been allowed to do it.*

83.   Rewrite the following in the past perfect tense.

1. Wir konnten es.
2. Ich mußte abfahren.
3. Er wollte es.
4. Sie mochten keinen Kuchen.
5. Sie sollte mich anrufen.
6. Durftest du sie besuchen?
7. Ich wollte nicht davon sprechen.

8. Ihr durftet es ja wissen.
9. Sie konnte das Fenster aufmachen.
10. Ich mußte zur Schule.
11. Wir mochten Peter nicht.
12. Wolltest du hinausgehen?
13. Ich konnte Russisch.
14. Er mußte den Wagen reparieren.

Future Tense

The future of modals is formed with a form of **werden** plus the infinitive plus the infinitive of the modal.

Er *wird* **wohl nicht** *fahren können.*	*He will probably not be able to go.*
Ich *werde* **nicht** *kommen dürfen.*	*I may not be allowed to come.*

84. Change the following to the future tense.

1. Sie können nicht schlafen.
2. Wir müssen den ganzen Tag studieren.
3. Er will es sehen.
4. Ich muß klingeln.
5. Ihr dürft nichts kaufen.

6. Kannst du es schicken?
7. Gudrun will nicht mitmachen.
8. Wollt ihr die Suppe probieren?
9. Sie dürfen nicht schreien.
10. Wir können nicht arbeiten.

DEPENDENT INFINITIVES

Simple Tenses—Present and Past

Like modals, the verbs **hören** (*to hear*), **sehen** (*to see*), **helfen** (*to help*), **lassen** (*to let, allow, leave*) can be used either by themselves or with the infinitive of another verb. This infinitive is referred to as a dependent infinitive. Note that the verb **lassen** means *to leave* when used by itself. When used with a dependent infinitive it means *to let* or *allow*. Compare the following:

Ich *lasse* **den Mantel hier.**	*I leave the coat here.*
Ich *lasse* **Robert** *kommen.*	*I let Robert come.*
Wir *hörten* **Musik.**	*We heard music.*
Wir *hörten* **Anita** *singen.*	*We heard Anita sing.*
Er *sah* **die Parade.**	*He saw the parade.*
Er *sah* **Inge** *kommen.*	*He saw Inge come.*
Hilfst **du Peter?**	*Are you helping Peter?*
Hilfst **du Peter** *schreiben?*	*Are you helping Peter write?*

85. Write sentences from the following, using the present tense.

1. Wir / lassen / das Bild / in der Schule.
2. Ich / helfen / Rita / den Hund / suchen.
3. Sehen / du / deine Schwester / arbeiten?
4. Hören / Sie / die Sonate?
5. Er / hören / seine Frau / schreien.

6. Lassen / ihr / Hans / gehen?
7. Die Leute / hören / uns / sprechen.
8. Ich / sehen / die Kirche.
9. Frau Berger / helfen / heute.
10. Er / lassen / Gerda / mitkommen.

Compound Tenses—Present Perfect and Past Perfect

When the verbs **hören, sehen, lassen, helfen** are used in the perfect tenses with a dependent infinitive, the double infinitive construction is used. If used without a dependent infinitive, the regular past participate is used. (See section on double infinitives.)

Compare the following:

Ich *habe* **das Lied** *gehört.*	*I heard the song.*
Ich *habe* **sie** *schreien hören.*	*I heard her scream.*
Wir *haben* **das Museum** *gesehen.*	*We saw the museum.*
Wir *haben* **Agnes** *malen sehen.*	*We saw Agnes paint.*
Hast **du das Buch dort** *gelassen?*	*Did you leave the book there?*
Hast **du Ute** *probieren lassen?*	*Did you let Ute try?*

86. Rewrite the following in the present perfect tense.

1. Ich ließ es liegen.
2. Wir hörten sie lachen.
3. Er sah seinen Freund.
4. Sie halfen Heinz das Auto reparieren.
5. Er hörte nichts.

6. Ich sah Pia reiten.
7. Sie hörten Sonja weinen.
8. Wir ließen die Zeitungen zu Hause.
9. Wir halfen den Kindern.
10. Vater ließ uns gehen.

Future Tense

When the future tense is formed with one of the preceding verbs and a dependent infinitive, the double infinitive construction occurs at the end of the sentence.

Ich *werde* **die Sängerin** *hören.*	*I shall hear the singer.*
Ich *werde* **das Kind** *weinen hören.*	*I shall hear the child cry.*
Wir *werden* **das Bild hier** *lassen.*	*We shall leave the painting here.*
Wir *werden* **das Bild** *hängen lassen.*	*We shall let the picture hang.*

87. Rewrite the following, adding the indicated words.

1. Er wird Peter sehen.   *schreiben*
2. Ich werde Otto hören.   *kommen*
3. Wir werden den Kindern helfen.   *zeichnen*
4. Wirst du Dieter sehen?   *lachen*
5. Sie werden Rainer hören.   *sprechen*
6. Werden Sie Anneliese helfen?   *lesen*
7. Ich werde den Mantel hier lassen.   *liegen*
8. Werdet ihr Großmutter hören?   *rufen*

Dependent Clauses

When the double infinitive construction occurs in dependent clauses, the conjugated form of the auxiliary **haben** or **werden** is not moved into last position as might be expected. Instead the auxiliary precedes the double infinitive.

Er sagt, daß er *hat kommen dürfen.*
Ich bin glücklich, weil ich Ursel *werde singen hören.*

88. Change the following main clauses to dependent clauses. Introduce the dependent clause with **Er sagt, daß . . .** Follow the model.

Ich habe Anna lachen sehen.
Er sagt, daß ich Anna habe lachen sehen.

1. Du hast die Jacke liegen lassen.
2. Wir haben Josef studieren helfen.
3. Sie haben Franz singen hören.
4. Ich habe es machen lassen.

5. Sie hat das Geschenk öffnen dürfen.
6. Du hast den Bleistift zurückgeben wollen.
7. Wir haben Peter kommen lassen.
8. Ihr habt das Auto bringen müssen.

Infinitives Preceded by zu (*to*)

Dependent infinitives are never preceded by **zu** (*to*) when used in the future tense, or when used with the modals or the verbs **sehen, hören, helfen, lassen.** However, dependent infinitives are preceded by **zu** (*to*) in the following instances.

After certain prepositions

The following prepositions introduce infinitive phrases in which the dependent infinitive is preceded by **zu** in German. Note that the gerund ending in -*ing* is used in English for the first two.

(an)statt . . . zu (*instead of . . . -ing*)

Wir haben gemalt, anstatt *zu studieren.*	*We were painting instead of studying.*

ohne . . . zu (*without . . . -ing*)

Er kam ins Zimmer, ohne *zu klopfen.*	*He came into the room without knocking.*

um . . . zu (*in order to*)

Sie ging hinaus, um den Brief *zu lesen.*	*She went outside in order to read the letter.*

Note that the dependent infinitive is in last position in German. The infinitive phrase is set off by a comma when it consists of more elements than **zu** plus infinitive.

When a separable prefix verb occurs in an infinitive phrase, **zu** comes between prefix and infinitive.

Er telefonierte, um uns ein*zu***laden.**	*He called in order to invite us.*

89. Complete the following with the German.

1. Er geht vorbei, _____ . *without seeing Norma*
2. Sie bleibt zu Hause, _____ . *instead of going to school*
3. Ich bin gelaufen, _____ . *in order to help Gertrud*
4. Sie sind gekommen, _____ . *without calling (anrufen)*
5. Ich gehe auf mein Zimmer, _____ . *in order to change*
6. Er hat telefoniert, _____ . *in order to invite the children*
7. Sie gibt es ihrem Bruder, _____ . *instead of bringing it to Helga*
8. Sie geht aus, _____ . *without putting on a coat*
9. Wir haben sie besucht _____ . *in order to ask*
10. Ich konnte das Gedicht, _____ . *without learning it*

With anticipatory da(r)- compounds followed by zu + dependent infinitive

Introductory phrases containing an anticipatory **da(r)-** compound are completed by an infinitive preceded by **zu.** In English **da(r)-** is not translated. Note that the infinitive is in last position in the German sentence.

Ich warte darauf, das Auto *zu* **sehen.**   *I am waiting to see the car.*
Er hofft darauf, sein Geld wieder*zu***finden.**   *He is hoping to find his money.*
Sie wartet darauf, sich *zu* **setzen.**   *She is waiting to sit down.*

90.   Complete the following with the correct German infinitive phrases. For all sentences, use the German clause appearing in the first example.

     1. Er denkt nicht daran, _____ .   *to apologize*
     2. *to ask us*
     3. *to help the children*
     4. *to tell the story*
     5. *to shave*
     6. *to come along*
     7. *to get it*
     8. *to take money*
     9. *to feed the dog*
    10. *to eat the cake*

Certain verbs introducing **zu** *+ infinitive*

    The following are some of the verbs introducing **zu** plus infinitive.

anfangen	*to start, begin*
aufhören	*to stop*
bitten	*to ask*
erlauben	*to allow*
etwas schön (nett, etc.**) finden**	*to find (consider) something pretty (nice, etc.)*
helfen	*to help*
hoffen	*to hope*
vergessen	*to forget*
versprechen	*to promise*
vorschlagen	*to propose*
wünschen	*to wish*

Er *hörte auf,* **Golf** *zu spielen.*   *He stopped playing golf.*
Ich *hoffe,* **euch bald** *zu sehen.*   *I hope to see you soon.*
Sie *findet es dumm,* **ihn** *zu fragen.*   *She considers it stupid to ask him.*

91.   Supply the correct infinitive phrases.

     1. Ich verspreche dir, dich oft _____ .   *anrufen*
     2. Er fängt an, seine Aufgaben _____ .   *schreiben*
     3. Sie vergaß, mir die Zeitung _____ .   *mitgeben*
     4. Sie hat mich gebeten, ihn auch _____ .   *einladen*
     5. Wir helfen dir gern, das Gras _____ .   *schneiden*
     6. Ich finde es toll, bei euch _____ .   *sein*
     7. Ich schlage vor, es _____ .   *lesen*
     8. Wir hoffen, Oma _____ .   *besuchen*
     9. Versprecht ihr, meinen Freund _____ ?   *begleiten*
    10. Er bittet, seine Mutter _____ .   *mitnehmen*
    11. Sie finden es schön, ihren Onkel _____ .   *sehen*
    12. Ich höre auf, die Geschichte _____ .   *glauben*

The verb **brauchen** + **nicht zu** + *dependent infinitive*

The form **brauchen** plus **nicht zu** plus infinitive corresponds to the English *not to have to*. This form is usually used instead of the negative form of **müssen**. Note that **nicht zu** plus infinitive occurs at the end of the sentence.

Muß ich kommen?	*Do I have to come?*
Nein, du *brauchst nicht zu kommen.*	*No, you don't have to come.*
Muß ich deinem Vater helfen?	*Do I have to help your father?*
Nein, du *brauchst* **ihm** *nicht zu helfen.*	*No, you don't have to help him.*
Müssen wir heute abend singen?	*Do we have to sing tonight?*
Nein, ihr *braucht* **heute abend** *nicht zu singen.*	*No, you don't have to sing tonight.*

92. Rewrite the following in the negative. Use the negative of **brauchen**.

1. Er muß studieren.
2. Ich muß lesen.
3. Wir müssen das Buch zurückgeben.
4. Sie muß arbeiten.
5. Ihr müßt es machen.
6. Du mußt Herbert helfen.
7. Ich muß Bert besuchen.
8. Renate muß lesen.
9. Sie müssen die Geschichte erzählen.
10. Ich muß es bestellen.

VERBS AS OTHER PARTS OF SPEECH

Infinitives Used as Nouns

German infinitives used as nouns are neuter in gender and are always capitalized. They often correspond to the English gerund, which ends in *-ing*.

Ihr *Lachen* **machte mich nervös.**	*Her laughing (laughter) made me nervous.*
Das viele *Rauchen* **ist ungesund.**	*Smoking a lot is unhealthy.*

The contraction **beim** plus infinitive noun means *while . . . -ing* or *in the act of.*

Er hat sich *beim Schwimmen* **verletzt.**	*He got hurt while swimming.*

93. Complete in German. For all sentences, use the German clause appearing in the first example.

1. Ich habe mich _____ amüsiert. *while walking*
2. *while dancing*
3. *while singing*
4. *while working*
5. *while painting*
6. *while repairing*
7. *while studying*
8. *while playing*
9. *while telephoning*
10. *while swimming*

Present Participles Used as Adjectives and Adverbs

The present participle is formed by adding **-d** to the infinitive. It can be used as an adjective or as an adverb. Remember to add adjective endings when appropriate.

Ist das *weinende* **Kind krank?**   *Is the crying child ill?*
Er kam *lachend* **ins Zimmer.**   *He came into the room laughing.*

94. Complete the following with the correct forms of the present participles.

1. Sie sieht _____ aus. *leiden*
2. Der _____ Student wartet auf den Professor. *lesen*
3. Wir brauchen ein Zimmer mit _____ Wasser. *fließen*
4. Hörst du den _____ Hund? *bellen*
5. _____ lief er ins Haus. *bluten*
6. Wie heißt die _____ Frau? *singen*
7. Kennst du den _____ Jungen? *weinen*
8. Dort liegt das _____ Kind. *schlafen*
9. Wer is das _____ Mädchen? *lächeln*
10. _____ geht er vorbei. *grüßen*

Past Participles Used as Adjectives and Adverbs

Many past participles of weak and strong verbs can be used as adjectives and adverbs.

Ich möchte ein *weichgekochtes* **Ei.**   *I would like a soft-boiled egg.*
Das Mädchen ist *verletzt.*   *The girl is hurt.*

95. Fill in the correct forms of the past participles.

1. Die _____ Stadt wird aufgebaut. *zerstören*
2. Die Suppe ist _____ . *anbrennen*
3. Was macht ihr mit dem _____ Geld? *stehlen*
4. Hier ist deine _____ Arbeit. *schreiben*
5. Frisch _____ Brötchen schmecken herrlich. *backen*
6. Wo ist die _____ Arbeit? *beginnen*
7. Das Tier ist _____ . *fangen*
8. Der _____ Hund schläft. *füttern*
9. Wo steht das _____ Auto? *reparieren*
10. Mach das _____ Fenster zu! *öffnen*

Participles Used as Nouns

Many present and past participles can be used as nouns. Such nouns are capitalized and take adjective endings.

Seine *Verwandte* **ist angekommen.**   *His relative (female) arrived.*
Der *Reisende* **hatte große Koffer.**   *The traveler had large suitcases.*

96. Complete with the correct adjective endings.

1. Wo sind die Verletzt_____ ?
2. Ein Gefangen_____ ist ausgebrochen.
3. Der Sterbend_____ ließ seine Kinder kommen.
4. Eine Verwundet_____ lag auf der Straße.
5. Wo wohnt der Gesandt_____ ?
6. Die Reisend_____ sind müde.
7. Die Verliebt_____ tanzen.

8. Das Gefroren_____ ist gut.
9. Wie heißt der Gefallen_____ ?
10. Das Neugeboren_____ schreit.

IMPERATIVES

Weak and Strong Verbs

The imperative expresses commands, requests, or orders. Just as there are three different forms of address **(Sie, ihr, du),** there are three corresponding imperative forms. The imperative verb is the first element in a command. However, it may be preceded by **bitte** (*please*). **Bitte** can also occur within the sentence or in last position. The word **doch** softens the command, corresponding to the English *why don't you?* In written German commands, an exclamation point is used.

```
Imperative = (Bitte) Verb + (Personal Pronoun if Required)
```

Study the examples of the imperative forms below:

Sie	Spielen Sie!	Helfen Sie mir!
ihr	Spielt!	Helft mir!
du	Spiel(e)!	Hilf mir!

Formal Commands (Singular and Plural)—Sie

The formal commands are formed by using the infinitive plus **Sie.** The pronoun **Sie** is always expressed.

Kommen Sie!	*Come.*
Bitte *parken Sie* **hier!**	*Please park here.*
Rauchen Sie **bitte nicht!**	*Please don't smoke.*
Antworten Sie **doch!**	*Why don't you answer?*
Herr Müller, *erzählen Sie* **die Geschichte bitte!**	*Mr. Müller, please tell the story.*
Meine Herren, *nehmen Sie* **bitte nichts!**	*Gentlemen, please don't take anything.*

Familiar Commands

Plural—ihr

The familiar plural command corresponds to the **ihr** form of the present tense. Note that the pronoun **ihr** is not expressed.

Macht **die Aufgaben!**	*Do your homework.*
Lest **doch den Roman!**	*Why don't you read the novel?*
Bitte *holt* **die Bücher!**	*Please get the books.*
Öffnet **bitte das Fenster!**	*Please open the window.*
Sprecht **langsamer bitte!**	*Talk slower, please.*
Kommt **doch am Abend!**	*Why don't you come in the evening?*

Singular—du

The familiar singular command is formed from the infinitive stem plus **-e.** In colloquial speech this **-e** is usually dropped (except in the cases noted below). Note that the pronoun **du** is not expressed.

Frag **deinen Vater!**	*Ask your father.*
Komm **mit deinem Bruder bitte!**	*Please come with your brother.*
Gudrun, bitte *kauf* **die Kamera!**	*Gudrun, please buy the camera.*
Trink **doch Wasser!**	*Why don't you drink water?*
Such **das Bild bitte!**	*Look for the picture, please.*
Geh **ins Zimmer!**	*Go into the room.*

97. Answer the following questions with formal commands. Follow the model.

      essen?   Ja, essen Sie bitte.

1.	schreiben?		6.	reden?
2.	schlafen?		7.	arbeiten?
3.	gehen?		8.	erzählen?
4.	tanzen?		9.	singen?
5.	lächeln?		10.	fahren?

98. Complete the following with the familiar plural commands.

1.	_____ es!	*finden*	9.	_____ dort!	*bleiben*
2.	_____ lauter!	*sprechen*	10.	_____ den Arzt!	*rufen*
3.	_____ weniger!	*trinken*	11.	_____ den Braten!	*essen*
4.	_____ den Mantel!	*holen*	12.	_____ das Geld!	*nehmen*
5.	_____ gut!	*schlafen*	13.	_____ langsamer!	*reiten*
6.	_____ das Auto!	*parken*	14.	_____ Milch!	*bestellen*
7.	_____ mehr!	*studieren*	15.	_____ bald!	*schreiben*
8.	_____ zur Schule!	*gehen*			

99. Rewrite the following commands, changing the plural to the singular.

1.	Singt lauter!		9.	Weint nicht!
2.	Kommt jetzt!		10.	Springt ins Wasser!
3.	Sucht das Geld!		11.	Schwimmt schneller!
4.	Bleibt hier!		12.	Sagt die Wahrheit!
5.	Macht es!		13.	Ruft die Polizei!
6.	Grüßt Tante Ida!		14.	Fragt den Lehrer!
7.	Geht ins Haus!		15.	Raucht nicht!
8.	Probiert die Wurst!			

Variations of the Familiar Singular Command

-e ending

When the infinitive stem ends in **-d, -t, -ig,** or **-m, -n** preceded by a consonant other than **-l** or **-r,** the **-e** ending is not dropped in the familiar singular command form.

Öffne **die Tür**	*Open the door.*
Entschuldige **bitte!**	*Excuse me, please.*
Antworte **bitte!**	*Answer, please.*
Wende **es!**	*Turn it.*
Atme **regelmäßig!**	*Breathe normally.*

Infinitives ending in **eln** *and* **-ern**

When the infinitive ends in **-eln,** and **e** preceding **-ln** is dropped and the **-e** ending is kept.

Klingle **nicht!**	*Don't ring.*
Lächle **doch!**	*Why don't you smile?*
Behandle **das Kind!**	*Treat the child.*

When the infinitive ends in **-ern,** the **-e** ending is kept.

Ändere **nichts!**	*Don't change anything.*
Füttere **die Katze!**	*Feed the cat.*
Wandere **nicht!**	*Don't hike.*

100. Answer the following with the familiar singular commands. Follow the model.

     arbeiten? Ja, arbeite!

1. warten?	8. es ändern?
2. reden?	9. es beobachten?
3. lächeln?	10. rechnen?
4. es füttern?	11. es schneiden?
5. ihn behandeln?	12. es sammeln?
6. es öffnen?	13. wandern?
7. antworten?	14. arbeiten?

Stem vowel **e** *changes to* **i** *or* **ie**

Those strong verbs that have a stem vowel change in the present tense from **e** to **i** or **ie** have the same change in the familiar singular command.

Gib **Gisela den Brief!**	*Give the letter to Gisela.*
Hilf **uns!**	*Help us.*
Iß **die Suppe!**	*Eat your soup.*
Sprich **langsamer!**	*Speak more slowly.*
Lies **doch das Buch!**	*Why don't you read the book?*
Nimm **nichts!**	*Don't take anything.*

101. Rewrite the following, changing the formal commands to the familiar singular commands.

1. Helfen Sie dem Kind!	7. Treffen Sie die Frau!
2. Sprechen Sie lauter!	8. Sterben Sie nicht!
3. Geben Sie es dem Lehrer!	9. Erschrecken Sie nicht!
4. Stehlen Sie nicht!	10. Essen Sie das Fleisch!
5. Lesen Sie die Zeitung!	11. Nehmen Sie den Schmuck!
6. Brechen Sie es nicht!	12. Vergessen Sie nichts!

Irregular Imperative Forms

The imperative forms of **haben, sein, werden, wissen** are slightly irregular. Study the following forms:

		haben	sein	werden	wissen
Formal	**Sie**	**Haben Sie!**	**Seien Sie!**	**Werden Sie!**	**Wissen Sie!**
Familiar plural	**ihr**	**Habt!**	**Seid!**	**Werdet!**	**Wißt!**
Familiar singular	**du**	**Hab(e)!**	**Sei!**	**Werde!**	**Wisse!**

102. Complete the following commands of the indicated verbs.

1. Peter und Hans, _____ keine Angst! *haben*
2. Ilse, _____ nicht frech! *sein*
3. Herr Koch, _____ ja nicht Krank! *werden*
4. Kinder, _____ morgen die Antwort! *wissen*
5. Frau Bucher, _____ bitte ruhig! *sein*
6. Du liebes Kind, _____ bald wieder gesund! *werden*
7. Christa, _____ nur vorsichtig! *sein*
8. Fritz, _____ doch Geduld! *haben*
9. Herr Knauer, _____ keine Angst! *haben*
10. Frau Bremer, _____ es nächste Woche! *wissen*
11. Kinder, _____ lieb! *sein*
12. Frau Sommer, _____ doch so nett! *sein*

First Person Command (*Let's*)

The idea of *let's* is expressed by using the first person plural. The pronoun **wir** follows the conjugated verb.

Singen wir!	*Let's sing.*
Gehen wir!	*Let's go.*
Fahren wir **mit dem Auto!**	*Let's go by car.*

103. Answer the following with the first person commands. Follow the model.

Pferd füttern? Füttern wir das Pferd!

1. Das Abendessen kochen?
2. Den Lehrer fragen?
3. Warme Milch trinken?
4. Wein kaufen?
5. Jetzt gehen?
6. Die Aufgaben schreiben?
7. Den Hund rufen?
8. Das Buch holen?
9. Viel arbeiten?
10. Nichts ändern?

Impersonal Imperative

Instructions to the public are expressed by an infinitive command form. The exclamation point is not necessary with such instructions. The infinitive command occurs in last position.

Bitte *anschnallen.*	*Please fasten your seat belts.*
Rechts *fahren.*	*Drive on the right side.*
Nicht *aufstehen.*	*Do not get up.*
Einfahrt *freihalten.*	*Keep the driveway clear.*

THE CONDITIONAL

Weak and Strong Verbs

The German conditional is formed with the auxiliary **würden** plus infinitive and corresponds to the English verb pattern *would* plus infinitive. The conditional expresses what would happen if it were not for another circumstance. As is customary for dependent infinitives, the infinitive of the conditional is in last position, unless it occurs in a dependent clause. Study the following:

ich würde sagen	wir würden sagen
du würdest sagen	ihr würdet sagen
er würde sagen	sie würden sagen

Sie *würden* **das Haus nicht** *kaufen*.	*They would not buy the house.*
Ich *würde* **dem Kind** *helfen*.	*I would help the child.*
Würdest **du das Geld** *nehmen?*	*Would you take the money?*
Er weiß, daß ich es *sagen würde*.	*He knows that I would say it.*

104. Rewrite the following in the conditional.

1. Wir nehmen nichts.
2. Bezahlst du?
3. Ich schwimme den ganzen Tag.
4. Sie arbeiten viel.
5. Er studiert nicht.
6. Fahrt ihr nach Deutschland?
7. Singen Sie laut?
8. Ich springe nicht ins Wasser.
9. Liest du das Buch?
10. Er repariert den Wagen.
11. Kommt ihr?
12. Sie bringen das Geschenk.
13. Helft ihr mir?
14. Ich gehe auch.
15. Tragen Sie die Jacke?
16. Laufen die Kinder?

Use of the Conditional

In both English and German the conditional is used in the conclusion of contrary-to-fact *if* clauses. It is used increasingly in place of the subjunctive in the conclusion of the condition in spoken and informal German. (See the section on the subjunctive.)

The conditional is also used as a polite form of request.

Würden **Sie bitte einen Moment** *warten?*	*Would you please wait a moment?*
Würdest **du mir bitte** *helfen?*	*Would you please help me?*
Würdet **ihr** *singen* **bitte?**	*Would you please sing?*

105. Rewrite in German, changing the commands to the conditional.

1. Kommen Sie bitte!
2. Nimm das bitte!
3. Bleibt hier bitte!
4. Fahren Sie bitte schneller!
5. Gib mir bitte das Messer!
6. Sprechen Sie bitte langsamer!
7. Gehen Sie bitte!
8. Park bitte das Auto!
9. Bestellt das Essen bitte!
10. Zeigen Sie es den Kindern bitte!
11. Besuchen Sie Ihren Vater bitte!
12. Warte hier bitte!

THE SUBJUNCTIVE

Whereas the *indicative mood* is used to make statements of fact, ask questions, and generally describe reality, the *subjunctive mood* is used in referring to conditions and situations that are contrary to fact, unlikely, uncertain or hypothetical. For example, the indicative is used for actions that have taken place, are taking place, or will very likely take place.

Er hat großen Hunger.	*He is very hungry.*
Ich weiß, daß sie krank ist.	*I know that she is ill.*
Wir werden ihn besuchen.	*We will visit him.*
Er hat es genommen.	*He took it.*

The subjunctive is used to express that a certain action has not or may not take place, because it is a supposition, conjecture, or desire, rather than a fact. When a statement is contrary to fact or when it implies a possibility rather than a probability, the subjunctive mood is used.

Ich wollte, er *wäre* **hier!**	*I wish he were here.*
Er sagte, er *würde* **keine Zeit haben.**	*He said he would have no time.*
Sie tut, als ob sie Geld *hätte*.	*She acts as if she had money.*

General Subjunctive and Special Subjunctive

In German there are two forms of the subjunctive—the *general subjunctive*, which is the form most commonly used, and the *special subjunctive*, which finds application in a much narrower range of situations, primarily for indirect speech in formal situations. The special subjunctive is also referred to as *subjunctive I*, since it is based on the infinitive stem, which is the first principal part of the verb. Similarly the general subjunctive is sometimes referred to as *subjunctive II* because it is based on the simple past tense, which is the second principle part of the verb.

Both forms of the subjunctive take the same set of personal endings. Unless otherwise indicated, the following sections discuss the general subjective, that is, subjunctive II.

The uses of the general subjunctive fall into four main categories:

(1)   Wishes

(2)   Contrary-to-fact conditions

(3)   Hypothetical statements and questions

(4)   Polite requests and questions

Each of these uses is explained below.

Present-Time Subjunctive

The present-time subjunctive is used to refer to wishes, unreal conditions, and hypothetical events in the present or future. It is formed by adding the subjunctive personal endings to the stem of the simple past. To find the past stem, just drop the **-en** from the simple past tense of the first person plural. Note that this same rule applies to both strong and weak verbs.

> *Present-Time Subjunctive = Past Stem + Subjunctive Personal Ending*

The subjunctive personal endings that must be added to the past stem are as follows:

	Singular	Plural
First person	-e	-en
Second person	-est	-et
Third person	-e	-en

Thus the fully conjugated present-time subjunctive for **sagen** is:

ich sagte	wir sagten
du sagtest	ihr sagtet
er sagte	sie sagten

Ich wollte, er *sagte* **mir die Wahrheit.**   *I wish he would tell me the truth.*

Weak Verbs

The German present-time subjunctive of weak verbs is identical with the simple past indicative. This is also true in English. The present-time subjunctive of all English verbs, except *to be*, is identical with the past indicative: *If* I had *the money* . . . ; *If* he lost *everything* . . . ; *but: If* we were *rich* . . . .

In English, as well as in German, these present-time subjunctive forms are ambiguous. Only the context makes clear whether the forms are used in the past indicative or the present subjunctive. For this reason the present conditional **würden** plus infinitive is often substituted for the subjunctive in

German. (See section on the conditional.) The German present-time subjunctive corresponds to the English present conditional *would* plus infinitive (*would run*) or to the present-time subjunctive (*ran*), depending on use. Although the present-time subjunctive looks like the simple past indicative, it always refers to present or future time.

106. Rewrite the following, substituting the present-time subjunctive for the present conditional.

1. Sie würden uns besuchen.
2. Wir würden viel machen.
3. Würdet ihr es kaufen?
4. Ich würde es erzählen.
5. Würdest du es zerstören?
6. Würden Sie dort arbeiten?
7. Ich würde ihn fragen.
8. Wir würden zahlen.
9. Er würde es glauben.
10. Ich würde es sagen.
11. Würdest du dort wohnen?
12. Würdet ihr es hören?
13. Sie würden es lernen.
14. Wir würden nicht weinen.
15. Ich würde bezahlen.
16. Er würde studieren.
17. Würdet ihr das Haus bauen?
18. Würden Sie dort spielen?
19. Sie würden alles hören.
20. Würdest du malen?

107. Write the German, using the present-time subjunctive.

1. I would cry.
2. We would play.
3. They would get it.
4. He would not believe it.
5. Children, would you study?
6. Gerda, would you buy flowers?
7. Mrs. Treibl, would you live there?
8. She would work.
9. We would learn.
10. They would try the soup.

Irregular Weak Verbs

The irregular weak verbs **brennen, kennen, nennen, rennen, senden, wenden** do not form the present-time subjunctive from their simple past tense stems but rather retain the vowel of the infinitive stem. These forms, however, are increasingly being replaced by the conditional (**würden** plus infinitive).

ich rennte	wir rennten
du renntest	ihr renntet
er rennte	sie rennten

Ich *wollte*, **die Kerze** *brennte* **den ganzen Tag.**   *I wished the candle would burn all day.*
Ich *wünschte*, **ich** *kennte* **die Frau besser.**   *I wished I knew the women better.*

The irregular weak verbs **bringen, denken, wissen** use the simple past tense stems but add an umlaut plus the subjunctive endings to form the present-time subjunctive.

ich brächte	ich dächte	ich wüßte
du brächtest	du dächtest	du wüßtest
er brächte	er dächte	er wüßte
wir brächten	wir dächten	wir wüßten
ihr brächtet	ihr dächtet	ihr wüßtet
sie brächten	sie dächten	sie wüßten

Ich *wünschte*, **er** *dächte* **nicht daran.**   *I wished he would not think of it.*
Ich *wünschte*, **sie** *brächte* **ihm nichts.**   *I wished she wouldn't bring him anything.*
Ich *wünschte* **wir** *wüßten* **alles.**   *I wished we would know everything.*

108. Rewrite the following, substituting the present-time subjunctive for the present conditional.

1. Das Hause würde brennen.
2. Würdet ihr daran denken?
3. Ich würde etwas bringen.
4. Würdest du es nennen?
5. Sie würden schnell rennen.

6. Wir würden es wissen.
7. Ich würde den Brief senden.
8. Wir würden das Blatt wenden.
9. Ich würde das wissen.
10. Würdest du das Buch bringen?

Strong Verbs

The present-time subjunctive of strong verbs is also formed by adding the subjunctive endings **-e**, **-est, -en, -et, -en** to the simple past tense stems. However, those verbs containing the vowels **a, o, u** in the past stems add an umlaut.

No Umlaut		Umlaut	
ich bliebe	wir blieben	ich nähme	wir nähmen
du bliebest	ihr bliebet	du nähmest	ihr nähmet
er bliebe	sie blieben	er nähme	sie nähmen
Umlaut		*Umlaut*	
ich flöge	wir flögen	ich führe	wir führen
du flögest	ihr flöget	du führest	ihr führet
er flöge	sie flögen	er führe	sie führen

Ich *wünschte*, **er** *käme* **am Samstag.** — I wished he would come on Saturday.
Ich *wünschte*, **wir** *flögen* **nach Paris.** — I wished we would fly to Paris.
Ich *wünschte*, **du** *gingest* **nach Hause.** — I wished you would go home.
Ich *wünschte*, **ich** *führe* **in die Schweiz.** — I wished I would go to Switzerland.
Ich *wünschte*, **sie** *schrieben* **die Karte.** — I wished they would write the card.

109. Write sentences from the following, using the present-time subjunctive.

1. ich / schreiben / das Gedicht.
2. wir / trinken / nichts.
3. lassen / du / ihn / gehen?
4. die Alten / gehen / zur Kirche.
5. die Sonne / scheinen / nicht.
6. die Studenten / lesen / das Buch.
7. er / fliegen / auch.
8. schlafen / du / lange?
9. ich / geben / Anna / alles.
10. er / laufen / schnell.

11. die Leute / fahren / mit dem Auto.
12. wir / schreien / laut.
13. er / schneiden / das Haar.
14. ich / bleiben / hier.
15. wir / kommen / auch.
16. nehmen / du / das Papier?
17. ich / essen / Brot.
18. das Pferd / ziehen / den Schlitten.
19. er / verlieren / das Geld.
20. wir / springen / hoch.

Irregular Strong Verbs

The following strong verbs modify their past tense stem vowels to form the present-time subjunctive.

helfen   ich hülfe   sterben   ich stürbe
stehen   ich stünde   werfen   ich würfe

These forms, however, are rarely used; the **würden** plus infinitive construction is generally used in their place in informal German.

Ich *stünde* dort.	*I would stand there.*
Wer *hülfe* dem Kind?	*Who would help the child?*
Wir *würfen* den Ball.	*We would throw the ball.*
Er *stürbe* vor Angst.	*He would die of fright.*

110. Write in German using the present-time subjunctive.

1. He would die.
2. They would help.
3. We would throw the ball.
4. She would stand here.
5. I would help.
6. They would die.
7. We would stand here.
8. Helga, would you help?

Auxiliaries haben *and* sein

Study the following:

ich hätte	wir hätten	ich wäre	wir wären
du hättest	ihr hättet	du wärest	ihr wäret
er hätte	sie hätten	er wäre	sie wären

Ich *hätte* kein Geld.	*I would not have any money.*
Wir *hätten* Ferien.	*We would have a vacation.*
Er *wäre* zu klein.	*He would be too small.*
Wärest du dort?	*Would you be there?*

111. Change the indicative to the subjunctive.

1. Wir haben kein Auto.
2. Ich bin reich.
3. Sie haben keine Ferien.
4. Du bist nicht glücklich.
5. Ich habe keinen Hund.
6. Sie ist böse.
7. Sie sind nicht intelligent.
8. Ihr habt kein Geld.
9. Er hat nichts.
10. Habt ihr Geld?
11. Wir sind krank.
12. Hast du Angst?
13. Wir haben alles.
14. Seid ihr müde?
15. Bist du froh?
16. Ich bin arm.

Modal Verbs

Modal auxiliary verbs retain the vowels of the infinitive in the stems of the present-time subjunctive. Note the consonant change in **mögen.**

dürfen	ich dürfte	*might, would be permitted, may I?, could I?* (in polite questions)
können	ich könnte	*were able, would be able*
mögen	ich möchte	*would like*
müssen	ich müßte	*ought to, would have to*
sollen	ich sollte	*should, would have to*
wollen	ich wollte	*wanted, would want to*

The subjunctive form of the modals is frequently used to express possibility or opinions and to phrase questions politely. In English the modals are usually expressed with *would* plus the meaning of the modal.

Du *solltest* **zu Hause bleiben.**   *You should stay at home.*
Müßtest **du nicht arbeiten?**   *Wouldn't you have to work?*
Möchtest **du ein Stück Kuchen?**   *Would you like a piece of cake?*
Dürfte **ich es sehen?**   *Could I see it?*

112. Restate the following. Use the present-time subjunctive to form polite requests or questions.

1. Können Sie mir helfen?	6. Kann ich ein Stück nehmen?
2. Willst du auch zeichnen?	7. Mußt du nicht lernen?
3. Mußt ihr nicht studieren?	8. Wollt ihr den Film sehen?
4. Darf er mitgehen?	9. Kann sie es holen?
5. Sollst du Marianne besuchen?	10. Darf ich bleiben?

113. Complete the following with the correct present-time subjunctive forms of **mögen.**

1. _____ du noch etwas?	6. _____ du dort leben?
2. Ich _____ Schokolade.	7. _____ Sie etwas haben?
3. Wir _____ gehen.	8. Ich _____ fliegen.
4. Die Kinder _____ reiten.	9. _____ ihr essen?
5. _____ Sie mitmachen?	10. _____ du etwas bestellen?

Wishes

Contrary-to-fact wishes

Contrary-to-fact wishes may be introduced by the present-time subjunctive of verbs of wishing, e.g., **ich wollte, ich wünschte.** When using a contrary-to-fact wish, the speaker expresses his or her dissatisfaction with an actual situation and expresses how he or she would like it to be.

Fact	**Er ist nicht zu Hause.**	*He is not at home.*
Wish	*Ich wollte,* **er wäre zu Hause.**	*I wish he were at home.*

114. Rewrite the following using the present-time subjunctive. Change the fact to a contrary-to-fact wish. Start with **Ich wollte . . . .** Follow the model.

Sie ist krank.   Ich wollte, sie wäre nicht krank.

1. Er bleibt dort.	8. Du kaufst dir nichts.
2. Sie können abfahren.	9. Sie weint.
3. Wir leben in einem Dorf.	10. Ich bin arm.
4. Ich habe Zahnweh.	11. Wir haben es.
5. Ihr arbeitet so viel.	12. Er nimmt es.
6. Ich muß studieren.	13. Er sieht Paula.
7. Wir sind nicht zu Hause.	14. Sie besuchen Oma.

Contrary-to-fact wishes introduced by **wenn** (*if*)

When the contrary-to-fact wish is expressed within a **wenn** (*if*) clause, the conjugated verb is in last position, as is required in dependent clauses. Such wishes often contain the words **nur** or **doch,** corresponding to the English *only.*

Wenn sie nur daran *glaubten!*   *If only they believed in it.*
Wenn er doch nicht *rauchte!*   *If only he wouldn't smoke.*
Wenn ich es nur nicht tun *müßte!*   *If only I didn't have to do it.*

115.   Form wishes from the following. Start with **Wenn**. Follow the model.

> **ich / nur mehr Geld / haben**
> **Wenn ich nur mehr Geld hätte!**

1. wir / nur in München / sein.
2. er / nur das Fenster / öffnen.
3. ihr / doch ein Auto / kaufen.
4. die Leute / nur nicht so laut / schreien.
5. ich / nur alles / wissen.

6. er / nur nicht krank / sein.
7. die Kinder / nur zu Hause / bleiben.
8. ich / nur Deutsch / können.
9. ihr / nur mehr / haben.
10. Georg / nur nicht / abfahren.

Contrary-to-fact wishes not introduced by **wenn**

The introductory **wenn** of the preceding wishes can also be omitted. In that case the conjugated verb is in first position.

> *Hätte* **ich nur mehr Zeit!**   *If only I had more time.*
> *Gäbe* **es nur besseres Essen!**   *If only there were better food.*
> *Dürfte* **ich nur heimgehen!**   *If only I could go home.*

116.   Rewrite the following, omitting **wenn**.

1. Wenn sie nur die Wahrheit sagte!
2. Wenn ich doch schlafen könnte!
3. Wenn er nur das Auto reparierte!
4. Wenn sie nur nicht so viel tränken!
5. Wenn er doch schwiege!

6. Wenn wir nur keine Angst hätten!
7. Wenn du nur hier wärest!
8. Wenn er nur hier bliebe!
9. Wenn sie es nur glaubte!
10. Wenn ihr nur mehr lerntet!

Conditional sentences
Contrary-to-fact conditions

Conditional sentences consist of a conditional clause, introduced by **wenn** (*if*), and a conclusion. The verbs in a conditional sentence may be in the indicative or the subjunctive mood.

If the speaker wants to express that the condition is factual, real, or fulfillable, the indicative is used.

> **Wenn ich Geld** *habe, kaufe* **ich es.**   *If I have money, I'll buy it.*
>   *When I have money, I'll buy it.*

In this sentence, the speaker does not yet have money, but there is a good probability that he or she will have it in the future.

If a condition is contrary to fact, unreal, or unfulfillable, the subjunctive is used.

> **Wenn ich Geld** *hätte, kaufte* **ich es.**   *If I had money, I would buy it.*

With the use of the subjunctive mood of the verb, the speaker expresses that he or she does not have the money now, nor is he or she likely to have it in the future. In the preceding sentence, the present-time subjunctive was used in both the condition and the conclusion.

Variations from the above patterns are possible in German. The present conditional is frequently used to replace the ambiguous subjunctive form of weak verbs.

machte **ich eine Weltreise.**

Wenn ich reich *wäre,*   or

würde **ich eine Weltreise** *machen.*

In colloquial speech, the present conditional is increasingly used to replace the subjunctive of strong verbs in the conclusion of the conditional sentence.

zöge **ich den Pelzmantel an.**

Wenn es kälter *wäre,*   or

würde **ich den Pelzmantel** *anziehen.*

The present-time subjunctive of **haben, sein,** and the modal verbs is not replaced by the present conditional.

117. Replace the present-time subjunctive in the conclusion with the conditional. Repeat the italicized clauses where indicated.

1. *Wenn ich kein Geld hätte*, arbeitete ich.
2. ..., wohnte ich nicht hier.
3. ..., gäbe ich dir nichts.
4. ..., flöge ich nicht nach Hamburg.
5. ..., bestellte ich mir nichts.
6. *Wenn er käme*, tränken wir Kaffee.
7. ..., unterhielten wir uns.
8. ..., freute ich mich.
9. ..., zöge ich mich um.
10. ..., fürchtete ich mich nicht.

118. Complete the following with the correct present-time subjunctive forms of the indicated verbs.

1. Wenn ich Zeit _____, _____ ich dir.   *haben, helfen*
2. Wenn er hier _____, _____ ich glücklich.   *sein, sein*
3. Wenn Ute etwas _____, _____ sie es.   *sehen, beschreiben*
4. Wenn du zu Hause _____, _____ wir dich.   *bleiben, besuchen*
5. Wenn ihr _____, _____ ihr es.   *studieren, wissen*
6. Wenn wir Essen _____, _____ wir es.   *bestellen, essen*
7. Wenn du Deutsch _____, _____ du es.   *lernen, können*

Omission of **wenn** in contrary-to-fact conditional sentences

The conjugated verb is in first position of the sentence when **wenn** is omitted.

Wäre **das Radio kaputt, (dann)** *würde* **er es** *reparieren.*
If the radio were broken, (then) he would fix it.

Machtest **du das Fenster** *auf,* **(dann)** *würde* **es kalt** *werden.*
If you opened the window, (then) it would get cold.

119. Rewrite the following, omitting the introductory **wenn.** Add **dann.**

1. Wenn du mir hülfest, wäre ich froh.
2. Wenn er käme, bliebe ich dort.
3. Wenn wir ihn fragten, würde er uns antworten.
4. Wenn sie es wollte, gäbe ich es ihr.
5. Wenn ich Angst hätte, würde ich schreien.

120. Write the German, using the present-time subjunctive in both clauses. Omit **wenn.**

1. If I were ill, I would stay at home.
2. If we knew it, we would tell Alexander.

3. If she had money, she would buy the coat.
4. If they worked, they would be happier.
5. If he arrived, I would pick him up.

Clauses introduced by als ob

The subjunctive is used in clauses introduced by **als ob** or **als wenn** (*as if*), because the speaker makes an unreal comparison. Note that if the word **ob** is omitted, the verb follows **als**.

Er sieht aus, *als ob* **er krank wäre.**	*He looks as if he were ill.*
Sie tun, *als ob* **sie Angst hätten.**	*They act as if they were afraid.*
Sie sehen aus, *als* **wären Sie krank.**	*You look as if you were ill.*

121. Complete the following with the correct present-time subjunctive forms.

1. Wir tun, als ob wir Zeit _____ . *haben*
2. Du tust, als ob du sie _____ . *lieben*
3. Er tut, als ob er ins Haus _____ . *gehen*
4. Sie tun, als ob sie krank _____ . *sein*
5. Ich tue, als ob ich bleiben _____ . *wollen*
6. Ich tue, als ob ich es _____ . *können*
7. Sie tut, als ob sie hier _____ . *bleiben*
8. Sie tun, als ob sie _____ . *arbeiten*
9. Er tut, als ob er alles _____ . *sehen*
10. Wir tun, als ob wir es _____ . *nehmen*

Hypothetical statements and questions

Study the use of the present-time subjunctive in the following examples.

So etwas *täte* **sie nicht.**	*She wouldn't do something like that.*
Tätest **du so etwas?**	*Would you do something like that?*
Das *wäre* **schrecklich!**	*That would be terrible!*

Polite requests and questions

Könntest **du mir bitte etwas Geld leihen?**	*Could you please lend me some money?*
Möchten **Sie noch ein Stück Kuchen?**	*Would you like another piece of cake?*
Würden **Sie mir das Messer geben?**	*Would you give me the knife?*

Past-Time Subjunctive

The past-time subjunctive is used to refer to wishes, unreal conditions, and hypothetical events relating to any time in the past. It is formed with the subjunctive forms of **hätte** or **wäre** plus the past participle.

> *Past-Time Subjunctive = Subjunctive II of* **haben** *or* **sein** (**hätte** *or* **wäre**) + *Past Participle*

Study the following:

ich hätte gesungen	wir hätten gesungen
du hättest gesungen	ihr hättet gesungen
er hätte gesungen	sie hätten gesungen
ich wäre gegangen	wir wären gegangen
du wärest gegangen	ihr wäret gegangen
er wäre gegangen	sie wären gegangen

The German past-time subjunctive corresponds to the English *had* plus participle (*had run, had gone*) or to the English past conditional *would* plus *have* plus past participle (*would have run, would have gone*), depending on use. Since the past-time subjunctive in German is not ambiguous, there is no need to use the past conditional.

The past-time subjunctive is used with contrary-to-fact wishes, contrary-to-fact conditional clauses, and **als ob** clauses referring to past time.

Wenn sie nur *mitgeholfen hätte!*	*If only she had helped.*
Hätte **ich nur den Roman** *gelesen!*	*If only I had read the novel.*
Wenn wir *studiert hätten, hätten* **wir die Antworten** *gewußt.*	*If we had studied, we would have known the answers.*
Wäre **er krank** *gewesen, hätte* **er nicht** *gearbeitet.*	*If he had been ill, he wouldn't have worked.*
Sie tut, als ob sie dort *gewesen wäre.*	*She acts as if she had been there.*

122. Write wishes in the past-time subjunctive. Change the fact to a contrary-to-fact wish. Follow the model.

Ich hatte keinen Schlüssel.
Wenn ich nur einen Schlüssel gehabt hätte!

1. Wir waren nicht in der Schule.
2. Du hast nicht angerufen.
3. Ich habe nicht gebadet.
4. Er hatte keine Angst.
5. Ihr seid nicht gekommen.

123. Rewrite the following wishes, omitting **wenn.**

1. Wenn du nur geschrien hättest!
2. Wenn wir ihr nur begegnet wären!
3. Wenn ich nur hingegangen wäre!
4. Wenn er nur nicht gestorben wäre!
5. Wenn sie nur geschrieben hätte!

124. Complete the following with the past-time subjunctive of the indicated verbs.

1. Wenn er alles _____ _____, _____ er keinen Hunger _____. *essen, haben*
2. Wenn du es _____ _____, _____ ich es nicht _____. *zurückbringen, holen*
3. Wenn ihr das Fenster _____ _____, _____ ihr euch nicht _____. *zumachen, erkälten*
4. Wenn du mich _____ _____, _____ ich es dir _____. *anrufen, sagen*
5. Wenn das Kind nicht so _____ _____, _____ es nicht so laut _____. *bluten, schreien*

125. Rewrite the following, omitting **wenn.**

  1. Wenn es geklingelt hätte, hätten wir aufgemacht.
  2. Wenn du angerufen hättest, wäre ich gekommen.
  3. Wenn wir es gefunden hätten, hätten wir es wieder zurückgegeben.
  4. Wenn ihr geschrieben hättet, hätten wir euch dort getroffen.

126. Write the German.

  1. He acts as if he had bought it.
  2. They act as if they had not slept.
  3. She acts as if she had been ill.
  4. He acts as if he had come along.

Modal auxiliaries

   When the modal auxiliary is used with a dependent infinitive in the past-time subjunctive, the double infinitive construction is used.

   Hätte **ich es nur** *machen können!*   *If only I could have done it!*

   If the double infinitive occurs in a **wenn** clause or an **als ob** clause, the auxiliary **hätte** precedes the double infinitive.

   Wenn ich nur *hätte kommen dürfen!*
   Wenn du es *hättest machen wollen,* **wäre ich glücklich gewesen.**
   Sie tun, als ob sie alles *hätten tun dürfen.*

127. Rewrite the following, adding the indicated modals.

  1. Wäre er nur geblieben! *dürfen*
  2. Wenn ich doch nicht gegangen wäre! *müssen*
  3. Er tut, als ob er es gesehen hätte! *können*
  4. Du tust, als ob ich es geschrieben hätte. *sollen*
  5. Wenn ich geritten wäre (*wollen*), hätte ich es dir gesagt.
  6. Hätte er nur gesungen! *können*
  7. Wenn du nur nichts gegessen hättest! *wollen*
  8. Wenn wir gefragt hätten (*dürfen*), hätten wir die Antwort gewußt.
  9. Hätte sie nur geholfen! *können*
 10. Sie tun, als ob sie auf mich gewartet hätten. *müssen*

Indirect Speech

   There are two ways of reporting what another person has said. One method is to quote the exact words of the original speaker. In written materials quotation marks set off the speaker's exact words. (Note the placement of the opening quotation marks in German.)

   Sie sagte: „Er hat die Schlüssel gefunden."   *She said: "He found the keys."*

   It is, however, also possible to report the substance of the original speaker's utterance as an indirect quotation. Note the difference in word order in the two examples below.

   Sie sagte, *daß* **er die Schlüssel** *gefunden*   *She said that he had found the*
   hätte.   *keys.*
   Sie sagte, er *hätte* **die Schlüssel** *gefunden.*   *She said he had found the keys.*

In the examples of indirect speech, the use of the subjunctive makes it clear that the information reported here is secondhand and that the speaker is merely passing it on. The use of the special subjunctive can imply a certain skepticism, or it can merely be a device to distance the speaker from events for which he or she was not present.

Note also that the use of the subjunctive to indicate indirect speech can be continued throughout long passages without any other signal that the entire passage is an indirect quotation.

Direct quotation

> **Robert sagt:** „Heidi *ist* **zu spät gekommen, und** *meine* **Freunde** *sind* **ohne sie ins Kino gegangen. Dies** *ist nichts Ungewöhnliches, sie* **kommt immer zu spät.** *Ich habe* **kein Verständnis dafür. So etwas** *ärgert mich* **maßlos. Sie** *muß* **sich bessern.**"

Indirect speech

> **Robert sagte, Heidi** *sei* **zu spät gekommen, und** *seine* **Freunde** *seien* **ohne sie ins Kino gegangen. Dies** *sei* **nichts Ungewöhnliches, sie** *käme* **immer zu spät.** *Er habe* **kein Verständnis dafür. So etwas** *ärgere ihn* **maßlos. Sie** *müsse* **sich bessern.**

As illustrated by the passages above, not only have the verb forms been changed from the indicative to the special subjunctive (subjunctive I), but indirect speech also requires logical changes in the pronouns and possessive adjectives used, e.g., changing *I* to *he*, *my* to *his*, etc.

In English the subjunctive is not used for indirect speech. The indicative is used for both direct and indirect quotations. It should be noted, however, that the indicative is also heard in indirect speech in German, particularly if there is absolutely no doubt regarding the accuracy of the information reported.

> **Ingo sagte:** „*Ich bin* **glücklich.**"   **Ingo sagte,** *daß er* **glücklich** *ist*.

In colloquial German there is an increasing tendency in indirect speech either to use the general subjunctive or to avoid subjunctive forms altogether and use the indicative.

In formal writing, however, the special subjunctive has been the preferred form in indirect speech, unless the form in the special subjunctive was identical with the present indicative. In such cases the special subjunctive was replaced by the general subjunctive forms. In current practice, however, the general subjunctive is being used more and more in indirect speech.

Special Subjunctive

Present-time subjunctive of weak and strong verbs

The subjunctive endings **-e, -est, -e, -en, -et, -en** are added to the infinitive stems of both weak and strong verbs.

Weak Verbs		Strong Verbs	
ich sage	wir sagen	ich gehe	wir gehen
du sagest	ihr saget	du gehest	ihr gehet
er sage	sie sagen	er gehe	sie gehen

All verbs except **sein** follow the above pattern.

Special subjunctive of **sein**

Study the following:

ich sei	wir seien
du seiest	ihr seiet
er sei	sie seien

128. Rewrite the following, using the present-time tense of the special subjunctive. Where indicated, substitute different words for the italicized words.

1. Sie sagt, er *wäre* in Kanada.
2. ... bliebe ...
3. ... wohnte ...
4. ... studierte ...
5. ... arbeitete ...
6. Sie sagt, sie *gäbe* uns etwas.
7. ... kaufte ...
8. ... brächte ...
9. ... holte ...
10. ... schickte ...
11. ... schenke ...
12. Er sagte, ich *hätte* nichts.
13. ... wüßte ...
14. ... könnte ...
15. ... wollte ...
16. ... fände ...
17. ... tränke ...
18. ... äße ...

Past-time subjunctive (subjunctive I)

The past-time of the special subjunctive is formed with a form of **sein** or **haben** + past participle.

Past-Time Subjunctive = Subjunctive I of **haben** *or* **sein** (**habe** *or* **sei**) + *Past Participle*

Study the following:

ich habe gesehen	wir haben gesehen
du habest gesehen	ihr habet gesehen
er habe gesehen	sie haben gesehen
ich sei gegangen	wir seien gegangen
du seiest gegangen	ihr seiet gegangen
er sei gegangen	sie seien gegangen

129. Rewrite the following, changing the general to the special subjunctive. Repeat the italicized clause where indicated.

1. *Er sagt*, er hätte schon geschrieben.
2. ..., ich wäre ins Kino gegangen.
3. ..., sie wäre im Krankenhaus gewesen.
4. ..., er hätte etwas geholt.
5. ..., ich hätte es repariert.
6. ..., er hätte nicht kommen dürfen.

Use of the special subjunctive

The use of the special subjunctive is rather limited. Some German speakers use it in indirect statements; others never use it. Moreover, the special subjunctive is mainly used in the first and third person singular.

Whether the present-time or the past-time of the subjunctive is used in the indirect quotation depends on the tense of the verb in the direct quotation.

When the original statement is in the present tense, the present-time of the general or the special subjunctive is used. In German, unlike in English, the tense of the introductory verb does not influence the choice of the subjunctive form in the indirect statement. The verb of the framing clause, i.e., **er sagt,** etc., may be any tense in German. Study the following:

Direct Statement	Indirect Statement	
„Ich *bin* **krank.**"	**Er sagt,** **Er sagte,** **Er hat gesagt,** **Er hatte gesagt,**	er *sei* (*wäre*) **krank.**

When the verb of the original statement is in the future tense, the present-time subjunctive or the present conditional may be used in the indirect statement:

„Ich *werde* **ihn** *fragen*."

Sie sagt,
Sie sagte,   sie *würde* **ihn** *fragen*.
Sie hat gesagt,   sie *frage* (*fragte*) **ihn.**
Sie hatte gesagt,

When the verb of the original statement is in the simple past, the present perfect, or the past perfect, the past-time subjunctive is used:

Direct Statement	Indirect Statement	
„Ich *kam* **gestern** *an*." „Ich *bin* **gestern** *angekommen*." „Ich *war* **gestern** *angekommen*."	**Er sagt,** **Er sagte,** **Er hat gesagt,** **Er hatte gesagt,**	er *sei* (*wäre*) **gestern** *angekommen*.

130. Change the direct statements to indirect ones. Start with **Sie sagte, ...** Use the general subjunctive.

1. „Mutter ist krank gewesen."
2. „Großvater hatte Geld."
3. „Peter hat Angst."
4. „Sie war allein."
5. „Er hatte ihn gesehen."
6. „Christa war nach Köln gefahren."
7. „Onkel Werner ist in Hamburg."
8. „Ich hatte dich besucht."

131. Change the preceding to indirect statements, using the special subjunctive. Start with **Er hat gesagt, . . .**

PASSIVE VOICE

The passive voice in German consists of a form of **werden** plus the past participle of the main verb. Note that all tenses in German can be expressed in the passive.

In German, as in English, passive constructions shift the emphasis from the subject of the active sentence to the direct object. What had been the direct object of the active sentence becomes the subject of the passive sentence. In an active sentence the subject performs an action, whereas in a passive sentence the subject is acted upon by an agent that was the subject of the active sentence. This agent might or might not be expressed in the passive sentence. If the agent is expressed in a passive construction in German, it is preceded by either **von** or **durch.** If an agent is a person, it is preceded by **von** followed by the dative case. If the agent is an impersonal means by which something is done, it is preceded by **durch** followed by the accusative case. In English the word *by* is used to introduce the agent whether it is a person or an impersonal means.

Active	**Die Eltern fragen den Jungen.**	*The parents ask the boy.*
Passive	**Der Junge** *wird von den Eltern gefragt.*	*The boy is asked by his parents.*
Active	**Der Sturm zerstört die Ernte.**	*The storm is destroying the harvest.*
Passive	**Die Ernte** *wird durch den Sturm zerstört.*	*The harvest is destroyed by the storm.*

However, many passive sentences in German do not express an agent. They simply consist of a subject and the passive verb pattern.

Die Tür *wird geschlossen.*	*The door is (being) closed.*
Die Vorlesung *wird gehalten.*	*The lecture is (being) held.*

In German the indirect object of the active sentence cannot become the subject of the passive sentence. It must remain the indirect object. The German passive construction does not need a subject. **Es** may be placed in first position of the sentence. It functions merely as a filler and not as a subject. Otherwise the indirect object or other elements may be in first position when no subject is present.

Active	**Der Arzt hilft dem Verwundeten.**	*The doctor is helping the wounded (man).*
Passive	**Dem Verwundeten** *wird* **vom Arzt geholfen.**	*The wounded man is being helped by the doctor.*
	Es wird **dem Verwundeten vom Arzt** *geholfen.*	*The wounded man is helped by the doctor.*

Present Tense

The present tense of the passive is constructed from the present tense of **werden** plus the past participle of the main verb.

> **Present Tense of Passive = Present Tense of werden + Past Participle**

Study the following:

ich werde gefragt	wir werden gefragt
du wirst gefragt	ihr werdet gefragt
er wird gefragt	sie werden gefragt

132. Complete the following with the correct present passive, preposition, and article or contraction, when necessary.

1. Das Brot _____ _____ Bäcker _____. *backen*
2. Die Kranke _____ _____ Arznei _____. *retten*
3. Das Abendessen _____ schon _____. *servieren*
4. Die Bücher _____ _____ ihm _____. *anschauen*
5. Es _____ _____ uns _____. *nehmen*
6. Dem Kranken _____ _____ Arzt _____. *helfen*
7. Die Aufgabe _____ _____ dem Mädchen _____. *schreiben*
8. Die Wäsche _____ _____ Mutter _____. *waschen*

9. Das Loch _____ _____ den Männern _____. *graben*
10. Das Hotel _____ _____ die Bombe _____. *zerstören*
11. Wir _____ _____ Vater _____. *sehen*
12. Ich _____ _____ dem Jungen _____. *schlagen*
13. Er _____ _____ seiner Freundin _____. *hören*
14. Das Haus _____ _____ den Sturm _____. *zerstören*
15. Das Auto _____ _____ dem Mechaniker _____. *reparieren*

113. Change the active to the passive voice.

1. Der Hund beißt das Kind.   4. Er füttert das Pferd.
2. Das Feuer zerstört das Haus.   5. Der Vater hilft dem Kranken.
3. Meine Freunde trinken den Kaffee.

Past Tense

The simple past tense of the passive is constructed from the past tense of **werden** plus the past participle of the main verb.

> Past Tense of Passive = Past Tense of **werden** + Past Participle

Study the following:

ich wurde gefragt	**wir wurden gefragt**
du wurdest gefragt	**ihr wurdet gefragt**
er wurde gefragt	**sie wurden gefragt**

Wir *wurden* **von ihm** *gesehen*.   *We were seen by him.*
Die Geschichte *wurde* **von dem Lehrer**   *The story was told by the*
   erzählt.   *teacher.*
Wann *wurdest* **du** *gefragt*?   *When were you asked?*

134. Change the following to the past passive tense.

1. Wir werden abgeholt.
2. Die Rechnung wird von Renate bezahlt.
3. Wirst du beobachtet?
4. Das Auto wird geparkt.
5. Es wird schon von den Leuten gemacht.
6. Das Museum wird von der Klasse besucht.
7. Das Wort wird von dem Studenten buchstabiert.
8. Ich werde gesehen.
9. Die Maschine wird von dem Mechaniker repariert.
10. Das Haus wird durch die Bombe zerstört.

135. Write the German.

1. He was seen.   5. It was washed by my aunt.
2. The window was opened by Marlene. 6. We were helped by the boy.
3. They were asked by their father. 7. I was observed.
4. She was heard.   8. The city was destroyed by a bomb.

Compound Tenses

Present Perfect and Past Perfect

The simple present tense and the simple past tense of the auxiliary verb **sein** are used in a the formation of the present perfect and the past perfect passive. The past participle of **werden** is **geworden.** The **ge-** prefix of the past participle is dropped in these tenses. Thus the perfect tenses in the passive consist of a form of **sein** plus the past participle of the verb plus **worden.**

> *Present Perfect Passive = Present Tense of* **sein** *+ Past Participle of Main Verb +* **worden**

Study the following:

ich bin gefragt worden	wir sind gefragt worden
du bist gefragt worden	ihr seid gefragt worden
er ist gefragt worden	sie sind gefragt worden

> *Past Perfect Passive = Past Tense of* **sein** *+ Past Participle of Main Verb +* **worden**

Study the following:

ich war gefragt worden	wir waren gefragt worden
du warst gefragt worden	ihr wart gefragt worden
er war gefragt worden	sie waren gefragt worden

Das Auto *ist* **vom Mechaniker** *repariert* **worden**.	*The car was repaired by the mechanic.*
Ich *bin* **von meiner Mutter** *gefragt worden*.	*I was asked by my mother.*
Das Haus *war* **von meinem Bruder** *verkauft* **worden**.	*The house was sold by my brother.*

136. Rewrite the following in the present perfect tense.

1. Das Museum wurde 1911 erbaut.
2. Der Löwe wurde vom Wärter gefüttert.
3. Es wurde ihr darüber erzählt.
4. Das Kleid wurde rot gefärbt.
5. Es wurde ihm gegeben.
6. Du wurdest überall gesucht.
7. Ich wurde von ihm gesehen.
8. Das Restaurant wurde durch das Feuer zerstört.
9. Er wurde vom Arzt behandelt.
10. Die Kinder wurden von den Hunden gebissen.

Future Tense

The future passive is formed by the present tense of **werden** plus the past participle of the verb plus **werden.**

> *Future Passive = Present Tense of* **werden** *+ Past Participle of Main Verb +* **werden**

Study the following:

ich werde gefragt werden	wir werden gefragt werden
du wirst gefragt werden	ihr werdet gefragt werden
er wird gefragt werden	sie werden gefragt werden

Er *wird* **wohl** *abgeholt werden.*   *He will probably be picked up.*
Die Möbel *werden* **wohl** *gebracht werden.*   *The furniture will probably be delivered.*
Ich *werde* **von meinem Freund** *besucht*   *I'll be visited by my friend.*
   werden.

The future passive is used chiefly to express probability.

When an adverb of time referring to the future occurs in the sentence, the present passive is preferred.

   Die Äpfel *werden morgen* **von den Männern** *gepflückt.*
   The apples will be picked by the men tomorrow.

137.   Rewrite the following in the future passive. Omit the adverb of time.

   1.   Das Haus wird nächstes Jahr von meinen Freunden gebaut.
   2.   Die Geschichte wird morgen erzählt.
   3.   Der Patient wird bald durch Medikamente geheilt.
   4.   Das Geschenk wird morgen abend von den Kindern bewundert.
   5.   Die Rechnung wird später von meinem Vater bezahlt.
   6.   Der Brief wird morgen geholt.
   7.   Das Haus wird am Sonntag beobachtet.
   8.   Der Brief wird morgen vom Lehrer geschrieben.
   9.   Rudi wird nächsten Monat gefragt.
   10. Franz wird in einer Stunde abgeholt.

Substitute for the Passive

Passive constructions are not used as frequently in German as they are in English. Especially in spoken German, the active construction is preferred. One common substitute for the passive is an active sentence containing the indefinite pronoun **man** as subject. **Man** can only be used in an active sentence. However, such sentences are often rendered as passive sentences in English. Compare the following. Note that the subject of the passive sentence becomes the direct object in the active sentence.

Passive	**Ich** *bin gesehen worden.*	*I was seen.*
Active	*Man hat* **mich** *gesehen.*	
Passive	**Peter** *wird gefragt.*	*Peter is asked.*
Active	*Man fragt* **Peter.**	
Passive	**Der Wagen** *wurde repariert.*	*The car was repaired.*
Active	*Man reparierte* **den Wagen.**	
Passive	**Das Haus** *wird* **wohl** *verkauft werden.*	*The house will probably be sold.*
Active	**Man** *wird* **wohl das Haus** *verkaufen.*	

138. Rewrite the following, using **man**.

1. Die Ruine wird zerstört.
2. Wir werden angerufen.
3. Das Essen wird bestellt.
4. Die Geschichte wurde erzählt.
5. Der Arzt wurde geholt.
6. Der Katalog wurde geschickt.
7. Das Bild ist verkauft worden.
8. Der Mann ist angerufen worden.
9. Der Brief war geschrieben worden.
10. Die Limonade war getrunken worden.
11. Die Stadt wird wohl aufgebaut werden.
12. Das Auto wird wohl geparkt werden.

Passive versus False (or Apparent) Passive

In German, unlike in English, a distinction is made between the action itself and the state resulting from the action. The English sentence *it was taken* may express the action or the result of the action. In German such ambiguity is not possible. The action or process is expressed by the genuine passive, formed by **werden** plus the past participle.

Es *wird* **gekocht.**	*It is (being) cooked.*
Es *wurde* **gezählt.**	*It was (being) counted.*

If the German speaker wants to express the result of that action, the verb **sein** plus the past participle is used. Such a construction is referred to as the false or apparent passive. Note that it describes a state of being rather than a process.

Es *ist* **gekocht.**	*It is cooked.*
Es *war* **gezählt.**	*It was counted.*

Compare the following forms of the true passive and the apparent passive.

	Process	*Result*
Present	**Es** *wird* **gebaut.**	**Es** *ist* **gebaut.**
Simple past	**Es** *wurde* **gebaut.**	**Es** *war* **gebaut.**
Present perfect	**Es** *ist* **gebaut** *worden.*	**Es** *ist* **gebaut** *gewesen.*
Past perfect	**Es** *war* **gebaut** *worden.*	**Es** *war* **gebaut** *gewesen*
Future	**Es** *wird* **gebaut** *werden.*	**Es** *wird* **gebaut.**

139. Express the following in the genuine passive.

1. It is found.
2. It was destroyed.
3. It was shown.
4. It was saved.
5. It is repaired.
6. It is begun.
7. It will be cut.
8. It had been built.
9. It was paid.
10. It is said.

140. Express the preceding in the apparent passive.

SPECIAL MEANINGS OF CERTAIN VERBS

kennen, wissen, können

The verb *to know* can be expressed in German by three different verbs.

kennen—*to know people* or *things* (to be acquainted with)

Ich *kenne* diese Stadt.	*I know this city.*
Hast **du ihn gut** *gekannt?*	*Did you know him well?*

wissen—*to know a fact.* This verb frequently introduces dependent clauses.

Er *wußte* **es schon.**	*He already knew it.*
Weißt **du, wo er wohnt?**	*Do you know where he lives?*

können—*to know how* (to have mastered something)

Er *kann* **gut Deutsch.**	*He knows German well.*
Ich *habe* **die Aufgabe** *gekonnt.*	*I knew the lesson.*

141. Fill in the correct forms of **kennen, wissen,** or **können,** using the present tense.

1. Seit wann _____ du deinen Freund?
2. Ich _____ die Schauspielerin.
3. Wir _____ auch Englisch.
4. _____ ihr, wo er wohnt?
5. Er _____, daß sie krank ist.
6. Das Mädchen _____ uns nicht.
7. Ich _____, wo er ist.
8. _____ du Deutsch?
9. _____ ihr den Präsidenten?
10. Die Kinder _____, daß ich hier bin.

142. Write the German.

1. We know the president.
2. They know French.
3. Inge, did you know my aunt?
4. I know the answer.
5. He knows everything.

liegen, sitzen, stehen

These three verbs are used intransitively (they cannot be followed by a direct object). They denote location and, if used with the either/or prepositions (accusative/dative), are followed by the dative case. All three are strong verbs.

liegen—*to lie*

Sie *liegt* **studenlang im Bett.**	*She lies in bed for hours.*
Er *hat* **unter dem Auto** *gelegen.*	*He was lying under the car.*

sitzen—*to sit*

Warum *sitzt* **du hinter ihr?**	*Why are you sitting behind her?*
Er *hat* **dort** *gesessen.*	*He was sitting there.*

stehen—*to stand*

Sie *standen* **unter dem Apfelbaum.**	*They were standing under the apple tree.*
Sie *steht* **vor dem Bild.**	*She is standing in front of the picture.*

legen, setzen, stellen

In contrast to the preceding verbs, these three verbs are followed by the accusative case when used with accusative/dative prepositions. All three are weak verbs and can be used reflexively.

legen, sich legen—*to lay, put, lie down*

Ich *habe* **es auf den Tisch** *gelegt.*	*I put it on the table.*
Er *legte sich* **aufs Sofa.**	*He lay down on the sofa.*

setzen, sich setzen—*to set, sit down*

Sie *setzt* **das Baby in den Hochstuhl.**	*She sits the baby in the highchair.*
Setz dich **auf den Boden!**	*Sit down on the floor.*

stellen, sich stellen—*to place, put (oneself), stand*

Wer *hat* **die Vase auf den Tisch** *gestellt?*	*Who put the vase on the table?*
Stell dich **neben mich!**	*Stand (place yourself) beside me.*

143. Complete the following with the correct forms of **liegen** or **legen.** Use the simple present tense.

1. Wo _____ das Buch?
2. Ich _____ auf dem Boden.
3. _____ er noch im Bett?
4. Warum _____ du dich nicht aufs Sofa?
5. Anna, _____ die Zeitung auf den Tisch!
6. Wir _____ unter dem Baum.
7. Er _____ das Messer neben den Teller.
8. Ich _____ das Papier auf den Tisch.

144. Complete the following with the appropriate forms of **sitzen** or **setzen.** Use the simple present tense.

1. Er _____ sich vor Günther.
2. Wo _____ ihr?
3. Ich _____ mich ins Auto.
4. Peter _____ sich neben seine Tante.
5. Wohin _____ du dich?
6. Ich _____ auf dem Sofa.
7. Er _____ neben dem Mädchen.
8. _____ du in der Küche?

145. Complete the following with the correct forms of **stehen** or **stellen.** Use the simple present tense.

1. Die Leute _____ an der Haltestelle.
2. Wohin _____ Mutter die Vase?
3. Ich _____ mich hinter Martin.
4. _____ du dich neben den Jungen?
5. Ich _____ den Teller auf den Tisch.
6. Wo _____ dein Freund?
7. Wir _____ den Stuhl ins Zimmer.
8. _____ du vor dem Auto?

lassen

The verb **lassen** can be used with or without a dependent infinitive. When it is used without a dependent infinitive, it has the meaning of *to leave* (*something someplace*). The past participle is prefixed with **ge-** in this case.

Ich *lasse* **den Hund zu Hause.**	*I leave the dog at home.*
Er *hat* **sein Auto in der Garage** *gelassen*.	*He left his car in the garage.*

When **lassen** is used with a dependent infinitive, it means *to let* or *allow* (*to let someone do something*). In this case the double infinitive construction is used in the compound tenses.

Bitte *laßt* **ihn doch** *gehen!*	*Please let him go.*
Er *hat* **mich** *mitkommen lassen*.	*He allowed me to come along.*

146. Complete the following with the appropriate German verb forms. Use the simple present tense.

1. Wir _____ die Kinder dort.   *leave*
2. Er _____ Irene hier _____.   *allow to live*
3. Herr Weiß, bitte _____ Sie Marianne _____!   *let go*
4. Ich _____ Herbert _____.   *let sing*
5. _____ du das Auto in der Garage?   *leave*
6. Frau Hauptmann _____ ihre Tochter _____.   *allow to call*
7. Thomas, _____ den Mantel hier!   *leave*
8. Ich _____ die Tasche zu Hause.   *leave*

147. Rewrite the following in the present perfect tense.

1. Wir lassen die Kinder spielen.
2. Er läßt das Fahrrad dort.
3. Läßt du die Jacke zu Hause?
4. Sie lassen uns mitmachen.
5. Rudi läßt Inge mitmachen.
6. Ich lasse die Katze im Garten.

Chapter 8

Negative Words and Constructions

NEGATION

In German negation is most commonly expressed by the negative adverb **nicht**. The word **nicht** can be used to negate an entire sentence or individual units within a sentence.

Nicht in Final Position

Nicht always *follows:*

> (1) The inflected form of the verb (the form with the personal ending)
> (2) Noun objects (direct or indirect objects)
> (3) Pronoun objects (direct or indirect objects)
> (4) Adverbs of definite time

Study the examples below. Note that in each example in this chapter, the sentence is first presented in the affirmative and then negated.

> *Subject + verb*

Sie liest.   **Sie liest** *nicht.*
Anton fragte.   **Anton fragte** *nicht.*

> *Subject + verb + direct object (noun or pronoun)*

Wir besuchten die Dame.   **Wir besuchten die Dame** *nicht.*
Gisela holte es.   **Gisela holte es** *nicht.*
Wir freuten uns.   **Wir freuten uns** *nicht.*

> *Subject + verb + direct object (pronoun) + indirect object (noun or pronoun)*

Sie gab es dem Kind   **Sie gab es dem Kind** *nicht.*
Ich erklärte es ihr.   **Ich erklärte es ihr** *nicht.*

> *Subject + verb + indirect object (noun or pronoun) + direct object (noun)*

Ich gab dem Jungen die Birne.   **Ich gab dem Jungen die Birne** *nicht.*
Werner kaufte ihr die Vase   **Werner kaufte ihr die Vase** *nicht.*

> *Subject + verb + objects + adverb of time*

Er besuchte uns heute.   **Er besuchte uns heute** *nicht.*

1. Rewrite the following sentences in the negative.

1. Er kennt den Herrn.
2. Wir geben es den Leuten.
3. Ich wasche mich.
4. Heinz weiß es.
5. Sie kamen vorgestern.

6. Ich kaufe den Mantel.
7. Sie nimmt es.
8. Er dankt mir.
9. Ich zeige ihr den Roman.
10. Wir rauchen.

Nicht Preceding Certain Other Elements in the Sentence

Nicht *precedes* most other elements:

---

(1) Predicate adjectives

(2) Predicate nouns

(3) Separable prefixes

(4) Noninflected verb forms (past participles in compound tenses, dependent infinitives, double infinitives)

(5) Adverbs (except those of definite time)

(6) Prepositional phrases

Predicate adjectives and nouns

Er ist krank.   **Er ist** *nicht* **krank.**
Das sind meine Kinder.   **Das sind** *nicht* **meine Kinder.**

Separable prefixes

Das Flugzeug flog ab.   **Das Flugzeug flog** *nicht* **ab.**

Past participles

Sie sind gefahren.   **Sie sind** *nicht* **gefahren.**

Dependent infinitives

Wir hören sie lachen.   **Wir hören sie** *nicht* **lachen.**
Ich darf kommen.   **Ich darf** *nicht* **kommen.**
Ich hoffe, es zu sehen.   **Ich hoffe, es** *nicht* **zu sehen.**

Double infinitives

Er hat es machen wollen.   **Er hat es** *nicht* **machen wollen.**

Adverbs of place or prepositional phrases

Er wohnte hier.   **Er wohnte** *nicht* **hier.**
Wir sind im Wohnzimmer   **Wir sind** *nicht* **im Wohnzimmer.**
Ich freue mich darauf.   **Ich freue mich** *nicht* **darauf.**

When a past participle and a prepositional phrase or adverb of place occur in the same sentence, **nicht** precedes the prepositional phrase or adverb of place.

Ich habe im Sand gelegen.   **Ich habe** *nicht* **im Sand gelegen.**
Er war zu Hause gewesen.   **Er war** *nicht* **zu Hause gewesen.**
Sie hat dort gespielt.   **Sie hat** *nicht* **dort gespielt.**

Nicht in Dependent Clauses

Since German word order requires the inflected form of the verb to be in final position in a dependent clause (see exception at pp. 189–190, 245), **nicht** must precede the verb or verb combination at the end of a dependent clause.

Ich weiß, daß er arbeitet.	**Ich weiß, daß er** *nicht* **arbeitet.**
Sie sagt, daß er kommen kann.	**Sie sagt, daß er** *nicht* **kommen kann.**
Ich hoffe, daß er es gesehen hat.	**Ich hoffe, daß er es** *nicht* **gesehen hat.**

2. Rewrite in the negative

1. Sie haben gespielt.
2. Ich wollte die Rechnung bezahlen.
3. Wir haben sie schreien hören.
4. Maria hat neben dem Hotel gewartet.
5. Ich weiß, daß er fliegen will.
6. Das ist meine Tante.
7. Er sagt, daß er sie gesucht hätte.
8. Das Mädchen fährt heim.
9. Wir sind zur Schule gegangen.
10. Ich bin dort geblieben.
11. Wir sind im Kino.
12. Ich sehe sie kommen.
13. Er kommt mit.
14. Ihr könnt es sehen.
15. Sie sind reich.
16. Er hat hier gewartet.
17. Wir haben es geholt.
18. Das sind meine Bücher.
19. Ich hoffe, Inge zu sehen.
20. Du hast sie genommen.

Nicht with sondern

As noted above, when **nicht** is used to negate a specific sentence unit, it precedes the element it negates. In this case, **nicht** is often followed by a clause introduced by the coordinating conjunction **sondern** (*but rather, but on the contrary*). (See Chapter 10.) Note that **sondern** is used only if the first clause is negated *and* a contrast is stated. Note also that whenever the two clauses share any of the same elements, it is not necessary to repeat these elements.

Sie raucht *nicht* **Zigaretten,** *sondern* **Zigarren.**	*She doesn't smoke cigarettes, but cigars.*
Er hat *nicht* **sie besucht,** *sondern* **ihre Schwester.**	*He didn't visit her but her sister.*
Sie singt *nicht,* *sondern* **spielt die Gitarre.**	*She doesn't sing, but plays the guitar.*
Sie geht *nicht* **ins Kino,** *sondern* **ins Theater.**	*She's not going to the movies, but to the theater.*

3. Rewrite the following in the negative, placing **nicht** in the appropriate position. Take your cue from the clause introduced by **sondern**. Follow the model.

> **Er hat das Flugzeug gesehen. _____, sondern gehört.**
> **Er hat das Flugzeug nicht gesehen, sondern gehört.**

1. Sie ist bei ihrer Tante geblieben. _____, sondern bei ihrer Schwester.
2. Er hat das Auto repariert. _____, sondern das Fahrrad.
3. Wir haben das rote Buch gekauft. _____, sondern das blaue.
4. Ich brauche den Löffel. _____, sondern das Messer.
5. Ihr habt das Radio gewonnen. _____, sondern gestohlen.
6. Ich lese die Zeitung. _____, sondern den Roman.

Nicht with Interrogative

The rules for negation with **nicht** also apply to the position of **nicht** in a negative interrogative construction.

Arbeitest du?	**Arbeitest du** *nicht?*
Gehst du mit?	**Gehst du** *nicht* **mit?**
Hast du ihn dort kennengelernt?	**Hast du ihn** *nicht* **dort kennengelernt?**

4. Rewrite the following in the negative.

1. Habt ihr ihnen geholfen?
2. Sind sie abgefahren?
3. Holt sie es?
4. Macht sie mit?
5. Darfst du bleiben?
6. Hast du ihn gefragt?
7. Ist das dein Freund?
8. Hast du mitgesungen?
9. Rasiert er sich?
10. Hat sie es vergessen?
11. Willst du ihm helfen?
12. War das seine Frau?
13. Ist sie schön?
14. Kaufst du die Blumen?
15. Kann er sich daran erinnern?

ANSWERING AFFIRMATIVE AND NEGATIVE QUESTIONS—Ja, doch

When the answer to an affirmative question is affirmative, **ja** is used.

Fährst du nach Hause?	*Ja*, **ich fahre nach Hause.**
Kann sie lesen?	*Ja*, **sie kann lesen.**

When the answer to an affirmative question is negative, **nein** is used.

Fährst du nach Hause?	*Nein*, **ich fahre nicht nach Hause.**
Kann sie lesen?	*Nein*, **sie kann nicht lesen.**

When the answer to a negative question is affirmative, **doch** is used instead of **ja**.

Fährst du *nicht* **nach Hause?**	*Doch*, **ich fahre nach Hause.**
Kann sie *nicht* **lesen?**	*Doch*, **sie kann lesen.**

5. Answer the following questions, using **ja** or **doch**.

1. War er krank?
2. Ist er nicht gestorben?
3. Hast du es gekonnt?
4. Braucht ihr es nicht?
5. Hat er es nicht gefressen?
6. Ist sie nicht intelligent?

THE NEGATIVE FORM OF brauchen

The negative form of **brauchen** (**brauchen** plus **nicht zu** plus infinitive) is usually preferred to the negative form of **müssen** to express *not to have to* (see Chapter 7, p. 192).

Muß er hier bleiben?
Nein, er *braucht nicht* **hier** *zu* **bleiben.**
Muß er Cornelia helfen?
Nein, er *braucht* **Cornelia** *nicht zu* **helfen.**

6. Rewrite the following in the negative.

1. Sie muß kommen.
2. Hans muß schreiben.
3. Ihr müßt abfahren.
4. Wir müssen gehen.
5. Ich muß studieren.
6. Sie müssen arbeiten.
7. Wir müssen springen.
8. Du mußt den Roman lesen.

OTHER NEGATIVE WORDS

The following negatives follow the same rules for position that apply to **nicht**.

gar nicht—*not at all*

Das ist *gar nicht* **teuer.**   *That is not at all expensive.*

nicht mehr—*no more, no longer, anymore*

Sie wohnen *nicht mehr* **hier.**   *They don't live here anymore.*

nie—*never*

Er hilft uns *nie.*   *He never helps us.*

noch nicht—*not yet*

Wir haben uns *noch nicht* **umgezogen.**   *We haven't changed yet.*

noch nie—*not ever, never*

Wir waren *noch nie* **dort.**   *We were never there.*

7. Rewrite the following, adding the German equivalents of the English words.

1. Er fragt uns. *never*
2. Wir sind müde. *not at all*
3. Sie wohnt in Bonn. *no longer*
4. Ich kann fahren. *not yet*
5. Er hat sie gesehen. *not ever*
6. Er hilft. *never*
7. Sie geht ins Kino. *no more*
8. Er war in Deutschland. *not ever*
9. Wir sind nach Hause geflogen. *not yet*
10. Sie sind freundlich. *not at all*
11. Ich habe Schnecken gegessen. *not ever*
12. Er kennt mich. *no longer*
13. Sie lernte den Präsidenten kennen. *never*
14. Wir machen mit. *not at all*
15. Er hat die Sammlung verkauft. *not yet*

Negative Article kein-

Kein- (*no, not any, not a*) precedes a noun object or a predicate noun. It is used when the noun in the affirmative statement has an indefinite article or no article. **Kein** takes the same ending as the indefinite article. (See Chapter 5.)

Er hat einen Bruder.   **Er hat** *keinen* **Bruder.**
Wir trinken Milch.   **Wir trinken** *keine* **Milch.**

When the noun in the affirmative is preceded by a definite article, a **"der"** word, or a possessive adjective, the negative **nicht** is used instead.

Dieses Bier schmeckt gut.   **Dieses Bier schmeckt** *nicht* **gut.**
Meine Tochter ist hier.   **Meine Tochter ist** *nicht* **hier.**
Der Hund bellt.   **Der Hund bellt** *nicht.*

8. Rewrite the following in the negative, using **kein-** or **nicht.**

1. Er erzählte ein Märchen.
2. Wir besuchten eine bekannte Stadt.
3. Er hat unser Kind gesehen.
4. Hat sie Blumen gekauft?
5. Trinkt er Wasser?
6. Ich habe einen warmen Mantel.
7. Das sind Haselnüsse.
8. Ich habe mich auf die Ferien gefreut.
9. Wir essen Bananen.
10. Ich habe einen Freund.
11. Ich kenne den Herrn.
12. Sie singt das Lied.
13. Er hat Kinder.
14. Dieser Ring ist teuer.
15. Hier liegt ein Buch.
16. Wer ißt Brot?
17. Das ist ein Tachometer.
18. Die Lehrerin schreibt.
19. Ist die Milch sauer?
20. Ich habe Zeit.

Pronouns nichts, niemand

Nichts (*nothing*) and **niemand** (*nobody*) are used only in the singular. **Nichts** has no endings, and no endings are required for **niemand** (note, however, that endings are sometimes used with **niemand.** E.g., Ich habe niemanden gesehen.) **Nichts** can be followed by a neuter adjective used as a noun.

Er hat *nichts* **gekauft.**   *He bought nothing.*
Er gab mir *nichts* **Kostbares.**   *He gave me nothing valuable.*
Ich kenne *niemand*.   *I know nobody.*

9. Write the German.

1. He can see nothing.
2. Nobody helps us.
3. I have nothing old.
4. They know nothing.
5. He asks nobody.

Chapter 9

Interrogative Words and Constructions

GENERAL QUESTIONS

Formation of Questions by Inversion

General questions are questions that can be answered by **ja** (*yes*) or **nein** (*no*). This type of question is formed by simply *inverting the subject and the verb* of the declarative sentence so that the verb is in first position. No interrogative word or phrase is used in forming this type of question. In German any subject–verb combination may be inverted to form a general question.

Compare the following patterns:

```
Statement = Subject + Verb (+Remainder of Sentence).
```

$$S \quad + \quad V \quad (+remainder\ of\ sentence).$$
Das Kind   kommt   (nach Hause).

```
General Question = Verb + Subject (+Remainder of Sentence)?
```

$$V \quad + \quad S \quad (+remainder\ of\ sentence)?$$
Kommt   das Kind   (nach Hause)?

Note: In English a general question usually requires the use of an auxiliary verb (such as *to do, to be,* e.g. *Does she sing? Is he going too?*), whereas in German in the simple tenses (simple present, simple past) the main verb is used by itself to introduce such questions (**Singt sie? Kommt er auch?**). In the compound tenses in German, however, it is the auxiliary verb (i.e., the verb form taking the personal ending) that is inverted and put in first position to introduce a general question.

Simple Tenses

Statement	*Question*
Robert reparierte das Auto.	*Reparierte* **Robert das Auto?**
Horst, du bist krank.	**Horst,** *bist* **du krank?**
Sie fährt auch mit.	*Fährt* **sie auch mit?**
Konrad kann Deutsch.	*Kann* **Konrad Deutsch?**

1. Change the following statements into questions.

1. Er kommt morgen.
2. Herbert bringt es zurück.
3. Er setzte sich aufs Bett.
4. Du weißt alles.
5. Die Männer arbeiteten viel.
6. Ihr braucht es.
7. Ihr amüsiert euch.
8. Petra bestellte auch Bier.
9. Die Touristen besichtigen das Schloß.
10. Er will nicht.
11. Du hörst nichts.
12. Sie muß in die Stadt.
13. Sie bleiben dort.
14. Er rauchte viel.
15. Du schwimmst nicht.

Compound Tenses and Dependent Infinitives

In compound tenses the subject and the auxiliary verb bearing the personal endings are inverted to form a question. In sentences containing dependent infinitives, the modal or similarly used verb, such as **hören, sehen, helfen, lassen,** is inverted with the subject. The dependent infinitive is in last position in questions.

Statement	*Question*
Er würde helfen.	*Würde* **er** *helfen?*
Robert, du hast es gesehen.	**Robert,** *hast* **du es** *gesehen?*
Ihr hättet gelesen	*Hättet* **ihr** *gelesen?*
Sie hat sich niedergesetzt.	*Hat* **sie sich** *niedergesetzt?*
Du kannst es machen.	*Kannst* **du es** *machen?*
Sie sehen ihren Vater kommen.	*Sehen* **sie ihren Vater** *kommen?*

2. Form questions from the following.

1. Er hat schon geschrieben.
2. Sie haben sich gestern kennengelernt.
3. Ihr habt alles verloren.
4. Sie wird es aufmachen.
5. Du darfst es nehmen.
6. Er hat sich verletzt.
7. Ihr werdet euch umziehen.
8. Du hättest es gekauft.
9. Er ist gestorben.
10. Sie können nicht dort bleiben.
11. Du läßt Peter helfen.
12. Sie sieht die Kinder spielen.
13. Er hat die Geschichte erzählt.
14. Ihr habt die Oper gesehen.
15. Sie haben immer studiert.

Use of doch in Answer to Negative Questions

In the answer to a negative question, **doch** is used instead of **ja. Doch** is stressed when used this way. (See p. 224.)

Hast du *kein* **Buch?**	*Doch,* **natürlich habe ich ein Buch.**
Könnt ihr *nicht* **lesen?**	*Doch,* **wir können lesen.**
Bist du *nicht* **krank?**	*Doch,* **ich bin krank.**

3. Form questions from the following, taking the cue from the answers. Follow the model.

Kannst du nicht schwimmen? Doch, ich kann schwimmen.

1. _____ ? Doch, er ist hier.
2. _____ ? Doch, ich fahre mit.
3. _____ ? Doch, wir dürfen nach Bonn fahren.
4. _____ ? Doch, ich komme mit.
5. _____ ? Doch, sie hilft den Kindern.

SPECIFIC QUESTIONS

Specific questions are questions that ask for specific information. In both English and German this type of question is introduced by an interrogative word or phrase that seeks information about time, manner, place, or cause (as well as who or what may be the actor or the recipient of some action).

Interrogative Adverbs and Adverbial Expressions

When a question is introduced by an adverb or an adverbial expression, the subject and verb are also inverted. However, in this case the verb is not in first position in the sentence, but is in second position following the interrogative adverb or adverbial expression that introduces the question.

Compare the following patterns:

> *Statement = Subject + Verb (+Remainder of Sentence).*

S	+	*V*	(+*remainder of sentence*).
Das Kind		**kommt**	**(nach Hause).**

> *Specific Question = Interrogative + Verb + Subject (+Remainder of Sentence)?*

I	+	*V*	+	*S*	(+*remainder of sentence*)?
Wann		**kommt**		**das Kind**	**(nach Hause)?**
Warum		**kommt**		**das Kind**	**(nach Hause)?**
Wie		**kommt**		**das Kind**	**(nach Hause)?**
Um wieviel Uhr		**kommt**		**das Kind**	**(nach Hause)?**

The following interrogative adverbs are used to introduce questions.

Wann?	*When?*	**Wie oft?**	*How often?*
Warum?	*Why?*	**Wieviel?**	*How much? How many?*
Wie?	*How?*	**Wie viele?**	*How many?*
Wie lange?	*How long?*	**Um wieviel Uhr?**	*At what time?*

Wann **kommt der Zug an?**	*When is the train arriving?*
Warum **hast du nichts gesagt?**	*Why didn't you say anything?*
Wie **ist das Wetter?**	*How is the weather?*
Wie lange **bleibst du dort?**	*How long are you staying there?*
Wie oft **besuchst du sie?**	*How often do you visit her?*
Wieviel **kostet es?**	*How much does it cost*
Wieviel (Wie viele) **Hunde habt ihr?**	*How many dogs do you have?*
Um wieviel Uhr **kommst du?**	*At what time are you coming?*

Wieviel *or* wie viele

Wieviel (*how much*) is used in specific questions and before singular nouns; **wie viele** (*how many*) is used before plural nouns.

Wieviel **kostet das?**	*How much does it cost?*
Wieviel **Zeit hast du?**	*How much time do you have?*
Wieviel **Geld hast du?**	*How much money do you have?*
Wie viele **Kinder sind hier?**	*How many children are here?*
Wie viele **Äpfel has du gegessen?**	*How many apples did you eat?*

Note: In colloquial speech one often hears **wieviel** when strictly speaking we would expect to hear **wie viele**.

Wieviel (Wie viele) **Planeten gibt es?**	*How many planets are there?*
Wieviel (Wie viele) **Katzen hast du?**	*How many cats do you have?*

4. Complete the following with the appropriate interrogative adverbs or adverbial expressions.

1. Sie fliegt morgen ab. _____ fliegt sie ab?
2. Peter ist klug. _____ ist Peter?
3. Er besucht uns dreimal die Woche. _____ besucht er uns?
4. Der Film war lang. _____ war der Film?
5. Ich habe zehn Minuten gewartet. _____ hast du gewartet?
6. Das Hemd kostet zehn Mark. _____ kostet das Hemd?
7. Er heißt Hans. _____ heißt er?
8. Ich habe es dreimal gesehen. _____ hast du es gesehen?
9. Ich bleibe eine Woche dort. _____ bleibst du dort?
10. Er kommt um drei Uhr. _____ kommt er?
11. Sie ist am Nachmittag gekommen. _____ ist sie gekommen?
12. Wir kommen nächste Woche. _____ kommt ihr?
13. Ich komme nicht, weil ich krank bin. _____ kommst du nicht?
14. Wir treffen Johann um zehn Uhr. _____ trefft ihr Johann?
15. Er kommt im Sommer. _____ kommt er?

Wo, woher, wohin

In German there are three different interrogatives to ask about place: **wo, wohin, woher.** These words are *not* interchangeable; each has its own distinct meaning.

The interrogative **wo** asks about *location* (*in what place?*). Normally **wo** is used when there is no movement (or only movement or activity within a place). The answer usually contains a preposition followed by the dative case.

Wo **seid ihr?**	**Wir sind in der Schule.**
Wo **wandert er?**	**Er wandert im Wald.**
Wo **ist das Buch?**	**Es liegt auf dem Tisch.**

The interrogative **wohin** asks about *destination* or *direction* (*to what place?*). **Wohin** expresses movement to or toward a place. The answer usually contains a preposition followed by the accusative case.

Wohin **geht ihr?**	**Wir gehen ins Theater.**
Wohin **fahren wir?**	**Wir fahren in die Stadt.**

The interrogative **woher** asks about *origin* (*from what place?*).

Woher **kommst du?**	**Ich komme aus dem Wald.**
Woher **kommst du?**	**Ich komme aus den USA.**

Note: Although modern English uses the word *where* for all of these situations, earlier English made the same distinctions as German (*where, whence = from where, whither = to where*).

5. Complete the following with **wo, wohin,** or **woher.**

1. Bärbel ist in Düsseldorf. _____ ist Bärbel?
2. Ich komme aus Zürich. _____ kommst du?
3. Wir fahren nach England. _____ fahrt ihr?
4. Er kommt von seiner Großmutter. _____ kommt er?
5. Wir gehen ins Kino. _____ geht ihr?
6. Ich fahre in die Stadt. _____ fährst du?
7. Wir sind in der Küche. _____ seid ihr?
8. Therese kommt aus Deutschland. _____ kommt Therese.

9.   Anna läuft ins Geschäft. _____ läuft Anna.
10. Ich bin hinter dem Haus. _____ bist du?

Review

6. Form questions using the interrogative words that will elicit the italicized elements in the responses. Follow the model.

Anna kommt *morgen*. Wann kommt Anna?

1. Sie fährt *nach Kanada*.
2. Sie bringen es *übermorgen*.
3. Alexander besuchte uns *dreimal*.
4. Heute ist es *heiß*.
5. Sie ist *in Holland*.

6. Er sieht mich *zweimal am Tag*.
7. Ella kommt *aus München*.
8. Sie bleiben *drei Monate* dort.
9. Sie sind *in Köln*.
10. Es kostet *zehn Mark*.

Interrogative Pronouns

Wer, wen, wem, wessen

The interrogative pronoun **wer** (*who*) is used when questions refer to people. **Wer** takes the same case endings as the definite article **der.** Study the following forms:

Nominative	**Wer?**	*Who?*
Accusative	**Wen?**	*Whom?*
Dative	**Wem?**	*Whom?*
Genitive	**Wessen?**	*Whose?*

Note: There are no plural forms of these interrogative pronouns. The answers, however, may be in the singular or the plural.

Wer **kommt?**	*Who is coming?*
Wen **hast du gesehen?**	*Whom did you see?*
Für *wen* **kaufst du es?**	*For whom are you buying it?*
Wem **gehört die Kamera?**	*To whom does the camera belong?*
Bei *wem* **bleibst du?**	*With whom are you staying?*
Wessen **Mantel ist das?**	*Whose coat is that?*

Was

The interrogative pronoun **was** is used in questions referring to things, ideas, or actions. The form **was** is the same for the nominative and the accusative. There are no dative, or genitive singular forms and there is no plural. The answers, however, may be in the singular or the plural.

Was **ist das?**	*What is that?*
Was **machst du?**	*What are you doing?*

7. Complete the following with the correct interrogative pronouns.

1. _____ hat er dir gegeben?
2. _____ bringst du Blumen?
3. _____ habt ihr gegessen?
4. Bei _____ hast du gewohnt?
5. _____ arbeitet dort?
6. Mit _____ gehst du?
7. _____ besucht ihr?
8. _____ Wagen ist das?
9. Für _____ machst du das?
10. Von _____ hast du das?

11. _____ hast du geholfen?
12. _____ habt ihr getroffen?
13. _____ kann das machen?
14. _____ hat sie gedankt?
15. _____ Hut liegt dort?
16. Zu _____ geht ihr?
17. Gegen _____ bist du?
18. _____ Buch ist das?
19. _____ sagte er?
20. _____ tust du?

Wo- *compounds*

The interrogative pronoun **was** is usually avoided after dative and accusative prepositions. Instead, **wo(r)-** is prefixed to the preposition to form the question. (See Chapter 3.)

Worauf **wartest du?**	*What are you waiting for?*
Wovor **fürchten Sie sich?**	*What are you afraid of?*
Wofür **interessierst du dich?**	*What are you interested in?*

Wo- compounds can be used with all accusative and dative prepositions except **entlang, ohne, außer, gegenüber, seit, hinter, neben, zwischen.**

   Wo- compounds cannot refer to people. The interrogative pronouns must be used in such cases.

An wen **erinnerst du dich?**	**An Hedwig.**
Woran **erinnerst du dich?**	**An letzten Sommer.**

8. Complete the following with the correct prepositions plus interrogative pronouns or **wo-** compounds. Take your cue from the answers.

1. _____ sprecht ihr?   von dem Sportwagen
2. _____ repariert er?   die Uhr
3. _____ fahrt ihr?   mit dem Zug
4. _____ habt ihr gefragt?   Herrn Böll
5. _____ habt ihr gefragt?   nach dem Weg
6. _____ brauchst du Geld?   für die Karten
7. _____ hofft er?   Auf gutes Wetter
8. _____ hast du das gekauft?   für Susi
9. _____ wundert er sich?   über Ursula
10. _____ brauchst du?   den Schlüssel
11. _____ sprecht ihr?   mit Frau Kröger
12. _____ interessiert er sich?   für moderne Musik
13. _____ liegt es?   in der Schachtel
14. _____ brauchst du das?   zum Reparieren
15. _____ setzt du dich?   hinter die dicke Dame

Welch- (*which, which one*)

The interrogative **welch-** may be used attributively as an interrogative adjective or as an interrogative pronoun. **Welch-** takes the same endings as the definite article. All forms in the singular and plural are used.

Interrogative Adjective	*Interrogative Pronoun*
Welches **Haus gehört euch?**	*Welches* **möchtest du haben?**
Welchen **Wein hat er getrunken?**	*Welchen* **hat sie gekauft?**
Mit *welchem* **Auto wollen wir fahren?**	**Aus** *welchem* **ist sie gestiegen?**
Welche **Blumen soll ich abschneiden?**	*Welche* **kann er bringen?**

9. Complete the following with the correct forms of **welch-**.

1. _____ Kinder haben es genommen?
2. Bei _____ Leuten seid ihr geblieben?
3. Nach _____ Straße hat er gefragt?
4. _____ Teppich habt ihr gekauft?
5. Aus _____ Land kommt er?
6. _____ Buch gehört dir?
7. Mit _____ Studentin kommst du zusammen?
8. Für _____ Roman interessierst du dich?
9. In _____ Haus wohnen Sie?
10. _____ Blume gefällt dir?
11. _____ Wagen ist kaputt?
12. _____ Kette hat er gekauft?

10. Complete the following with the correct forms of the interrogative pronoun **welch-**. Take your cue from the statements. Follow the model.

Hier sind schöne Äpfel. Welchen möchtest du haben?

1. Dort sind viele Hunde. _____ gehört dir?
2. Ich habe zwei Autos. Mit _____ möchtest du fahren?
3. Wir besuchen unsere Tanten. Für _____ kaufst du ein Geschenk?
4. Dort sind viele Taschen. _____ gehört dir?
5. Dort liegen viele Bleistifte. _____ brauchst du?

11. Rewrite in the plural.

1. Welches nimmst du?
2. Welche hat er gekauft.
3. Von welcher erzählt er?
4. Welchen brauchst du?
5. Für welche kauft er es?

Interrogative Adjective

Was für ein- (*what kind of*) is usually used as an interrogative adjective. In the singular, the indefinite article **ein-** takes adjective endings. The adjective endings are determined by the way the noun that follows is used grammatically in the sentence. **Für** does not act as a preposition in these expressions. In the plural the expression is **was für**.

Was für eine **Maschine habt ihr gekauft?**	**Eine Drehmaschine.**
Mit *was für einem* **Herrn hast du gesprochen?**	**Mit einem alten Herrn.**
Was für **Leute sind das?**	**Das sind Touristen.**

12. Express in German.

1. What kind of car is that?
2. What kind of girl is that?

3. With what kind of people does he go to Germany?
4. In what kind of house do they live.
5. What kind of books does he write?

Chapter 10

Word Order and Conjunctions

WORD ORDER

There are four basic sentence types in German, each with its own characteristic word order. These basic sentence types are:

> (1) Declarative sentences (statements)
> (2) Interrogative sentences (questions)
> (3) Imperative sentences (commands)
> (4) Exclamatory sentences (exclamations)

In general, word order in German is more flexible than in English. This is possible because German contains many grammatical clues such as case, gender, and verb endings that permit one to analyze the relationships between the words in a sentence without having to depend primarily on word order. English, which in most cases lacks these grammatical markers, depends more on word order to clarify the relationships between the words in a sentence.

Although in some respects there is more flexibility in German word order, there are nonetheless cardinal rules for word order that must be followed in forming sentences.

Statements

Regular Word Order (S + V)

The regular word order used in declarative sentences in German is as follows:

> *Statements (Regular Word Order) = Subject + Verb (+ Other Sentence Parts).*

Simple tenses

In statements in the simple present or simple past tense, the verb is in second position, preceded by the subject and followed by the objects and other sentence parts. The subject may be a noun, pronoun, or other noun phrase. Words such as **danke, ja, nein, doch** do not affect word order.

Subject	*Conjugated Verb*	*Other Sentence Parts*
Der Mann	**ist**	**unser Lehrer.**
Die Erde	**dreht**	**sich um die Sonne.**
Ja, mein kleiner Bruder	**gab**	**ihm das Buch.**

Compound tenses

In statements containing compound tenses, the conjugated verb, that is, the verb form with the personal ending, or the auxiliary is in second position. The dependent infinitive, the double infinitive, or the past participle is in last position, preceded by the other sentence parts.

Subject	Conjugated Verb	Other Sentence Parts	Infinitives or Past Participles
Doch, Inge	wird	ihm	helfen.
Meine Eltern	wollten	sich einen Ofen	kaufen.
Ich	habe	es ihr	zeigen wollen.
Seine Schwester	hat	ihm gestern das Buch	gekauft.
Das rote Auto	wurde	von ihm	gestohlen.

Separable prefixes

Simple tenses

In simple tenses the prefix is separated from the verb and occurs in last position.

Subject	Conjugated Verb	Other Sentence Parts	Prefix
Wir	gehen	jeden Sonntag	spazieren.
Die Studenten	kamen	mit dem Zug	an.

Compound tenses

In compound tenses the prefix is attached to the verb and occurs in last or next-to-last position.

Subject	Conjugated Verb	Other Sentence Parts	Infinitives or Past Participles
Er	wird	bald	heimgehen.
Ich	habe	das Geschenk	aufmachen dürfen.
Der Junge	ist	gestern abend	weggelaufen.

1. Form sentences from the following. Start with the subjects.

1. vor einer Stunde / der Schnellzug / angekommen / ist.
2. bei uns / bleibt / Norma.
3. mitmachen / will / der kleine Junge.
4. von ihm / wurde / zurückgebracht / die Goldkette.
5. wir / ihn / können / haben / sehen.
6. mit Klaus / Gerda / geht / spazieren.
7. den Jungen / der Hund / beißt.
8. es / ich / habe / dürfen / kaufen.
9. die Geschichte / wird / er / erzählen.
10. er / mich / kommen / sieht.

2. Rewrite the following sentences, using the present perfect tense.

1. Sie mußten schneller laufen.
2. Wir machten die Schachtel auf.
3. Er wollte nicht heimgehen.
4. Ich wollte es ihm zeigen.
5. Seine Großeltern brachten es mit.
6. Mein Vater ließ mich gehen.
7. Er konnte gut singen.
8. Der Alte setzte sich auf die Bank.
9. Ich hörte die Kinder schreien.
10. Der Zug fuhr vor einer Stunde ab.

Inverted Word Order (X + V + S)

Simple tenses

As noted above, German word order is in some respects quite flexible, and it is not required that the subject be the first component of a sentence. For special emphasis the direct object, indirect object, adverb, prepositional phrase, or any other logical unit can be placed in first position, which is here denoted by X. However, when the subject is no longer the first element in a declarative sentence, the regular S + V word order changes:

Statements (Inverted Word Order) = X + Verb + Subject (+ Other Sentence Parts).

Note that although the conjugated verb remains in second position, the order of the subject and verb is inverted, and the subject is followed by any other sentence parts that may be present.

Compound verbs

If the verb is a compound verb, the conjugated form of the auxiliary verb is in second position and the past participle, dependent infinitive, or double infinitive is in final position.

In the case of separable prefix verbs, the separable prefix is attached to the verb stem in the infinitive and past participle (see Chapter 7). These separable prefix forms are placed in final position, just like any other past participle or infinitive.

It is important to remember that the X element can be of any length. It can be a single word, a prepositional phrase, a dependent clause, or even a combination of long and involved dependent clauses. However, *no matter how long this X element is, the subject and the verb of the main clause that follows must be inverted.*

Any Element	Conjugated Verb	Subject	Other Sentence Parts
Vor zwei Tagen	**reiste**	**mein Freund**	**nach Indien.**
Trotz des Regens	**sind**	**wir**	**mit ihm ausgegangen.**
Dadurch	**wollte**	**er**	**viel Geld gewinnen.**
Nach dem Essen	**will**	**sie**	**abfahren.**
Wie immer	**hat**	**sie**	**ihn warten lassen.**
Wenn ich Zeit hätte,	**besuchte**	**ich**	**sie.**
Weil sie krank war,	**kam**	**sie**	**nicht.**

Thus the X element can be as simple as **gestern** (*yesterday*), **heute** (*today*), or **am Mittwoch** (*on Wednesday*), or as complex as **nach einer gut vorbereiteten und wohl schmeckenden Mahlzeit** (*after a well-prepared and good tasting meal*) or **weil er immer geglaubt hatte, daß er nicht genug Geld hatte, um eine lange Reise zu machen** (*because he had always believed that he did not have enough money to take a long trip*).

Questions

Specific Questions (X + V + S?)

Specific questions (sometimes referred to as *informational questions*) are questions that ask for particular information. This type of question is introduced by an interrogative word or phrase seeking specific information: **Wann? Warum? Wo? Wie? Wovon? Wieso? Um wieviel Uhr?** Specific questions also follow the word order pattern below:

Specific Questions = X (Interrogative) + Verb + Subject (+ Other Sentence Parts)?

Interrogative Adverb	Conjugated Verb	Subject	Other Sentence Parts
Wann	**hat**	**das Konzert**	**begonnen?**
Wohin	**habt**	**ihr**	**es gelegt?**

3. Rewrite the following, starting the sentences with the italicized elements.

    1. Wir wollten *das Auto* in Deutschland kaufen.

2. Sie kommen *heute* zurück.
3. Er hat es *im Kino* vergessen.
4. Er ist am Abend *meistens* müde.
5. Meine Eltern waren *leider* zu Hause.
6. Ich konnte *wegen meiner Erkältung* nicht kommen.
7. Wir haben es *gestern abend* gemacht.
8. Sie fahren *mit dem Zug* in die Schweiz.
9. Das Museum ist *im Zentrum.*
10. Ich habe es *oft* hören müssen.

4. Form questions from the following, using the present tense. Start the questions with the interrogative adverbs.

1. Wann / du / zumachen / das Fenster?
2. Was / das Kind / dürfen / wissen?
3. Wieviel / die Kamera / kosten?
4. Wo / die Leute / wollen / wohnen?
5. Warum / du / nicht / niedersetzen / dich?
6. Wohin / du / fahren / mit dem Auto?
7. Worauf / die Bücher / sollen / liegen?
8. Woher / die Kinder / kommen?

5. Rewrite the following, starting with the italicized dependent clauses.

1. Ich kann nicht mit ins Kino, *weil ich viel zu tun habe.*
2. Sie las ein Buch, *als ihre Mutter ins Zimmer kam.*
3. Ich werde meine Tante besuchen, *wenn ich Zeit habe.*
4. Ich habe viel lernen müssen, *während ich studierte.*
5. Du sollst deiner Großmutter helfen, *bevor du abreist.*

Variations in the position of the noun subject

In sentences using inverted word order, the noun subject may be preceded by a pronoun object. An accusative, dative, or reflective pronoun may thus come between the subject and the verb. When the subject is a pronoun, this variation is not possible. Then the object pronoun must follow the subject.

Wo hat *dich* **Peter kennengelernt?**
   or
Wo hat Peter *dich* **kennengelernt?**

Gestern abend hat *ihm* **Anton geholfen.**
   or
Gestern abend hat Anton *ihm* **geholfen.**

Am Sonntag hat *sich* **Paula schön angezogen.**
   or
Am Sonntag hat Paula *sich* **schön angezogen.**

Wo hat er *dich* **gesehen?**
Warum gibst du *ihm* **etwas?**

6. Rewrite the following. Place the pronouns before the subject when possible.

1. Morgen bringt er mir die Leiter.
2. Vor einer Woche hat Axel uns besucht.
3. Im Theater hat Konrad sich amüsiert.
4. Jeden Tag schickt Mutter ihr etwas.
5. Wo hat Ursel dich getroffen?
6. Wann kannst du es machen?
7. Warum helft ihr mir nicht?
8. Gestern hat Vater uns etwas gebracht.
9. Um neun Uhr trifft ihr Freund sie.
10. In der Stadt kaufte ich ihm die Krawatte.

General Questions (V + S?)

General questions (sometimes referred to as *alternative questions*) are questions that ask whether something is true or false. They can be answered by **ja** (*yes*) or **nein** (*no*). This type of question is formed by inverting the subject and the verb of the declarative sentence so that the conjugated form of the verb is in first position.

> General Questions = Verb + Subject (+ Other Sentence Parts)?

In the case of compound verbs, the infinitives, the past participle, and the separable prefix are in last position.

Note: No interrogative word or phrase is used in forming this type of question.

Kennst **du meine Freundin?**	*Do you know my girlfriend?*
Hat **er es nehmen dürfen?**	*Was he permitted to take it?*
Wirst **du ihn dort treffen?**	*Will you meet him there?*
Kommt **er bald heim?**	*Is he coming home soon?*

When the verb is in first position, the noun subject may be preceded or followed by a pronoun object.

Hat ihn **dein Bruder gesehen?**
  or
Hat **dein Bruder** *ihn* **gesehen?**

7. Rewrite the following, changing the statements to questions. Place the pronoun objects before the subjects when possible.

1. Du hast ihm den Brief geschrieben.
2. Peter kennt mich.
3. Gerda wollte das Museum besuchen.
4. Ihr helft ihm den Baum pflanzen.
5. Herr Klein macht die Tür auf.
6. Er kann Deutsch.
7. Erika hat sich bei ihr entschuldigt.
8. Du hast dir das schnelle Auto gekauft.
9. Ihr habt es ihm genommen.
10. Man hat dich gefragt.

Commands (V(+ S))

The imperative verb is the first element in commands in German. The subject is not expressed in the second person singular (**du**) and second person plural (**ihr**) imperative forms (informal commands). In formal commands the subject (**Sie**) is expressed directly after the imperative verb. The subject in the **wir** commands is expressed, also directly following the imperative verb. Separable prefixes are in final position.

> Commands = Verbs (+ Subject) (+ Other Sentence Parts)!

Commands are generally indicated by an exclamation mark.

Geh **hinters Haus!**	*Go behind the house.*
Steht **bitte** *auf!*	*Please get up.*
Setzen **Sie** *sich* **bitte!**	*Please sit down.*
Fahren **wir mit dem Motorrad!**	*Let's go by motorcycle.*
Bitte *fahren* **Sie bald** *ab!*	*Plese depart soon.*
Macht auf!	*Open up.*

8. Complete the following with the correct forms of the familiar singular and plural commands.

1. _____ mir das Bild! *zeigen*
2. _____ uns die Tür! *öffnen*
3. _____ ihn! *fragen*

4. _____ bald _____ ! *heimkommen*
5. _____ es sofort _____ ! *nachmachen*

9. Write formal commands. Follow the model.

> **darauf warten? Ja, warten Sie darauf!**

1. das Bier trinken?
2. das Lied singen?
3. darüber lachen?

4. es mir schicken?
5. den warmen Mantel anziehen?

Exclamations

Exclamations are utterances expressing great feeling, surprise, irritation, and a whole range of other emotional responses. Exclamations do not have to be complete sentences, as the examples demonstrate. They are generally indicated by an exclamation mark.

> **Was für ein braves Mädchen!**
> **So was ärgerliches!**
> **Wie lieb von dir!**

COORDINATING CONJUNCTIONS—Regular Word Order

A coordinating conjunction links words, phrases, or clauses that are parallel and equal. Because coordinating conjunctions are merely links and do not become a part of any of the clauses they connect, they have no effect on the word order of the clauses they introduce. In the normal case a coordinating conjunction is followed by regular word order according to the pattern:

> *Word Order with Coordinating Conjunctions =*
> *Subject + Verb (+ Rest of Sentence) + Coordinating Conjunction + Subject*
> *+ Verb (+ Other Sentence Parts)*

If, however, another element X (adverb, prepositional phrase, etc.) directly follows the coordinating conjunction, the word order of the clause following the conjunction will be inverted. This is not due to the coordinating conjunction, but rather to the rule X + V + S.

In written texts coordinating conjunctions are usually preceded by a comma.

> **Er singt Lieder,** *und* **ich spiele Gitarre.**

However, a comma is not used before **und** and **oder** when either the subject or the verb of the main clauses is identical but is not expressed in the second clause.

Er singt Lieder *und* spielt die Gittare.
Er spielt Klavier *und* Gitarre.

Note: Coordinating conjunctions never change their form.
The most common coordinating conjunctions are:

aber—*but*

> **Er mußte hier bleiben, *aber* ich durfte ins Kino gehen.**
> *He had to stay here, but I could go to the movies.*

denn—*because, since, for*

> **Sie geht nicht mit, *denn* sie ist krank.**
> *She isn't going along because she is ill.*

oder—*or*

> **Sag ihm die Wahrheit, *oder* er wird sie von mir hören.**
> *Tell him the truth, or he'll hear it from me.*

sondern—*but (on the contrary)*

> **Sondern** follows a negative.

> **Sie fuhr *nicht* in die Stadt, *sondern* sie blieb zu Hause.**
> *She did not go downtown, but she stayed home.*

und—*and*

> **Ich habe im Gras gelegen, *und* er hat gearbeitet.**
> *I was lying in the grass, and he was working.*

10.   Combine the following sentences with the indicated coordinating conjunctions.

     1.   Er ist arm. Seine Eltern sind reich.   *aber*
     2.   Ich freute mich. Er wollte sofort mit der Arbeit anfangen.   *denn*
     3.   Wir sind nicht dort geblieben. Wir sind ausgegangen.   *sondern*
     4.   Sei vorsichtig! Es geht kaputt.   *oder*
     5.   Ich spiele Golf. Er spielt Tennis.   *und*
     6.   Er ist glücklich. Er hat Geld gewonnen.   *denn*
     7.   Wir sind nicht in Deutschland. Wir sind in Spanien.   *sondern*
     8.   Du kannst zu Hause bleiben. Ich muß zur Schule.   *aber*
     9.   Er trinkt Milch. Ich trinke Limonade.   *und*
     10.   Er kommt zu uns. Wir gehen zu ihm.   *oder*

SUBORDINATING CONJUNCTIONS—Verb in Final Position

Subordinating conjunctions introduce dependent clauses (sometimes also referred to as subordinate clauses) and establish the relationship between the main clause and the dependent clause or clauses in the sentence. A dependent clause is not a complete sentence and cannot stand alone.

Unlike the coordinating conjunctions, the subordinating conjunctions do become a part of the clause they introduce, and they do have an effect on the word order of the clause. Thus the conjugated verb is normally placed in final position at the end of a dependent clause. The pattern for dependent clause word order is:

> Dependent Clause Word Order =
> Subordinating Conjunction + Subject (+ Other Sentence Parts) + Verb

All dependent clauses introduced by subordinating conjunctions are separated from the main clause by a comma.

Er weiß, *daß* **ich zu Hause** *bin*.
Weil **ich mich nicht gut** *fühle*, **bin ich heute zu Hause geblieben.**

Note: Like the coordinating conjunctions, the subordinating conjunctions never change their form. The most common subordinating conjunctions include:

als—*when*

Als **er ins Zimmer** *kam*, **standen alle auf.**
When he came into the room, everyone got up.

als ob—*as if*

Sie sieht aus, *als ob* **sie krank** *gewesen wäre*.
She looks as if she had been ill.

bevor—*before*

Bevor **du ins Kino** *gehst*, **mußt du mir noch helfen.**
Before you go to the movies, you have to help me.

bis—*until*

Ich arbeitete, *bis* **ich müde** *wurde*.
I worked until I became tired.

da—*since, as*

Ich mußte warten, *da* **sie noch nicht** *angezogen war*.
I had to wait since she wasn't dressed yet.

damit—*in order to, so that*

Ich rufe ihn an, *damit* **er nicht** *kommt*.
I'll call him so that he won't come.

daß—*that*

Ich weiß, *daß* **er einen Hund** *hat*.
I know that he has a dog.

je . . . desto—*the* (comparative) *. . . the* (comparative)

Je mehr **er Klavier** *spielt*, *desto weniger* **Fehler macht er.**
The more he plays the piano, the fewer mistakes he makes.

Je länger **sie in den USA** *lebt*, *desto besser* **spricht sie Englisch.**
The longer she lives in the USA, the better she speaks English.

This two-part subordinating conjunction is always used with the comparative.

Note the word order used with this two-part conjunction. The clause beginning with **je** has its verb in final position, as is expected for dependent clauses introduced by subordinating conjunctions, whereas the clause introduced by **desto** follows the X + V + S rule for word order.

nachdem—*after*

> **Er grüßte mich,** *nachdem* **ich ihn** *gegrüßt hatte.*
> *He greeted me after I had greeted him.*

ob—*whether, if*

> **Sie wollen wissen,** *ob* **sie** *rauchen dürfen.*
> *They want to know whether they may smoke.*

obwohl—*although*

> **Er ging,** *obwohl* **es sein Vater** *verboten hatte.*
> *He went although his father forbade it.*

seit, seitdem—*since*

> *Seitdem* **wir weniger Geld** *haben,* **bleiben wir öfters zu Hause.**
> *Since we have less money, we stay home more often.*

während—*while*

> **Ich arbeitete,** *während* **er einen Roman** *las.*
> *I worked while he was reading a novel.*

weil—*because*

> **Wir konnten nichts kaufen,** *weil* **wir kein Geld** *hatten.*
> *We couldn't buy anything because we had no money.*

wenn—*when*

> *Wenn* **er nach Hause** *kommt,* **gehen wir ins Theater.**
> *When he comes home, we can go to the theater.*

Als, wenn, wann

The English *when* can be expressed three ways in German: **als, wenn, wann.** Each has a definite use, and they are not interchangeable.

Als refers to a single action in the past. It is used with the simple past, the present perfect, or the past perfect tense.

> **Ich freute mich,** *als* **er die Goldmedaille** *gewann.*
> *I was glad when he won the gold medal.*

Wenn corresponds to English *if* in conditional clauses. In time clauses it may be rendered with *when*. It is then used with the present tense, referring to the future.

> *Wenn* **ich Zeit hätte,** *würde* **ich schwimmen gehen.**
> *If I had time, I would go swimming.*

> **Ich gehe schwimmen,** *wenn* **es heiß** *wird.*
> *I'll go swimming when it gets hot.*

Wenn may also be used with the simple past tense. It then has the meaning of *whenever.*

> *Wenn* **er hier** *war,* **gingen wir spazieren.**
> *Whenever he was here, we went for a walk.*

Wann is an interrogative, meaning *when.* It is used in direct and indirect questions.

Wann **erwartest du ihn?**   *When do you expect him?*
Weißt du, *wann Ilse* kommt?   *Do you know when Ilse is coming?*

11. Write the German, using the correct forms of **wenn, als,** or **wann.**

    1. When are you reading the book?
    2. When she is ill, she stays home.
    3. Whenever he visited me, he brought me something.
    4. Do you know when he is arriving?
    5. When it got cold, I went into the house.
    6. If he had more money, he would go to Germany.

12. Rewrite the following, introducing the second sentence with the indicated subordinating conjunction.

    1. Sie hat Kopfweh. Die Kinder haben viel Lärm gemacht.   *weil*
    2. Er ist in Berlin. Seine Frau ist noch hier.   *während*
    3. Ich fragte ihn. Sie sind wieder gesund.   *ob*
    4. Es war sehr kalt. Wir waren in Alaska.   *als*
    5. Sie konnte gut Deutsch. Sie hatte in Deutschland studiert.   *nachdem*
    6. Wir kauften alles. Wir hatten viel Geld gewonnen.   *da*
    7. Wir blieben im Wald. Es wurde dunkel.   *bis*
    8. Konrad mußte mithelfen. Er konnte ausgehen.   *bevor*
    9. Er trägt einen Pullover. Er erkältet sich nicht.   *damit*
    10. Sie ist immer müde. Sie kann nicht gut schlafen.   *seitdem*

13. Complete the following with the correct German conjunctions.

    1. Ich weiß, _____ er in Köln ist.   *that*
    2. _____ es kalt ist, trägt er keinen Mantel.   *although*
    3. Ich wartete, _____ er fertig war.   *until*
    4. Sie tut, _____ sie reich wäre.   *as if*
    5. Weißt du, _____ sie dort ist?   *whether*
    6. _____ wir arbeiten, haben wir keine Zeit.   *since*
    7. _____ weniger sie ißt, desto schlanker wird sie.   *the*
    8. Er studiert, _____ er alles weiß.   *so that*
    9. Ich konnte nicht kommen, _____ ich in Rom war.   *since*
    10. Wir waren im Theater, _____ du studiert hast.   *while*

WORDS FUNCTIONING AS SUBORDINATING CONJUNCTIONS—Verb in Final Position

Dependent clauses can also be introduced by words functioning as subordinating conjunctions, such as relative pronouns, interrogative pronouns, and interrogative adverbs. These constructions also require dependent clause word order with the conjugated verb in final position. Remember, separable prefixes are always prefixed to the verb in dependent clauses.

Relative Pronouns and Interrogatives

The conjugated verb is in last position in relative clauses and in indirect questions introduced by interrogative words.

Dort steht der Student, *den* **ich in Paris kennengelernt** *habe*.

Du bekommst alles, *was* **du** *willst*.
Weißt du, *wann* **der Zug** *ankommt?*
Ich möchte wissen, *wieviel* **du davon getrunken** *hast*.

14. Rewrite the following, changing the direct questions to indirect ones. Start with **Ich weiß nicht,** ...
Follow the model.

    1. Wo hat er gewohnt?   4. Warum bringt er es mit?
    2. Wieviel muß sie noch machen?   5. Worüber wird er erzählen?
    3. Wovon lebt er?

15. Combine the two sentences, using the correct form of the relative pronoun **der.** Follow the model.

    Kennst du die Leute? Du hast ihnen das Bild gezeigt.
    Kennst du die Leute, denen du das Bild gezeigt hast?

    1. Wo ist der Mantel? Ich habe ihn gekauft.
    2. Die Kinder spielen mit der Puppe. Er hat sie mitgebracht.
    3. Dort steht das Flugzeug. Ich fliege damit ab.
    4. Hilfst du dem Mädchen? Sein Vater ist gestorben.
    5. Wo sind die Karten. Er hat sie mir geschenkt.

Haben or werden with the Double Infinitive

If a double infinitive construction occurs in a dependent clause, the conjugated form of the auxiliary **haben** or **werden** does not move to last position. Instead the conjugated verb precedes the double infinitive.

    Ich freute mich, weil er *hat kommen können*.
    Ich weiß, daß er sie *wird singen hören*.

16. Rewrite the following, changing the verb to the present perfect. Follow the model.

    Weißt du, ob er schreiben wollte?
    Weißt du, ob er hat schreiben wollen?

    1. Er ist glücklich, weil er gehen durfte.
    2. Ich glaube, daß er fragen wollte.
    3. Kennst du den Mann, den ich schreien hörte?
    4. Weißt du, ob er arbeiten mußte?
    5. Ich weiß, was er machen sollte.

Conditional Sentences

Any real or contrary-to-fact condition may start with **wenn** or with the conjugated verb. When the conjugated verb is in first position, the infinitives, the past participle, and the separable prefix move to last position.

    Wenn **er nach Hause** *käme*, **wäre ich froh.**
    Käme **er nach Hause, wäre ich froh.**
    Wenn **sie abfahren** *will*, **rufe ich das Taxi.**
    Will **sie abfahren, rufe ich das Taxi.**

17. Rewrite the following, omitting **wenn.**

    1. Wenn ich daran denke, bestelle ich es.
    2. Wenn er es gewollt hätte, hätte ich es ihm gekauft.
    3. Wenn es kalt wird, heizen wir das Haus.
    4. Wenn du mitmachen willst, mußt du dich umziehen.
    5. Wenn ich es ihr wegnehme, weint sie.

Main Clauses Following Dependent Clauses

When the main clause follows the dependent clause, the conjugated verb is in first position of that main clause.

Wenn ich Zeit hätte, *besuchte* **ich sie.**
Weil sie krank war, *kam* **sie nicht.**

18. Rewrite the following, starting with the dependent clause.

    1. Ich konnte es nicht machen, da ich keine Zeit hatte.
    2. Sie spielte Klavier, als er ins Zimmer kam.
    3. Ich werde euch besuchen, wenn ich das Auto habe.
    4. Ich mußte viel schlafen, während ich krank war.
    5. Du mußt mir helfen, bevor du gehst.

POSITION OF THE OBJECT

Noun and pronoun objects are usually arranged in the following manner, regardless of the position of the verb:

Dative nouns precede accusative nouns.

Der Professor erklärte *den Studenten das Problem*.

Pronoun objects precede noun objects, regardless of their case.

Weißt du, ob sie *es ihren Eltern* **zeigt?**
Hast du *dir die Hände* **gewaschen?**
Sie kauft *ihm das Auto*.

19. Rewrite the following, changing the dative noun objects to pronouns.

    1. Wir zeigten der Dame die Lampe.
    2. Wann hat er dem Hasen die Karotte gegeben?
    3. Ich habe meiner Tante eine Vase geschenkt.
    4. Hat er seinem Sohn das Motorrad gekauft?
    5. Wer hat den Leuten das Geld genommen?
    6. Weißt du, ob er den Kindern die Schokolade gegeben hat?

20. Rewrite the preceding exercise, changing the accusative noun objects to pronouns.

Accusative pronoun objects precede dative pronoun objects.

Wir bestellten *es uns*.
Ich war krank, als er *sie mir* **brachte.**

21. Rewrite the following, changing both noun objects to pronouns.

    1. Willst du deiner Mutter das Gedicht vorlesen?
    2. Wann hat er seinen Eltern den Brief gebracht?
    3. Weißt du, ob er seinem Vater die Geschichte erzählt hat?
    4. Wann hat er den Touristen das Museum gezeigt?
    5. Ich habe Frau Hartmann die Zeitschrift gegeben.

Pronoun objects may precede or follow noun subjects if the subject is not in first position.

Ich glaube, daß *ihn der Leher* **gesehen hat.**
Er weiß, warum *Angelika mir* **das Geschenk gegeben hat.**
Kann *dir der Junge* **helfen?**
Hat *das Mädchen sich* **verletzt?**

22. Rewrite the following, placing the pronoun objects before the subjects.

    1. Gibt Peter dir den Ring?
    2. Warum kann Ursula uns nicht besuchen?
    3. Kennt der Professor ihn?
    4. Hat Frau Schafft sich schon umgezogen?
    5. Sie weint, weil die Leute sie auslachten.

POSITION OF THE ADVERB

Adverbs follow pronoun objects.

Ich habe es *ihr gestern* **gebracht.**
Hast du *sie dort* **getroffen?**

Adverbs may precede or follow noun objects. The item of greater news value follows the item of less news value.

Ich weiß, daß du *deinem Freund gestern* **geschrieben hast.**
Ich weiß, daß du *gestern deinem Freund* **geschreiben hast.**

23. Rewrite the following, changing the noun objects to pronouns.

    1. Er sieht täglich seine Freunde.
    2. Wir geben natürlich den Leuten alles zurück.
    3. Sie besucht abends ihre Freundin.
    4. Ich habe wirklich den Schauspieler getroffen.
    5. Er kann leider seine Eltern nicht abholen.

If more than one adverb or adverbial phrase is used in a sentence, they occur in the following order: time, manner, place.

Ich bin *um acht Uhr mit dem Zug nach Bonn* **gefahren.**

24. Answer the following questions with complete sentences, incorporating the cues in your answers.

1. Wann bist du nach Hause gekommen?   *am Nachmittag*
2. Wo trefft ihr sie um zehn Uhr?   *im Hotel*
3. Wann warst du dort?   *jeden Tag*
4. Mit wem gehst du heute abend spazieren?   *mit Ursel*
5. Wie bist du in die Stadt gefahren?   *sehr schnell*
6. Womit seid ihr gestern ins Kino gefahren?   *mit dem alten Wagen.*

If there are several time expressions in one sentence, the general time precedes the specific time.

Er ist *gestern vormittag um elf Uhr* **gekommen.**

25. Answer the following questions affirmatively. Follow the model.

War er gestern abend hier? um sieben Uhr
Ja, er war gestern abend um sieben Uhr hier.

1. Besucht ihr mich morgen?   *um drei Uhr*
2. Fahrt ihr diesen Sommer in die Berge.   *im Juli*
3. Gehst du nächste Woche ins Theater?   *am Mittwoch*
4. Fliegt ihr heute abend ab?   *um sechs Uhr*
5. Bist du morgen zu Hause?   *zwischen sieben und acht Uhr*

Answers

Chapter 1

1. See German alphabet on p. 1.

2. See German alphabet on p. 1.

3. See list of code words developed by the German Post Office on p. 2.

4.
1.	wann	6.	lang
2.	hastig	7.	Bank
3.	rasch	8.	Ball
4.	Stadt	9.	Gedanke
5.	Hand	10.	Handtasche

5.
1.	beten	6.	fehlen
2.	Kopfweh	7.	Mehlwurm
3.	Vorlesung	8.	Seemann
4.	dem	9.	mehr
5.	Regenwasser	10.	Beet

6.
1.	Dienstag	6.	ihnen
2.	mir	7.	Bier
3.	Lieder	8.	Briefträger
4.	ihm	9.	hier
5.	wir	10.	antik

7.
1.	Spott	6.	Norden
2.	morgen	7.	Oktett
3.	Segelsport	8.	Stock
4.	offen	9.	Topf
5.	sorgfältig	10.	Wochentag

8.
1.	Fuß	6.	Natur
2.	Stuhl	7.	Bluse
3.	Kuh	8.	Anzug
4.	gut	9.	Ruhm
5.	Juli	10.	trug

9.
1.	älter	6.	Bett
2.	Eltern	7.	fern
3.	Wände	8.	kälter
4.	Unterwäsche	9.	beschäftigen
5.	ändern	10.	Ärzte

10.
1.	blöd	6.	Böhmen
2.	Möbel	7.	Fön
3.	Löwe	8.	Föhn
4.	aushöhlen	9.	Öl
5.	öd	10.	Vermögen

11.
1.	Müller	4.	benützen
2.	müssen	5.	Früchte
3.	Mütter	6.	schüchtern

7.	beglückern	9.	Müll
8.	Lücke	10.	Idyll

12.
1.	sich	6.	Nichte
2.	nichts	7.	leichter
3.	schlecht	8.	Becher
4.	besichtigen	9.	Löcher
5.	wöchentlich	10.	Bäuche

13.
1.	gewesen	6.	Besuch
2.	Käsekuchen	7.	Eisen
3.	Nase	8.	sechzehn
4.	also	9.	so
5.	ansehen	10.	Süden

14.
1.	<u>A</u>bend	6.	Phanta<u>sie</u>
2.	<u>Leu</u>te	7.	<u>Su</u>ppe
3.	Mu<u>sik</u>	8.	Univer<u>si</u>tät
4.	<u>sa</u>gen	9.	be<u>en</u>den
5.	Bäcke<u>rei</u>	10.	stu<u>die</u>ren

15.
1. Telefonbe / antworter
2. Post / amt
3. eines / Abends
4. in / Aachen
5. was / eßt / ihr?
6. auf / Englisch
7. Ebbe / und Flut
8. Verkehrs / ampel
9. be / enden
10. die / Ei / erkuchen

16.
1.	bak-ken	6.	Re-stau-rants
2.	Würst-chen	7.	lang-wei-lig
3.	Om-ni-bus	8.	Ha-se
4.	Pro-gram-me	9.	au-ßer
5.	Ra-dier-gum-mi	10.	Wasch-lap-pen

Chapter 2

1.
1.	Der	11.	Der
2.	Das	12.	Das
3.	Die	13.	Die
4.	Der	14.	Die
5.	Das	15.	Das
6.	Die	16.	Der
7.	Das	17.	Der
8.	Die	18.	Das
9.	Der	19.	Die
10.	Die	20.	Das

2.
1.	Der	2.	Der

3. Der, der
4. Der
5. Der
6. Der

7. Der
8. Der
9. Der, der
10. Der

17 Die
18. Die

19. Die
20. Die

3.
1. Die, die
2. Die, die
3. Die
4. Die
5. Die

6. der
7. Die
8. Die
9. Die
10. Die

10.
1. Das
2. das
3. Das
4. das
5. Das

6. Das
7. das
8. Das
9. Das
10. Das

4.
1. die
2. der
3. _____
4. Die
5. Das

6. Die
7. Die
8. _____
9. das
10. Die

11.
1. Die, das
2. Die, das, der
3. Die
4. Der
5. Die
6. Das
7. Der, der
8. die
9. Die, die
10. Die

11. Das, das
12. Der
13. Die, die
14. der, der
15. Die
16. Das
17. Die
18. Die
19. Der
20. Der

5.
1. Das
2. Das
3. der
4. Das
5. Das

6. Das
7. Das
8. Das
9. Das
10. Das

12.
1. Der
2. Die
3. Der
4. Der
5. Das
6. das
7. Die
8. Das

9. Die
10. Der
11. Das
12. Der
13. Die
14. Die
15. Das

6.
1. Das
2. das
3. Der
4. Der
5. Der
6. Der
7. Der
8. Der
9. Das
10. Der, die

11. Die
12. Das
13. die
14. Der
15. Der
16. Die
17. Die
18. Die
19. Das
20. Der

13.
1. Der Geburtstagskuchen
2. Der Wintermantel
3. Der Autobus
4. Das Hotelzimmer
5. Der Sportsmann
6. Die Blumenvase
7. Das Kinderzimmer
8. Der Krankenwagen
9. Die Straßenlampe
10. Die Universitätsprofessorin
11. Das Tagebuch
12. Die Mitgliedskarte
13. Die Wasserfarbe
14. Das Staatsexamen
15. Die Zahnbürste
16. Der Rotstift
17. Die Rundfahrt
18. Der Schnellimbiß
19. Der Sitzplatz
20. Das Segelboot

7.
1. Der
2. das
3. Der
4. Die, der, das
5. Der
6. Der, das
7. Der
8. Der, der
9. Der

10. der
11. Das
12. Der
13. Der
14. die
15. Der
16. Die, die
17. Das
18. das

8.
1. Der
2. Der
3. Der
4. Der
5. Der

6. Der
7. Der
8. Der
9. Der
10. Der

14.
1. Das Obst ist frisch.
2. Die Musik ist modern.
3. Das Fleisch ist frisch.
4. Die Butter ist teuer.
5. Der Honig ist süß.
6. Die Milch ist sauer.
7. Das Vieh ist hungrig.
8. Das Gold ist kostbar.

9.
1. Die
2. die
3. Die
4. Die
5. Die
6. Die
7. Die
8. Die

9. die
10. Die
11. Die
12. Die
13. Die
14. Die
15. Die
16. die

15.
1. Die Kissen sind weich.
2. Die Onkel kommen.
3. Die Töchter sind klein.
4. Die Zimmer sind kalt.
5. Die Brüder rauchen.
6. Die Mäntel sind neu.
7. Die Fenster sind geschlossen.
8. Die Äpfel sind rot.
9. Die Lehrer sind alt.
10. Die Koffer sind aus Leder.
11. Die Messer sind rostig.
12. Die Segel sind weiß.
13. Die Teller stehen dort.
14. Die Schlüssel sind alt.
15. Die Fräulein sind hübsch.
16. Die Mütter warten.
17. Die Wagen stehen hier.
18. Die Theater sind modern.
19. Die Löffel sind teuer.
20. Die Schüler lernen.

16.
1. Die Würste schmecken gut.
2. Die Monate sind lang.
3. Die Hände sind naß.
4. Die Gedichte sind kurz.
5. Die Hunde sind braun.
6. Die Züge kommen an.
7. Die Tische sind aus Holz.
8. Die Städte sind modern.
9. Die Berge sind hoch.
10. Die Tiere sind verletzt.
11. Die Kriege sind brutal.
12. Die Söhne sind groß.
13. Die Briefe sind interessant.
14. Die Schuhe sind aus Leder.
15. Die Tage sind kurz.
16. Die Freunde lachen.
17. Die Nächte sind kalt.
18. Die Jahre gehen vorüber.

17.
1. Die Würmer sind lang.
2. Die Bücher sind interessant.
3. Die Eier schmecken gut.
4. Die Länder sind neutral.
5. Die Gläser sind kalt.
6. Die Blätter sind grün.
7. Die Männer rauchen.
8. Die Häuser sind teuer.
9. Die Kleider passen nicht.
10. Die Kinder weinen.
11. Die Völker sind hungrig.
12. Die Bilder sind billig.
13. Die Lieder sind melodisch.
14. Die Götter sind alt.

18.
1. Die Herren sind alt.
2. Die Damen sind freundlich.
3. Die Katzen sind schwarz.
4. Die Nationen sind progressiv.
5. Die Jungen sind hier.
6. Die Studentinnen lernen.
7. Die Türen sind offen.
8. Die Straßen sind breit.
9. Die Studenten sind arm.
10. Die Freundinnen sind krank.
11. Die Hasen sind weiß.
12. Die Blumen blühen.
13. Die Fabriken sind grau.
14. Die Tassen sind gelb.
15. Die Wohnungen sind kalt.
16. Die Präsidenten sind alt.
17. Die Namen sind lang.
18. Die Antworten sind falsch.
19. Die Helden sind stark.
20. Die Zeitungen liegen hier.

19.
1. Die Kameras sind teuer.
2. Die Bars sind geschlossen.
3. Die Radios sind kaputt.
4. Die Hotels sind teuer.
5. Die Sofas sind weich.
6. Die Parks sind groß.
7. Die Jobs sind interessant.
8. Die Fotos sind alt.

20.
1. Die Firmen sind bekannt.
2. Sind die Wörter auf der Liste?
3. Die Bänke sind im Park.
4. Die Dramen sind interessant.
5. Die Museen sind modern.
6. Die Busse kommen.
7. Die Banken sind geschlossen.
8. Die Zentren sind groß.

21.
1. Der Teller ist weiß.
2. Die Lehrerin ist hübsch.
3. Das Glas ist leer.
4. Der Mantel hängt hier.
5. Das Zimmer ist warm.
6. Der Student lernt.
7. Das Geschäft ist geschlossen.
8. Die Nacht ist lang.
9. Der Held ist bekannt.
10. Die Bar ist billig.
11. Das Gymnasium ist progressiv.
12. Das Sofa ist rot.
13. Die Mutter ist freundlich.
14. Das Segel ist weiß.
15. Die Stadt ist übervölkert.
16. Das Radio ist kaputt.
17. Die Zeitung ist alt.
18. Der Mann ist krank.
19. Die Hand ist schmutzig.
20. Das Theater ist modern.
21. _____
22. _____

22.
1. _____
2. Die Schuhe sind schwarz.
3. Die Freundinnen sind nett.
4. _____
5. Die Äpfel sind sauer.
6. Die Schlüssel sind rostig.
7. Die Mädchen sind freundlich.
8. Die Busse sind rot.
9. Die Mütter schreiben.
10. Die Würste sind lecker.
11. Die Autos sind neu.
12. Die Briefe sind lang.
13. Die Hände sind naß.
14. Die Zimmer sind groß.
15. Die Tiere sind wild.
16. Die Gläser sind teuer.
17. Die Bücher sind interessant.
18. Die Straßen sind eng.
19. Die Freunde sind reich.
20. Die Lieder sind kurz.

23.
1. Die
2. Der
3. das
4. Der
5. Die
6. Das
7. das
8. Die
9. Der
10. Der

24.
1. Diese
2. Dieser
3. dieses
4. Dieser
5. Diese
6. Dieses
7. dieses
8. Diese
9. Dieser
10. Dieser

25.
1. Diese Länder sind reich.
2. Welche Männer kommen?
3. Jene Häuser sind alt.
4. Wo sind die Zeitungen?
5. Welche Studentinnen sind hübsch?
6. Jene Frauen sind krank.
7. Dort liegen die Äpfel.
8. Diese Mädchen lernen.
9. Diese Städte sind modern.
10. Wo sind die Bücher?

26.
1. ein
2. Eine
3. ein
4. Ein
5. ein
6. eine
7. eine
8. Eine
9. ein
10. ein

27.
1. kein
2. Keine
3. kein
4. Kein
5. kein
6. keine
7. keine
8. Keine
9. kein
10. kein

28.
1. e
2. _____
3. _____
4. e

5. _____
6. _____
7. _____
8. _____
9. e
10. e

29.
1. Ist das seine Firma?
2. Sein Job ist schwer.
3. Sein Glas ist leer.
4. Sein Hund bellt.
5. Wo ist seine Frau?
6. Sein Auto ist neu.
7. Sein Bus kommt.
8. Sein Drama ist lang.
9. Wo ist sein Junge?
10. Seine Freundinnen ist hübsch.

30.
1. Meine Freundin lachen.
2. Ihre Brüder sind krank.
3. Wo sind seine Lehrer?
4. Deine Messer liegen dort.
5. Wo sind unsere Schlüssel?
6. Sind das eure Häuser?
7. Wo sind Ihre Zeitungen?
8. Dort sind meine Onkel.
9. Sind das deine Kinder?
10. Wo sind eure Lehrerinnen?

31.
1. e, e
2. _____
3. e
4. _____
5. es
6. e
7. er, _____
8. _____
9. e
10. e

32.
1. den
2. das
3. die
4. die
5. das
6. das
7. die
8. den
9. das
10. den

33.
1. diesen
2. dieses
3. diese
4. diese
5. dieses
6. dieses
7. diese
8. diesen
9. dieses
10. diesen

34.
1. Wir kennen die Dichter.
2. Ich bekomme die Briefe.
3. Er kauft die Würste.
4. Ich sehe die Tiere.
5. Sie treffen die Freunde.
6. Wir besuchen die Städte.
7. Ich kenne die Berge.
8. Er schreibt die Gedichte.
9. Ich kaufe die Blumen.
10. Wir singen die Lieder.

35.
1. einen
2. eine
3. ein
4. ein
5. einen
6. eine

7. einen   9. ein
8. einen   10. eine

36.
1. keinen   6. keine
2. keine   7. keinen
3. kein   8. keinen
4. kein   9. kein
5. keinen   10. keine

37.
1. Kaufst du unser Auto?
2. Ich sehe unsere Katze.
3. Wir besuchen unser Kind.
4. Er ruft unseren Lehrer.
5. Ich nehme unseren Schlüssel.
6. Wir kennen unsere Lehrerin.

38.
1. en   6. e
2. e   7. e
3. en   8. _____
4. _____   9. _____
5. e   10. e

39.
1. Hat er meine Bilder?
2. Brauchst du deine Bücher?
3. Seht ihr unsere Freundinnen?
4. Ich nehme seine Zeitungen.
5. Hast du deine Mäntel?
6. Wir kennen ihre Kinder.
7. Ich habe ihre Schuhe.
8. Verkaufst du unsere Wagen?
9. Sie brauchen ihre Freunde.
10. Treffen Sie Ihre Lehrer?

40.
1. en, en   6. en, n
2. en, en   7. en, en
3. en, en   8. en, en
4. en, n   9. en, n
5. en, n   10. en, n

41.
1. e, en   11. _____, es
2. _____   12. e, en, en
3. en, n   13. e, en
4. en, n   14. ____, ____, e
5. er, _____, en   15. e, e
6. e, en   16. e
7. er, _____, e   17. e
8. as, e   18. en, n
9. e, en   19. e, es
10. er, _____   20. en

42.
1. dem   6. dem
2. der   7. dem
3. dem   8. der
4. dem   9. dem
5. der   10. der

43.
1. jenem   4. jenem
2. jener   5. jener
3. jenem   6. jenem

7. jenem   9. jenem
8. jener   10. jener

44.
1. einer   6. einer
2. einer   7. einem
3. einem   8. einem
4. einer   9. einem
5. einem   10. einem

45.
1. keiner   6. keiner
2. keiner   7. keinem
3. keinem   8. keinem
4. keiner   9. keinem
5. keinem   10. keinem

46.
1. er   6. er
2. em   7. em
3. er   8. em
4. em   9. er
5. em   10. em

47.
1. keinem   6. unserer
2. unserem   7. jenem
3. dieser   8. jedem
4. meinem   9. seiner
5. eurer   10. Ihrer

48.
1. em, en   5. em, n
2. em, en   6. em, n
3. em, en   7. em, en
4. em, n   8. em, n

49.
1. Schreibst du deinen Freundinnen?
2. Er hilft jenen Kindern.
3. Es gefällt seinen Lehrern.
4. Sie zeigt es ihren Brüdern.
5. Er antwortet den Männern.
6. Ich hole den Babys Milch.
7. Es gehört diesen Jungen.
8. Wir glauben den Frauen.
9. Sie dankt ihren Freunden.
10. Es gehört euren Studenten.

50.
1. jenen   6. dieser
2. meinem   7. Welchem
3. unseren   8. keinem
4. ihrem   9. einem
5. deinen   10. jedem

51.
1. _____, em   9. er, em, ie
2. er, ie   10. _____, er
3. en   11. en, n, en
4. er   12. er, em
5. es, er   13. en, _____
6. e, em, en   14. em, ie
7. em, es   15. en, n, e
8. en

52.
1. der, _____   2. des, s

3. des, s
4. des, es
5. der, _____
6. des, es

7. des, ns
8. des, n
9. des, es
10. des, en

3. Das
4. Die
5. Die

6. Der
7. Der
8. Die

53.
1. dieser, _____
2. dieses, s
3. dieses, s
4. dieses, es
5. dieser, _____

6. dieses, es
7. dieses, ns
8. dieses, n
9. dieses, es
10. dieses, en

61.
1. Der
2. die
3. Die
4. die
5. Der
6. Der

7. der
8. Das
9. die
10. Die
11. _____
12. Das

54.
1. eines, en
2. eines, n
3. eines, es
4. eines, en
5. eines, s

6. eines, s
7. einer, _____
8. eines, s
9. eines, n
10. einer, _____

62.
1. das
2. das
3. die

4. die
5. das
6. die

55.
1. seines, s
2. meiner, _____
3. unseres, en
4. eures, n
5. ihres, s

6. deiner, _____
7. ihrer, _____
8. meines, es
9. seines, es
10. Ihrer, _____

63.
1. die
2. die
3. die
4. den

5. das
6. den
7. den
8. die

56.
1. Die Kinder jener Frauen sind krank.
2. Die Sitze seiner Autos sind bequem.
3. Das sind die Fotos unserer Töchter.
4. Die Bücher jener Studenten liegen hier.
5. Wann beginnt der Bau eurer Häuser?
6. Die Museen dieser Städte sind modern.
7. Die Kleider meiner Freundinnen sind neu.
8. Der Wagen der Herren steht dort.
9. Die Betonung der Namen ist schwer.
10. Die Gemälde jener Museen sind bekannt.

64.
1. die
2. die
3. Die
4. das
5. Die
6. Der
7. den
8. Der
9. die

10. Die
11. die
12. Die
13. Das
14. Die
15. Das
16. die
17. die
18. Die

57.
1. Die Schneide von diesem Messer ist scharf.
2. Die Dokumente von unserem Präsidenten sind im Museum.
3. Wir haben die Hälfte von dem Gedicht gelesen.
4. Hier ist ein Bild von meinen Freunden.
5. Der Preis von dem Auto ist zu hoch.

65.
1. Ich habe Fieber.
2. Er ist Lehrer.
3. Sie ist eine gute Lehrerin.
4. Hat er Zahnweh?
5. Er ist als Student in Berlin.
6. Er ist Professor.
7. Sie wird Pianistin.
8. Wir haben Halsweh.

58.
1. Das Wasser jenes Sees ist eiskalt.
2. Peters Hund bellt.
3. Die Ohren solcher Hasen sind sehr lang.
4. Die Mutter des Mädchens steht dort.
5. Die Produkte dieser Fabrik sind teuer.

66.
1. ie, es, es, en
2. es, es, er, _____, en
3. ie, es, s
4. _____, e
5. e, er, er, _____
6. e, e
7. e, en, _____, _____
8. er, es, n
9. em, en, en
10. es, er, es, s

59.
1. ie, er, _____
2. as, er, _____
3. ie, es, es
4. es, s
5. ie, es, s
6. ie, es, es
7. s
8. er, es, s

9. ie, er , _____
10. ie, es, n
11. ie, er, _____
12. as, es, es
13. ie, er, _____
14. en, es, en
15. en, es, s

67.
1. Wir haben keine Fotos.
2. Wo sind seine Brüder?
3. Wer hat jene Bilder genommen?
4. Welche Lieder soll ich singen?
5. Wer hilft den Babys?
6. Das gefällt den Mädchen.
7. Meine Freundinnen kommen.
8. Unsere Autos sind rot.

60.
1. Der

2. Die

9. Wann kommen Ihre Töchter?
10. Die Kinder unserer Lehrer sind hier.
11. Wo sind unsere Hotels?
12. Manche Länder sind arm.
13. Wo sind die Museen?
14. Die Bücher der Studenten liegen hier.
15. Werden diese Geschichten euren Freunden gefallen?

68.
1. _____
2. _____
3. _____
4. das
5. Die
6. Die
7. ein
8. Der
9. die
10. Der
11. den
12. die
13. Der
14. Das
15. die
16. _____

Chapter 3

1.
1. durch
2. entlang
3. um
4. gegen
5. ohne
6. bis
7. für
8. für
9. durch
10. ohne

2.
1. en
2. s
3. en
4. e
5. en
6. e
7. s
8. e
9. ie
10. s
11. s
12. e
13. e
14. en
15. e
16. s
17. e
18. ie
19. ie
20. e

3.
1. meine
2. ihren
3. unsere
4. seinen
5. jenen
6. diese
7. ihren
8. euer

4.
1. mit, nach
2. bei
3. zum
4. seit
5. gegenüber
6. Nach, zur
7. von
8. mit
9. von
10. von

5.
1. em
2. er
3. em
4. m
5. em
6. em
7. m
8. _____
9. er
10. Der
11. em
12. em
13. en, _____
14. er
15. em
16. en
17. vom
18. em
19. er
20. en

6.
1. seiner
2. einem
3. jenem
4. einem
5. Dieser
6. unserem
7. eurem
8. dem
9. der
10. dem
11. meiner
12. seinem
13. ihren
14. deiner

7.
1. im
2. die
3. unters
4. unseren
5. im
6. der
7. Am
8. ins
9. diesem
10. die
11. Im
12. einem
13. ans
14. deinen
15. seinen
16. jener
17. Am
18. ins
19. deine
20. dem
21. im
22. meinen
23. ihren
24. Im
25. hinters
26. den
27. einem
28. eurem
29. meinem
30. deine
31. jenem
32. unsere
33. ins
34. den
35. der

8.
1. darin
2. damit
3. daneben
4. dabei
5. darunter
6. dahinter
7. daran
8. darauf
9. darüber
10. dazu
11. danach
12. davon

9.
1. herein
2. hinaus
3. hinein
4. herein
5. heraus
6. herein
7. hinein
8. hinaus
9. hinein
10. heraus

10.
1. Womit
2. Worauf
3. Worin
4. Woran
5. Woraus
6. Wovon
7. Worum
8. Worüber
9. Wovor
10. Wozu
11. Worauf
12. Wobei
13. Wogegen
14. Womit
15. Wofür

11.
1. er
2. er
3. es
4. er
5. es
6. er
7. er
8. er
9. es
10. er
11. er
12. es
13. es
14. er
15. er
16. er
17. es
18. er

19. es   20. er

12.
1. Seiner
2. des
3. des
4. die
5. der
6. den
7. der
8. Der
9. Des
10. dem

13.
1. ie
2. im, nach
3. en
4. er
5. em
6. es
7. _____
8. ie
9. ie
10. er
11. ie
12. em
13. es
14. em
15. em
16. es
17. m
18. er
19. ie
20. em
21. e
22. e
23. es
24. as (ums)
25. en, nach

14.
1. Worin
2. Wozu
3. Womit
4. Wogegen
5. Worüber
6. Worauf
7. Wovon
8. Wovor

15.
1. darin
2. daneben
3. davor
4. darauf
5. darunter

Chapter 4

1.
1. er
2. du
3. Sie
4. sie
5. du
6. Ihr
7. Es
8. Sie
9. ihr
10. Sie
11. Sie
12. Sie
13. Sie
14. Sie
15. es
16. ihr
17. Sie
18. du

2.
1. er, ihn
2. sie, sie
3. wir, sie
4. sie, es
5. sie, sie
6. er, sie
7. ich, ihn
8. sie, sie
9. ich, es
10. wir, ihn
11. ich, dich
12. er, sie
13. wir, ihn
14. ich, es

3.
1. Renate braucht es.
2. Wir kaufen ihn.
3. Ich setzte mich neben sie.
4. Wir essen sie.
5. Ich darf ihn lesen.
6. Wer hat ihn gefüttert?

4.
1. Ja, er hat dich erkannt.
2. Ja, er schreibt uns.
3. Ja, ich habe es für dich gekauft.
4. Ja, er geht ohne uns.
5. Ja, wir können euch dort besuchen.

5.
1. Er gab es ihr.
2. Wir helfen ihm.
3. Gibst du ihm das Futter?
4. Wir unterhielten uns mit ihr.
5. Er erzählte von ihm.
6. Wohnst du bei ihnen?
7. Ich schrieb ihnen Ansichtskarten.
8. Sie holte ihm Medizin.
9. Es gehört ihnen.
10. Sie bringen ihr Essen.
11. Es gefällt ihm.
12. Ich kaufe ihr etwas.
13. Er kommt von ihm.
14. Wir stehen hinter ihm.

6.
1. Ja, er hat mir etwas gebracht.
2. Ja, ich zeige euch die Stadt.
3. Ja, wir sagen euch die Wahrheit.
4. Ja, er hat mir geholfen.
5. Ja, ich bringe dir etwas mit.
6. Ja, er hat mir dafür gedankt.
7. Ja, sie hat uns geholfen.
8. Ja, ich kaufe (wir kaufen) ihm etwas.
9. Ja, das Bild gefällt mir.
10. Ja, wir kaufen dir den Wagen.

7.
1. Er gab es seiner Mutter.
2. Ich habe ihr ein Paket geschickt.
3. Sie zeigte sie ihrem Kind.
4. Sie erzählen ihnen die Neuigkeit.
5. Sie bringen sie den Kranken.
6. Er kauft sie seiner Tante.
7. Ich schreibe ihm eine Karte.
8. Sie glaubt ihm die Geschichte.
9. Ich gebe sie der Dame.
10. Wir kaufen ihnen Geschenke.

8.
1. Wir bringen es ihm.
2. Ich hole ihn ihm.
3. Wir erzählten sie ihnen.
4. Er gibt ihn ihm.
5. Er hat sie ihr geglaubt.
6. Johann zeigte es ihnen.
7. Der Professor erklärte sie ihnen.
8. Ich kaufe sie ihnen.
9. Er schreibt sie ihm.
10. Dieter holt es ihm.

9.
1. Ja, er hat sie mir geschenkt.
2. Ja, ich habe sie ihnen gezeigt.
3. Ja, er hat sie uns gekauft.
4. Ja, ich bringe ihn dir.

5. Ja, sie hat ihn uns gegeben.

10. 1. Hilft ihnen Ellen?
2. Ich glaube, daß es Maria gekauft hat.
3. Wir wissen nicht, ob er sie besichtigt hat.
4. Ich habe Zeit, weil ihn Norma abholt.
5. Morgen kauft ihr Susi den Pullover.

11. 1. Jeden Tag holt Pia ihm die Zeitung.
2. Ich weiß, wann Peter ihr geholfen hat.
3. Bringt Gabriele es?
4. Hat er es genommen?
5. Weißt du, wo Dieter sie getroffen hat?

12. 1. Er lachte über sie.
2. Wir sprechen von ihnen.
3. Er fragt nach ihr.
4. Was weißt du von ihm?
5. Er denkt an sie.
6. Warten Sie auf ihn?
7. Warum hast du Angst vor ihm?
8. Wir sprechen über ihn
9. Ich habe von ihm gehört.
10. Er lädt sie zu ihnen ein.

13. 1. dir   8. dich
2. ihm   9. euch
3. uns   10. mich
4. sie   11. uns
5. uns   12. dir
6. ihm   13. sie
7. dir   14. Sie

14. 1. Ja, ich denke daran.
2. Ja, ich liege darunter.
3. Ja, ich warte auf sie.
4. Ja, wir sprechen darüber.
5. Ja, ich spreche von ihr.
6. Ja, ich fahre damit.
7. Ja, ich stehe davor.
8. Ja, ich warte darauf.
9. Ja, wir stehen neben ihnen.
10. Ja, er denkt an sie.
11. Ja, sie fragt nach ihr
12. Ja, ich sitze hinter ihm.
13. Ja, ich arbeite damit.
14. Ja, wir fahren mit ihnen.
15. Ja, ich weiß etwas davon.
16. Ja, ich habe Angst vor ihm.

15. 1. mich   6. sich
2. sich   7. dich
3. uns   8. dich
4. euch   9. mich
5. sich   10. sich

16. 1. euch   3. sich
2. mir   4. dir

5. mir   8. mir
6. dir   9. dir
7. sich   10. uns

17. 1. Heute morgen haben sich die Kinder weh getan.
2. Auf die Ferien freut sich Max.
3. Wegen des Unfalls hat sich der Beamte verspätet.
4. Vor einer Stunde hat Vater sich das Auto gekauft.
5. An seine Ferien erinnert sich mein Freund.
6. Am Abend putzt Barbara sich die Zähne.
7. Ein Motorrad kauft sich Herr Obermeyer.
8. Am Morgen rasiert sich Vater.

18. 1. deine   6. seine
2. eurer   7. ihren
3. unsere   8. unserem
4. mein(e)s   9. meinen
5. deinen   10. ihrem

19. 1. der dort (da)   4. dem hier
2. dem hier   5. die hier
3. die dort (da)   6. denen dort (da)

20. 1. diese dort (da) 4. dieser hier
2. diesem hier   5. dieses hier
3. diese dort (da)

21. 1. niemand (en)   10. einem nichts
2. etwas   11. viel
3. Wenige   12. wenig
4. einigen   13. Jemand
5. Jeder   14. andere
6. nichts   15. einige (mehrere)
7. Man   16. Viele (Manche)
8. Viele   17. alles
9. alle   18. Man

22. 1. das   5. der
2. der   6. das
3. die   7. die
4. die   8. der

23. 1. den   5. die
2. die   6. die
3. den   7. das
4. das   8. den

24. 1. Liest du das Buch, das er gebracht hat?
2. Brauchst du die Zeitung, die auf dem Tisch liegt?
3. Kennst du den Herrn, den wir getroffen haben?
4. Heute kam der Junge, der uns damals geholfen hatte.
5. Kennst du die Leute, die dort spazierengehen?

6. Wo sind die Blumen, die ich gekauft
    habe?

25. 1. dem   5. der
         2. dem   6. der
         3. denen   7. denen
         4. dem   8. dem

26. 1. Dort sitzt der Tourist, welchem du das
             Essen bringen sollst.
         2. Kennst du meine Geschwister, bei welchen
             ich wohne?
         3. Die Leiter, auf welcher er steht, ist kaputt.
         4. Hier ist das Auto, mit welchem wir
             spazierenfahren.
         5. Der Stuhl, auf welchem du sitzt, ist alt.

27. 1. deren   5. deren
         2. dessen   6. deren
         3. dessen   7. dessen
         4. deren   8. dessen

28. 1. Wer   4. Was
         2. Was   5. Wer
         3. Wer

29. 1. was   5. was
         2. wo   6. was
         3. wo   7. wo
         4. was   8. was

30. 1. Der Stuhl, worauf du sitzt, ist eine Rarität.
         2. Wir besuchen das Haus, worin Goethe
             geboren wurde.
         3. Ist das das Spielzeug, womit sie sich so
             amüsiert?
         4. Dort ist die Kirche, wonach er fragte.
         5. Sind das die Bücher, wofür du dich
             interessierst?
         6. Wo ist der Brief, worauf er wartet?
         7. Das Problem, worüber ihr sprecht, ist
             schwer.
         8. Wo ist die Ruine, wovon er erzählt?

31. 1. was   14. Wer
         2. den   15. das
         3. Wer   16. die
         4. dem   17. wo
         5. deren   18. denen
         6. das   19. deren
         7. dem   20. was
         8. den   21. die
         9. wo   22. die
        10. der   23. dem
        11. das   24. was
        12. was   25. dem
        13. dessen

Chapter 5

1. 1. das   6. Die
        2. der   7. den
        3. der   8. den
        4. den   9. den
        5. dem   10. die

2. 1. Dieser Mantel dort gehört mir.
        2. Wir holen etwas für dieses Mädchen hier.
        3. Ich helfe diesem Mann da.
        4. Es liegt unter diesen Büchern da.
        5. Mit diesem Wagen hier fahren wir nicht.
        6. Ursula hat diese Kamera da.
        7. Ich schlafe nicht in diesem Bett da.
        8. Kennst du diesen Mann dort?
        9. Diese Frauen hier kaufen nichts.
       10. Er kauft diese Blumen hier.

3. 1. heiß   9. häßlich
        2. süß   10. billig
        3. faul   11. dick
        4. lang   12. langsam
        5. krank   13. schlecht
        6. reich   14. alt
        7. schmutzig   15. klein
        8. leicht

4. 1. er, e   5. er, e
        2. as, e, e   6. er, e, e
        3. es, e   7. er, e
        4. ie, e   8. er, e

5. 1. Welche deutsche
        2. Jenes kleine
        3. Jedes neue
        4. die junge
        5. dieser amerikanische
        6. jener blonde
        7. das dünne, rote
        8. jeder gesunde
        9. das leere
       10. jene große
       11. der interessante
       12. Diese kalte

6. 1. Jener französische Dichter ist weltbekannt.
        2. Der rote Bus wartet.
        3. Manches deutsche Drama ist lang.
        4. Wieviel kostet jenes schnelle Auto?
        5. Jedes moderne Museum braucht Geld.
        6. Welche alte Maschine ist kaputt?
        7. Wo ist die weiße Katze?
        8. Wo steht die frische milch?

7. 1. es, e   5. en, en
        2. ie, e   6. e, e, e
        3. en, en   7. en, en
        4. es, e   8. en, en

8.
1. die lange
2. jenes moderne
3. diesen großen
4. Welchen interessanten
5. das scharfe
6. die kleine
7. jenes fremde, junge
8. jedes kranke
9. den schmutzigen
10. jenen heißen
11. den großen, blonden
12. jenen klugen

9.
1. Er restaurierte manches historische Haus.
2. Wer hat den alten Lederkoffer?
3. Bring dieses schmutzige Glas in die Küche!
4. Wir kaufen jenes schnelle Motorboot.
5. Welchen roten Apfel möchtest du?
6. Wir wandern durch die kleine Stadt.
7. Sie bringt Blumen für das kranke Kind
8. Ich brauche jede neue, deutsche Briefmarke.

10.
1. em, en
2. er, en
3. em, en
4. em, en, en
5. er, en
6. em, en
7. er, en
8. em, en

11.
1. jenem internationalen
2. jeder interessanten
3. dieser netten
4. dem schmutzigen
5. jenem kurzen
6. dem großen, amerikanischen
7. welchem fremden
8. der hübschen
9. jenem reichen
10. dem kleinen
11. jeder kranken
12. dem häßlichen

12.
1. Wir schlafen in dem modernen Schlafwagen.
2. Mit welcher neuen Schreibmaschine soll ich schreiben?
3. Er wohnt bei jener netten Dame.
4. Der Ball liegt unter dem blauen Sessel.
5. Trink nicht aus jenem roten Glas!
6. Wir gehen bei diesem kalten Wetter nicht aus.
7. Wer sitzt auf der alten, rostigen Bank?
8. Wir bekamen von manchem amerikanischen Studenten Post.

13.
1. es, en
2. er, en
3. es, en
4. es, en
5. er, en
6. es, en
7. es, en
8. er, en

14.
1. des blauen
2. jenes exotischen
3. des deutschen
4. dieses billigen
5. der kranken
6. dieses bequemen
7. jener bekannten
8. dieser kleinen
9. der dicken
10. des gesunden
11. jenes großen
12. jener interessanten

15.
1. Wo ist der Besitzer dieses schmutzigen Mantels?
2. Die Gedichte manches deutschen Dichters sind kompliziert.
3. Die Mutter jenes kranken Kindes ist hier.
4. Der Park ist jenseits des großen Monuments.
5. Trotz dieser starken Explosion gab es keine Verwundete.
6. Die Straßen jener alten Stadt sind eng.
7. Die Zimmer der neuen Wohnung sind modern.

16.
1. Welche deutschen Städte hat er besucht?
2. Ohne diese warmen Kleider fahre ich nicht.
3. Wir steigen auf jene bekannten Berge.
4. Es gehört jenen interessanten, jungen Frauen.
5. Er schenkt etwas in alle leeren Gläser.
6. Ich liege unter den schattigen Bäumen.
7. Er erzählt den kleinen Mädchen Geschichten.
8. Ich komme um der kranken Lehrer willen.
9. Alle gesunden Patienten dürfen nach Hause.
10. Sie hat die grünen Äpfel.

17.
1. dem dunklen
2. die bittere
3. jenen teuren (teueren)
4. dieses hohen
5. die saubere
6. die saure (sauere)
7. das saubere
8. dieses teure (teurer)
9. die sauren (saueren)
10. dieser hohe
11. Nürnberger
12. Frankfurter
13. Dortmunder
14. Berliner
15. Kölner

18.
1. ie, en, en, en
2. en, en, em, en
3. en, en, er, en
4. ie, e, em, en
5. es, en
6. ie, e, em, en, en
7. e, en, m, en
8. en, en, as, e
9. ie, e, es, e
10. er, e, es, e

19.
1. Dieses deutsche   jener netten
2. Alle eleganten   diese kurzen
3. Jener blonde   dieses teure (teuere)
4. Die hübsche   dem dicken
5. Der neue   des teuren (teueren)
6. die schmutzigen   des kleinen
7. Jener amerikanische   diese billige
8. Der schwarze   dem runden
9. Die jungen   der dunklen
10. Die hungrige   den großen

20.
1. _____, er
2. e, e, e
3. e, e
4. _____, er
5. e, e
6. _____, es
7. _____, er
8. e, e
9. e, e, e
10. _____, es
11. _____, er
12. _____, es
13. _____, er
14. _____, es
15. e, e
16. _____, er

21.
1. Wo ist ein weiches Kissen?
2. Ein alter Freund ist hier.
3. Wann schläft ein wildes Tier?
4. Eine neue Maschine steht dort.
5. Hier ist ein schmutziger Teller.
6. Wo ist ein kleines Buch?
7. Hier liegt eine deutsche Zeitung.
8. Wieviel kostet ein schnelles Auto?

22.
1. Mein altes Radio ist kaputt.
2. Wo wohnt deine nette Freundin?
3. Wieviel kostet Ihr neuer Wagen?
4. Wann kommt sein reicher Onkel?
5. Das ist keine enge Straße.
6. Ist unser deutsches Foto interessant?
7. Wo ist eure schmutzige Wäsche?
8. Hier ist ihr alter Wein.

23.
1. en, en
2. _____, es
3. e, e, e, e
4. e, e
5. en, en, en
6. e, e
7. en, en, en
8. _____, es
9. e, e
10. e, e
11. _____, es
12. _____, es

24.
1. Er kauft einen häßlichen Teppich.
2. Wann bekommst du einen neuen Mantel?
3. Wir besuchen eine historische Stadt.
4. Siehst du ein rotes Auto?
5. Ich kaufe es für ein krankes Kind.
6. Er geht durch einen langen Tunnel.
7. Der Bus fuhr gegen eine alte Mauer.
8. Ich möchte ein weißes Bonbon.

25.
1. Sie geht in ihre dunkle Wohnung.
2. Wir verkaufen unser blaues Sofa.
3. Haben Sie ein billiges Zimmer?
4. Ich habe einen bequemen Stuhl.
5. Braucht er seine neue Kamera?
6. Wir gehen durch einen langen Tunnel.
7. Ich schreibe einen kurzen Brief.
8. Kennst du keine hübsche Studentin?

26.
1. em, en
2. em, en, en
3. er, en
4. em, en
5. er, en, en
6. er, en
7. em, en
8. er, en
9. er, en
10. em, en
11. er, en
12. em, en

27.
1. Er sitzt auf einem harten Stuhl.
2. Sie wohnt in einem modernen Haus.
3. Ich bin bei einer netten Frau.
4. Sie spielt mit einem süßen Baby.
5. Wir stehen neben einem großen Mann.
6. Ich liege auf einem weichen Bett.
7. Hilfst du einem fremden Mann?
8. Sie kommt von einer langen Reise zurück.

28.
1. Er kam mit einem interessanten Freund.
2. Wir kennen uns seit unserer glücklichen Kindheit.
3. Er schnitt das Brot mit seinem scharfen Messer.
4. Warum sitzt du auf einem unbequemen Stuhl?
5. Die Katze liegt auf meinem schwarzen Mantel.
6. Sie kommt aus ihrem dunklen Zimmer.
7. Was steht in seinem langen Brief?
8. Sie sitzt in meinem neuen Auto.

29.
1. einer dunklen
2. meines alten
3. seiner schlimmen
4. eines amerikanischen
5. ihrer wichtigen
6. eures kranken
7. deiner neuen
8. eines teuren (teueren)

30.
1. Das ist die Frau eines bekannten Dichters.
2. Es ist die Geschichte eines fremden Volkes.
3. Der Preis eines antiken Perserteppichs ist hoch.
4. Ich singe die Melodie eines deutschen Liedes.
5. Der Direktor einer großen Fabrik kommt.

31.
1. Trotz meiner langen Reise war ich nicht müde.
2. Die Farbe deines neuen Pullovers ist hübsch.
3. Sie ist die Frau eines amerikanischen Präsidenten.
4. Hier ist das Foto seines bekannten Bruders.
5. Wo ist das Haus Ihres reichen Onkels?
6. Wir konnten wegen seiner langen Verspätung nicht essen.
7. Der Bus ist jenseits eines hohen Turm(e)s.

32.
1. Er hat keine teuren Ringe gekauft.
2. Er glaubt seinen kleinen Söhnen.
3. Ich telefonierte mit meinen deutschen Freundinnen.
4. Unsere neuen Nähmaschinen waren teuer.
5. Wer hat meine roten Bleistifte?
6. Wegen seiner faulen Brüder darf er nicht kommen.
7. Wir trinken keine kalten Getränke.
8. Wo sind ihre warmen Jacken?
9. Willst du deine alten Lehrer busuchen?
10. Wo sind eure progressiven Gymnasien?

33.
1. _____, er, e, e
2. er, en, _____, er
3. ie, e, em, en
4. er, en, es, en
5. en, en, er, en, e, en
6. e, e, em, en
7. e, e, er, en
8. as, e, e, e
9. _____, es, en, en
10. en, en, ie, e
11. e, en, e, e
12. em, en, ie, en

34.
1. der jungen   einen interessanten
2. mein kranker   unserem guten
3. ihrem kleinen   die leere
4. deine reiche   dieses teure (teuere)
5. jener langen   ihre neuen
6. das neue   des bekannten
7. meine amerikani-   keinen bitteren
   schen
8. sein kaputtes   die dunkle
9. ihren netten   eine kurze
10. Die armen   ihrer kalten

35.
1. Welch   5. Solch
2. viel   6. viel
3. wenig   7. solch
4. viel   8. Wenig

36.
1. armes   3. Leibe
2. bittere   4. viel schmutzige

5. Lieber   10. kaltes
6. wenig deutsches 11. Lieber
7. Guter alter   12. armer
8. gutes   13. teures (teueres)
9. neues   14. typische

37.
1. Welch interessantes Gedicht!
2. Das ist teures Leder.
3. Frische Butter schmeckt gut.
4. Moderne Musik ist schnell.
5. Ist das billiger Schmuck?
6. Kalte Limonade ist erfrischend.
7. Du süßes Baby!

38.
1. viel saure (sauere)
2. wenig schwarzes
3. Guten Gute Guten
4. große
5. weißen
6. wenig süßen
7. schönes
8. schwarzen
9. dünnes
10. Frische holländische
11. pikanten französichen
12. große
13. viel amerikanisches
14. viel heißes

39.
1. Was hast du gegen klassiche Musik?
2. Leg es in kaltes Wasser!
3. Ich esse frisches Brot.
4. Wir brauchen deutsches Geld.
5. Er hat großen Hunger.
6. Warum trinkst du kalten Kaffee?
7. Sie nimmt braunen Zucker.
8. Sie hat viel teuren Schmuck.

40.
1. großer
2. langer
3. guter
4. viel warmer
5. großem
6. schönem sonnigem
7. rostfreiem
8. großer
9. wenig weißem
10. viel heißem
11. bitterem kaltem
12. hartem

41.
1. Bei schlechtem Wetter fliege ich nicht.
2. Wer schreibt mit grüner Kreide?
3. Nach kurzer Zeit wurde es still.
4. Das Messer ist aus rostfreiem Stahl.
5. Warum schwimmst du in eiskaltem Wasser?
6. Der Dieb kam bei hellichtem Tag.

7. Ich kenne ihn seit langer Zeit.
8. Er trank nichts außer viel starkem Kaffee.

42.
1.	klassischer	6.	wahrer
2.	dichten	7.	langer
3.	freundlicher	8.	neuen
4.	Traurigen	9.	großer
5.	alten	10.	kurzer

43.
1. Trotz bitterer Kälte spielten die Kinder im Schnee.
2. Er ist Liebhaber moderner Musik.
3. Der Preis guten alten Weins ist hoch.
4. Wegen schlechten Wetters hat er Verspätung.
5. Trotz guter Ausbildung fand er keine Stelle.
6. Trotz netter Hilfe kam sie nicht vorwärts.

44.
1.	es, es	9.	es
2.	em	10.	er
3.	er	11.	e
4.	er	12.	en
5.	e	13.	e, en, en
6.	e, er	14.	em
7.	em	15.	es
8.	es		

45.
1.	einige	4.	viele
2.	Andere	5.	Wenige
3.	Mehrere	6.	Viele

46.
1. gelbe
2. viele gute
3. einige bekannte
4. braune
5. einige graue
6. Mehrere große frische
7. andere neue
8. Alte
9. wenige teure (teuere)
10. Manche kleine bunte

47.
1. alten
2. einigen deutschen
3. netten
4. einigen amerikanischen
5. mehreren kleinen
6. schmutzigen
7. dicken
8. vielen intelligenten
9. anderen alten
10. wenigen fremden

48.
1. einiger hoher
2. mehrerer wilder
3. alter
4. vieler alter
5. einiger reicher
6. mancher primitiver
7. hoher
8. armer
9. herbstlicher
10. einiger moderner

49.
1.	er	11.	en
2.	e, e	12.	en, en
3.	em	13.	em
4.	er, e, e	14.	en
5.	e, e	15.	e, e
6.	en, en, e	16.	e, e
7.	er	17.	em
8.	e	18.	er, er
9.	er, e	19.	en
10.	es	20.	e

50.
1.	kochende	6.	fließendem
2.	bellenden	7.	sterbenden
3.	kommenden	8.	brennenden
4.	weinende	9.	leidende
5.	Fliegende	10.	schreiende

51.
1.	gekochte	6.	geschnittenen
2.	geöffneten	7.	Vereinigten
3.	geschriebene	8.	angebrannte
4.	gefrorenen	9.	bezahlte
5.	reparierte	10.	zebrochene

52.
1.	Kleinen	6.	Reichen
2.	Blonde	7.	Arme (Armen)
3.	Schnelle	8.	Kranken
4.	Alten	9.	Hübsche
5.	Fremden	10.	Glücklichen

53.
1.	e	9.	e
2.	en	10.	en
3.	e	11.	en
4.	e	12.	e
5.	er	13.	e
6.	e	14.	e
7.	en	15.	en
8.	e	16.	en

54.
1.	Billiges	6.	Persönliches
2.	Neues	7.	Altes
3.	Süßes	8.	Modernes
4.	Interessantes	9.	Kaltes
5.	Gutes	10.	Wichtiges

55.
1.	Seine	6.	Ihr
2.	Unsere	7.	Ihre
3.	Ihr	8.	eure
4.	mein	9.	Unser
5.	dein	10.	Ihre

56.
1.	unseren	4.	eure
2.	meine	5.	Ihre
3.	dein	6.	ihren

7. sein
8. meine

9. unser
10. eure

57.
1. er
2. er
3. em
4. en
5. em

6. em
7. er
8. en
9. em
10. em

58.
1. seines
2. ihrer
3. unseres
4. meiner
5. ihres

6. deines
7. eures
8. Ihrer
9. unseres
10. ihrer

59.
1. seine
2. mein
3. deine
4. Ihre
5. unsere
16. ihrer

7. seinem
8. eure
9. Ihrem
10. eure
11. Meine
12. seiner

60.
1. länger — am längsten
2. teurer — am teuersten
3. größer — am größten
4. schneller — am schnellsten
5. mehr — am meisten
6. härter — am härtesten
7. öfter — am öftesten
8. schärfer — am schärfsten
9. lieber — am liebsten
10. höher — am höchsten

61.
1. mehr als
2. dicker als
3. größer als
4. teuer als
5. lieber als

6. höher als
7. netter als
8. jünger als
9. dunkler als
10. härter als

62.
1. Der Februar ist kürzer als der Januar.
2. Das Kleid ist teurer als die Bluse.
3. Der Vater ißt mehr als das Baby.
4. Ute kann besser Spanisch als Marianne.
5. Im Haus ist es wärmer als im Garten.
6. Das Auto fährt schneller als das Motorrad.
7. Robert ist ärmer als Manfred.
8. Mein Vater ist stärker als mein Bruder.
9. Die Lilie ist schöner als die Geranie.
10. Die Limonade ist kälter als das Wasser.
11. Der Kaffee ist heißer als der Tee.
12. Die Schule ist näher als die Kirche.

63.
1. Es wird immer dunkler.
2. Sie wird immer älter.
3. Er fährt immer schneller.
4. Die Tage werden immer länger.
5. Es kommt immer näher.

64.
1. Ich springe am höchsten.
2. Karl ist am größten.
3. Wir singen am besten.
4. Meine Mutter spricht am schnellsten.
5. Sabine ist am kränksten.
6. Mein Bruder spart am meisten.
7. Die Kirche ist am nächsten.
8. Klaus und ich gehen am langsamsten.
9. Unsere Nachbarn sind am reichsten.
10. Der Rock ist am kürzesten.

65.
1. Der Brocken ist hoch. Das Matterhorn ist höher. Die Zugspitze ist am höchsten.
2. Ich trinke Wasser gern. Ich trinke lieber Limonade. Ich trinke Bier am liebsten.
3. Das Gedicht ist lang. Die Geschichte ist länger. Der Roman ist am längsten.
4. Der Vogel fliegt schnell. Der Hubschrauber fliegt schneller. Das Düsenflugzeug fliegt am schnellsten.
5. Der Apfel ist sauer. Die Orange ist saurer. Die Zitrone ist am sauersten.
6. Das Brot schmeckt gut. Der Kuchen schmeckt besser. Dir Torte schmecket am besten.
7. Hans arbeitet viel. Josef arbeitet mehr. Franz arbeitet am meisten.
8. Das Wollkleid ist warm. Die Jacke ist wärmer. Der Wintermantel ist am wärmsten.

66.
1. Deine Nägel sind so lang wie Katzenkrallen.
2. Pia ist so groß wie Inge.
3. Die Jacke ist nicht so warm wie der Mantel.
4. Deine Augen sind so blau wie der Himmel.
5. Heute ist es so kalt wie im Winter.
6. Peter ist so stark wie Max.
7. Die Hose ist so teuer wie der Pullover.
8. Großmutter is so alt wie Großvater.
9. Renate schreit so laut wie ich.
10. Mein Bruder schreibt so viel wie sein Freund.

67.
1. schönere
2. teurere
3. schärfere
4. ärmere

5. jüngerer
6. kleineres
7. besserer
8. kälteres

68.
1. wärmeren
2. stärkeren
3. schärferes
4. größere

5. bessere
6. mehr
7. kleinere
8. ältere

69.
1. Wir sind in einer kleineren Wohnung.
2. Er kommt aus einem bekannteren Museum.

3. Er fährt mit einem schnelleren Wagen.
4. Wir helfen einem kränkeren Patienten.
5. Sie erzählt von einer besseren Zeit.
6. Er spricht mit einer kleineren Frau.

70.
1. höheren
2. jüngeren
3. älteren
4. stärkeren
5. kleineren
6. kälteren

71.
1. nächste
2. höchste
3. wärmste
4. teuerstes
5. dünnste
6. härteste
7. bester
8. älteste

72.
1. jüngsten
2. modernste
3. stärksten
4. teuerste
5. beste
6. meisten
7. intelligentesten
8. kleinste

73.
1. teuersten
2. kürzesten
3. ärmsten
4. wärmsten
5. jüngsten
6. neuesten
7. teuersten
8. stärkstem

74.
1. besten
2. teuersten
3. ältesten
4. jüngsten
5. längsten
6. hübschesten

75.
1. e
2. e
3. en
4. _____
5. en
6. e
7. _____
8. e
9. en
10. en
11. e
12. en
13. en
14. en
15. e
16. en
17. en
18. e
19. en
20. e

76.
1. Er ist sehr alt.
2. Sie haben sehr gute Lehrer.
3. Er ist ein sehr intelligenter Mann.
4. Es ist sehr kalt.
5. Sie singt sehr schön.

77.
1. nun, jetzt
2. heute
3. selten
4. gestern
5. nie
6. abends
7. damals
8. täglich
9. bald
10. immer
11. manchmal
12. morgens

78.
1. natürlich
2. gern
3. leider
4. nicht
5. so
6. wirklich
7. zu
8. ziemlich
9. schon
10. Vielleicht

79.
1. da, dort
2. oben
3. drinnen
4. draußen
5. hier
6. weg
7. links
8. hinten
9. rechts
10. überall

80.
1. Er bleibt natürlich hier.
2. Maria wohnt nicht unten.
3. Karl sieht uns täglich.
4. Wir waren gestern wirklich drinnen.
5. Ich arbeite abends nicht draußen.
6. Vater suchte dich damals überall.
7. Wir sitzen manchmal gern dort.
8. Ich habe morgens wirklich großen Hunger.
9. Sie ist jetzt ziemlich dick.
10. Sie sind heute leider weg.

81.
1. Wir trinken nie Wein.
2. Sie war heute schon hier.
3. Ich bin abends nicht dort (da).
4. Sie sind jetzt leider oben.
5. Sie ist morgens immer drinnen.
6. Er war damals hier.
7. Ich sitze immer draußen.
8. Er ist vielleicht hinten.
9. Ich bin selten weg.
10. Sie ist sicherlich überall.

82.
1. noch
2. denn
3. doch
4. doch
5. Doch
6. noch einen
7. ja
8. doch

Chapter 6

1.
1. acht
2. sechzehn
3. einundzwanzig
4. vierunddreißig
5. einundfünfzig
6. sechsundfünfzig
7. siebzig
8. neunundachtzig
9. einundneunzig
10. hundert
11. hunderteins
12. neunhundertsechsunddreißig
13. tausendzweihundertvierundsiebzig
14. neunzehnhundertachtzig
15. zweitausendeinunddreißig
16. zehn Millionen
17. acht komma neun
18. siebzehn komma einundsechzig
19. zwanzig Mark dreißig
20. hunderteinundneunzig Mark siebenundsechzig

2. 1. achten   6. der Achte
     2. zweites   7. fünfte
     3. vierte   8. der Erste
     4. erste   9. des Fünfzehnten
     5. dritten   10. dem Zweiten

3. 1. Wer hat meine Hälfte?
     2. dreiviertel Pfund
     3. ein halbes Glas
     4. ein Drittel der Arbeit
     5. zwei einviertel Stunden
     6. fünf Achtel der Bevölkerung
     7. eineinhalb Pfund (anderthalb) (ein und ein halbes)
     8. ein Zwanzigstel
     9. ein Viertel des Brotes
    10. ein halbes Pfund

4. 1. am Mittwoch
     2. im Herbst
     3. im August
     4. am Dienstag
     5. im Winter
     6. im Mai
     7. an dem Donnerstag
     8. am Freitag
     9. im Frühling
    10. am Montag
    11. am Samstag
    12. im Sommer
    13. im Juli
    14. in dem September
    15. an dem Montag
    16. am Sonntag

5. 1. Er hat am 20. (zwanzigsten) Januar Geburtstag.
     2. Heute ist der 13. (dreizehnte) Oktober 1996.
     3. Ich komme am Freitag, den 9. (neunten) März an.
     4. Er ist 1970 gestorben.
     5. Ich habe am 10. (zehnten) Dezember Geburtstag.
     6. Im Jahre 1980.
     7. 30. 5. 1998.
     8. Sie hat am 10. (zehnten) August Geburtstag.
     9. Ich komme am 2. (zweiten) Februar an.
    10. Heute ist der 3. (dritte) März 1996.
    11. Er ist 1975 gestorben.

6. 1. Es ist acht Uhr abends.
     2. Es ist halb elf Uhr vormittags.
     3. Es ist (ein) Viertel nach fünf.
     4. Es ist fünf nach halb acht.
     5. Es ist fünfundzwanzig nach sechs. (Es ist fünf vor halb sieben.)
     6. Es ist (ein) Viertel vor fünf. (Es ist drei Viertel fünf.)
     7. Es ist zwanzig nach elf. (Es ist zehn vor halb zwölf.)
     8. Es ist zehn nach drei.
     9. Es ist ein Uhr nachmittags.
    10. Es ist zwölf Uhr mittags.

7. 1. Es ist zwanzig Uhr dreißig.
     2. Es ist dreizehn Uhr.
     3. Es ist ein Uhr.
     4. Es ist vierundzwanzig Uhr.
     5. Es ist null Uhr fünfunddreißig.
     6. Es ist einundzwanzig Uhr fünfundzwanzig.
     7. Es ist zwölf Uhr vierzig.
     8. Es ist zehn Uhr fünfundvierzig.
     9. Es ist vierzehn Uhr.
    10. Es ist dreiundzwanzig Uhr.

8. 1. Um fünf Uhr.
     2. Um zwei Uhr.
     3. Um halb vier Uhr.
     4. Um sieben Uhr.
     5. Um elf Uhr

9. 1. am morgen   4. am Mittag
     2. Am Nachmittag   5. am Abend
     3. In der Nacht

10. 1. Ja, ich bin immer abends hier.
     2. Ja, ich habe immer sonntags Zeit.
     3. Ja, ich gehe immer mittwochs mit.
     4. Ja, ich schreibe immer nachmittags.
     5. Ja, ich fahre immer morgens zur Schule.

11. 1. Er kommt morgen abend.
     2. Er war gestern nachmittag zu Hause.
     3. Otto, hast du gestern abend geschlafen?
     4. Sie kommen übermorgen.
     5. Sie ist heute morgen abgefahren.
     6. Er kommt morgen nachmittag.

12. 1. en   4. en, en
     2. en   5. e
     3. e   6. e, e

13. 1. er   6. er
     2. em   7. en
     3. em   8. em
     4. en   9. em
     5. em   10. em

14. 1. eines Tages
     2. eines Nachts
     3. eines Abends
     4. eines Nachmittags
     5. eines Morgens

15.
1. en
2. es, s
3. um
4. heute abend
5. im
6. ie, e
7. am
8. es
9. In der Nacht
10. Morgen nachmittag
11. in einem Monat
12. Um
13. Am Morgen
14. vor einer Woche (vor acht Tagen)
15. sonntags
16. am Mittag
17. In vierzehn Tagen (In zwei Wochen)
18. eines Tages
19. e, e
20. heute morgen

5. Wohin reist du?
6. Was haßt du?
7. Wo sitzt du?
8. Beißt du in den Apfel?

4.
1. klettert
2. wandern
3. bewundere
4. behandelt
5. fütterst
6. ändern
7. lächle
8. behandeln
9. klingelt
10. sammeln
11. behandle
12. füttern
13. sammle
14. klettern

5.
1. Schläfst du die ganze Nacht?
2. Er wächst schnell.
3. Wäschst du die Wäsche?
4. Ich halte die Ballons.
5. Was trägt er zum Ball?
6. Laßt du mich gehen?
7. Ich backe Brot.
8. Warum gräbt er ein Loch?
9. Er schlägt das Kind.
10. Das Tier säuft Wasser.
11. Er bläst ins Feuer.
12. Wohin läufst du?
13. Er fällt.
14. Fängst du den Ball?
15. Ich schlafe schön.
16. Was trägst du?

Chapter 7

1.
1. Hörst
2. trinken
3. kommt
4. schicke
5. singt
6. brennt
7. fliege
8. bellt
9. bleibt
10. Denkst
11. weint
12. stehen
13. beginnt
14. bringt
15. renne
16. parkt
17. schreit
18. Rauchen
19. Kennt
20. Liebst
21. studiert
22. besuchen
23. holt
24. springt
25. ruft
26. riecht
27. schreiben
28. Steigt
29. glaubt
30. probiere
31. telefoniert
32. höre
33. brauchen
34. wohnt
35. holen
36. gehen

2.
1. wartet
2. Schneidest
3. arbeitet
4. bittest
5. Begegnest
6. reitet
7. Findet
8. Rechnet
9. redest
10. rettet
11. öffnet
12. Beobachtet
13. atmest
14. ordnet
15. blutet
16. Sendest
17. antwortest
18. wendet
19. Arbeitest
20. Badest

3.
1. Wie heißt du?
2. Was mixt du?
3. Du tanzt gut.
4. Warum grüßt du mich nicht?

6.
1. Hilfst du mir?
2. Er stirbt bald.
3. Siehst du uns?
4. Ich esse Suppe.
5. Der Hund frißt.
6. Was gibst du ihm?
7. Ich spreche gern.
8. Er sieht uns.
9. Er steht beim Haus.
10. Gehst du auch?
11. Was nimmst du?
12. Wann triffst du uns?
13. Was liest er?
14. Warum erschrickst du?
15. Was bricht er?
16. Was stiehlst du?
17. Was wirft er?
18. Warum hilft er nicht?
19. Was vergißt er?
20. Empfiehlst du dieses Hotel?

7.
1. bin
2. ist
3. sind
4. sind
5. seid
6. Sind
7. ist
8. Bist

8.
1. haben
2. habe
3. Hast
4. haben

5. Habt   7. haben
6. hat   8. hast

9. 1. werde schon wieder gesund.
2. werdet schon wieder gesund.
3. wirst schon wieder gesund.
4. wird schon wieder gesund.
5. werden schon wieder gesund.
6. werden schon wieder gesund.
7. wird schon wieder gesund.
8. werden schon wieder gesund.

10. 1. wissen   5. weiß
2. wissen   6. Weißt
3. wißt   7. weiß
4. weiß   8. wissen

11. 1. tust   5. Tut
2. tue   6. Tun
3. tun   7. tun
4. tut   8. tut

12. 1. Ja, ich komme morgen.
2. Ja, er hat übermorgen Geburtstag.
3. Ja, wir gehen morgen abend ins Theater.
4. Ja, ich fliege im Juli nach Frankfurt.
5. Ja, ich fahre nächstes Jahr nach Regensburg.
6. Ja, ich besuche dich heute in acht Tagen.
7. Ja, ich bin nächsten Monat in Deutschland.
8. Ja, ich bin morgen abend zu Hause.
9. Ja, wir haben nächste Woche Zeit.
10. Ja, sie spielt nächsten Samstag Golf.

13. 1. warte   6. kenne
2. wohnt   7. sind
3. ist   9. fliegt
4. arbeiten   9. regnet
5. Singst   10. Schreibt

14. 1. Ich lese schon seit einer Stunde.
2. Er studiert schon zehn Tage.
3. Ich bin seit fünf Minuten hier.
4. Ich kenne ihn schon sechs Jahre.
5. Ich telefoniere schon zwanzig Minuten.

15. 1. gräbst   12. frißt
2. komme   13. fahrt
3. läuft   14. fängt
4. änderst   15. wasche
5. füttern   16. grüßen
6. Seid   17. Sind
7. wird   18. wissen
8. reist   19. schläfst
9. arbeitet   20. wird
10. Liest   21. steht
11. atmen   22. studieren

23. blutest   27. gibst
24. klingle   28. sieht
25. heißt   29. behandeln
26. ißt   30. sitzt

16. 1. Sie spielten.
2. Er wohnte in Köln.
3. Wir glaubten daran.
4. Ich studierte gern.
5. Der Hund bellte.
6. Ich bezahlte die Rechnung.
7. Man gratulierte ihm.
8. Wir brauchten Milch.
9. Meine Eltern bauten es.
10. Das Telefon klingelte.

17. 1. maltest   6. reparierte
2. besichtigten   7. zeigten
3. fragten   8. besuchtet
4. schenkte   9. kauften
5. lernten   10. störte

18. 1. Ich atmete ganz regelmäßig.
2. Man tötete ihn.
3. Wir retteten den Verunglückten.
4. Du öffnetest die Tür.
5. Sie begegneten ihren Eltern.
6. Paul beobachtete den Vogel.
7. Ich arbeitete gern.
8. Er ordnete die Bücher.
9. Sie antwortete nicht.
10. Sie bluteten stark.

19. 1. Er wußte das nicht.
2. Ich sandte ihm einen Brief.
3. Es brannte dort.
4. Wir brachten Geschenke.
5. Sie dachten daran.
6. Die Kinder rannten.
7. Man nannte es.
8. Ich kannte ihn auch.
9. Sie wußten die Antwort.
10. Du kanntest uns.

20. 1. Sie litt.
2. Er schlief schon.
3. Sie schrieben Briefe.
4. Wir ritten gerne.
5. Ich schrie laut.
6. Das Buch fiel auf den Boden.
7. Der Zug hielt dort.
8. Ludwig blieb dort.
9. Sie schwiegen immer.
10. Wir litten sehr.
11. Er schrieb die Aufgabe.
12. Sie schwieg nicht.
13. Ihr schnittet ins Papier.
14. Die Sonne schien.

15. Man lieh dem Kind das Buch.
16. Der Hund biß das Mädchen.

21.
1. Ich ließ Gudrun gehen.
2. Das Pferd lief am schnellsten.
3. Hubert ritt den ganzen Tag.
4. Wir liehen Gisela das Buch.
5. Der Rattenfänger fing Ratten.
6. Ich schnitt ins Fleisch.
7. Meine Eltern schrieben den Brief.
8. Wir schrien nicht.

22.
1. flog
2. verlor
3. roch
4. schlossen
5. schoß
6. frorst
7. wog
8. zogen
9. floß
10. floht
11. soffen
12. flog
13. hob
14. bogen

23.
1. aßen
2. gewann
3. sprang
4. sahen
5. kam
6. las
7. nahm
8. sprangen
9. tat
10. sank
11. band
12. starb
13. gaben
14. saßen
15. sah
16. begann
17. schwammen
18. stank
19. traft
20. bat
21. warf
22. sprachst
23. sahen
24. stahl
25. traf
26. halfen
27. standen
28. vergaß
29. maß
30. traten

24.
1. Der Hund fraß das Futter.
2. Die Bücher lagen auf dem Tisch.
3. Wir sprangen aus dem Fenster.
4. Ich saß auf einem Stuhl.
5. Die Sängerin sang die Arie.
6. Die Kinder tranken keinen Wein.
7. Er fand die Diamantbrosche.
8. Wir kamen um acht Uhr.
9. Ich sah Monika im Kino.
10. Er tat alles.

25.
1. Die Lehrerinnen fuhren in die Stadt.
2. Ich schlug ihn nicht.
3. Die Arbeiterin grub ein Loch.
4. Wir trugen Lederhosen.
5. Dad Baby wuchs schnell.
6. Tante Ida wusch die Bettwäsche.
7. Er trug etwas.
8. Ich fuhr mit dem Zug.

26.
1. war
2. warst
3. war
4. Warst

5. waren
6. Wart
7. waren
8. waren
9. Wart
10. war

27.
1. Hattest
2. hatten
3. hatten
4. hatte
5. Hattest
6. Hattet
7. Hattest
8. hatte
9. Hattet
10. Hatten

28.
1. wurden
2. wurden
3. wurde
4. wurde
5. wurde
6. wurde
7. wurdest
8. Wurdet
9. Wurde
10. wurdet

29. Peter besuchte mich gestern. Wir tranken Limonade. Er aß auch ein Stück Schokoladenkuchen. Wir fuhren ins Zentrum. Wir trafen dort seine Freunde und (wir) gingen ins Kino. Der Film war prima. Er gefiel mir sehr. Wir kamen um acht Uhr nach Hause. Wir spielten eine Stunde CDs und sprachen über Musik. Meine Mutter machte noch Wurstbrote. Peter ging danach nach Hause.

30.
1. schlief, las
2. lächelte, sang
3. aßen, tanzten
4. schrieb, klingelte
5. kaufte, traf
6. gingen, wurde
7. lachte, erzählte
8. waren, kamst
9. half, arbeitete
10. schwammen, schnitt

31.
1. Wir fuhren gewöhnlich in die Schweiz.
2. Ich war immer krank.
3. Die Damen tranken gewöhnlich Tee.
4. Die Schauspielerin wurde immer nervös.
5. Wir gingen sonntags gewöhnlich zur Kirche.
6. Er arbeitete immer.
7. Karin trank gewöhnlich Limonade.
8. Wir gaben den Kindern immer Geld.
9. Ich half Renate immer.
10. Wir spielten gewöhnlich moderne Musik.

32.
1. wurdest
2. litt
3. arbeitete
4. öffnete
5. reparierte
6. besichtigten
7. Wart
8. sah
9. schlief, kam
10. Hattest
11. waren
12. nahm
13. trank, war
14. zeigten
15. klingelte
16. lief

17. wusch   19. waren
18. vergaß   20. las, studierte

6. Wir haben das Paket gesandt.
7. Habt ihr den höchsten Berg genannt?
8. Ich habe das Blatt gewandt.

33.
1. haben . . . gefragt
2. haben . . . gewohnt
3. haben . . . geglaubt
4. Hast . . . gekauft
5. hat . . . geliebt
6. haben . . . gehört
7. habe . . . gesucht
8. haben . . . geraucht
9. habt . . . geparkt
10. hast . . . geweint
11. Hast . . . gelegt
12. hat . . . geschenkt
13. habe . . . gekämmt
14. habt . . . gelernt
15. haben . . . gesagt

34.
1. habt . . . bezahlt
2. Hast . . . verkauft
3. haben . . . repariert
4. hat . . . erzählt
5. habe . . . studiert
6. haben . . . probiert
7. hat . . . zerstört
8. Hat . . . gehört
9. Hast . . . telefoniert
10. haben . . . bestellt
11. hat . . . besucht
12. hat . . . entdeckt
13. hat . . . erklärt
14. hast . . . zerstört
15. hat . . . entschuldigt

35.
1. Wir haben viel studiert.
2. Hast du Geld gebraucht?
3. Warum hat der Hund gebellt?
4. Er hat viel gearbeitet.
5. Man hat das Haus zerstört.
6. Haben Sie den Jungen gesucht?
7. Habt ihr oft geträumt?
8. Sie hat sehr laut geatmet.
9. Ich habe stark geblutet.
10. Die Kinder haben gerne gebadet.
11. Wo habt ihr gewohnt?
12. Ich habe Papier geholt.
13. Wir haben die Bücher auf den Tisch gelegt.
14. Sie hat oft telefoniert.
15. Die Katze hat dem Mädchen gehört.
16. Wer hat dafür bezahlt?

36.
1. Er hat meine Schwester gekannt.
2. Die Kinder haben die Antwort gewußt.
3. Ich habe Blumen gebracht.
4. Hast du daran gedacht?
5. Die Häuser haben gebrannt.

37.
1. sind . . . gerannt
2. seid . . . gereist
3. bin . . . geklettert
4. Ist . . . gereist
5. Seid . . . gewandert
6. bin . . . gerannt
7. sind . . . begegnet
8. ist . . . gereist
9. Bist . . . geklettert
10. bin . . . begegnet

38.
1. Hast . . . gelesen
2. hat . . . geschlagen
3. habe . . . gegeben
4. habt . . . gesehen
5. haben . . . gebacken
6. habe . . . gemessen
7. hat . . . gefressen
8. haben . . . gegraben
9. hat . . . getragen
10. habe . . . gewaschen
11. Habt . . . gefangen
12. hat . . . gegessen
13. Hast . . . gelassen
14. habt . . . geschlafen

39.
1. Mein Bruder ist schnell gefahren.
2. Bist du ins Haus getreten?
3. Wir sind schon wieder gewachsen.
4. Seid ihr nach Bremen gefahren?
5. Die Kinder sind immer gewachsen.
6. Ich bin gestern gefahren.
7. Seid ihr ins Haus gelaufen?
8. Wann bist du gekommen?
9. Die Leute sind schnell gelaufen.
10. Ich bin ins Wasser gefallen.

40.
1. Bist du oft geritten?
2. Wir haben laut geschrien.
3. Warum habt ihr nicht geschrieben?
4. Die Sonne hat geschienen.
5. Warum hat er gebissen?
6. Seid ihr lange geblieben?
7. Die Kranken haben gelitten.
8. Warum habt ihr geschwiegen?
9. Bist du auf die Leiter gestiegen?
10. Ich habe dir Geld geliehen.
11. Er hat dem Kind die Haare geschnitten.
12. Habt ihr nicht gelitten?
13. Ich habe nicht geschrien.
14. Hast du den Brief geschrieben?

41.
1. Hast . . . verloren
2. hat . . . gerochen

3. Seid . . . geflogen
4. hat . . . gewogen
5. hast . . . geschossen
6. hat . . . gezogen
7. ist . . . geflohen
8. ist . . . geflossen
9. hast . . . geschlossen
10. haben . . . gefroren
11. hat . . . gebogen
12. hat . . . gelegen
13. hat . . . gesoffen
14. habe . . . verloren

42.
1. Die Sonne ist ins Meer gesunken.
2. Die Vorlesung hat begonnen.
3. Seid ihr von der Brücke gesprungen?
4. Ich habe das Lied gesungen.
5. Bist du über die Nordsee geschwommen?
6. Er hat den Preis gewonnen.
7. Das Gas hat gestunken.
8. Hast du den Hund an den Baum gebunden?
9. Die Männer sind über die Hürde gesprungen.
10. Habt ihr oft gesungen?
11. Ich habe Wasser getrunken.
12. Wir haben gestern begonnen.
13. Er hat auf dem Sofa gesessen.
14. Habt ihr die Frau gebeten?
15. Wer hat den Schmuck gefunden?
16. Er hat kaltes Bier getrunken.

43.
1. Habt ihr sie getroffen?
2. Sie haben den Ball geworfen.
3. Warum hast du es in Stücke gebrochen?
4. Ich habe ihr geholfen.
5. Das Kind hat nichts genommen.
6. Der Verletzte ist gestorben.
7. Warum hast du gestohlen?
8. Frau Knauer, Sie haben zu schnell gesprochen.
9. Wir haben dem Kranken geholfen.
10. Hast du viel gesprochen?
11. Bist du ins Kino gegangen?
12. Ich habe hier gestanden.
13. Wir haben die Suppe empfohlen.
14. Der Kran hat das Auto gehoben.
15. Was hast du getan?

44.
1. Hast du Hunger gehabt?
2. Ich bin krank gewesen.
3. Wir haben Hunger gehabt.
4. Sie sind immer dicker geworden.
5. Er ist wieder gesund geworden.
6. Wann sind Sie dort gewesen?
7. Ich habe Kopfweh gehabt.
8. Wir sind naß geworden.
9. Bist du auch müde gewesen?

10. Ich bin böse geworden.
11. Habt ihr Geld gehabt?
12. Ich habe Sorgen gehabt.
13. Sie ist unglücklich gewesen.
14. Die Pferde sind unruhig gewesen.
15. Bist du nervös geworden?
16. Seid ihr krank gewesen?

45.
1. Haben . . . besichtigt
2. hat . . . gegeben
3. hast . . . gewohnt
4. hat . . . gekauft
5. haben . . . gekannt
6. hast . . . gebacken
7. Habt . . . gesehen
8. haben . . . geschrien
9. hat . . . telefoniert
10. habe . . . gearbeitet
11. Habt . . . bestellt
12. bist . . . begegnet
13. hat . . . geschwiegen
14. haben . . . verloren
15. hat . . . gefressen
16. bist . . . gewachsen
17. Seid . . . gesprungen
18. habe . . . geträumt
19. hat . . . zerstört
20. Hast . . . studiert
21. bist . . . gekommen
22. habe . . . erzählt
23. Habt . . . gegessen
24. Haben . . . gewartet
25. haben . . . getrunken
26. haben . . . verkauft
27. Hast . . . geblutet
28. bin . . . gestiegen
29. hat . . . gesagt
30. hat . . . repariert
31. Hast . . . empfohlen
32. ist . . . gesunken
33. habt . . . getroffen
34. hast . . . geschlafen
35. haben . . . geschlossen

46.
1. Wir hatten getanzt.
2. Hattest du gesungen?
3. Sie waren gefahren.
4. Hattet ihr gefragt?
5. Man hatte es genommen.
6. Sie hatten viel getrunken.
7. Hattest du studiert?
8. Ich hatte es repariert.
9. Wann war er gekommen?
10. Er hatte mich besucht.
11. Hattest du den Wagen gewaschen?
12. Konrad war dort geblieben.
13. Ich hatte die Jacke getragen.
14. Sie war in Rom gewesen.

15. Hatte er dem Kranken geholfen?
16. Wir hatten gearbeitet.

47. 1. Wir waren arm, denn wir hatten alles
    verloren.
 2. Sie hatte Angst, denn sie war schon oft im
    Krankenhaus gewesen.
 3. Ich wußte alles, denn ich hatte viel
    studiert.
 4. Sie bestellten viel, denn sie hatten den
    ganzen Tag nichts gegessen.
 5. Laura war traurig, denn ihr Freund hatte
    sie nicht besucht.
 6. Sie waren schwach, denn sie waren krank
    gewesen.
 7. Ich war müde, denn ich hatte schlecht
    geschlafen.
 8. Wir hatten Durst, denn wir hatten nichts
    getrunken.
 9. Es roch nach Wein, denn er hatte die
    Flasche zerbrochen.
10. Ich hatte kein Geld, denn ich hatte viel
    gekauft.

48. 1. Werdet . . . bleiben
 2. Wirst . . . telefonieren
 3. werden . . . glauben
 4. werde . . . bezahlen
 5. wird . . . lesen
 6. werden . . . machen
 7. Werdet . . . helfen
 8. werden . . . schreiben
 9. werde . . . öffnen
10. Wirst . . . kaufen
11. werdet . . . bestellen
12. wird . . . kommen
13. werde . . . vergessen
14. werden . . . biegen
15. werden . . . schreien
16. wirst . . . frieren

49. 1. Wir werden das Auto bringen.
 2. Ich werde nach Berlin fahren.
 3. Wirst du kommen?
 4. Er wird das Gedicht schreiben.
 5. Werdet ihr euren Eltern das Haus zeigen?
 6. Sie werden arbeiten.
 7. Ich werde bei Inge essen.
 8. Wirst du es kaufen?

50. 1. Sie wird vielleicht krank sein.
 2. Wir werden wohl kommen.
 3. Sie werden vielleicht weinen.
 4. Kinder, ihr werdet wohl Hunger haben.
 5. Peter, du wirst es wohl wissen.
 6. Ich werde wohl gehen.
 7. Er wird wohl arbeiten.
 8. Sie werden vielleicht helfen.

51. 1. Ihr werdet wohl getanzt haben.
 2. Sie werden wohl gekommen sein.
 3. Maria wird wohl geschlafen haben.
 4. Wir werden es wohl nicht gesehen haben.
 5. Du wirst wohl nicht gefragt haben.
 6. Er wird wohl das Gedicht geschrieben
    haben.
 7. Sie wird sich wohl gefreut haben.
 8. Du wirst wohl lange gewartet haben.

52. 1. bekommt   7. Gefällt
 2. zerbreche   8. Besucht
 3. verkauft   9. erkläre
 4. verstehen   10. Erzählst
 5. empfange   11. empfehlen
 6. bestellt   12. vergißt

53. 1. Wir haben das Wort verstanden.
 2. Es hat mir nicht gefallen.
 3. Sie haben die Wahrheit gestanden.
 4. Warum ist es zerfallen?
 5. Ich habe das Examen bestanden.
 6. Wer hat dich besucht?
 7. Habt ihr das Haus verkauft?
 8. Er hat den Brief empfangen.
 9. Warum hast du alles erzählt?
10. Was hat er entdeckt?

54. 1. steigt . . . ein
 2. kommen . . . zusammen
 3. fahre . . . mit
 4. ziehst . . . an
 5. Legt . . . nieder
 6. lernen . . . kennen
 7. kommst . . . zurück
 8. gehe . . . hin
 9. steht . . . auf
10. fahren . . . spazieren

55. 1. Er aß alles auf.
 2. Ich schrieb das Lied ab.
 3. Wir lernten ihn kennen.
 4. Arnim sammelte für die Armen ein.
 5. Die Kinder machten alles nach.
 6. Wer machte das Fenster zu?
 7. Wie nähte er das Leder zusammen?
 8. Wann gingen die Studenten heim?

56. 1. Gisela, lauf nicht weg!
 2. Frau Bayer, machen Sie schnell zu!
 3. Konrad, fahr bitte mit!
 4. Ursula und Theo, tretet leise ein!
 5. Frau Breuer, stehen Sie langsam auf!
 6. Helga, komm doch her!
 7. Mutter, mach die Schachtel zu!
 8. Arno, schau es nicht an!

57. 1. Wir werden fortgehen.

2. Ich werde hinausgehen.
3. Er wird es zurückbringen.
4. Sie werden nichts wegnehmen.
5. Wirst du ausgehen?
6. Ich werde das Album anschauen.

58.
1. Sie haben auch mitgelacht.
2. Wir haben bei ihr nachgeschaut.
3. Ich habe ihn kennengelernt.
4. Der Zug ist bald angekommen.
5. Wir sind spazierengegangen.
6. Ich bin mit ihm heimgefahren.
7. Gudrun ist dann aufgestanden.
8. Sie haben bald nachgeschaut.

59.
1. war . . . eingestiegen
2. hatte . . . ausgemacht
3. hatten . . . abgeschrieben
4. hatten . . . niedergelegt
5. Wart . . . zusammengekommen
6. hatte . . . kennengelernt
7. waren . . . fortgeblieben
8. hatte . . . zugehört

60.
1. Ich weiß, daß er fortgegangen ist.
2. Ich weiß, daß sie herkommen wird.
3. Ich weiß, daß wir morgen abfliegen.
4. Ich weiß, daß ihr Peter kennengelernt habt.
5. Ich weiß, daß der Zug angekommen war.
6. Ich weiß, daß ich nachkomme.
7. Ich weiß, daß er ausging.
8. Ich weiß, daß wir heimkommen werden.
9. Ich weiß, daß du mitfährst.
10. Ich weiß, daß er nachgeschaut hatte.

61.
1. Ich zeige dem Kind das Buch.
2. Er schickt deiner Mutter eine Karte.
3. Wir glauben dem Mann.
4. Ich bringe der Studentin den Roman.
5. Dankst du deinem Lehrer?
6. Wir helfen unserer Großmutter.
7. Das Haus gehört meinen Eltern.
8. Antwortet ihr der Lehrerin?
9. Maria kauft ihrer Freundin eine Kette.
10. Der Wagen gehört meinem Bruder.
11. Wer holt dem Kranken eine Pille?
12. Die Blumen gefallen unserer Tante.
13. Warum gratulierst du deiner Schwester?
14. Er schenkt dem Baby eine Puppe.
15. Wir schicken dem Präsidenten einen Protest.
16. Die Kinder folgen dem Großvater.

62.
1. er		5. em
2. em		6. er
3. ie		7. er
4. em, e		8. em

9. er	14. er
10. em	15. en
11. er	16. er, e
12. en	17. em
13. er	18. er

63.
1. interessiere mich
2. unterhalten uns
3. regst dich . . . auf
4. setzt . . . euch
5. erkälte mich
6. stellst . . . dich vor
7. ziehen sich um
8. freut sich
9. legt sich
10. freuen uns
11. rasiert sich
12. amüsiere mich
13. bewegt sich
14. Freust . . . dich
15. Wascht . . . euch
16. entscheidet sich
17. verspäte mich
18. Erinnern . . . sich
19. zieht sich . . . an
20. Entschuldigst . . . dich

64.
1. Er hat sich vor Pferden gefürchtet.
2. Wir haben uns für die Sammlung interessiert.
3. Sie haben sich ganz nett benommen.
4. Habt ihr euch über das Geschenk gefreut?
5. Ich habe mich schon umgezogen.
6. Wir haben uns heute vorgestellt.
7. Hast du dich oft erkältet?
8. Sie hat sich schon gewaschen.
9. Die Männer haben sich rasiert.
10. Habt ihr euch verspätet?

65.
1. Ich habe mich auf seine Ankunft gefreut.
2. Wir legen uns aufs Bett.
3. Ich habe mich am Freitag verletzt.
4. Ich interessiere mich für Briefmarken.
5. Ich habe mich schon an die Arbeit gewöhnt.
6. Er hat sich im Winter erkältet.
7. Ich wundere mich über die Explosion.
8. Die Kinder fürchten sich vor dem Gewitter.

66.
1. Reg dich nicht auf. Regen Sie sich nicht auf.
2. Kinder, verspätet euch nicht!
3. Peter, erkälte dich nicht!
4. Herr Ziegler, stellen Sie sich vor!
5. Setzen wir uns!
6. Gisela, wasch dich!
7. Mädchen, entschuldigt euch!

8. Frau Klein, beeilen Sie sich!
9. Ute, fürchte dich nicht vor dem Hund!
10. Vater, rasier dich!

67.
1. _____   6. _____
2. sich   7. uns
3. mich   8. _____
4. sich   9. _____
5. sich   10. _____

68.
1. tust dir . . . weh
2. putzen uns
3. kaufe mir
4. wascht . . . euch
5. bildet sich . . . ein
6. setzt sich . . . auf
7. bestellt sich
8. stelle mir . . . vor
9. kaufen uns
10. holt sich
11. tun sich weh
12. bildet euch . . . ein
13. wasche mir
14. Nehmt . . . euch
15. machst . . . dir

69.
1. Ich stelle mir das Haus vor.
2. Ich habe mir das Papier geholt.
3. Wir bestellen uns das Essen bald.
4. Ich habe mir am Fuß weh getan.
5. Die Gäste ziehen sich im Schlafzimmer an.
6. Gisela bildet sich etwas ein.

70.
1. Herr Müller, bestellen Sie sich das Buch!
2. Kinder, putzt euch die Zähne!
3. Peter und Heinz, kauft euch etwas!
4. Marlene, tu dir nicht weh!
5. Kinder, wascht euch die Hände!
6. Frau Wimmer, nehmen Sie sich etwas!

71.
1. dürfen   5. darf
2. dürfen   6. darfst
3. darfst   7. Dürft
4. Darf   8. darfst

72.
1. Er muß schwer arbeiten.
2. Sie müssen Brot holen.
3. Mußt du studieren?
4. Müssen Sie heute singen?
5. Wir müssen aufstehen.
6. Wann müßt ihr im Büro sein?
7. Die Kinder müssen zu Hause bleiben.
8. Ich muß das Essen bestellen.

73.
1. Ich kann die Geschichte nicht glauben.
2. Könnt ihr morgen mitkommen?
3. Wir können unserem Freund nicht helfen.
4. Max kann gut tanzen.

5. Kannst du langsamer sprechen?
6. Ich kann alles hören.

74.
1. mag   5. Mögt
2. mag   6. mag
3. mögen   7. mögen
4. Magst   8. mögen

75.
1. Wir wollen helfen.
2. Ich will es nicht sehen.
3. Er will kommen.
4. Wollen sie schlafen?
5. Ursel, willst du gehen?
6. Sie will studieren.
7. Erika und Franz, wollt ihr arbeiten?
8. Ich will das Museum besuchen.

76.
1. Ich soll dem Kind etwas kaufen.
2. Er soll schnell kommen.
3. Sollst du die Wahrheit sagen?
4. Die Studenten sollen lernen.
5. Man soll nicht stehlen.
6. Wir sollen nicht kommen.
7. Sollt ihr bleiben?
8. Ich soll das Auto reparieren.

77.
1. Wir können Englisch.
2. Ich mag keine Suppe.
3. Sie müssen nach Hause.
4. Kann er Deutsch?
5. Sie muß in die Stadt.
6. Er mag keine Milch.

78.
1. Wir wollten mitmachen.
2. Ich mochte keinen Reis.
3. Konntest du bleiben?
4. Durftet ihr denn rauchen?
5. Du konntest nicht heimgehen.
6. Luise wollte bezahlen.
7. Warum wollten Sie helfen?
8. Mußtest du studieren?
9. Ich wollte es sehen.
10. Konntet ihr das machen?

79.
1. Konntet ihr ihm helfen?
2. Ich wollte etwas kaufen.
3. Sollte er auch mitmachen?
4. Wir mußten ihn anrufen.
5. Die Kinder mochten kein Gemüse.
6. Durftest du nicht gehen?

80.
1. Herr Maier, wollten Sie schlafen?
2. Durftet ihr rauchen?
3. Konntest du ausgehen?
4. Mochtet ihr Bananen?
5. Frau Lang, sollten Sie daran glauben?
6. Mußtet ihr helfen?
7. Solltest du es kaufen?

8. Wolltet ihr fragen?
9. Durftest du mitmachen?
10. Konntet ihr es sehen?
11. Mußten Sie alles nehmen?
12. Solltet ihr Bier bestellen?
13. Mochtest du keine Milch?
14. Wollten Sie Konrad kennenlernen?

81.
1. Ich habe ihn nicht gemocht.
2. Sie hat nach Köln gewollt.
3. Hast du das gedurft?
4. Wir haben zur Schule gemußt.
5. Hat er das gekonnt?
6. Die Leute haben nicht gemocht.
7. Ihr habt doch Deutsch gekonnt.
8. Sie haben Englisch gekonnt.
9. Ich habe zur Arbeit gemußt.
10. Wir haben es gedurft.
11. Hast du keine Limonade gemocht?
12. Ich habe in die Stadt gesollt.

82.
1. Wir haben nicht mitfahren sollen.
2. Ich habe nicht schreiben können.
3. Habt ihr hier bleiben müssen?
4. Warum hat er anrufen wollen?
5. Ich habe es bringen dürfen.
6. Man hat Musik hören können.
7. Sie haben nicht aufstehen mögen.
8. Warum hast du es zerstören wollen?
9. Er hat es sehen dürfen.
10. Habt ihr dort parken wollen?
11. Ich habe heimgehen wollen.
12. Hast du zu Hause bleiben müssen?
13. Sie haben gut lesen können.
14. Hubert hat studieren müssen.
15. Wir haben Maria helfen wollen.
16. Haben Sie schwimmen können?

83.
1. Wir hatten es gekonnt.
2. Ich hatte abfahren müssen.
3. Er hatte es gewollt.
4. Sie hatten keinen Kuchen gemocht.
5. Sie hatte mich anrufen sollen.
6. Hattest du sie besuchen dürfen?
7. Ich hatte nicht davon sprechen wollen.
8. Ihr hattet es ja wissen dürfen.
9. Sie hatte das Fenster aufmachen können.
10. Ich hatte zur Schule gemußt.
11. Wir hatten Peter nicht gemocht.
12. Hattest du hinausgehen wollen?
13. Ich hatte Russisch gekonnt.
14. Er hatte den Wagen reparieren müssen.

84.
1. Sie werden nicht schlafen können.
2. Wir werden den ganzen Tag studieren müssen.
3. Er wird es sehen wollen.
4. Ich werde klingeln müssen.

5. Ihr werdet nichts kaufen dürfen.
6. Wirst du es schicken können?
7. Gudrun wird nicht mitmachen wollen.
8. Werdet ihr die Suppe probieren wollen?
9. Sie werden nicht schreien dürfen.
10. Wir werden nicht arbeiten können.

85.
1. Wir lassen das Bild in der Schule.
2. Ich helfe Rita den Hund suchen.
3. Siehst du deine Schwester arbeiten?
4. Hören Sie die Sonate?
5. Er hört seine Frau schreien.
6. Laßt ihr Hans gehen?
7. Die Leute hören uns sprechen.
8. Ich sehe die Kirche.
9. Frau Berger hilft heute.
10. Er läßt Gerda mitkommen.

86.
1. Ich habe es liegen lassen.
2. Wir haben sie lachen hören.
3. Er hat seinen Freund gesehen.
4. Sie haben Heinz das Auto reparieren helfen.
5. Er hat nichts gehört.
6. Ich habe Pia reiten sehen.
7. Sie haben Sonja weinen hören.
8. Wir haben die Zeitungen zu Hause gelassen.
9. Wir haben den Kindern geholfen.
10. Vater hat uns gehen lassen.

87.
1. Er wird Peter schreiben sehen.
2. Ich werde Otto kommen hören.
3. Wir werden den Kindern zeichnen helfen.
4. Wirst du Dieter lachen sehen?
5. Sie werden Rainer sprechen hören.
6. Werden Sie Anneliese lesen helfen?
7. Ich werde den Mantel hier liegen lassen.
8. Werdet ihr Großmutter rufen hören?

88.
1. Er sagt, daß du die Jacke hast liegen lassen.
2. Er sagt, daß wir Josef haben studieren helfen.
3. Er sagt, daß sie Franz haben singen hören.
4. Er sagt, daß ich es habe machen lassen.
5. Er sagt, daß sie das Geschenk hat öffnen dürfen.
6. Er sagt, daß du den Bleistift hast zurückgeben wollen.
7. Er sagt, daß wir Peter haben kommen lassen.
8. Er sagt, daß ihr das Auto habt bringen müssen.

89.
1. Ohne Norma zu sehen.
2. anstatt zur Schule zu gehen.
3. um Gertrud zu helfen.

4. ohne anzurufen.
5. um mich umzuziehen.
6. um die Kinder einzuladen.
7. anstatt es Helga zu bringen.
8. ohne einen Mantel anzuziehen.
9. um zu fragen.
10. ohne es zu lernen.

90.
1. sich zu entschuldigen.
2. uns zu fragen.
3. den Kindern zu helfen.
4. die Geschichte zu erzählen.
5. sich zu rasieren.
6. mitzukommen.
7. es zu holen.
8. Geld zu nehmen.
9. den Hund zu füttern.
10. den Kuchen zu essen.

91.
1. anzurufen
2. zu schreiben
3. mitzugeben
4. einzuladen
5. zu schneiden
6. zu sein
7. zu lesen
8. zu besuchen
9. zu begleiten
10. mitzunehmen
11. zu sehen
12. zu glauben

92.
1. Er braucht nicht zu studieren.
2. Ich brauche nicht zu lesen.
3. Wir brauchen das Buch nicht zurückzugeben.
4. Sie braucht nicht zu arbeiten.
5. Ihr braucht es nicht zu machen.
6. Du brauchst Herbert nicht zu helfen.
7. Ich brauche Bert nicht zu besuchen.
8. Renate braucht nicht zu lesen.
9. Sie brauchen die Geschichte nicht zu erzählen.
10. Ich brauche es nicht zu bestellen.

93.
1. beim Gehen
2. beim Tanzen
3. beim Singen
4. beim Arbeiten
5. beim Malen
6. beim Reparieren
7. beim Studieren
8. beim Spielen
9. beim Telefonieren
10. beim Schwimmen

94.
1. leidend
2. lesende
3. fließendem
4. bellenden
5. Blutend
6. singende
7. weinenden
8. schlafende
9. lächelnde
10. Grüßend

95.
1. zerstörte
2. angebrannt
3. gestohlenen
4. geschriebene
5. gebackene
6. begonnene
7. gefangen
8. gefütterte
9. reparierte
10. geöffnete

96.
1. en
2. er
3. e
4. e
5. e
6. en
7. en
8. e
9. e
10. e

97.
1. Ja, schreiben Sie bitte!
2. Ja, schlafen Sie bitte!
3. Ja, gehen Sie bitte!
4. Ja, tanzen Sie bitte!
5. Ja, lächeln Sie bitte!
6. Ja, reden Sie bitte!
7. Ja, arbeiten Sie bitte!
8. Ja, erzählen Sie bitte!
9. Ja, singen Sie bitte!
10. Ja, fahren Sie bitte!

98.
1. Findet
2. Sprecht
3. Trinkt
4. Holt
5. Schlaft
6. Parkt
7. Studiert
8. Geht
9. Bleibt
10. Ruft
11. Eßt
12. Nehmt
13. Reitet
14. Bestellt
15. Schreibt

99.
1. Sing lauter!
2. Komm jetzt!
3. Such das Geld!
4. Bleib hier!
5. Mach es!
6. Grüß Tante Ida!
7. Geh ins Haus!
8. Probier die Wurst!
9. Wein nicht!
10. Spring ins Wasser!
11. Schwimm schneller!
12. Sag die Wahrheit!
13. Ruf die Polizei!
14. Frag den Lehrer!
15. Rauch nicht!

100.
1. Ja, warte!
2. Ja, rede!
3. Ja, lächle!
4. Ja, füttere es!
5. Ja, behandle ihn!
6. Ja, öffne es!
7. Ja, antworte!
8. Ja, ändere es!
9. Ja, beobachte es!
10. Ja, rechne!
11. Ja, schneide es!
12. Ja, sammle es!
13. Ja, wandere!
14. Ja, arbeite!

101.
1. Hilf dem Kind!
2. Sprich lauter!
3. Gib es dem Lehrer!
4. Stiehl nicht!

5. Lies die Zeitung!
6. Brich es nicht!
7. Triff die Frau!
8. Stirb nicht!
9. Erschrick nicht!
10. Iß das Fleisch!
11. Nimm den Schmuck!
12. Vergiß nichts!

102.
1.	habt	7.	sei
2.	sei	8.	hab
3.	werden Sie	9.	haben Sie
4.	wißt	10.	wissen Sie
5.	seien Sie	11.	seid
6.	werde	12.	seien Sie

103.
1. Kochen wir das Abendessen!
2. Fragen wir den Lehrer!
3. Trinken wir warme Milch!
4. Kaufen wir Wein!
5. Gehen wir jetzt!
6. Schreiben wir die Aufgaben!
7. Rufen wir den Hund!
8. Holen wir das Buch!
9. Arbeiten wir viel!
10. Ändern wir nichts!

104.
1. Wir würden nichts nehmen.
2. Würdest du bezahlen?
3. Ich würde den ganzen Tag schwimmen.
4. Sie würden viel arbeiten.
5. Er würde nicht studieren.
6. Würdet ihr nach Deutschland fahren?
7. Würden Sie laut singen?
8. Ich würde nicht ins Wasser springen.
9. Würdest du das Buch lesen?
10. Er würde den Wagen reparieren.
11. Würdet ihr kommen?
12. Sie würden das Geschenk bringen.
13. Würdet ihr mir helfen?
14. Ich würde auch gehen.
15. Würden Sie die Jacke tragen?
16. Würden die Kinder laufen?

105.
1. Würden Sie bitte kommen?
2. Würdest du das bitte nehmen?
3. Würdet ihr bitte hier bleiben?
4. Würden Sie bitte schneller fahren?
5. Würdest du mir bitte das Messer geben?
6. Würden Sie bitte langsamer sprechen?
7. Würden Sie bitte gehen?
8. Würdest du bitte das Auto parken?
9. Würdet ihr bitte das Essen bestellen?
10. Würden Sie es bitte den Kindern zeigen?
11. Würden Sie bitte Ihren Vater besuchen?
12. Würdest du bitte hier warten?

106. 1. Sie besuchten uns.

2. Wir machten viel.
3. Kauftet ihr es?
4. Ich erzählte es.
5. Zerstörtest du es?
6. Arbeiteten Sie dort?
7. Ich fragte ihn.
8. Wir zahlten.
9. Er glaubte es.
10. Ich sagte es.
11. Wohntest du dort?
12. Hörtet ihr es?
13. Sie lernten es.
14. Wir weinten nicht.
15. Ich bezahlte.
16. Er studierte.
17. Bautet ihr das Haus?
18. Spielten Sie dort?
19. Sie hörten alles.
20. Maltest du?

107.
1. Ich weinte.
2. Wir spielten.
3. Sie holten es.
4. Er glaubte es nicht.
5. Kinder, studiertet ihr?
6. Gerda, kauftest du Blumen?
7. Frau Treibi, wohnten Sie dort?
8. Sie arbeitete.
9. Wir lernten.
10. Sie probierten die Suppe.

108.
1. Das Haus brennte.
2. Dächtet ihr daran?
3. Ich brächte etwas.
4. Nenntest du es?
5. Sie rennten schnell.
6. Wir wüßten es.
7. Ich sendete den Brief.
8. Wir wendeten das Blatt.
9. Ich wußte das.
10. Brächtest du das Buch?

109.
1. Ich schriebe das Gedicht.
2. Wir tränken nichts.
3. Ließ du ihn gehen?
4. Die Alten gingen zur Kirche.
5. Die Sonne schiene nicht.
6. Die Studenten lasen das Buch.
7. Er flöge auch.
8. Schliefest du lange?
9. Ich gäbe Anna alles.
10. Er liefe schnell.
11. Die Leute führen mit dem Auto.
12. Wir schrien laut.
13. Er schnitte das Haar.
14. Ich bliebe hier.
15. Wir kämen auch.
16. Nähmest du das Papier?

17. Ich äße Brot.
18. Das Pferd zöge den Schlitten.
19. Er verlöre das Geld.
20. Wir sprängen hoch.

110.
1. Er stürbe.
2. Sie hülfen.
3. Wir würfen den Ball.
4. Sie stünde hier.
5. Ich hülfe.
6. Sie stürben.
7. Wir stünden hier.
8. Helga, hülfest du?

111.
1. Wir hätten kein Auto.
2. Ich wäre reich.
3. Sie hätten keine Ferien.
4. Du wärest nicht glücklich.
5. Ich hätte keinen Hund.
6. Sie wäre böse.
7. Sie wären nicht intelligent.
8. Ihr hättet kein Geld.
9. Er hätte nichts.
10. Hättet ihr Geld?
11. Wir wären krank.
12. Hättest du Angst?
13. Wir hätten alles.
14. Wäret ihr müde?
15. Wärest du froh?
16. Ich wäre arm.

112.
1. Könnten Sie mir helfen?
2. Wolltest du auch zeichnen?
3. Müßtet ihr nicht studieren?
4. Dürfte er mitgehen?
5. Solltest du Marianne besuchen?
6. Könnte ich ein Stück nehmen?
7. Müßtest du nicht lernen?
8. Wolltet ihr den Film sehen?
9. Könnte sie es holen?
10. Dürfte ich bleiben?

113.
1. Möchtest
2. möchte
3. möchten
4. möchten
5. Möchten
6. Möchtest
7. Möchten
8. möchte
9. Möchtet
10. Möchtest

114.
1. Ich wollte, er bliebe nicht dort.
2. Ich wollte, sie könnten nicht abfahren.
3. Ich wollte, wir lebten in keinem Dorf.
4. Ich wollte, ich hätte kein Zahnweh.
5. Ich wollte, ihr arbeitetet nicht so viel.
6. Ich wollte, ich müßte nicht studieren.
7. Ich wollte, wir wären zu Hause.
8. Ich wollte, du kauftest dir etwas.
9. Ich wollte, sie weinte nicht.
10. Ich wollte, ich wäre nicht arm.

11. Ich wollte, wir hätten es nicht.
12. Ich wollte, er nähme es nicht.
13. Ich wollte, er sähe Paula nicht.
14. Ich wollte, sie besuchten Oma nicht.

115.
1. Wenn wir nur in München wären!
2. Wenn er nur das Fenster öffnete!
3. Wenn ihr doch ein Auto kauftet!
4. Wenn die Leute nur nicht so laut schrien!
5. Wenn ich nur alles wüßte!
6. Wenn er nur nicht krank wäre!
7. Wenn die Kinder nur zu Hause blieben!
8. Wenn ich nur Deutsch könnte!
9. Wenn ihr nur mehr hättet!
10. Wenn Georg nur nicht abführe!

116.
1. Sagte sie nur die Wahrheit!
2. Könnte ich doch schlafen!
3. Reparierte er nur das Auto!
4. Tränken sie nur nicht so viel!
5. Schwiege er doch!
6. Hätten wir nur keine Angst!
7. Wärest du nur hier!
8. Bliebe er nur hier!
9. Glaubte sie es nur!
10. Lerntet ihr nur mehr!

117.
1. würde ich arbeiten.
2. würde ich nicht hier wohnen.
3. würde ich dir nichts geben.
4. würde ich nicht nach Hamburg fliegen.
5. würde ich mir nichts bestellen.
6. würden wir Kaffee trinken.
7. würden wir uns unterhalten.
8. würde ich mich freuen.
9. würde ich mich umziehen.
10. würde ich mich nicht fürchten.

118.
1. hätte, hülfe
2. wäre, wäre
3. sähe, beschriebe
4. bliebest, besuchten
5. studiertet, wüßtet
6. bestellten, äßen
7. lerntest, könntest

119.
1. Hülfest du mir, dann wäre ich froh.
2. Käme er, dann bliebe ich dort.
3. Fragten wir ihn, dann würde er uns antworten.
4. Wollte sie es, dann gäbe ich es ihr.
5. Hätte ich Angst, dann würde ich schreien.

120.
1. Wäre ich krank, bliebe ich zu Hause.
2. Wüßten wir es, erzählten wir es Alexander.
3. Hätte sie Geld, kaufte sie den Mantel.
4. Arbeiteten sie, wären sie glücklicher.
5. Käme er an, holte ich ihn ab.

121.
1. hätten
2. liebtest
3. ginge
4. wären
5. wollte
6. könnte
7. bliebe
8. arbeiteten
9. sähe
10. nähmen
11. schenke
12. habe
13. wisse
14. könne
15. wolle
16. finde
17. trinke
18. esse

122.
1. Wenn wir nur in der Schule gewesen wären!
2. Wenn du nur angerufen hättest!
3. Wenn ich nur gebadet hätte!
4. Wenn er nur Angst gehabt hätte!
5. Wenn ihr nur gekommen wäret!

123.
1. Hättest du nur geschrien!
2. Wären wir ihr nur begegnet!
3. Wäre ich nur hingegangen!
4. Wäre er nur nicht gestorben!
5. Hätte sie nur geschrieben!

124.
1. gegessen hätte, hätte . . . gehabt
2. zurückgebracht hättest, hätte . . . geholt
3. zugemacht hättet, hättet . . . erkältet
4. angerufen hättest, hätte . . . gesagt
5. geblutet hätte, hätte . . . geschrien

125.
1. Hätte es geklingelt, hätten wir aufgemacht.
2. Hättest du angerufen, wäre ich gekommen.
3. Hätten wir es gefunden, hätten wir es wieder zurückgegeben.
4. Hättet ihr geschrieben, hätten wir euch dort getroffen.

126.
1. Er tut, als ob er es gekauft hätte.
2. Sie tun, als ob sie nicht geschlafen hätten.
3. Sie tut, als ob sie krank gewesen wäre.
4. Er tut, als ob er mitgekommen wäre.

127.
1. Hätte er nur bleiben dürfen!
2. Wenn ich doch nicht hätte gehen müssen!
3. Er tut, als ob er es hätte sehen können.
4. Du tust, als ob ich es hätte schreiben sollen.
5. Wenn ich hätte reiten wollen, hätte ich es dir gesagt.
6. Hätte er nur singen können!
7. Wenn du nur nichts hättest essen wollen!
8. Wenn wir hätten fragen dürfen, hätten wir die Antwort gewußt.
9. Hätte sie nur helfen können!
10. Sie tun, als ob sie auf mich hätten warten müssen.

128.
1. sei
2. bleibe
3. wohne
4. studiere
5. arbeite
6. gebe
7. kaufe
8. bringe
9. hole
10. schicke

129.
1. er habe schon geschrieben
2. ich sei ins Kino gegangen
3. sie sei im Krankenhaus gewesen
4. er habe etwas geholt
5. ich habe es repariert
6. er habe nicht kommen dürfen

130.
1. Sie sagte, Mutter wäre krank gewesen.
2. Sie sagte, Großvater hätte Geld gehabt.
3. Sie sagte, Peter hätte Angst.
4. Sie sagte, sie wäre allein gewesen.
5. Sie sagte, er hätte ihn gesehen.
6. Sie sagte, Christa wäre nach Köln gefahren.
7. Sie sagte, Onkel Werner wäre in Hamburg.
8. Sie sagte, ich hätte dich besucht.

131.
1. Er hat gesagt, Mutter sei krank gewesen.
2. Er hat gesagt, Großvater habe Geld gehabt.
3. Er hat gesagt, Peter habe Angst.
4. Er hat gesagt, sie sei allein gewesen.
5. Er hat gesagt, er habe ihn gesehen.
6. Er hat gesagt, Christa sei nach Köln gefahren.
7. Er hat gesagt, Onkel Werner sei in Hamburg.
8. Er hat gesagt, ich habe dich besucht.

132.
1. wird vom . . . gebacken
2. wird durch . . . gerettet
3. wird . . . serviert
4. werden von . . . angeschaut
5. wird von . . . genommen
6. wird vom . . . geholfen
7. wird von . . . geschrieben
8. wird von . . . gewaschen
9. wird von . . . gegraben
10. wird durch . . . zerstört
11. werden von . . . gesehen
12. werde von . . . geschlagen
13. wird von . . . gehört
14. wird durch . . . zerstört
15. wird von . . . repariert

133.
1. Das Kind wird von dem (vom) Hund gebissen.
2. Das Haus wird durch das (durchs) Feuer zerstört.
3. Der Kaffee wird von meinen Freunden getrunken.
4. Das Pferd wird von ihm gefüttert.

5. Dem Kranken wird von dem (vom) Vater geholfen.

134.
1. Wir wurden abgeholt.
2. Die Rechnung wurde von Renate bezahlt.
3. Wurdest du beobachtet?
4. Das Auto wurde geparkt.
5. Es wurde schon von den Leuten gemacht.
6. Das Museum wurde von der Klasse besucht.
7. Das Wort wurde von dem Studenten buchstabiert.
8. Ich wurde gesehen.
9. Die Maschine wurde von dem Mechaniker repariert.
10. Das Haus wurde durch die Bombe zerstört.

135.
1. Er wurde gesehen.
2. Das Fenster wurde von Marlene geöffnet.
3. Sie wurden von ihrem Vater gefragt.
4. Sie wurde gehört.
5. Es wurde von meiner Tante gewaschen.
6. Uns wurde von dem Jungen geholfen. (Es wurde uns von dem Jungen geholfen.)
7. Ich wurde beobachtet.
8. Die Stadt wurde durch eine Bombe zerstört.

136.
1. Das Museum ist 1911 erbaut worden.
2. Der Löwe ist vom Wärter gefüttert worden.
3. Es ist ihr darüber erzählt worden.
4. Das Kleid ist rot gefärbt worden.
5. Es ist ihm gegeben worden.
6. Du bist überall gesucht worden.
7. Ich bin von ihm gesehen worden.
8. Das Restaurant ist durch das Feuer zerstört worden.
9. Er ist vom Arzt behandelt worden.
10. Die Kinder sind von den Hunden gebissen worden.

137.
1. Das Haus wird von meinen Freunden gebaut werden.
2. Die Geschichte wird erzählt werden.
3. Der Patient wird durch Medikamente geheilt werden.
4. Das Geschenk wird von den Kindern bewundert werden.
5. Die Rechnung wird von meinem Vater bezahlt werden.
6. Der Brief wird geholt werden.
7. Das Haus wird beobachtet werden.
8. Der Brief wird vom Lehrer geschrieben werden.
9. Rudi wird gefragt werden.
10. Franz wird abgeholt werden.

138.
1. Man zerstört die Ruine.
2. Man ruft uns an.
3. Man bestellt das Essen.
4. Man erzählte die Geschichte.
5. Man holte den Arzt.
6. Man schickte den Katalog.
7. Man hat das Bild verkauft.
8. Man hat den Mann angerufen.
9. Man hatte den Brief geschrieben.
10. Man hatte die Limonade getrunken.
11. Man wird wohl die Stadt aufbauen.
12. Man wird wohl das Auto parken.

139.
1. Es wird gefunden.
2. Es wurde zerstört.
3. Es wurde gezeigt.
4. Es wurde gerettet.
5. Es wird repariert.
6. Es wird begonnen.
7. Es wird geschnitten werden.
8. Es war gebaut worden.
9. Es wurde bezahlt.
10. Es wird gesagt.

140.
1. Es ist gefunden.
2. Es war zerstört.
3. Es war gezeigt.
4. Es war gerettet.
5. Es ist repariert.
6. Es ist begonnen.
7. Es wird geschnitten.
8. Es war gebaut gewesen.
9. Es war bezahlt.
10. Es ist gesagt.

141.
1. kennst
2. kenne
3. können
4. Wißt
5. weiß
6. kennt
7. weiß
8. Kannst
9. Kennt
10. wissen

142.
1. Wir kennen den Präsidenten.
2. Sie können Französisch.
3. Inge, hast du meine Tante gekannt?
4. Ich weiß die Antwort.
5. Er weiß alles.

143.
1. liegt
2. liege
3. Liegt
4. legst
5. leg
6. liegen
7. legt
8. lege

144.
1. setzt
2. sitzt
3. setze
4. setzt
5. setzt
6. sitze
7. sitzt
8. Sitzt

145. 1. stehen
2. stellt
3. stelle
4. Stellst

5. stelle
6. steht
7. stellen
8. Stehst

146. 1. lassen
2. läßt . . . wohnen
3. lassen . . . gehen
4. lasse . . . singen
5. Läßt
6. läßt . . . rufen (anrufen)
7. laß
8. lasse

147. 1. Wir haben die Kinder spielen lassen.
2. Er hat das Fahrrad dort gelassen.
3. Hast du die Jacke zu Hause gelassen?
4. Sie haben uns mitmachen lassen.
5. Rudi hat Inge mitmachen lassen.
6. Ich habe die Katze im Garten gelassen.

Chapter 8

1. 1. Er kennt den Herrn nicht.
2. Wir geben es den Leuten nicht.
3. Ich wasche mich nicht.
4. Heinz weiß es nicht.
5. Sie kamen vorgestern nicht.
6. Ich kaufe den Mantel nicht.
7. Sie nimmt es nicht.
8. Er dankt mir nicht.
9. Ich zeige ihr den Roman nicht.
10. Wir rauchen nicht.

2. 1. Sie haben nicht gespielt.
2. Ich wollte die Rechnung nicht bezahlen.
3. Wir haben sie nicht schreien hören.
4. Maria hat nicht neben dem Hotel gewartet.
5. Ich weiß, daß er nicht fliegen will.
6. Das ist nicht meine Tante.
7. Er sagte, daß er sie nicht gesucht hätte.
8. Das Mädchen fährt nicht heim.
9. Wir sind nicht zur Schule gegangen.
10. Ich bin nicht dort geblieben.
11. Wir sind nicht im Kino.
12. Ich sehe sie nicht kommen.
13. Er kommt nicht mit.
14. Ihr könnt es nicht sehen.
15. Sie sind nicht reich.
16. Er hat nicht hier gewartet.
17. Wir haben es nicht geholt.
18. Das sind nicht meine Bücher.
19. Ich hoffe, Inge nicht zu sehen.
20. Du hast sie nicht genommen.

3. 1. Sie ist nicht bei ihrer Tante geblieben . . .
2. Er hat nicht das Auto repariert . . .
3. Wir haben nicht das rote Buch gekauft . . .
4. Ich brauche nicht den Löffel . . .
5. Ihr habt das Radio nicht gewonnen . . .
6. Ich lese nicht die Zeitung . . .

4. 1. Habt ihr ihnen nicht geholfen?
2. Sind sie nicht abgefahren?
3. Holt sie es nicht?
4. Macht sie nicht mit?
5. Darfst du nicht bleiben?
6. Hast du ihn nicht gefragt?
7. Ist das nicht dein Freund?
8. Hast du nicht mitgesungen?
9. Rasiert er sich nicht?
10. Hat sie es nicht vergessen?
11. Willst du ihm nicht helfen?
12. War das nicht seine Frau?
13. Ist sie nicht schön?
14. Kaufst du die Blumen nicht?
15. Kann er sich nicht daran erinnern?

5. 1. Ja, er war krank.
2. Doch, er ist gestorben.
3. Ja, ich habe es gekonnt.
4. Doch, wir brauchen es.
5. Doch, er hat es gefressen.
6. Doch, sie ist intelligent.

6. 1. Sie braucht nicht zu kommen.
2. Hans braucht nicht zu schreiben.
3. Ihr braucht nicht abzufahren.
4. Wir brauchen nicht zu gehen.
5. Ich brauche nicht zu studieren.
6. Sie brauchen nicht zu arbeiten.
7. Wir brauchen nicht zu springen.
8. Du brauchst den Roman nicht zu lesen.

7. 1. Er fragt uns nie.
2. Wir sind gar nicht müde.
3. Sie wohnt nicht mehr in Bonn.
4. Ich kann noch nicht fahren.
5. Er hat sie noch nie gesehen.
6. Er hilft nie.
7. Sie geht nicht mehr ins Kino.
8. Er war noch nie in Deutschland.
9. Wir sind noch nicht nach Hause geflogen.
10. Sie sind gar nicht freundlich.
11. Ich habe Schnecken noch nie gegessen.
12. Er kennt mich nicht mehr.
13. Sie lernte den Präsidenten nie kennen.
14. Wir machen gar nicht mit.
15. Er hat die Sammlung noch nicht verkauft.

8. 1. Er erzählte kein Märchen.
2. Wir besuchten keine bekannte Stadt.
3. Er hat unser Kind nicht gesehen.
4. Hat sie keine Blumen gekauft?
5. Trinkt er kein Wasser?

6. Ich habe keinen warmen Mantel.
7. Das sind keine Haselnüsse.
8. Ich habe mich nicht auf die Ferien gefreut.
9. Wir essen keine Bananen.
10. Ich habe keinen Freund.
11. Ich kenne den Herrn nicht.
12. Sie singt das Lied nicht.
13. Er hat keine Kinder.
14. Dieser Ring ist nicht teuer.
15. Hier liegt kein Buch.
16. Wer ißt kein Brot?
17. Das ist kein Tachometer.
18. Die Lehrerin schreibt nicht.
19. Ist die Milch nicht sauer?
20. Ich habe keine Zeit.

9. 1. Er kann nichts sehen.
2. Niemand hilft uns.
3. Ich habe nichts Altes.
4. Sie wissen nichts.
5. Er fragt niemand.

Chapter 9

1. 1. Kommt er morgen?
2. Bringt Herbert es zurück?
3. Setzte er sich aufs Bett?
4. Weißt du alles?
5. Arbeiteten die Männer viel?
6. Braucht ihr es?
7. Amüsiert ihr euch?
8. Bestellte Petra auch Bier?
9. Besichtigen die Touristen das Schloß?
10. Will er nicht?
11. Hörst du nichts?
12. Muß sie in die Stadt?
13. Bleiben sie dort?
14. Rauchte er viel?
15. Schwimmst du nicht?

2. 1. Hat er schon geschrieben?
2. Haben sie sich gestern kennengelernt?
3. Habt ihr alles verloren?
4. Wird sie es aufmachen?
5. Darfst du es nehmen?
6. Hat er sich verletzt?
7. Werdet ihr euch umziehen?
8. Hättest du es gekauft?
9. Ist er gestorben?
10. Können sie nicht dort bleiben?
11. Laßt du Peter helfen?
12. Sieht sie die Kinder spielen?
13. Hat er die Geschichte erzählt?
14. Habt ihr die Oper gesehen?
15. Haben sie immer studiert?

3. 1. Ist er nicht hier?
2. Fährst du nicht mit?

3. Dürft ihr nicht nach Bonn fahren?
4. Kommst du nicht mit?
5. Hilft sie nicht den Kindern?

4. 1. Wann
2. Wie
3. Wie oft
4. Wie
5. Wie lange
6. Wieviel
7. Wie
8. Wie oft
9. Wie lange
10. Um wieviel Uhr
11. Wann
12. Wann
13. Warum
14. Um wieviel Uhr
15. Wann

5. 1. Wo
2. Woher
3. Wohin
4. Woher
5. Wohin
6. Wohin
7. Wo
8. Woher
9. Wohin
10. Wo

6. 1. Wohin fährt sie?
2. Wann bringen sie es?
3. Wie oft besuchte uns Alexander?
4. Wie ist es heute?
5. Wo ist sie?
6. Wie oft sieht er dich?
7. Woher kommt Ella?
8. Wie lange bleiben sie dort?
9. Wo sind sie?
10. Wieviel kostet es?

7. 1. Was
2. Wem
3. Was
4. wem
5. Wer
6. wem
7. Wen
8. Wessen
9. wen
10. wem
11. Wem
12. Wen
13. Wer
14. Wem
15. Wessen
16. wem
17. wen
18. Wessen
19. Was
20. Was

8. 1. Wovon
2. Was
3. Womit
4. Wen
5. Wonach
6. Wofür
7. Worauf
8. Für wen
9. Über wen
10. Was
11. Mit wem
12. Wofür
13. Worin
14. Wozu
15. Hinter wen

9. 1. Welche
2. welchen
3. welcher
4. Welchen
5. welchem
6. Welches
7. welcher
8. welchen
9. welchem
10. Welche
11. Welcher
12. Welche

10. 1. Welcher   4. Welche
     2. welchem   5. Welchen
     3. welche

11. 1. Welche nimmst du?
     2. Welche hat er gekauft?
     3. Von welchen erzählt er?
     4. Welche brauchst du?
     5. Für welche kauft er es?

12. 1. Was für ein Auto ist das?
     2. Was für ein Mädchen ist das?
     3. Mit was für Leuten fährt er nach Deutschland?
     4. In was für einem Haus wohnen sie?
     5. Was für Bücher schreibt er?

Chapter 10

1. 1. Der Schnellzug ist vor einer Stunde angekommen.
     2. Norma bleibt bei uns.
     3. Der kleine Junge will mitmachen.
     4. Die Goldkette wurde von ihm zurückgebracht.
     5. Wir haben ihn sehen können.
     6. Gerda geht mit Klaus spazieren.
     7. Der Hund beißt den Jungen.
     8. Ich habe es kaufen dürfen.
     9. Er wird die Geschichte erzählen.
     10. Er sieht mich kommen.

2. 1. Sie haben schneller laufen müssen.
     2. Wir haben die Schachtel aufgemacht.
     3. Er hat nicht heimgehen wollen.
     4. Ich habe es ihm zeigen wollen.
     5. Seine Großeltern haben es mitgebracht.
     6. Mein Vater hat mich gehen lassen.
     7. Er hat gut singen können.
     8. Der Alte hat sich auf die Bank gesetzt.
     9. Ich habe die Kinder schreien hören.
     10. Der Zug ist vor einer Stunde abgefahren.

3. 1. Das Auto wollten wir in Deutschland kaufen.
     2. Heute kommen sie zurück.
     3. Im Kino hat er es vergessen.
     4. Meistens ist er am Abend müde.
     5. Leider waren meine Eltern zu Hause.
     6. Wegen meiner Erkältung konnte ich nicht kommen.
     7. Gestern abend haben wir es gemacht.
     8. Mit dem Zug fahren sie in die Schweiz.
     9. Im Zentrum ist das Museum.
     10. Oft habe ich es hören müssen.

4. 1. Wann machst du das Fenster zu?
     2. Was darf das Kind wissen?
     3. Wieviel kostet die Kamera?
     4. Wo wollen die Leute wohnen?
     5. Warum setzt du dich nicht nieder?
     6. Wohin fährst du mit dem Auto?
     7. Worauf sollen die Bücher liegen?
     8. Woher kommen die Kinder?

5. 1. Weil ich viel zu tun habe, kann ich nicht mit ins Kino.
     2. Als ihre Mutter ins Zimmer kam, las sie ein Buch.
     3. Wenn ich Zeit habe, werde ich meine Tante besuchen.
     4. Während ich studierte, habe ich viel lernen müssen.
     5. Bevor du abreist, sollst du deiner Großmutter helfen.

6. 1. _____
     2. Vor einer Woche hat uns Axel besucht.
     3. Im Theater hat sich Konrad amüsiert.
     4. Jeden Tag schickt ihr Mutter etwas.
     5. Wo hat dich Ursel getroffen?
     6. _____
     7. _____
     8. Gestern hat uns Vater etwas gebracht.
     9. Um neun Uhr trifft sie ihr Freund.
     10. _____

7. 1. Hast du ihm den Brief geschrieben?
     2. Kennt mich Peter?
     3. Wollte Gerda das Museum besuchen?
     4. Helft ihr ihm den Baum pflanzen?
     5. Macht Herr Klein die Tür auf?
     6. Kann er Deutsch?
     7. Hat sich Erika bei ihr entschuldigt?
     8. Hast du dir das schnelle Auto gekauft?
     9. Habt ihr es ihm genommen?
     10. Hat man dich gefragt?

8. 1. Zeig (Zeigt)
     2. Öffne (Öffnet)
     3. Frag (Fragt)
     4. Komm . . . heim (Kommt . . . heim)
     5. Mach . . . nach (Macht . . . nach)

9. 1. Ja, trinken Sie das Bier!
     2. Ja, singen Sie das Lied!
     3. Ja, lachen Sie darüber!
     4. Ja, schicken Sie es mir!
     5. Ja, ziehen Sie den warmen Mantel an!

10. 1. Er ist arm, aber sein Eltern sind reich.
     2. Ich freute mich, denn er wollte sofort mit der Arbeit anfangen.
     3. Wir sind nicht dort geblieben, sondern wir sind ausgegangen.
     4. Sei vorsichtig, oder es geht kaputt!

5. Ich spiele Golf, und er spielt Tennis.
6. Er ist glücklich, denn er hat Geld gewonnen.
7. Wir sind nicht in Deutschland, sondern wir sind in Spanien.
8. Du kannst zu Hause bleiben, aber ich muß zur Schule.
9. Er trinkt Milch, und ich trinke Limonade.
10. Er kommt zu uns, oder wir gehen zu ihm.

11.
1. Wann liest du das Buch?
2. Wenn sie krank ist, bleibt sie zu Hause.
3. Wenn er mich besuchte, brachte er mir etwas.
4. Weißt du, wann er ankommt?
5. Als es kalt wurde, ging ich ins Haus.
6. Wenn er mehr Geld hätte, führe er nach Deutschland (würde er nach Deutschland fahren).

12.
1. Sie hat Kopfweh, weil die Kinder viel Lärm gemacht haben.
2. Er ist in Berlin, während seine Frau noch hier ist.
3. Ich fragte ihn, ob sie wieder gesund sind.
4. Es war sehr kalt, als wir in Alaska waren.
5. Sie konnte gut Deutsch, nachdem sie in Deutschland studiert hatte.
6. Wir kauften alles, da wir viel Geld gewonnen hatten.
7. Wir blieben im Wald, bis es dunkel wurde.
8. Konrad mußte mithelfen, bevor er ausgehen konnte.
9. Er trägt einen Pullover, damit er sich nicht erkältet.
10. Sie ist immer müde, seitdem sie nicht gut schlafen kann.

13.
1. daß
2. obwohl
3. bis
4. als ob
5. ob
6. Seit (dem)
7. Je
8. damit
9. da
10. während

14.
1. Ich weiß nicht, wo er gewohnt hat.
2. Ich weiß nicht, wieviel sie noch machen muß.
3. Ich weiß nicht, wovon er lebt.
4. Ich weiß nicht, warum er es mitbringt.
5. Ich weiß nicht, worüber er erzählen wird.

15.
1. Wo ist der Mantel, den ich gekauft habe?
2. Die Kinder spielen mit der Puppe, die er mitgebracht hat.
3. Dort steht das Flugzeug, mit dem ich abfliege.
4. Hilfst du dem Mädchen, dessen Vater gestorben ist?
5. Wo sind die Karten, die er mir geschenkt hat?

16.
1. Er ist glücklich, weil er hat gehen dürfen.
2. Ich glaube, daß er hat fragen wollen.
3. Kennst du den Mann, den ich habe schreien hören?
4. Weißt du, ob er hat arbeiten müssen?
5. Ich weiß, was er hat machen sollen.

17.
1. Denke ich daran, bestelle ich es.
2. Hätte er es gewollt, hätte ich es ihm gekauft.
3. Wird es kalt, heizen wir das Haus.
4. Willst du mitmachen, mußt du dich umziehen.
5. Nehme ich es ihr weg, weint sie.

18.
1. Da ich keine Zeit hatte, konnte ich es nicht machen.
2. Als er ins Zimmer kam, spielte sie Klavier.
3. Wenn ich das Auto habe, werde ich euch besuchen.
4. Während ich krank war, mußte ich viel schlafen.
5. Bevor du gehst, mußt du mir helfen.

19.
1. Wir zeigten ihr die Lampe.
2. Wann hat er ihm die Karotte gegeben?
3. Ich habe ihr eine Vase geschenkt.
4. Hat er ihm das Motorrad gekauft?
5. Wer hat ihnen das Geld genommen?
6. Weißt du, ob er ihnen die Schokolade gegeben hat?

20.
1. Wir zeigten sie der Dame.
2. Wann hat er sie dem Hasen gegeben?
3. Ich habe sie meiner Tante geschenkt.
4. Hat er es seinem Sohn gekauft?
5. Wer hat es den Leuten genommen?
6. Weißt du, ob er sie den Kindern gegeben hat?

21.
1. Willst du es ihr vorlesen?
2. Wann hat er ihn ihnen gebracht?
3. Weißt du, ob er sie ihm erzählt hat?
4. Wann hat er es ihnen gezeigt?
5. Ich habe sie ihr gegeben.

22.
1. Gibt dir Peter den Ring?
2. Warum kann uns Ursula nicht besuchen?
3. Kennt ihn der Professor?
4. Hat sich Frau Schafft schon umgezogen?
5. Sie weint, weil sie die Leute auslachten.

23.
1. Er sieht sie täglich.
2. Wir geben ihnen natürlich alles zurück.
3. Sie besucht sie abends.
4. Ich habe ihn wirklich getroffen.

5. Er kann sie leider nicht abholen.

24. 1. Ich bin am Nachmittag nach Hause gekommen.
2. Wir treffen sie um zehn Uhr im Hotel.
3. Ich war jeden Tag dort.
4. Ich gehe heute abend mit Ursel spazieren.
5. Ich bin sehr schnell in die Stadt gefahren.
6. Wir sind gestern mit dem alten Wagen ins Kino gefahren.

25. 1. Ja, wir besuchen dich morgen um drei Uhr.
2. Ja, wir fahren diesen Sommer im Juli in die Berge.
3. Ja, ich gehe nächste Woche am Mittwoch ins Theater.
4. Ja, wir fliegen heute abend um sechs Uhr ab.
5. Ja, ich bin morgen zwischen sieben und acht Uhr zu Hause.

Verb Chart

PRINCIPAL PARTS OF VERBS

Below is a list of the most commonly used strong and irregular verbs.

Infinitive	Simple Past	Past Participle	Present Stem Vowel	English
backen	backte (old: buk)	gebacken	bäckt	to bake
beginnen	begann	begonnen		to begin
beißen	biß	gebissen		to bite
biegen	bog	gebogen		to bend
binden	band	gebunden		to bind
bitten	bat	gebeten		to ask
bleiben	blieb	(ist) geblieben		to stay
brechen	brach	gebrochen	bricht	to break
brennen	brannte	gebrannt		to burn
bringen	brachte	gebracht		to bring
denken	dachte	gedacht		to think
dürfen	durfte	gedurft	darf	to be allowed
essen	aß	gegessen	ißt	to eat
fahren	fuhr	(ist) gefahren	fährt	to go, drive
fallen	fiel	(ist) gefallen	fällt	to fall
fangen	fing	gefangen	fängt	to catch
finden	fand	gefunden		to find
fliegen	flog	(ist) geflogen		to fly
fliehen	floh	(ist) geflohen		to flee
fließen	floß	(ist) geflossen		to flow
fressen	fraß	gefressen	frißt	to eat (of animals)
frieren	fror	gefroren		to freeze, be cold
geben	gab	gegeben	gibt	to give
gehen	ging	(ist) gegangen		to go
gewinnen	gewann	gewonnen		to win
graben	grub	gegraben	gräbt	to dig
haben	hatte	gehabt	hat	to have
halten	hielt	gehalten	hält	to hold, stop
helfen	half	geholfen	hilft	to help
kennen	kannte	gekannt		to know
kommen	kam	(ist) gekommen		to come
können	konnte	gekonnt	kann	can, to be able
lassen	ließ	gelassen	läßt	to let, leave
laufen	lief	(ist) gelaufen	läuft	to run, walk
leiden	litt	gelitten		to suffer
leihen	lieh	geliehen		to loan
lesen	las	gelesen	liest	to read

liegen	lag	gelegen		to lie
messen	maß	gemessen	mißt	to measure
mögen	mochte	gemocht	mag	to like
müssen	mußte	gemußt	muß	must, to have to
nehmen	nahm	genommen	nimmt	to take
nennen	nannte	genannt		to name, call
reiten	ritt	(ist) geritten		to ride
rennen	rannte	(ist) gerannt		to run
riechen	roch	gerochen		to smell
saufen	soff	gesoffen	säuft	to drink (of animals)
scheinen	schien	geschienen		to shine, seem
schießen	schoß	geschossen		to shoot
schlafen	schlief	geschlafen	schläft	to sleep
schlagen	schlug	geschlagen	schlägt	to hit
schließen	schloß	geschlossen		to close
schneiden	schnitt	geschnitten		to cut
schreiben	schrieb	geschrieben		to write
schreien	schrie	geschrien		to scream
schweigen	schwieg	geschwiegen		to be silent
schwimmen	schwamm	(ist) geschwommen		to swim
sehen	sah	gesehen	sieht	to see
sein	war	(ist) gewesen	ist	to be
senden	sandte	gesandt		to send
singen	sang	gesungen		to sing
sinken	sank	(ist) gesunken		to sink
sitzen	saß	gesessen		to sit
sollen	sollte	gesollt	soll	ought, to be supposed to
sprechen	sprach	gesprochen	spricht	to talk, speak
springen	sprang	(ist) gesprungen		to jump
stehen	stand	gestanden		to stand
stehlen	stahl	gestohlen	stiehlt	to steal
steigen	stieg	(ist) gestiegen		to climb
sterben	starb	(ist) gestorben	stirbt	to die
stinken	stank	gestunken		to stink
tragen	trug	getragen	trägt	to wear, carry
treffen	traf	getroffen	trifft	to meet
treten	trat	(ist) getreten	tritt	to step
trinken	trank	getrunken		to drink
tun	tat	getan		to do
verlieren	verlor	verloren		to lose
wachsen	wuchs	(ist) gewachsen	wächst	to grow
waschen	wusch	gewaschen	wäscht	to wash
wenden	wandte	gewandt		to turn
werden	wurde	(ist) geworden	wird	to become
werfen	warf	geworfen	wirft	to throw
wiegen	wog	gewogen		to weigh
wissen	wußte	gewußt	weiß	to know
wollen	wollte	gewollt	will	to want to
ziehen	zog	gezogen		to pull

Index

Accusative case, 36–38
  accusative pronouns, 71
  with accusative prepositions, 52–53
  accusative reflexive pronouns, 76
  direct objects, 36–37, 176
  with either/or (accusative/dative) prepositions, 57–60
  time expressions in the accusative case, 37, 134
Accusative prepositions, 52–53
Accusative reflexive pronouns, 178–180
Address, forms of, 69, 137
Adjectives:
  adjective endings following **der**-words, 90–95
  adjective endings following **ein-**words, 97–101
  as nouns, 111–112
  attributive adjectives, 90
  city names as adjectives, 96
  comparison of adjectives, 115–116, 119–120
  demonstrative adjectives:
    der, das, die, 88
    dieser, dieses, diese, 88
  descriptive adjectives, 89
  following **der**-words, review chart, 96
  following **ein-**words, review chart, 102
  neuter adjectives used as nouns, 112–113
  past participles as adjectives, 110–111, 194
  possessive adjectives, 113–114
  predicate adjectives, 89
  present participles as adjectives, 110, 193–194
  special adjective forms, 95
  superlative of adjectives, 115–116, 119
  taking no adjective endings, 89, 95–96
  unpreceded adjectives, 103–110
  unpreceded adjectives, review chart, 109
Adverbs, 122–125
  adverbs of time, 134
  comparison of adverbs, 115–116
  customary action, 134
  position of adverbs, 247–248
  superlative of adverbs, 116
Alphabet, German, 1
Articles, 32–47
  cases of, 32–47
  definite, 32–34
  indefinite, 32–34
  special uses of the definite article:
    with general and abstract nouns, 48
    with geographical names, 48
    with parts of the body, articles of clothing, 49
    with weights, measures and expressions of time, 49

Attributive adjectives, 90
Auxiliaries:
  haben, 145, 155, 166–167, 197, 203
  modal, 184–189, 203–204
  sein, 145, 155, 166–167, 197, 203
  werden, 145, 155, 166–167, 197, 198–199, 214–215
Capitalization, 14
  in correspondence, 69
Case (*see* Nominative, Accusative, Dative, Genitive)
  review of case endings for **der** and **ein** words, 47
City names as adjectives, 96
Clauses:
  contrary-to-fact, 199, 204–206
  dependent, 190, 198–199, 204–205, 241–246
  independent (using coordinating conjunctions), 240–241
  infinitive, 189, 190–193
  relative, 244–245
  subordinate (*see* Clauses, dependent)
Commands (*see* Imperative)
Comparative of adjectives, 115–117
Comparative of adverbs, 116–117
Comparison of equality, 119
Comparison of inequality, 117
Compound nouns, 22–23
Conditional, 198–199, 245
Conjunctions:
  coordinating, 240–241
  subordinating, 241–244
Contractions, 53, 56, 59–60
Contrary-to-fact wishes, 204
Conversational past, 155–156
Coordinating conjunctions, 240–241
Countries, names of, 16–17, 48
Customary action, 134

Da-compounds, 62, 75–76
Dates, 130–131
Dative verbs, 39–40
Dative case, 39–42
  dative personal pronouns, 72
  dative reflexive pronouns, 77
  indirect object, 39–40
  time expressions in the dative case, 135
  with dative prepositions, 54–56
  with dative reflexive verbs, 181–183
  with dative verbs, 39–40
  with either/or (accusative/dative) prepositions, 57–60

Days of the week, 129
Definite article, 32
    adjectives following, 90–96
    omission of, 50
    with abstract nouns, 48
    with parts of body, clothing, 49
    with names of streets, mountains, lakes, countries, 48
    with weights, measures, time, 49
Definite time, 134
Demonstrative pronouns, 78–79
Dependent clauses, 190, 198–199, 204–205, 241–246
Dependent infinitive:
    with anticipatory **da(r)**-compounds, 191–192
    with modal auxiliaries, 184
    with other verbs, 189–190
    with **zu,** 191–193
der-words, 32–34, 90
    adjectives following der-words, 90–96
    case endings of, 32–47
Diminutives, 14
Direct address, 35
Direct objects, 36–37, 176
Direct quotations, 210
Double infinitive, 188, 245

ein-words, 32–34
    adjectives following ein-words, 97–102
    case endings of, 32–48
    possessive adjectives, 33
Either/or prepositions, 57–60

First person commands, 198
Flavoring particles, 124–125
Forms of address, 69
    formal/informal, 137
Fractions, 128–129
Future perfect tense, 171
Future tense, 169–170

Gender, 14
    countries, 16–17
    of compound nouns, 22–23
    of nouns, 14–22
    noun endings indicating, 18–21
General questions, 227–228
Genitive case, 43–45
    genitive of proper names, 45
    substitute for genitive case, 46
    time expressions in the genitive case, 44, 135
    with genitive prepositions, 64–65

haben, 145, 155, 166–167, 197, 203
Hypothetical statements, 207

Immer plus comparative, 118
Imperatives, 195–198
Impersonal imperative, 198
Indefinite article, 32–34
    adjectives following indefinite article, 97–102
    case endings of, 32–47
Indefinite time expressions, genitive, 135
Independent clauses (using coordinating conjunctions), 240–241
Indirect object, 39–40, 176
Indirect speech, 209–212
Infinitive:
    dependent:
        with modal auxiliaries, 184
        with other verbs, 189–190
    double, 188
    as nouns, 21, 193
Inseparable prefix verbs, 171–172
Interrogatives, 227–233
    interrogative adverbs, 229–230
    interrogative pronouns, 231
Inverted word order, 236–237
Irregular verbs, 137–138
    stem vowel changes, past participle, 161–166
    stem vowel changes, past tense, 150–154
    stem vowel changes, present tense, 143–145
Irregular weak verbs, 149–150, 160, 201

Know – kennen, wissen, können, 217–218

lassen, 220
liegen – legen, 218–219

Modal auxiliaries, 184–189, 203–204, 209

Narrative past, 155–156
Negation, 221–226
Nominative case, 33–35, 90, 97, 104
    nominative pronouns, 69–70
    predicate nominative, 34–35
Noun suffixes indicating gender, 18–21
Nouns, 14–33
    adjectives used as nouns, 20
    capitalization, 14
    compound nouns, 22–24
    dative endings, 42

Nouns (*Cont.*):
  genitive endings, 44–45
  infinitives used as nouns, 21
  n-nouns, 38, 42, 45
  participles used as nouns, 194
Numbers, 126–129
  cardinal, 126
  dates, 129–131
  decimals, 127
  fractions, 128–129
  ordinal numbers, 127–128
  time, 131–133

Passive voice, 212–217
  substitutes for the passive, 216
Past participle, 157–166, 171–172, 175, 187–188
Past perfect tense, 168–169
Past-time subjunctive, 207–209
Person, 69
Personal pronouns, 69–74
Plurals of nouns, 25–31
Polite requests, 199, 207
Possession, 43–45, 46
Possessive adjectives, 113–114
Predicate adjectives, 89
Predicate nominative, 34–35
Prefixes (*see* Separable prefix verbs, Inseparable
  prefix verbs)
Prepositions:
  accusative, 52–53
  contractions, 53, 56, 59–60
  da- and **wo**-compounds with, 62–63
  dative, 54–56
  either/or (accusative/dative), 57–60
  genitive, 64–65
Present participles as adjectives, 110
Present perfect tense, 157–166
Present-time subjunctive, 200–206
Pronouns:
  case, accusative, 71
  case, dative, 72
  case, nominative, 69–70
  demonstrative, 78–79
  indefinite, 79–81
  indefinite relative, 85–86
  interrogative, 231
  personal, 69–74
  possessive, 78
  reflexive, 76–77
  relative, 82–86
Pronunciation of German, 3–10
  consonants, 5–8
  diphthongs, 4–5
  glottal stop, 8
  vowels, 3–4
Proper names showing possession, 45

Questions:
  (*see* Interrogatives, General questions, Specific
    questions)

Reflexive pronouns, 76–77
Reflexive verbs with separable prefixes, 180
Regular verbs (*see* Verbs)
Relative clauses, 244–245
Relative pronouns, 82–86
  indefinite relative pronouns, 85–86
  wo-compounds in relative clauses, 87

Seasons, 130
sein, 145, 155, 166–167, 197, 203
Sentence types, 235–240
Separable prefix verbs, 172–176
setzen-sitzen, 60–61
Simple past tense, 148–157
Simple present tense, 138–146
Singular nouns, 24
sitzen-setzen, 218–219
Specific questions, 228–231
stehen-stellen, 218–219
stellen-stehen, 60–61
Stress, 8–9
Strong verbs, 137–138
  stem vowel changes, past participle, 161–166
  stem vowel changes, past tense, 150- 154
  stem vowel changes, present tense, 143–145
Subjunctive:
  general subjunctive (subjunctive II), 200
  indirect speech, 209–212
  past-time subjunctive, 207–209
  present-time subjunctive, 200–206
  special subjunctive (subjunctive I), 200
Subordinating conjunctions, 241–244
Suffixes, noun, 18–21
Superlative of adjectives, 115–119
Superlative of adverbs, 115–118
Syllabification, 9–10

Telling time, 131–133

Unpreceded adjectives, 103–110

Verb + preposition combinations, 74–75
Verbs:
  conditional, 198–199, 205–206
  dative verbs, 176–177

Verbs (*Cont.*):
dependent infinitives, 189–191
false passive, 217
future perfect tense, 171
future tense, 169–170
imperatives, 195–198
indirect speech, 209–212
infinitives, 189–193
   as nouns, 193
   with anticipatory **da(r)**-compounds, 191–192
   with **zu,** 191–193
inseparable prefix verbs, 171–172
intransitive, 137, 161
irregular verbs, chart, 285–286
irregular verbs, **sein, haben, werden, wissen, tun,** 145
irregular weak verbs, 150
modal auxiliary verbs, 184–189
passive voice, 212–217
past participle formation, 158–160, 162–166
past perfect tense, 168–169
personal endings, 137, 139–143, 148–149, 150
phrasal verbs (*see* Verbs, verb + preposition)
present perfect tense, 157–166
reflexive verbs, 178–183
separable prefix verbs, 172–176
simple past tense, 148–157
simple present tense, 138–146
strong verbs, 137–138
   stem vowel changes, past participle, 161–166
   stem vowel changes, past tense, 150–154
   stem vowel changes, present tense, 143–145
subjunctive, 199–212
substitutes for the passive, 216
transitive, 137
verb plus preposition, 177
weak verbs, 137–138

Verb tense usage notes:
continued action into the present, 146
conversational past, 155–156
customary past occurrence, 157
future for probability, 170
narrative past, 155–156
past perfect, 168–169
present perfect for conversation, 158
present tense for future, 146
simple past, 155–157

werden, 145, 155, 166–167, 197, 198–199, 214–215
Wo-compounds, 63, 87, 232
Word order:
in commands, 239–240
in conditional sentences, 245
in dependent clauses, 241–242
in exclamations, 240
in prepositional phrases, 66
in questions:
   general questions, 239
   specific questions, 237–238
in statements:
   inverted word order, 236–237
   regular word order, 235–236
position of adverbs, 123–124, 247–248
position of objects, 246–247
position of pronoun, objects, 73–74
with coordinating conjunctions, 240–241
with reflexives, 77
with subordinating conjunctions, 241–244
with words acting as subordinating conjunctions, 244–245